KT-563-242

THE BIG TRIP

HOW TO USE THIS BOOK

This book is designed to provide information you need to turn your travel dreams into concrete plans. The first part, Travel Smarts, looks at everything you need to know to get started, including what to expect when you arrive in your destination and all the paperwork you'll need to organise beforehand. The Tailoring Your Trip section is about organising your trip in a way that works for you and suits your interests – do you want to work to make some travel cash, volunteer in a community or take on the festival circuit? It's worth reading to see what's out there.

For more specific planning there are the destination chapters in the book's third part. These chapters look at the regions of the world and are a good place to start if you can't make up your mind where to go. Finally, there's the Directories chapter, a list of contact information for useful organisations, divided into sections: British Travellers for Brits, North American Travellers for US citizens and Canadians, and Australasian Travellers for Australians and New Zealanders.

We've made this book as up-to-date as we can, but remember that prices do go up, currencies fall and a million other things can happen before this book even hits a bookshelf. But the secret of good travelling is to stay flexible and stay up to date.

INTRODUCTION

It started with the Grand Tour. Way back in the 17th century, upper-class British kids would complete their education by heading over to parts of Europe to experience museums, paintings and, more importantly, wines that they'd only studied or read about in school. For a few months they'd tour the continent, though most only went as far as Italy (probably something to do with the wine). All of them returned with enough stories, souvenirs and sores to last a lifetime.

Fast-forward a couple of hundred years. Cheap flights have meant that even more people are taking a year off and seeing a world outside of school books and dull history lessons. Whether it's a gap year, an overseas experience (OE), an exchange program, a working holiday, a sabbatical, a year out or a year off, people want to head off to India, Italy, Israel or a thousand places in between to see what the world is really like. Today there are even more reasons to head overseas.

WHY GO?

But hang on, can't you just see all of that on TV or find out everything you need to know about the world on wikipedia? Only if you want to fake it. There's no substitute for getting out there seeing, hearing, tasting, touching and smelling what the world is. Some of the smells and tastes won't be good BTW, but at least you'll have done it. You can shut the most boring book-smart expert up at parties just by saying 'Have you actually been there?'

For many travellers, what starts out as a vacation ends up a vocation, a passion becomes a profession. Take the economics graduate who thought he was bound to work in an accounting firm but did a stint with a music distribution company during his gap year. He was so inspired he's been in music business ever since, so his year off changed his future entirely.

Sarah Bruce was a traveller who didn't just have a year off but used the time to check out a field she might be interested in. 'I volunteered overseas for five months with Trekforce Expeditions. This really changed my perspective and my priorities and it opened a door for me to work in the charity sector, doing marketing.'

The jobs you do, the people you meet and the experiences you have can show you careers and

ESCAPING THE PARENT TRAP

So maybe your parents aren't so keen on you going away for months on end. They're probably making noises about going to university, settling down or getting a good job in a bank. They really need to move on. Here are our best arguments to stop them fretting and get them shelling out for airline tickets:

✪ **PROTECTIVE RESEARCH** If you can tell them about the place you're visiting, it can be reassuring. Everyone's going to freak out when they don't know where someone's going, but if you can explain your itinerary it will seem more real. Helpful facts ('They all speak English.', 'There's more than 30,000 tourists every year and they all seem okay.' or 'It's one of the safest cities in Central America.') can also be useful. You can even get them to read a few chapters of this book so they can see you're taking this trip seriously.

✪ **GET INVOLVED** Get your parents to help out with the planning and show them a detailed itinerary – they can even check progress on your blog. Show them you've got a budget and you have a time limit on the trip. You can always change itineraries later, but let them know when you do veer off the itinerary to save the grey hairs and panicked phone calls.

✪ **PHONE HOME** Create a schedule for phoning home, texting or whatever (there are more tips in Part One, p70). Make sure it's reasonable (calling every hour is crazy but only ringing once a month could lead to parental tears) and stick to it.

✪ **ON COURSE** Prove you're committed to the trip by doing a course (see Part Four, Directories, for more clues on this). Learning to speak a language, taking a first-aid course or even picking up some basic travel skills are all good ways to show that you're taking this seriously.

✪ **INSURANCE IS REASSURANCE** Show them you're prepared for the bad stuff by getting good travel insurance that will cover any emergencies.

✪ **CAREER BUILDING** This is your trump card. Explain that this trip could help your career and point to a few people whose careers have been helped by travel.

---

life choices you never would have seen back home. Opportunities open up when you're travelling. But as Tom Hall warns us, 'The trip didn't answer my questions about what I wanted to do with my life but it remains the source of some of my happiest memories.' Today Tom manages Lonely Planet's London office, so perhaps travelling did nudge him slightly in the direction of a career choice.

But it's not all about work. Just like those Grand Tourists of hundreds of years ago, you'll also gather friends and experiences that will be valuable for the rest of your life. Whenever someone mentions Thailand you'll remember a full-moon party, or if you meet a New Zealander, Canadian or Scot you'll be able to tell them stories of drinking in their pubs and laughing with

people from their country. These intangibles will stay with you your whole life.

Then there's the confidence building. Just to know that you've worked out how to catch a bus in Prague or protected yourself from malaria in Cambodia makes the problems you'll face back home at university or work seem simpler. As Amanda Akass sees it, 'Once you have trekked through the Andes in the freezing cold, scared off muggers in Rio, or been lost in a jungle at night, you feel you can do anything!' Fighting off muggers isn't a must-have skill for many gigs, but if you mention it in a job interview, they'd be too scared not to give you the job.

Plus after being in school since you were five, you've definitely earned a bit of time off.

WHY NOT GO?

We're not going to bullshit you: no trip is always easy. Travel brochures can turn out to be studio-shot lies and there will be times when you'll be broke, sick or just lonely and homesick. But with a bit of preparation you can minimise the lows and maximise the highs.

Before you go there's always the money to think about. Travel can be expensive and even studying at university comes with a pretty big price tag. We've got a few tips on making your dollars, pounds, euros and baht go further (see p33), but you may have to prioritise and work out how long you can afford to be away. Would you rather spend your time working in a London pub with a few short hops over to Europe? Or would you rather volunteer in Laos helping street kids? Or do you just want to trek to Machu Picchu then take your sore feet home? After balancing up time and money, should your gap year really be a gap month? Either way, we've got you covered and can help you come up with a budget that will make it work.

Lots of travellers worry about personal safety. You only have to switch on the news to know that there are some places in the world that you don't want to visit. And we want to steer you away from the really dangerous places in the world (see p43). For everything else, we'll prepare you as best we can by giving you the word on some of the everyday dangers.

And then there's the environmental concern. Aeroplanes do produce hefty carbon emissions and tourists can bring problems to sensitive regions. This book will show you how to keep your carbon footprint tiny and how to respect the countries you're visiting to prevent damage to fragile environments and cultures (see p75). We also believe that travel can help developing nations if it's done responsibly – not every visitor needs to be an invader. At the risk of getting all Brady Bunch on you, travel should bring the world closer together.

STILL GOING?

Despite the worries, millions of people are still hitting the road every year and discovering what the world is really like behind the headlines and outside the school books. You'll find out that all the clichés about travel changing you are true, and you'll come back with memories that are worth more than any holiday snaps or souvenirs.

The practical tips in this book aim to get you from dreaming to doing and back again. From planning to coming home, we've pulled together enough tips from travellers to inspire you and get you there safely. There are world highlights so can you plan an itinerary to suit. There's also advice on job hunting and visas.

But in all the planning and preparing the best advice we can give you is from Lonely Planet's founder, Tony Wheeler, who left everything he knew in Britain to go overland from England to Australia and ended up turning travel into big business. After years of travelling the world what would Tony say? 'Just go.'

20 BIG TRIP
TRAVEL EXPERIENCES

OUR AUTHORS HAND-PICKED THEIR FAVOURITE
SPOTS IN THEIR FAVOURITE REGIONS.

SCALING THE SUMMIT OF MT KILIMANJARO (TANZANIA, SEE P272)
The famous snows may be thinning, but the rooftop of Africa still affords stunning views,
probably because it's the highest peak on the continent.

HAVING A ROYAL KILTED KNEES-UP AT EDINBURGH FRINGE FESTIVAL (SCOTLAND, SEE P169)
Imagine the maddest Scots getting all their friends over for a week of comedy and kooky arts. That's what you get with Fringe – the wild and weird all crammed into a medieval city that never sleeps.

DONKEY TREKKING INTO THE GRAND CANYON (USA, SEE P243)
With only the slap of saddlebags and your own footsteps you could be in a Western movie, not at the biggest and busiest canyon the world has to offer.

COMING TO THE CHILLED OASIS OF THE TAJ MAHAL
(INDIA, SEE P225) Even the bustling touts hold this ancient mausoleum in awe and as you get closer, the lotus design, the gold spire and the sacred Muslim moon are all drawn in detail.

INVENTING NEW COLOURS IN THE CORALS OF GREAT BARRIER REEF (AUSTRALIA, SEE P182)

The world's largest coral reef can be explored by glass-bottomed boat, but if you strap on the snorkel you'll see the colours up close and feel the tickle as rare fish get friendly.

CHANNEL-SURFING THROUGH NEW YORK CITY (USA, SEE P243)

From the *Seinfeld* deli to the fashionista fantasy set of *Zoolander* to the Empire State's memorable turn in *King Kong*, New York is just waiting for you to shout 'Action!'

HIKING TO JAW-DROPPING IGUAZÚ FALLS (ARGENTINA, PARAGUAY, BRAZIL, SEE P258)

Most impressive are the gargling waters at Garganta del Diablo (Devil's Throat) that divide Argentina and Brazil, but you're bound to be impressed anywhere along this stretch of cascading water.

GETTING HISTORIC AT THE ACROPOLIS (GREECE, SEE P166)

The great 'sacred rock' has towered over Athens for thousands of years in tribute to the ancient Greek gods, so explore it early in the morning to get a feel for the majesty and to avoid unholy crowds.

HEATING UP AT THE BURNING MAN FESTIVAL (USA, SEE P245)

Black Rock Desert in Nevada is overrun with hippies, artists and all the right kind of rabble for this trippy festival that includes nude cycling and incinerating a big wicker dude.

TAKING A CAMEL RIDE TO THE PYRAMIDS OF GIZA (EGYPT, SEE P272)

Seeing the mythical pyramids bouncing before you as your dromedary crosses the desert is the only way to arrive at the ruins that were the world's biggest buildings in their day.

TAKING THE PLUNGE DIVING AT KO PHI PHI (THAILAND, SEE P213) Clear waters and plentiful coral make for some of the world's sweetest snorkelling, plus scuba divers can go deeper with the *King Cruiser* wreck and there are some impressive limestone formations to explore.

HIKING THE DEPTHS OF TIGER LEAPING GORGE (CHINA, SEE P198) Follow the roughest stretch of the Yangzi River in the shadow of Jade Dragon Snow Mountain through the hamlets of the Naxi people.

MARVELLING AT THE LIMESTONE KARSTS OF HALONG BAY (VIETNAM, SEE P214) Whether you soak it up from a beachside restaurant or take on the waters in an old-school junk, you'll have to visit a couple of times to see the many colours of the limestone.

TREATING THE WHOLE CITY AS YOUR FANCY DRESS PARTY WITH COSPLAY GANGS OF TOKYO (JAPAN, SEE P198) From the latest manga superheroine to old-school Goths, get your kookiest duds on at Harajuku and other hotspots throughout Tokyo.

EXPLORING THE ARTSY TREASURE HOUSE OF THE HERMITAGE (RUSSIA, SEE P298) Possibly swiped at the end of WWII, these St Petersburg treasures have been hiding out in the Paris of the East just waiting for you to discover them.

RE-ENACTING CHE GUEVARA'S *MOTORCYCLE DIARIES* THROUGH SOUTH AMERICA (SEE P265)
Rev an old bike out of Buenos Aires and head south through Chile, draw inspiration at Machu Picchu (pictured) and finish by
volunteering in Peru (Guevara visited a leper colony). Witnessing all this inspired young Che to become a revolutionary.

RUBBING NOSES WITH MAORI AT A *HANGI* IN ROTORUA (NEW ZEALAND, SEE P183) Rotorua might be crowded but the traditional feast cooked in the geothermal heat of the earth will soon make you feel at home before traditional dancing kicks off.

WILDLIFE-SPOTTING ON THE GALÁPAGOS ISLANDS (ECUADOR, SEE P258) The islands that evolution forgot have the unique giant tortoises, but there are also some pretty freaky iguanas, cute penguins and flocks of weird birds to discover.

CLIMBING TO THE TOP OF ANGKOR WAT (CAMBODIA, SEE P213) From up the top you can see the scattered pieces of the Khmer empire's history in dozens of temples, palaces and monuments buried in the jungle.

TRAVEL SMARTS

JOIN THE FESTIVITIES AT THE WORLD'S LARGEST WINTER CARNIVAL (P245) IN QUÉBEC CITY, CANADA.

GET PLANNING

If you're tired of wandering past travel agents, looking wistfully at the prices and thinking 'One day...', then it's time to get serious. Travel is always on everyone's list of things to do, but why not put it as your number-one priority? Planning might sound boring but once you start buying guidebooks, imagining your itinerary and working out where to go, you'll feel like you're actually doing it.

TIMING

As well as finding the right time for your destination (see the destination chapters in Part Three for details on when to visit specific regions), you need to find the right time for *you*. Travelling is a great way to finish off high-school or university study, or if you've got long breaks in your study you can take a trip. Many people use the time while they're away to work out what to do next, whether it's between jobs or after school. Finishing study offers the advantage of fewer responsibilities and plenty of free time to plan what you'll do.

The downsides are that you may fall out of step with some of your friends – you might be starting university a year later or entering the job market after them. At the time this might seem like a big difference, but if you stay in touch with your buddies at the other end,

they might help you get a job or tell you which courses to avoid. Some would-be travellers worry that stepping out of their careers to travel will interrupt their climb up the corporate ladder, but the corporate ladder can wait. While you may miss some opportunities by being overseas, you'll also see even more possibilities – you might find out that you want to study overseas or volunteer (see p143).

The classic 'gap year' (as it's known in the UK) occurs just before university study, and it can start as soon as you drop your pen for the last exam and finish just in time for enrolment. It's a good idea to give yourself time to relax before heading away. And you'll need to raise some money to get you through your trip. You can get a rough idea of costs by heading to the Money & Costs chapter (p33), which will be helpful for working out when you can ditch that summer job.

CHOOSING YOUR DESTINATIONS

India, Cuba and Thailand are perennial favourites with travellers, but you should go your own way. Are there places you've always wanted to see or know more about? You might be inspired by something you studied, such as the ruins of ancient Greece or crumbling Aztec ziggurats. Some people travel to find out more about their ancestors, while others just like the cost-cutting of sleeping on relatives' couches. Two other top ways to target potential destinations are to follow the festival scene (see p111) or head into the great outdoors with some hiking, cycling or other activities (see p105).

Most travellers look at doing several stops, including a destination where they can work (see p115) to get cashed up before heading out again. The round-the-world ticket (see p90) can be the perfect way to skip around the globe. You could decide to team up with your best buddy or the love of your life to travel together, which may mean that you'll have to plan an itinerary together. A good alternative can be to look at doing some legs of your journey alone and meeting up to travel together at certain points. If your boyfriend would rather surf in Indonesia while you explore China, it's easy enough to meet up in Hong Kong before heading on to Europe. Check the Who With chapter (see p83) for a few more ideas on travelling with friends and partners.

RESEARCHING YOUR DESTINATIONS

Once you've hit on a few destinations to visit you can start finding out a little more about them, including the best time to visit and the local customs and culture. You'll get a closer look at what the destination has to offer and start working out which towns or cities you'll include on your itinerary – are you more New York than New England, more Milan than Ko Pha-Ngan?

There's a more serious side to research, including details such as immunisations, visas and other precautions, which will be different depending on where you go. Be sure to check travel advisories (see p41) before you travel.

INTERNET

Chances are you'll have started your research by googling a few destinations, probably while you should have been working or writing an essay. The quality of the information you'll find will vary, though the internet can have some of the most up-to-date information from travellers. **Lonely Planet's Thorn Tree** (www.lonely planet.com/thorntree) is a good example, as travellers

post questions about destinations they're interested in and they're often answered by travellers who've recently been to the same places. You'll probably also come across **Lonely Planet's Destinations** (www .lonelyplanet.com/destinations), with profiles of every destination in the world. The **CIA Factbook** (www .cia.gov/library/publications/the-world-factbook) has a more technical look around the globe, including comments on roads and telecommunications. **Virtual Tourist** (www.virtualtourist.com) is a user-generated site with loads of reviews and tips from other travellers.

Tourism Websites

Another popular place to gather information is from tourism websites. You'll see when you read a few of them that they specialise in 'brochurese', a gushing language where every island is a 'secluded paradise' and even a hole in the ground can be described as 'a boutique getaway subterranean retreat'. They're good for basics and usually have plenty of inspiring pictures, but they're really trying to sell their destination. You can find tourist offices in your destination by visiting **Tourism Offices Worldwide Directory** (www.towd.com), which has links and addresses for most tourism offices in the world.

Online Travel Agents & Bookers

Several websites offer booking services and also provide destination guides, which can be a good way to get an idea of what a destination is like and what the major attractions are. Even if you don't book with them, they can give you some good ideas on places to head for or (if you want to get off the beaten track) avoid.

Here are a few:

- **Expedia** (www.expedia.com) Has links to various local sites.
- **Orbitz** (www.orbitz.com)
- **Travelocity** (www.travelocity.com)
- **Viator** (www.viator.com)

GUIDEBOOKS

Okay, so being a guidebook company we're always going to tell you that guidebooks are essential tools – they offer information on places to stay and eat, detail what to see, give you language basics and cultural insights. Still not convinced? Check the 10 Ways To Use

✪ **TO PREVENT SNORING** When sleeping in a crap hostel with battered flat pillows, just slip the guide into the pillowcase to give your head a few extra inches of elevation. No more snoring!

✪ **TO ESCAPE WITH YOUR LIFE** When some punk fronts you with a knife in Soho, just slam the book into his face as hard as you can and run like the wind.

✪ **AS TOILET PAPER** Not the best use for a book, but when it's either your hand or the paper you'll use the paper. Make sure it's for the places you've been to though, or you'll spend an unpleasant hour cleaning bits you still need!

✪ **AS KINDLING** When you're camping in a cave and your idiot brother forgot fire starters, you'll turn to your very dry and flammable guidebook for help.

✪ **AS BUG CONTROL** In a mosquito-infested hotel room, where everything is nailed down and the only thing heavy enough to smash the gigantic evil blood suckers is your guidebook, you won't mind a few blood splats on the cover.

✪ **TO BLOCK A MOUSE HOLE** When your girlfriend won't go to sleep because of the mouse hole in the corner of the room, you will be REALLY glad that your guidebook blocks it enough to reassure her so you can get some kip.

✪ **TO KEEP A WINDOW OPEN** When the temperature is hitting 40°C and you have no air conditioning and the window won't stay open, a guidebook is a great thing to use as a wedge.

✪ **AS ROACH MATERIAL** When the big man with the dreads and machete asks you for something he can roach, you'll give him the cover of your Jamaica guidebook. In about five minutes you won't care anyway.

✪ **AS INSULATION** If you're climbing and didn't bring enough warm clothes, you can layer pages from the guidebook inside your clothes and get some extra warmth.

✪ **TO GET GIRLS** For some reason, playing the little-boy-lost in the middle of a European city works wonders. A guidebook makes a perfect prop. Or so my better-looking brother tells me.

www.lonelyplanet.com

Your Guidebook boxed text (above) to see how reliant you could become on your guidebook for everything from security to toilet paper.

Before buying your guidebook you should work out a rough itinerary, so consider just browsing a bookshop or library until you have a good idea where you're heading. Multicountry books which cover areas such as Europe or Southeast Asia can keep your options open and you can always buy a new or used book on the road if you change your itinerary. Most travellers come prepared by buying a book before they head off so they can read up before they leave. It gets you excited about your destination before you get there.

Selecting Your Guidebook

There's a confusing array of guidebooks on the shelves in most bookshops, but flip through them and see which one suits you. As well as Lonely Planet, there are other popular brands including Rough Guides, Let's Go, Time Out, Moon, Frommer's, Fodor's and Footprint. Before parting with your hard-earned cash, ask your friends and family which books they've used.

When you're in the bookshop, read through the guidebooks a little and compare edition dates (latest may not always be best though, as having the latest book is no use if it's wrong), hard information and reviews. Which book has a style that suits you? Some guides are written for business travellers or families so they might not suit your idea of all-night partying. Some books will go into greater depth on activities such as hiking or surfing, so if you're basing your whole trip on doing these activities check the coverage in different books. You might also consider a specialised guidebook that concentrates on cycling or cultural travel.

Also think about how long you plan to spend in each destination, as this will influence the level of detail you will want from your guide. For example, in Lonely Planet's *Europe on a Shoestring*, London usually gets 18 pages, which is fine if you're going to be there on a short trip. If, on the other hand, you're staying a while and travelling around the country, the *Great Britain* book might be better as it gives London a whopping 75 pages. If you need even more depth, you should try a city guide, which gives the British capital around 430 pages, or if you're on a brief visit, *London*

Encounter has 244 pages, including a lot of snappy colour photographs.

TRAVEL AGENCIES

With internet booking becoming popular, the travel agent around the corner could be an endangered species. Good travel agencies offer things you can't get on the web, such as advice on where to go, and they also help with booking tricky connections and tell you which vaccinations you'll need. Their brochures can be a good source of free information and even if you don't want to go on an organised tour, you can get a good feel for a country's major sights from the full-colour pictures in these glossy publications. Travel consultants are often widely travelled and most will be happy to share their experiences with you. However, many consultants work on commission, so they may be keen to make the deal and won't want to waste too much time if it's not going to result in a booking.

MOTORCYCLES ARE A GREAT WAY TO SEE THE SIGHTS OF SOUTHEAST ASIA (SEE P214) – SUCH AS THE ROYAL PALACE, PHNOM PENH, CAMBODIA.

PAPERWORK

If travelling is all about being free, then why does paperwork take up so much time? It's boring but important stuff and it may mean waiting in a few long lines or reading lengthy documents, but you really can't leave home without it. The more you research the easier it will be once you're on the road – everyone's heard stories about travellers who get sent home at their destination's airport because they didn't have the right visa or their passport had expired. They're easy problems to avoid if you use the advance-planning tips in this chapter.

PASSPORTS

Famous for photos that make you look like a serial killer, a lunatic or both, passports are proof of your nationality and let you cross international borders. When you're overseas, it's your main form of ID, with visas and entry stamps showing that you have a legal right to be in a country.

You'll need to carry your passport with you in most destinations. You should avoid handing it over to anyone for long periods of time, though when checking in at hotels or hostels it's common to give it to the desk clerk to sign you in. When you apply for a visa, you'll entrust your passport to embassy staff, which can sometimes mean being without your passport for a period of a few weeks (see p27).

KEEPING A COPY

When you haven't got your passport in your hands, it can be reassuring to know that you have the details which will make it easy to replace. You should copy down your passport number and keep it safely in a separate place from your passport. Some travellers keep it in their journal, but putting it in an email to yourself is a good idea as well. You can leave the number with friends or family at home, so you can call them reverse-charge (see p73) if you lose everything. You can also scan or photocopy the photo page of your passport, which can be handy when you don't have photo ID.

EXPIRY DATES & BLANK PAGES

If you've already got a passport, check its expiry date. Most countries require that your passport is valid for at least six months even if you're only intending to stay for a few days. Some immigration officials might also want to plonk their entry and exit stamps on clean pages only (though usually if you ask nicely they'll put them on another page), and you'll need a full page for some visas, so make sure you've got enough pages left before you head off.

GETTING A PASSPORT

Getting a passport is a simple enough process no matter where you live. Your national government website will have details of where you can apply (see the Directories in Part Four), but many post offices should be able to give you forms and process your application. What you'll require in order to apply depends on your home country (so check websites for latest changes), but generally you'll need proof of citizenship (such as a birth certificate), photo ID (driving licence) and at least two identical photos of yourself (in a portrait style). You'll also need to pay a fee and provide any evidence of name change. Some countries have strict rules regarding the photos (no smiling, no hats etc) and their websites will be the best guide for this. In Australia, for example, photos must be signed by a guarantor. Some US outlets (they're listed on the US State Department site) include photography facilities, which will cost you a little more but can be a good way to ensure you get a useable photo.

You may be required to sit an interview in some countries, which is a straightforward process of checking your application and making sure that you have the correct documentation. Other countries let you apply online and you can post in relevant documents.

Costs

Depending on where you're from, you might have the option of getting more pages in your passport, which can push the price up. If you really get the travel bug, it can be worth getting a passport with more pages, but generally a cheaper one will do the trick. Some countries charge you extra if you want a fast-track service, so you can save a few bucks if you get organised in advance.

At the time of research, the cost of a passport was:
- **Australia** A$200–300
- **Canada** C$87–92
- **New Zealand** NZ$150–300
- **UK** £72–85
- **USA** US$100

Issuing Period & Fast Tracking

Again, different countries promise different results, though fast-track passports usually cost more. Sometimes there can be complications such as not having the right type of photos or not providing the correct information, which will blow out the application process, so check the details on the website.
- **Australia** 8–10 working days
- **Canada** 2–4 weeks (though 24 hours is possible by paying an additional $70)
- **New Zealand** 1 week or 3 days fast tracked
- **UK** 6 weeks
- **USA** 3–4 weeks

ELECTRONIC PASSPORTS

Most countries have already introduced the electronic passport, which has a small built-in computer chip that stores the passport holder's information, including a photograph. These passports are also called biometric passports, because they use facial-recognition technology so your face can be quickly scanned to see if you match the passport you're carrying. At the time of research no passports held fingerprint information, though the chips within an electronic passport have the capacity to hold this and other information.

Electronic passports are slightly more vulnerable to damage and most come with warnings not to bend, wet or fold your passport.

LOST OR STOLEN PASSPORTS

Although we advise you to keep your passport with you at all times, losing the passport is a fixable problem. You should report it straight away to your nearest embassy or high commission (which should be listed in your guidebook). If your country doesn't have diplomatic representation in the country you're in, you should try a neighbouring country. You may also need to notify local authorities, but check with embassy staff as there may be a quick way to resolve the situation. If your passport has been stolen, go straight to the police and ask for a police report which you can take to the embassy or consulate.

You'll generally have to show the embassy another form of photo ID, so they can issue an emergency passport. If you've got a photocopy or scan of your passport, this is the time to use it. Replacements usually cost a little more but will get to you quickly, and you may even be issued with an emergency passport on the same day.

If you had visas in your lost passport, you'll need to replace them by going to the nearest consulate of the issuing countries.

DUAL CITIZENSHIP

If you've got two passports, you can switch between them for more affordable visas and possibly even residence and the ability to work in another country. Every country has different rules about dual citizenship (and some may not allow it at all), so check the passport websites. You're usually eligible if your parents (and sometimes grandparents) were born in another country.

If you do travel with two passports, don't tell the immigration officials that you have dual citizenship. You should stick to the same passport when travelling between neighbouring countries – if you entered Thailand on a British passport, don't try to enter Malaysia on your Australian passport, or the officials will wonder how you got into the region.

VISAS

A visa is like getting a permission note from a country that says you're allowed to visit. Usually they're issued by the embassy, consulate or high commission of the country you're intending to visit. They're attached to or printed in your passport and require a photograph or two which will be kept on file and may be added to your passport.

Depending on your country's diplomatic relations with your destination, you may not even need to get a visa to enter a country (see below). You'll need to check though, because without a visa (or with the wrong kind) you might be sent home without even seeing more than the inside of the airport.

Applying in advance is usually the best idea, though most visas are active from the date of issue, so if you get a six-month visa to China and you visit seven months later, it will have expired. If you've got a loose itinerary it might be better to apply on the road. If you do apply in advance, however, you may be given greater choice of visas. In Romania, for example, you could be offered a six-month visa if you apply through the embassy, but if you lob up at the border you'll only have the option of a 30-day visa.

DO YOU NEED A VISA?

When you review your itinerary, remember that every country could potentially require a visa. Be aware that international relations often shift while you're away, so you may find that a country that was fine when you left could require a visa when you arrive at the border. The best place to find out the latest rules is the embassy site of your destination, and a good portal to many of these sites is **Project Visa** (http://projectvisa.com), which links to the visa pages in the maze of most embassy sites. You should search every destination you intend to visit and review the information just before you leave.

Commonly, countries that have trade agreements (such as the European Union) or are neighbours (such as Canada and the US) don't need visas between them. The Schengen Agreement between European countries, for example, allows many European nationals to travel freely between their countries, but it also means that non-Europeans need only apply for a single Schengen visa to visit several European destinations. The US recently introduced a Visa Waiver Program (VWP) for many countries it's friendly with, which only requires that you have an electronic passport (see p26) to enter the country for short-term visits.

TIPS

If you want to be really prepared, bring along a set of passport-sized pictures. These are good for visa applications, police reports if you get anything stolen, and other unforeseen paperwork. You don't have to get new pictures every year, but think of how cheap they are back home and how much of a pain it will be to find a place to get them done at 3am in Nepal.

APPLYING FOR VISAS

Applying for visas isn't necessarily a nightmare, though if you have to go to an embassy or organise an invite into a country (as is the case with Russia), it can require some preparation. Allow some time before you travel to organise your visas, just in case you get knocked back or need to supply more information. Don't forget to add visa costs into your budget (see Money & Costs, p33), as

they range from £10/US$20/A$22 to £50/US$100/A$110, though like passports they can cost more for rush jobs (see p26). An embassy website should tell you if you need to organise a visa in advance or if it's possible to get a visa on arrival.

Whether you visit the embassy or apply for a visa when you arrive, you'll need to make sure you have passport-style photos and money to buy your visa. Many embassies allow you to download application forms which you can bring with you to an interview or post them in with your passport. The forms generally ask for personal information (date of birth, mother's maiden name, marital status, occupation, etc) as well as information about your trip (length of stay, arrival/departure dates and, possibly, an address where you'll be staying), so if you have to apply at an embassy make sure you have this information with you. You'll also be asked which type of visa (see p29) you'll need. Some countries (Australia and Cambodia, for example) allow you to apply for basic tourist visas online, which saves you a lot of waiting in lines.

If you do have to go to the embassy, allow lots of time for long lines and arrive early. No matter how petty or bureaucratic they might seem, you should be polite and friendly to the embassy staff, partly because they can be helpful if they like you, but also because reviewing hundreds of applications is a hard job. Going to an embassy is still the preferred way to get a visa for many travellers, but if you do a postal application be prepared for it to take longer and don't expect to get too much help from embassy staff. ('All this information is on the website. Look it up there and then call me back if you have problems.')

Better travel agents may organise visas for you for an extra fee, so it's generally more affordable to organise it yourself. Using a travel agent is only useful when there are complicated applications, such as those requiring invitations or negotiating complex bureaucracy.

Of course, obtaining a visa when you land in a country is the easiest method with a transaction at the immigration desk, but never assume you can do this (unless you like the idea of being deported), especially if you're getting a working holiday visa (see p116). Visa requirements can change based on the transport you used to enter a country. For instance, if you fly into Laos you can get visas on arrival, but if you go overland you have to arrange them in advance (usually in Bangkok).

When you do get your visa (sometimes posted back to you, sometimes by a return visit to the embassy), check that the dates and details are correct. Mistakes do happen and you should make sure it's all okay before you leave.

Types of Visas

There are five basic visa types: transit, tourist, business, student and working holiday. You're most likely to use tourist, student or working holiday visas, though transit visas are worth thinking about for stopovers. The tourist visa usually lasts for 30 to 90 days and is designed for visitors who are taking in the sights and won't be working. If you're studying (usually at university level – short courses don't require a student visa), the student visa is for you. Your school at home or in your destination should help you apply for this.

The working holiday visa is just the ticket if you want to mix vocation and vacation. The idea behind this visa is that you're just working short-term and some visas won't allow you to work in your career field, so it can be important what you write as your occupation when you apply for this visa. In practice it's very difficult to police this ('Your field is landscape gardening – have you mowed any lawns while you've been in the country?'), but there are random crackdowns. For more on working holiday visas see p116.

The transit visa is for brief stays in a country when you're heading on somewhere else in the next day or two (some countries only allow one-day transit visas). If you're heading overland through a country or stopping over, then a transit visa will get you in and out in a hurry. Don't get a transit visa if there's a chance you might stay longer, because immigration people are tougher on transit visas than tourist visas.

Finally, business visas are for when you're working in a country and will require sponsorship by a company. They require major hoop-jumping on your part and from the company who will sponsor you, plus you'll be bonded to that company and unable to work anywhere else in the country. Because of these complications, most people only use these visas to relocate or do business in another country.

VISA QUIRKS

Visas are part of a bigger political game. You'll find that some countries won't allow visas because your own nation has been a little too critical of another nation's human-rights record or has imposed economic sanctions.

Two important quirks at the time of writing are in Israel and Cuba. The USA has a strict embargo imposed on Cuba, which includes limiting the number of US citizens it will allow to visit Cuba (limiting them to zero if possible). For non-US citizens this means you can't fly from the US to Cuba, but US citizens have the additional complication of what to do with their passports. Simply put, Cuban authorities will stamp a piece of paper rather than your passport, which could create some hassles on the way home.

Israel's officials are also happy to stamp a piece of paper rather than your passport. The reason behind this is that if you want to travel onwards in the Middle East, some countries won't let you in with an Israeli stamp. Countries such as Syria or Lebanon are particularly tough on this though Jordan and Egypt are cool. If you don't get the separate piece of paper stamped and want to travel further in the Middle East, you may have to look at getting a new passport.

Single or Multiple Entry?

A single-entry visa allows you to enter (and leave) a country once, while a multiple-entry visa lets you come and go several times. Another difference is

~ JOURNEY IN CYBERIA ~

You kids think travel is all about hooking up with Facebook friends in far-off lands, texting home for extra travel money (MUM DSPRT 4 CASH PLS SND ASAP) and booking your next hostel bed online. It wasn't always so easy. Eons ago when I was a hard-core traveller, things weren't so simple. You'd show up in a strange new country with little more than an outdated guidebook and the half-remembered suggestions from travellers you met the night before at a bar. Need money? No problem, change some on the street at the black-market rate.

Then one day everything changed. I was in Istanbul and needed to get to Vienna, fast. Istanbul in the 1990s was choc-a-bloc with 'bucket shops', handy little store fronts where you could buy a ticket to Kathmandu or Timbuktu. I never understood how a grubby backpacker like myself could walk into a bucket shop in Istanbul and, *voila!*, 10 minutes later, walk out with a valid ticket on an imminently departing plane to Vienna.

But this time it was different. My travel request would normally trigger a half-dozen heated exchanges over the telephone, as my heroic bucket man fought hard to wrangle me a cheap airplane ticket from Istanbul to Vienna. Go bucket man, go! But not this time. As I sat sipping the obligatory cup of apple tea, three sugars please, my bucket man calmly clicked a few buttons on his computer. Hey bucket man, what's that? Is that the newfangled World Wide Web?

Yes! It was true! My bucket man was playing it cool, but he couldn't hide the truth. My bucket man was making a booking on his computer. On the World Wide Website of Turkish Airlines. It was as simple as click, print and go! Oh, heroic bucket man, how you enlightened me that day. With just a few clicks of a mouse you taught me there's no magic to booking online travel. You drew back the curtain on your dark arts and exposed an Emerald City where I, too, could be king.

Scott McNeely is a recovering travel writer and, though they deny it, the former online publisher at Lonely Planet. Scott currently oversees the 'travel and things to do' website www.viator.com.

---

cost, which usually means that travellers opt for a single-entry visa. Multiple-entry visas come in handy if you're going to use one country as a base to visit neighbouring countries.

TICKETS

AIR

Travel doesn't feel real until you buy your ticket, right? But shopping around is always a good idea and buying at least three months in advance can be good for deals. Obviously, you'll need to have a good idea of where you're going to travel before you buy a ticket, but you'll need to have most of your cash saved up as well. You can make a deposit on most tickets to hold the fare, but you'll have to pay up before you travel (often a month before the flight). For types of tickets to suit your trip, head for the Transport Options chapter (p87).

Comparing Prices

You should definitely look at shopping around for flights once you know where you're going. Hopping between several budget airlines (see p92) can be cheaper than a round-the-world ticket (see p90), and going overland (see p95) can cut the price tag if you've got the extra time. Check your destinations with a couple of different airlines as well as with travel agents, who sometimes get special deals. Even if a deal looks perfect, shopping around can save you money that can be better spent on the road.

Airlines and online travel agents increasingly offer newsletters and alerts that you can subscribe to, and you can even be informed when specific destinations are on

---

sale. Signing up for a few of these services six months before you travel can give you a clearer idea of top fares.

Buying from Airlines

Going straight to an airline can be good if you've already looked around at other prices. Most airlines have online booking, which is quicker than standing in line at a travel agency and allows you to make special requests (see p62), but you might not be able to customise your flight very easily, particularly if you want to visit obscure destinations. Check the Air section in the Getting There portion for the region you'll be visiting (see destination chapters in Part Three) for details about which airlines fly there.

Buying from Online Bookers

The web has a few good comparison tools which are operated by online travel agents and search several airlines at once. Doing your own research, however, can often turn up better deals than a web spider. Here are a few reliable options:

○ **Ebookers** (www.ebookers.com)
○ **Expedia** (www.expedia.com)
○ **Farecast** (www.farecast.com)
○ **FareCompare** (www.farecompare.com)
○ **Kayak** (www.kayak.com)
○ **Lonely Planet Bookings & Services** (www.lonelyplanet.com/bookings/flights.do)
○ **Opodo** (www.opodo.com) European-based site.
○ **Travelocity** (www.travelocity.com)
○ **Viator** (www.viator.com)
○ **Zuji** (www.zuji.com) Asian-based site.

Buying from Travel Agents

If you want someone else to do the legwork and the web surfing, a travel agent can save you some stress. They'll generally have a good idea about the visa situation and will do some price comparing for you. They occasionally have access to better deals than you might be able to find on the web and can offer good packages that can include tours, insurance and other add-ons. If you're getting a round-the-world ticket, they can give you advice on the pricey destinations and suggestions on the best times to visit.

In addition to the regular variety, there are specialist travel agencies that cater for students. As well as other suggestions in the Directories (Part Four), these international agents offer excellent trips:

○ **STA Travel** (www.statravel.com)
○ **Student Flights** (www.studentflights.com)

OVERLAND

Planes, trains and auto-rickshaws will all be an option on your trips, but buying tickets in advance can be a good money saver. Many train passes are available only to foreigners, so when you arrive in the country it can be difficult to buy a pass like the Eurail ticket. See Transport Options (p95).

INSURANCE

Travel insurance seems like a waste of good drinking money, doesn't it? Except when you need it. Accidents happen, sickness can hit even the healthiest people, luggage gets stolen and there are a thousand other things that could really ruin your trip. Travel insurance at least prepares you for some of them. Many nations have reciprocal health agreements, so British travellers, for instance, can use Australian health services, but even in these cases having insurance can get you a ticket home. You may need to bring a health card from home to use another country's medical services.

TIPS

If you need to get a visa, find out at what times the embassy or consulate is open and what documentation you'll need. Get there ahead of this time and be prepared to queue. This preparation will prevent you from wasting days hanging around an embassy that's only open for an hour a week.

WHAT INSURANCE DO YOU NEED?

Travel-insurance policies are offered by travel agencies, general insurance companies and, increasingly, online. Read the fine print before handing over your hard-earned cash for any policy. Premiums get pricey when you want to visit Canada, the US or Japan, because of different health-care arrangements in these countries. Make sure your policy covers you for all the countries you'll be visiting.

Here are some other important factors to look for:

○ **Activity coverage** Study the list of activities you're covered for. Often you'll be allowed one or two bungee jumps within a policy but will have to pay twice as much if you want to go gliding, for instance. If you want to try snowboarding or scuba diving, ask about these activities because they're often not included. Also, look at the list of sports you're allowed to play.

○ **Cancellation** Good policies will cover you against flight and train cancellations, which can be handy when you have paid for prebooked accommodation.

○ **Extensions** If you decide to stay away for longer, ensure your policy can be easily extended while you're away, and that you only pay for the difference in cost between the two periods rather than having to take out a fresh policy for your additional time.

○ **Illegal activities** Most policies won't help you out if you get up to anything illegal. No policy covers for nuclear, chemical or biological warfare, but some policies do insure you against acts of terrorism.

○ **Luggage & valuables** If you're taking a laptop, mobile phone or other valuables, check that they'll be covered as some policies require you to declare these upfront by providing equipment serial numbers. Cheap policies may only cover a limited amount of valuables unless you pay more for the initial policy.

○ **Pre-existing conditions** If you've got high blood pressure, diabetes, asthma or any other illnesses, make sure they're covered. Usually you're okay if your condition is diagnosed and stable, but all policies vary.

○ **Receipts & serial numbers** Keep receipts and serial numbers at home for anything you might lose on your travels.

○ **Sufficient cover** Buy a policy that will cover repatriation – you really don't want a policy that only covers evacuation to the nearest regional medical facility rather than back to your home country. While you're at it, check how large your medical excess

will be (ie how much you have to pay before your insurance company will pick up the tab).

○ **Who pays?** Check whether your policy obliges you to pay on the spot and redeem the money later, or whether the company will pay the providers direct. If you have to claim later, you'll need to keep all documentation. If you have a medical problem, some policies will ask you to call a centre back home where an immediate assessment of your condition will be made.

Some policies also exclude countries based on travel advisories (see p41), so if your country isn't on the list of places covered there could be a good reason for it.

Before you go try out your travel-insurance company's 24-hour emergency hotline to make sure that it's working and easy to work your way through. Better to do this in advance rather than in an emergency.

There are hundreds of insurance companies out there, but here are a few that cater for travellers:

○ **Columbus Travel Insurance** (www.columbusdirect.com)
○ **IMG** (International Medical Group; www.imglobal.com)
○ **Lonely Planet Travel Insurance** (www.lonelyplanet.com/bookings/insurance.do)
○ **STA Travel** (www.statravel.com)
○ **Travelex** (www.travelex-insurance.com)

MONEY & COSTS

No-one likes penny-pinching, but saving money will let you travel longer. Some travellers go overboard with fixed budgets and draconian 'no splurge' rules, but we reckon you should use a budget as a guide only and give yourself a little bit of room to enjoy your trip. Would you really want to miss out on seeing whales thumping the ocean right next to your boat just to save a few dollars? Or say 'no, thanks' to a safari through Kenya, or hang out in a hostel rather than the hippest London club – all because your original budget didn't include it?

Good budgets allow for new possibilities and give you the chance to enjoy the odd bit of serendipity. Plus you could discover a few savings along the way or take a job to pay it off later (see p115). While you don't want to be throwing money away, being miserly and haggling over every last dong (stop snickering, that's what Vietnamese money is called) in a Hanoi market won't make you many friends among locals.

BUDGETING

The best way to start budgeting is to look at your expenses (see p34) while you're away and see how long the money you have will last. Guidebooks to your destination will give you a rough idea of prices, but beware as prices can go up very quickly, so make sure you've got the latest edition or consider looking on the internet for rough ideas on costs.

While you're reading a guidebook, look for activities you might want to do or a course that could make your trip more worthwhile (see p150). A tour could be the best way to get out of major cities if you don't have your own transport. Think about comfort levels. Do you want to blow some extra money on a plush Fijian resort after a couple of weeks of doing it tough island-hopping in the Pacific? It's difficult to plan for everything, so build a bit of 'fat' into the budget so you can stay in a nice hotel when you need to, or allow cash to get a taxi when you're in a hurry. Sometimes you'll have no choice but to spend more to get things done quickly – the Russian visa, for example, can almost double in price depending on how quickly you need it. Allow a little bit of money for emergencies such as missing a plane (you could require an extra flight), and if you don't have any emergencies you can blow it all on your way home.

No matter how thoroughly you plan it, no budget will capture everything, so overestimating can be a good idea – if the guidebook says a meal in Indonesia will cost 15,000Rp (£0.80/US$1.60/A$1.80), you might want to round it up in your currency (£1/US$2/A$2). This means you'll factor in a bit of fat for price changes and currency fluctuations, which can happen when your own currency falls on financial markets.

EXPENSES

Working out your expenses will give you a good idea of how much you'll spend. Start with the big-ticket items which are often closest to what you'll actually spend when you're away (as they won't change much and you can get a clear quote when you book).

BEFORE YOU GO
Plane Tickets
Your plane ticket will be the biggest pretrip expense. Prices depend on where you want to go and you can calculate them by doing a few experimental bookings on airline websites (see p31). You can do this well in advance of your trip, but beware that ticket prices will increase closer to your departure date, so booking when you see a bargain fare is just the ticket. Bargain fares can start a year before your departure date, and some airlines or travel agents will let you pay for your ticket in instalments provided you put down a deposit.

For approximate prices on round-the-world (RTW) tickets, check the Transport chapter (see p88–9). Don't forget the budget carriers (see p92) which offer deals year-round. Some airlines have mailing lists that will send you updates on flight prices and sales.

PAYPAL

If you're addicted to eBay, you'll already know about PayPal (www.paypal.com). This web-based financial tool lets people transfer money into and out of your bank or credit card accounts without giving them the account details, plus you can buy and sell almost anything online. It's a good alternative to wired money if you have easy access to the internet.

Factoring in airport taxes can jack up advertised prices of flights. Usually they'll be part of the final price of your ticket, but in some countries you might have to pay at the airport in the local currency (generally no more than £15/ US$30/A$35). This is often mentioned in the guidebook or you could call the airline for their word on it.

Visas
Don't forget visas when working out your expenses. Sometimes they're free, but if you get a few they add up to a hefty total. Cambodia, for example, charges £10/ US$20/A$21.50 for international flights, while Russian visas will set you back anything from £20/US$40/A$43 to £110/US$220/A$240, depending on how long you want to stay. Try to work out how long you'll stay so you can get the best-value visa, and avoid multiple-entry visas (see p29) as they can push costs up.

Travel Insurance
Skimp on insurance and it will come back to bite your bruised arse. A cheap policy is a waste of money and may not cover you for everything you'll be doing (see p31). On a first trip you should pay more for a reasonably comprehensive policy so you don't have to worry before you bungee jump off a cliff or go hang-gliding. If you're a member of the Hostelling International (see p40), you can get a 10% discount on insurance.

Immunisations
Go to your local travel clinic at least eight weeks before you depart to discuss which vaccinations you need. Some may be free but most will cost you. Depending on where you're going you might be limited to free shots, but if you're going to Southeast Asia you might be looking at several shots and some antimalarials. Go to Health & Safety chapter for more information on immunisations (see p43).

Equipment
Many travellers go crazy buying specialised gear and a new wardrobe before the trip. You probably won't need that outdoorsy fleece if you're going to Sydney, London or Los Angeles – in fact, locals will probably snicker at you. There are a few pieces of equipment which will make your trip easier (such as a money belt, padlock or small torch), but think about your destination and whether you'll really need the gear. Borrowing equipment or buying second-hand might be a good way to crunch costs.

OXPECKERS PERCHED ATOP AN IMPALA AT SOUTH AFRICA'S LARGEST GAME RESERVE, KRUGER NATIONAL PARK (P272).

Basic travel equipment (money belt, power adapter, lock and simple torch) will set you back £18/US$35/A$37.50, but if you throw in a pair of hiking shoes and a basic knife you'll be looking at £80/US$160/A$175. If you want to go camping, a two-person tent and sleeping bag will add £145/US$290/A$310 to your budget. It's easy to spend a lot here, so look really closely at your needs before you go and remember that if it's really vital you can probably buy it while you're away.

Lonely Planet's **online gear shop** (www.lonely planet.com/bookings/gear.do) has partners who can bundle up gear and send it to your home or to you while you're on the road.

Luggage

You'll need to invest in a good bag that will suit every moment of your trip (see Choosing Your Bag, p55), so add a little to your pretrip budget for this.

ON THE ROAD

The destination chapters (see Part Three) include costs, which will help you get an idea of basic on-the-road expenses, and once you've decided on a destination you can get a better idea with the help of a guidebook. Prices do go up, particularly in tourist hotspots, so some travellers get their estimates of on-the-road expenses and add 20%. Others monitor their budget as they go and adjust it as they discover new costs. ('Five bucks for a bottle of water? That wasn't in the budget.')

Accommodation

In terms of your on-the-road costs, where you bunk down will be your biggest expense. Work out how many nights you'll be staying in each type of accommodation and multiply this by the room rate. Don't forget to allow yourself a few nights in a motel or hotel for those days when you just want to get away from the hostel. You

THE TIPPING POINT

Just as you're wiping the corners of your mouth, tipping anxiety pounces on you. It starts by not knowing what sort of place you're in: Are they too homespun for tips? Are they so fancy that they'll be snooty if you don't leave a huge chunk of change?

Tipping varies from country to country and the best approach is to see what other people are doing around you. Remember, a tip is about appreciation, so leaving some money or saying 'Keep the change' is a good idea whenever you enjoyed the meal. You'll need to tip for most services in North America and 15% is the going rate for restaurants, taxis, bartenders and hairdressers (though fast-food places are tip-free). In Japan, however, tipping is seen as rude and appreciation is shown with gifts instead. In almost all countries porters and guides expect a tip and their wages are set accordingly.

Here are a few web resources that will help relieve tipping anxiety:

❂ **DENTON SOFTWARE (www.dentonsoftware .com)** Home of the free downloadable Tipper software that calculates your tip on a Palm device.

❂ **LOUSY TIPPERS (www.lousytippers.com)** A US site that names and shames bad tippers – check to see you're not there before someone deliberately sneezes in your sangria.

❂ **ORIGINAL TIPPING PAGE (www.tipping.org)** Features US tips for tattooists, DJs and everyone else, plus a few international rates.

❂ **TRAMEX TRAVEL TIP (www.tramex.com/tips/ tipping.htm)** Gives a list of 28 countries and their tipping rates and practices.

can make some savings by camping if you've got a tent, or by couchsurfing (see p104). And if that motel room is looking too pricey you can always share to drive costs down.

Travelling out of season is another way to cut costs and you can check the destination chapters for advice on off-season prices for specific places (see Part Three).

Booking ahead can sometimes be a good way to grab a bargain, but if you've got a flexible itinerary you can make savings by finding cheaper places as you travel.

Food & Drink

You'll need to account for at least three square meals a day in your budget calculations, plus a few coffees and snacks along the way. You can scrimp on some meals by cooking for yourself in hostel share kitchens which have basic facilities, and by stocking up at supermarkets for packed lunches when you're sightseeing. But allow yourself a few restaurant meals as well, otherwise your tastebuds might as well have stayed at home eating TV dinners.

A good approach is to allow for a restaurant meal about once a day so you don't miss out on sampling great Italian pasta, true Mexican burritos and a million other signature dishes. Whatever you do to save money, don't forget to factor in the odd tip (see boxed text, left).

Sightseeing

Admission fees for galleries and museums can add up, so look out for discounted or free days, plus having a student card usually gets you a discount.

Entertainment

Okay, so you'll need to think about a few club cover charges and maybe the odd ticket to a performance such as a Maori *hangi* (traditional feast and dancing) or a Japanese *noh* (opera), but there's also a lot of free entertainment that you can see on the street. Ask at a local tourist office for free events or check out posters and flyers around universities, libraries and other public venues.

Shopping

You'll definitely want to leave a small portion of your budget for souvenirs – from a Mexican poncho to a traditional Ghanian drum – but if you're going away for a while you'll probably also need to replace your clothes and other travel goods. There will be bargains in some countries, such as buying clothing in Asia and CDs in the US and Russia.

Communication

Email is usually affordable though other web-based communication can be good value, including Voice over Internet Protocol (VOIP) or a blog. The best way to do this is to save up your emails and blog updates until you find a really cheap internet café or good broadband connection. Phonecards are cheaper than normal phone calls, and texting is significantly cheaper than calling. Check the Staying in Touch chapter (p70) for all the options.

Laundry

Handwashing in the sink will save you some drinking money, though it can be time-consuming, and drying socks on a radiator can get stinky for your bunkmates. A weekly trip to a laundrette usually costs more in time than money, as you have to find a place and wait around while your clothes dry.

Transport

Getting around will add up, so many travellers rediscover walking to save money and see their destination from the street level. Public transport is the next best thing, with taxis coming in as a pricey last resort.

When you're budgeting you can often work out a few large trips (say, from one city to another by train) by looking on the web. Work out the costs of the big tickets and it might be more affordable to get a rail pass (see p95) or to use the hop-on/hop-off bus (see p96).

Activities

This is another important splurge, as you need to enjoy your trip as well as balance the budget. Camel trekking in Xinjiang (China) or sandboarding in Western Australia are as important to your trip experience as eating, so add these in the mix. Some travellers work in the hospitality industry in ski resorts or as diving instructors (see p115), which can be a good way to enjoy activities on your days off.

MONEY PRACTICALITIES

TAKING YOUR MONEY WITH YOU

Getting your life savings out of the bank is scary enough, but then you've got to work out how you can take it all with you. The general rule is to mix different methods, and if your credit card isn't accepted you have travellers cheques as a backup. Even your humble ATM card can be handy if you don't mind your bank getting their cut. Review the list of options below and you'll get a sense of each one's strengths and weaknesses.

Once you're on the road the best idea is to use a money belt (see p57) and look at some good personal security measures (see p50).

Debit Cards

These days getting money on the road can be a simple matter of using your debit card to withdraw cash from your bank account back home. Your bank card will usually have words such as Cirrus or Maestro on it to indicate which network you can use.

Search these popular networks to see if they cover your destinations:

○ **Mastercard/Cirrus** (www.mastercard.com)
○ **Mastercard/Maestro** (www.maestrocard.com)
○ **Visa/Plus** (http://visa.via.infonow.net/locator/global)

Exchange rates at ATMs are okay, but you'll get slugged with a bank transaction fee which can surprise you when you see the statement. It means you're often better off withdrawing large amounts to avoid multiple fees. However, carrying lots of cash can be worrying in terms of security (see p50).

Before you pack your debit card check that it's not going to expire while you're away, and contact your bank to let them know you're off overseas so they don't think your card's gone on a holiday by itself. Two other factors with cards are that they can be corrupted due to demagnetisation or scratching (keep them safe in your wallet or purse and they're usually okay) and that there's a problem of forgetting your PIN. In normal circumstances you might have no problems remembering your PIN, but when you're in a foreign country with jet lag the most basic things are hard to remember. If you do need to write it down in a diary, find a way to encode it so it doesn't look like a PIN number (write a sentence that has the numbers in it and that will help you remember it). Obviously, giving your PIN to strangers while you're away would be dumb and could leave you cashless.

Cash

Cold hard cash comes in handy. Savvy travellers usually get a small amount of their destination's local currency before they leave, usually just enough to get a taxi into town and pay for a few night's accommodation in case something goes wrong. If your bags get lost or the ATMs are out of action, those yuan you got before arriving in China will be more valuable than any transaction fees.

Carrying all your money in cash, though, would require a wheelbarrow in some countries and it's a lot less convenient if you lose your wallet or get mugged. Having a few spare notes stashed somewhere is fine for emergencies, but other means of carrying money are smarter and more secure. Changing cash can be difficult (see p38) and small amounts are almost unchangeable with commissions and other fees factored in – better to donate to a charity at the airport than hang onto them.

Credit Cards

The plastic fantastic really comes in handy in emergencies and can be good for big expenses, but look out for massive interest rates, especially if you won't be able to pay your card off using internet banking while you're away. Most travellers carry one or two cards to use when things get tough, but they usually rely on other means for daily transactions.

You can use credit cards to withdraw cash from ATMs, but this usually comes with a nasty fee that you'll also be paying interest on. Some merchants charge a fee for the onerous task of pushing your credit card through their machine, which makes credit cards less attractive for these functions.

The great advantage of credit cards is that they can be paid off by your parents or friends back home if things get tricky. You'll be able to check your balance online and call for help when you need it. Some credit cards also offer insurance on purchases made using the card, which is handy for large purchases but useless for getting a refund on a bad kebab.

Travellers Cheques

Many travellers appreciate the security of travellers cheques, though with credit cards getting easier to replace when stolen, travellers cheques are rarer. When you get travellers cheques, you sign them and then countersign them when they're cashed. If they get stolen in between they're worthless, and if you record the numbers of your travellers cheques you can get them replaced quickly when stolen or lost. They can come in handy when you're in a rural area that might not accept credit cards.

Now the downside: multiple commissions. You'll get hit with the first commission when you buy travellers cheques and a second one when you cash them. And the exchange rate you'll be offered always sucks. As with any transaction, count your bills carefully to make sure that someone hasn't taken an 'extra commission'. Still, for carrying larger amounts, they can be handy and are relatively easy to cash.

Travellers cheques are often available at banks and some post offices or you can search out some of these providers:

○ **American Express**
   (https://home.americanexpress.com)
○ **Thomas Cook** (www.thomascook.com)
○ **Travelex** (www.travelex.com)

Prepaid Travel Money

These cards run like card versions of travellers cheques and are offered by the same credit-card companies under names such as TravelMoney, Traveller's Cash and Cash Passport. They offer security similar to credit cards as you can cancel them quickly, and a free second card can come in handy.

The fees add up though, with one to put money on the card, another to use ATMs and another to convert currencies. ATM access can be handy, however, and you'll be saved the trouble of working out exchange rates (though the exchange rate you'll be given will suck as hard as with travellers cheques).

Wired Money

Also called 'money transfers', this is your real get-out-of-jail emergency option. You're better off using some of the other options before calling your parents or friends to wire you some money. Why are we so down on this method? Firstly, there's a whopping fee to wire the money, then there's trying to find the wired-money company's office and you'll have to pull out a government-issued piece of ID to get the money.

But when you're really in the shit, wired money is quick (it can take ten minutes to get to you) and you'll receive it in local currency so you can start spending as soon as you leave the wired-money office.

Wired-money companies include:
- **MoneyGram** (www.moneygram.com)
- **Western Union** (www.westernunion.com)

CHANGING MONEY

Whenever you change money, whether it's with a bank or a bloke on a street corner shouting 'Best price for US dollars!', moneychangers will take a cut. Make sure you know upfront how this will work. Most places take a percentage, though some may add a small fee and others just offer bad rates which cover their cut, so make sure you're clear on the rates before you make the deal.

Rules for changing money include:
- **Bigger is better** Change large amounts all at once rather than in several small transactions. This may mean having large amounts of cash on you, but dividing your money is the best idea (see p50).

- **Denominational switcheroos** Beware of getting too much local currency, as in some destinations it's almost worthless. In Cambodia, for example, most traders accept US dollars and will give you change in Cambodian riel which ironically aren't as well accepted in Cambodia. In Cuba, it's the opposite and you can save money using Cuban dollars, which is better than using the US cash. Check your guidebook for the best currency and ask for it in all exchanges.
- **Keep your receipts** Some destinations need you to hang onto these, but they also come in handy when you're trying to work out which place to go back to for a good rate.
- **Street dealers can be hustlers** If it seems too good to be true when a guy comes up to you on the street and offers you the greatest rate you've heard, it probably is.

CURRENCY CONVERSION

Currency exchange rates change daily and one day a moneychanger will offer a great rate, the next your country's currency nose-dives and you'll be wondering if the friendly folks at the moneychanger's aren't ripping you off. You can stay up-to-date online:
- **OANDA (www.oanda.com)** Has good currency converters and a printable cheat sheet that gives you rates.
- **XE (www.xe.com)** Also has a converter and an email alert of currency changes. Most travellers don't worry too much about daily exchange rates, but currency converters come into their own when you're switching countries and you need to know how many Chinese yuan you'll get for your Thai baht.

DISCOUNT CARDS

Discount cards will make it cheaper on the road and are available to students and young people. They offer good deals on everything from hostels to museums, so good that there's a roaring trade in fake cards in backpacker hangouts such as Bangkok and Cairo. It means you'll probably be asked for your student card from home when you're looking for a discount.

International Student Identity Card (ISIC)

The **ISIC** (www.isiccard.com) offers almost 40,000 discounts in over 100 countries, including everything from MP3s and cinemas to flights and carbon offsetting. Check their website for your destinations and see how much value you can get out of the card.

The ISIC card lasts for 16 months (September to the following December), is available to full-time students (there's no age limit) and costs £9/US$18/A$19.50. Applications are available online for UK residents with a list of your nearest branches on the site (usually travel agents such as STA Travel). You'll need to provide evidence you're a full-time student.

International Youth Travel Card (IYTC)

The IYTC is available from the **ISIC** site (www.isiccard.com) if you're under 26. It has almost as many benefits as the ISIC and is available to non-students for £9/US$18/A$19.50 for 12 months.

Euro<26 Youth Card

If you're under 26 and heading to Europe, the **Euro<26 youth card** (www.euro26.org) offers discounts on insurance, concerts, museums, transport and more in 35 different countries. Wherever you see the Euro<26 logo (a pink sign with a juggling Hercules), it indicates that the place offers advantages and discounts. It costs €14 (£11/US$21.50/A$23), lasts for a year and is available online.

Hostelling International (HI) membership

If you're going to stay in a hostel, then this card is crucial as it will give you a discount rate at **Hostelling International** (HI; www.hihostels.com) hostels as well as a few other discounts elsewhere. HI is so massive that even some independent hostels will sometimes give discounts to HI members to drag loyal members away from the chain. At last count they had over 4500 youth hostels worldwide, which can be searched through their website. You can get a membership card through your local branch for £16/US$28/A$32, which lasts for a year.

BARGAINING & HAGGLING

In most parts of the world the price on the tag is what you pay, but there are a few places out there in which bargaining is part of the transaction. Your guidebook should give you a good idea of whether it's okay in a given destination – it's definitely not cool for galleries, museums and often hotels. Markets are usually the venue for haggling though it's sometimes okay in retail stores.

At some point haggling stops being fun for everyone and becomes hard work for the seller who could be serving someone else while the annoying foreigner is trying to shave a few cents off the price. You'll rarely get prices the locals get, so stay polite and keep smiling so the seller enjoys haggling with you. Chances are they've seen all your tricks before ('I'm really walking away now. No, I really am.') and will have a price in mind when haggling starts off. Most importantly, keep some perspective. You're probably paying a lot less than you would at home and a little difference to you could mean a lot to the trader.

HEALTH & SAFETY

No matter where you're travelling it's likely that you will be an obvious target for scammers and shifty characters. As a foreigner, you'll probably have more money on you than most locals do, and you'll have less of an understanding of the culture. Then there's your immune system, which won't be tuned into the bacterial environment you're in. But there's no need to be alarmed. With a few simple precautions you can avoid most hassles and enjoy your trip without any incidents.

BEFORE YOU GO

Before you part with all that cash for a ticket, you should feel your destination is safe. The best way to do this is to research the destination and ask yourself if you're okay with the level of risk.

Once you've booked a ticket you'll need to make your predeparture medical plans. At least six weeks before you go (though eight is more realistic with difficult appointment times and busy schedules), you'll need to begin immunisations. As part of your packing regime, you'll need to start looking for a medical kit even if you're going somewhere safe – it'll come in handy for accidental scrapes, unexpected colds and even hangovers.

IS YOUR DESTINATION SAFE?

No matter where you go there's always some risk. Governments monitor these risks and offer regular updates on places they perceive have risks or potential incidents. While your own government will publish information specific to your nationality, we advise you to check a few of these updates to get a picture of the situation. You should also register for alerts about the country you're travelling to, if you can. This means that the info on any potential problems will be delivered into your inbox while you're on the road and you can work out if it's time to hightail it out of the country.

The best travel advisory services include:

- **British Foreign & Commonwealth Office** (www.fco.gov.uk/travel) Good warnings under 'Travel advice by country'.
- **Canadian Foreign Affairs and Trade** (www.international.gc.ca) Sort out your language choice, then click on 'Services for Travellers' for straight-up advice.
- **Safe Travel** (www.safetravel.govt.nz) New Zealand site that's also good for Pacific islands.
- **Smart Traveller** (www.smarttraveller.gov.au) Use the 'Subscribe' function to receive alerts from this branch of the Australian Department of Foreign Affairs and Trade (DFAT).

COME FACE TO FACE WITH MEMBERS OF THE TURKIC-SPEAKING UIGHUR PEOPLE IN KASHGAR MARKET (SEE P198), XINJIANG, CHINA.

○ **Bureau of Consular Affairs** (www.travel.state.gov) Navigate this US service by clicking on 'International Travel'; subscribe to the State Department Worldwide Caution Alert for regular updates.

PRETRAVEL CHECKUPS

Before you hit the road it's a good idea to get a checkup while you can still see your own doctor and find out if there are any health issues that might affect your trip. Even if you don't think you need any vaccinations, visit eight weeks before you go just for a checkup, which should give you plenty of time for tests or referrals to specialists if necessary.

While you're getting your jabs it's pretty easy to get a medical checkup. Ask your doctor about any medications you might need to take with you, and look at getting a bigger prescription to cover the trip. If you're doing any diving while you're away, you may need to get a certificate of fitness for some dive centres. Ask about any ongoing problems you might have, such as hay fever or asthma, and how they might be affected in some of the countries you'll be visiting.

Getting a dental check could save you a big bill while you're away, and if you're headed somewhere remote the last thing you want is to get a helicopter to fly in because your wisdom teeth are hurting. Your teeth will be hit with new pressures from life on the road, so best to make sure they're in good condition when you go.

If you wear glasses or contacts, you should check in with your optometrist before you go. Bring a good supply of cleaning solutions and a few disposable contacts, which will stay sterile until you crack them open. Even if you prefer contacts, take a spare pair of specs because you may need them. In some countries, prescription contacts are affordable, so consider stocking up.

IMMUNISATIONS

The expression 'prevention is better than cure' could have been coined for immunisations. The basic principle behind immunisations or vaccinations is that your body will be given a tiny amount of a virus, to build up immunity for when you're exposed to the whole nasty virus.

You'll need to get to your local doctor or a travel clinic at least eight weeks before you travel to ensure there's enough time to take full courses of immunisations. Doctors can generally advise on what jabs you'll need, but they'll probably just be looking at a site like **Centers for Disease Control and Prevention** (www.cdc.gov/travel) and clicking on your destination. You should check the Directories (Part Four) for other websites about immunisations to make sure you're well informed. It's also worth reviewing immunisations you may have had as a child, such as tetanus, diphtheria, tuberculosis and polio, to see if they need to be topped up.

If you can't complete a course of vaccinations, your protection against a disease won't be full, so make sure you organise a good schedule with your doctor well before you go. Of course, no matter how sweetly your doctor distracts you, needles will hurt and you may need to organise the rest of your day around experiencing minor side effects, such as slight fever and a numb arm.

If you need antimalarial drugs you may have to start your course of drugs before you go (see p45).

All your immunisations will be recorded on an official certificate and you may need to bring this with you, as some countries require you to show you've been immunised against yellow fever and other diseases. Some travellers even attach it inside their passports with elastic bands.

MEDICAL KIT

Medical kits are as essential as insurance – as soon as you don't have one, you'll realise how crucial they are. Travel clinics sell a range of medical kits with names such as 'overland', 'expedition', 'independent' or 'rock'n'roll', which are designed for all kinds of travellers. They usually cost between £30/US$50/A$55 and £50/US$100/A$110.

It can be slightly cheaper to make your own medical kit and tailor it to your destination. It's better to make the kit comprehensive and keep extras of some items for emergencies (you don't want to be hunting for a pharmacist at 4am to buy water-purifying tablets).

THINK TWICE

Unless you're an aid worker, several countries were no-go zones at the time of writing. This list is far from complete. Governments change, war-torn nations become peaceful and civil unrest can erupt suddenly, so check the latest travel advisories before you travel.

The following countries are the real bad boys with most travel advisories agreeing that they're off-limits for travel:
- ✪ Algeria
- ✪ Afghanistan
- ✪ Burundi
- ✪ Central African Republic
- ✪ Chad
- ✪ Colombia
- ✪ Haiti
- ✪ Iraq
- ✪ Somalia
- ✪ Sudan
- ✪ Yemen
- ✪ Zimbabwe

Following is a list of the medical-kit basics:
- Prescription medicines, including antibiotics and antimalarials.
- Antidiarrhoeals – loperamide is probably the most effective, or the preventive Pepto-Bismol.
- Antifungal cream.
- Antihistamine tablets for hay fever and other allergies or itching.
- Calamine cream or aloe vera for sunburn and other skin rashes.
- Cough and cold remedies, and sore-throat lozenges.
- Eye drops.
- Indigestion remedies such as antacid tablets or liquids.

- Insect repellent (DEET or plant-based) and permethrin (for treating mosquito nets and clothes).
- Laxatives (particularly if you're headed to an area where there's little fibre in the diet).
- Oral-rehydration sachets and a measuring spoon for making up your own solution.
- Over-the-counter cystitis treatment.
- Painkillers such as paracetamol and aspirin for pain and fever, and anti-inflammatory drugs such as ibuprofen.
- Sting-relief spray or hydrocortisone cream for insect bites.
- Sun screen and lip salve with sun block.
- Water-purifying tablets or water filter/purifier.

First-Aid Equipment

Stow this in your checked-in luggage because any-thing sharp will get confiscated if brought on as hand luggage:

- Antiseptic powder or solution (eg povidone-iodine) and/or antiseptic wipes.
- Bandages and safety pins.
- Digital (not mercury) thermometer.
- Gauze swabs and adhesive tape.
- Nonadhesive dressings.
- Scissors.
- Sticking plasters (adhesive bandages).
- Syringes and needles – ask your doctor for a note explaining why you have them to avoid any difficulties.
- Tweezers to remove splinters or ticks.
- Wound closure strips.

If you're going to really remote areas, you'll also need the following:

- Antibiotic eye and ear drops.
- Antibiotic pills or powder.
- Blister kit.
- Dental first-aid kit (either a commercial kit, or make up your own – ask your dentist for advice).
- Elasticated support bandage.
- Emergency splints (eg SAM splints).
- Triangular bandage for making an arm sling.
- Sterile kit with an intravenous-fluid giving set, blood-substitute solution and other intravenous fluids.

Health Documents

Here's a checklist of health-related information you might need to bring with you – some of it may not be relevant to your destination:

- Blood group.
- Contact details of your doctor back home.
- Copy of the prescription for any medication you take regularly.
- Details of any serious allergies (drug or otherwise).
- Health card or contact details for your national health service.
- Letter from your doctor explaining why you're carrying syringes in a medical kit.
- Prescription for glasses or contact lenses.
- Proof of yellow-fever immunisation.
- Summary of any important medical conditions you have.
- Travel-insurance emergency number and serial number of your policy (see Insurance, p31).
- Vaccination certificate.

STAYING HEALTHY ON THE ROAD

When you're away you'll be run down and off your guard for viruses and villains alike. There's no need to get paranoid if you take a few simple precautions and use some common sense.

MALARIA

This disease provokes much debate among travellers and the **Malaria Foundation International** website (www.malaria.org) is dedicated to its prevention. Aside from the backpacker myths (and you'll hear plenty of them, including the one about rubbing gin on yourself!), the facts are that malaria has been found in more than 100 countries globally and can be potentially fatal. The disease is commonly spread by mosquitoes, though not every mosquito bite results in malaria.

You're generally less at risk of getting malaria in Asia than in the more infamous malarial zones of sub-Saharan Africa and South America, though there are some high-risk areas in Asia. In many parts of Southeast Asia – especially areas of eastern Thailand and western Cambodia – there is a rise in resistance of the malarial parasite to commonly used antimalarial drugs. So the best prevention is to use several different preventive methods.

Antimalarial Pills

The bad news is that those crafty mosquitoes have developed resistance to several antimalarial pills, so a doctor will prescribe different pills from region to region. You need to start taking the pills before you leave, so that they'll reach maximum protective levels in your body before you arrive at your destination. This also gives any side effects (such as headaches and diarrhoea – check with your doctor before getting a prescription) a chance to work themselves out before you go. And you'll need to keep popping your pills after you get back or any parasites you picked up will go on a spree in your body. This can mean up to four weeks after you've left a malaria-prone area.

You can find a full list of antimalarial drugs and their possible side effects on the **Centers for Disease Control and Prevention** website (www.cdc.gov/malaria). You'll need to check on the latest developments because mosquitoes keep developing new immunities, but at the time of research some antimalarial drugs included:

○ **Atovaquone-proguanil (Malarone)**: Good for both prevention and treatment of malaria; not for very young children, and very expensive so not ideal for longer trips.

○ **Chloroquine plus Proguanil**: Long-standing drug generally not recommended in Asia and elsewhere due to resistance; useful if you can't take other drugs; can be difficult with other medications.

○ **Doxycycline:** No drug resistance reported yet, but it's probably only a matter of time; side effects include diarrhoea, sensitivity to sunlight and vaginal thrush; not for pregnant women or children under eight.

○ **Mefloquine (Lariam)**: Developed when chloroquine resistance was becoming widespread, though resistance has developed in Thailand and Cambodia; ask your doctor about side effects; note that it's not recommended during pregnancy.

Cover Up

The best way to stop a mosquito biting you is to not give it any flesh to bite. Even if you're taking antimalarials, you should take these simple precautions to avoid bites. Wearing long sleeves, long trousers and socks will leave only a small area exposed – in some countries this can just mean changing into your 'longs' at dusk and dawn, but in areas where you're preventing dengue-fever mosquitoes (such as Central America, Southeast Asia and even northern parts of Australia) you'll need 24-hour protection. Treating your clothes with permethrin will help repel the little monsters.

FIRST-AID COURSES

Depending on where you're going and how far off the beaten track you'll be, a predeparture first-aid course can be a good idea.

As well as listings in the Directories chapter (Part Four), try these international options:

❂ RED CROSS (www.redcross.int) Find your local Red Cross branch for first-aid courses that can include childcare and workplace specialisations.

❂ ST JOHN AMBULANCE (www.sja.org.uk, www.stjohn.org.au, www.sja.ca) With offices in the UK, Australia and Canada, this organisation conducts reliable first-aid courses.

Using a mosquito net at night is another essential, and often you'll be supplied with them in good hostels, but check for holes and protect your own net on your travels by rolling it in another bag. When buying your own net look for one that is treated in permethrin. If you're eating out, look for places that have mosquito coils (see p46) or bug zappers – the constant crackling might not make for great dining ambience, but it's better than slapping your dinner companion to get yet another mosquito.

Finally, biting insects are attracted by many variables: body heat, body odour, chemicals in your sweat, perfumes, scented soap and types of clothing, so consider avoiding perfumes and scented soaps as well as steering clear of activity that makes you hot and sweaty when you know mosquitoes will be around.

Repellents

Despite the many 'jungle strength' and 'mozzie blitzkrieg' brands on the market, the most effective mosquito repellents contain DEET (diethyltoluamide) – check the label for these magic letters and you'll be right. DEET is very effective against mosquitoes and other bugs and one application lasts up to four hours, although if you're sweating in the heat it won't last as long. The higher the concentration of DEET, the longer it will last. The optimal concentration is around 50%, although there are some longer-acting formulations with lower strengths of DEET. You should try a test dose before you travel in case of allergies or skin irritation. You'll use this on clothes and mosquito nets, so make sure it's not irritating, and the smell will become synonymous with your trip ('Ahhhh, DEET! I remember that smell better than Sri Lanka's curries!').

MALARIA & LONG-HAUL TRAVEL

If you're planning on travelling in a malaria-prone area for six months or more, antimalarial pills can get expensive. You have two main options: you can continue to take the usual antimalarials or you can decide not to take them. If you do decide to stop taking them (discuss this with your doctor before you go), you need to be extremely vigilant about avoiding mosquito bites, plus you need to be very clear about where your nearest doctor is and have a good idea of symptoms of malaria. Unless you're really conscientious, it can be easy to forget to take your pills. Unlike with other diseases, you don't build up immunity to malaria with time, so you're still at risk of getting it, even if you've been in a risk area for ages.

Lemon eucalyptus–based natural products have also been an effective alternative to DEET (although DEET is probably still your best bet in high-risk areas). Other natural repellents include citronella, but these tend to be less effective and last shorter (up to an hour), which makes them less practical.

There's a whole industry in repellents, including DEET-soaked wrist bands, electric vapour mats (that gradually burn chemicals), even electrified 'tennis racket' swats and, the traveller's favourite, mosquito coils. Although illegal in some countries and a bit of fire hazard, burning a mosquito coil while you sleep is often a good way to get rid of buzzing blights, plus they're relatively portable and usually available in camping shops. You can often buy them in mosquito-prone countries, but make sure that they don't contain formaldehyde as their active ingredient. Plug-ins, which go into a power socket and disperse slowly, are another option if you know there won't be blackouts or generator switch-offs.

EATING & DRINKING

Bali belly, Montezuma's revenge, the Rangoon runs and tourist trots – it's almost a rite of passage to get diarrhoea from eating something bad while you're on the road, but at the time it can really blow your plans. Most problems come from food, with poor hygiene usually to blame. Diarrhoea and dysentery (bloody diarrhoea) are transmitted in this way, but there are also diseases such as hepatitis A (common in travellers) and typhoid (uncommon).

Less-developed countries are particularly prone to it, but diarrhoea could equally strike in a café at home. When you travel, you'll being eating out more and relying on other people to prepare your food safely. There are a few simple precautions to minimise your risk of getting something nasty. Here are some food-and-drink hygiene tips:

- Avoid food that has been peeled, sliced or nicely arranged, as this means it has been handled a lot.
- Avoid ice cubes in drinks; they may have been made from contaminated water.
- Drink bottled water or canned drinks when you're not sure of water quality. This can mean brushing your teeth with bottled water as well.
- Eat only food that's freshly prepared and piping hot – avoid the hotel buffet like the plague.
- Raw fruit and vegetables are hard to clean. Only eat them if you know they've been washed in clean water or if you can safely peel them yourself. Bananas and papayas are good fruits to eat in the tropics.
- Remember that food can get contaminated from dirty dishes, cutlery, utensils and cups, and blenders or pulpers used for fruit juices are often suspect. Bring your own cup or spoon or clean those in the restaurant with a wet wipe.

- Tinned goods and powdered milk are usually safe (check 'best before' dates).
- Most breads and cakes are usually safe, though avoid cream-filled goodies because bugs such as salmonella love cream.

If you do find yourself with diarrhoea, don't panic. Traveller's diarrhoea usually strikes about the third day after you arrive and lasts about three to five days. As well as by poor hygiene, it can be caused by jet lag, strange food (including too much coffee) and your new lifestyle. It can make a comeback in the second week, though you will build up immunity so it should be less severe.

The most important aspect of treatment is to prevent dehydration by replacing lost fluid and to rest. You can drink most liquids, except alcohol, very sugary drinks, and dairy products. Oral-rehydration sachets can be useful but aren't essential if you're usually healthy. Starchy foods such as potatoes, plain rice or bread are believed to help fluid replacement, and you'll need to stick to a bland diet even after you start to feel better. Antidiarrhoeal tablets are of limited use, as they 'block you up', preventing your system from clearing out toxins and making certain types of diarrhoea worse. They're only really useful as a temporary stopping measure, for example if you have to go on a long bus journey.

Sometimes diarrhoea can be more serious, with blood, high fever and cramps (bacterial dysentery), or it can be persistent and bloody (amoebic dysentery) or persistent, explosive and gassy (giardia). All these diseases need treatment with specific antibiotics. If you're going to a remote area far from medical help, you may want to consider taking antibiotics with you for self-treatment of diarrhoea. However, it's generally better to seek medical advice to diagnose which type of diarrhoea you have and to decide which antibiotics you should be taking.

Safe Drinking Water

Even the clearest, cleanest water can harbour the nastiest illnesses, so water purity will be an issue in many countries. Water can carry diarrhoea, dysentery, hepatitis A and typhoid, particularly in countries where infrastructure is limited and shared water may not be actively monitored.

Drinking bottled water is the obvious answer. It's best to stick to major brands of bottled water (though 'pirate' brands do appear), and make sure the seal on the lid is not broken (as bottles can be refilled with water from any old river). If you're in any doubt, choose carbonated water (for example plain soda water), as this is harder to counterfeit.

Bottled water can be costly, not just to your pocket but also to the environment, with millions of discarded and unrecycled plastic bottles having a severe

URBAN MYTHS – FOOD

You'll hear a not-so-wise old traveller give you these tips on the road, but don't believe a word of it. Checking health conditions in a country you're visiting in a guidebook will help you out, but other travellers probably won't have any special medical knowledge.

✪ **ONE BITE AND YOU'RE SICK!** Your stomach's natural defences (mainly acid) can cope with small amounts of contaminated foods, so if you're not sure about something, just don't pig out on it.

✪ **IF IT SMELLS GOOD, IT'S ALL GOOD.** Bugs are just as attracted to those good smells as you are and smell really isn't an indicator of bacteria content.

✪ **GERMS CAN'T SURVIVE THE BURN OF SPICY FOOD.** The only reason to add spice is for flavour, and it can just disguise bacteria but won't kill them.

✪ **MILK IS ALWAYS GOOD FOR YOU – MY MOTHER TOLD ME.** Unpasteurised milk can transmit a lot of diseases, including TB and salmonella, though boiling it will kill off many bugs.

✪ **WHAT COULD GO WRONG WITH ICE CREAM – IT'S FROZEN, RIGHT?** Freezing can kill off bacteria, but if power cuts are a factor, the food may have been refrozen several times, making it vulnerable to bugs.

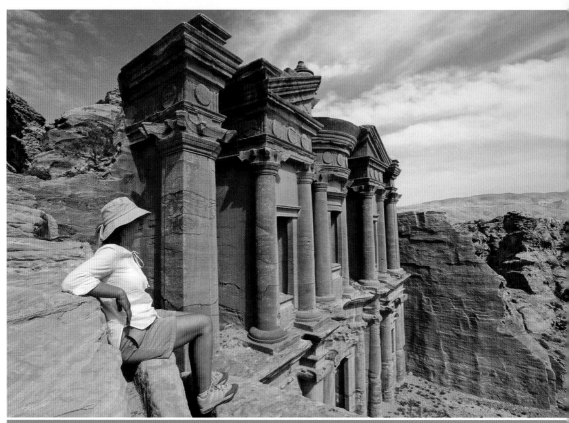

MENTIONED IN THE DEAD SEA SCROLLS, THE ANCIENT CITY OF PETRA (SEE P281), JORDAN, CONSISTS OF BUILDINGS HEWN OUT OF SANDSTONE CLIFFS.

environmental impact in many countries. If you're trekking or travelling off the beaten track, bottled water is just not practical and may not be available in remote areas. In these situations, you'll have to carry some means of making safe drinking water with you. Chlorine and iodine are the most popular chemicals, and at optimal concentrations both kill bacteria, viruses and most parasites (one exception is cryptosporidium). They're both available as tablets or liquids ('tincture' of iodine), and iodine is also available as crystals, usually at pharmacies, travel clinics and outdoor stores. They'll come with instructions about dosage and use, which you should follow closely or they may not be effective.

Make sure you have more than one means of purifying water in case one method fails (for example, take some iodine as well as a pump-action purifier).

If the water is cloudy, no chemical in the world can help you because organic matter neutralises the chemicals. This will happen when you're going off the beaten track and taking water from a surface source (ie river, puddle or lake), not from a tap. This is when you'll need a filter/purifier. There are tons of different types on the market, and they can be expensive and break down easily, but specialist outdoor shops can usually recommend good options.

ACCLIMATISATION

It can take awhile to adjust to a new destination, but changes in temperature and altitude require some special consideration. Your body has an amazing capacity to adjust, but you'll need to help it along in extreme circumstances.

Beating Heat

Avoiding serious problems such as heat exhaustion and heatstroke is all about drinking enough water to replace the amount you're sweating out. Cool water is best. Alcohol, tea and coffee, no matter how refreshing they seem, actually make you lose fluids. Don't wait until you feel thirsty before drinking; thirst is a very bad indicator of your fluid needs, and if you're thirsty, you're already dehydrated. Keep your own clean water (see p47), ideally in your own bottle to avoid plastic waste, and take regular drinks. If you sweat a lot, you may need to supplement your drinking with rehydration salts.

Physical activity will obviously make you hot, so your body will have to work even harder to stay cool during exercise. If you're active in a tropical climate, take it easy during the first week, building up slowly as you acclimatise. Avoid overexerting yourself (and this includes overeating) during the hottest part of the day; it's the perfect time for a siesta.

As far as clothing is concerned, you need to choose clothes that will protect your skin from the sun (and insects) but that won't make you too darn hot. Sunburn makes your body less able to cope with the heat. Loose, light-coloured clothing made of natural fibres such as cotton will help you cope with the heat – ironically, dark colours, though 'cooler', will absorb the heat more.

Tanning might be an option at home, but with different conditions (holes in the ozone layer over the southern hemisphere or higher altitude, for example) it's probably not worth it. As well as making you embarrassingly lobster-red on your first day, too much sun will age your skin and increase your risk of skin cancer. The best tip is to stay pale by covering up with clothes and hats. These provide by far the best protection from harmful rays (much better than any sun lotion). A wide-brimmed hat keeps damaging rays off all those easily forgotten bits: nose, ears, back of the neck, bald patch etc. Protect your eyes with sunglasses that block out UV rays. If you're using sun cream, make sure it's strong and waterproof and replace it as often as you need to. The sun is usually at its most intense between 11am and 3pm, so use it like locals do and have a rest in the shade.

Remember, you can:
○ Still get burnt on a cold day if the sun is shining.
○ Fry on a cloudy day (because clouds let through some UV radiation) and in the shade (from reflected light, often off water).
○ Sunburn through water (snorkelling can leave you smouldering).
○ Cover up with a T-shirt and don't forget to use plenty of water-resistant sun screen.

Cold Climate

Extreme cold, especially if you are trekking or just travelling through highland areas, can have as much impact as the sun. In the desert it can get freezing when the sun goes down, as there's nothing to retain the heat. Wearing the right gear is the best idea and if you're going in and out (which you will be if you're sightseeing in a museum, then heading somewhere else for lunch, for example), wearing several layers that you can remove as temperature changes is a good idea. Food equals heat, so make sure you eat regularly and get sufficient calories in cold climates.

Another chilling problem is dehydration (cold makes you urinate more) so, much like in a hot climate, you should drink water often. The cold can also give you constipation and sunburn (especially at high altitude). Worse problems are general body cooling (hypothermia), or localised cooling (usually affecting hands and feet), called 'frostbite'.

Altitude

Above 2000m the lack of oxygen tends to make you a little loopy, particularly if you fly straight to a high place such as Lhasa (Tibet), La Paz (Bolivia) or Cuzco (Peru). Symptoms of mild altitude sickness kick in when you first arrive and include headache, nausea, loss of appetite, difficulty sleeping and lack of energy. Mild symptoms of altitude sickness just require rest, but more serious cases can be fatal so should be treated quickly.

If you're trekking you'll need to look seriously into acute mountain sickness (AMS) and consult with your travel-health clinic or expedition organiser. An authoritative website with a good section about AMS is www.fitfortravel.scot.nhs.uk. Before you leave, check that your insurance covers altitude sickness. Discuss the effects of high altitude with your doctor if you have any ongoing illnesses such as asthma or diabetes, or if you're taking the contraceptive pill.

If you are trekking or climbing, the best way to prevent AMS is to ascend slowly. Sleep at a lower altitude than the greatest height you reached during the day, and allow extra time in your schedule for rest days. Drugs such as acetazolamide (trade name Diamox) are sometimes used to prevent AMS. However, taking drugs is no substitute for proper acclimatisation. If symptoms persist or worsen you must descend. You must never continue to climb if you have symptoms of AMS.

WOMEN'S HEALTH
Periods
Your cycle may be affected by time changes and the novelty of travelling, but, like jet lag, it should fall into synch with your new destination. You may find that your periods stop altogether when you're away – affected by change of routine and various stresses (but do a pregnancy test if you think you may be pregnant). Or they might become heavier. If you suffer from PMT, be prepared for it to be worse, especially when you're trapped on a local bus where you have to nurse your neighbour's chickens. Take plentiful supplies of remedies you find helpful, as they may not be available in your destination.

If you think you may need contraception, consider starting the pill before you leave – it can reduce PMT and makes periods lighter and regular.

Vaginal Infections
Hot weather and limited washing facilities make thrush (yeast infection) more likely when you're travelling. If you know you are prone to thrush, it's worth taking a supply of medication with you.

Sex with a new partner could result in acquiring a sexually transmitted disease (STD, also called STI for 'sexually transmitted infection'). Get any symptoms such as an abnormal vaginal discharge or genital sores checked out as soon as possible. Some STIs don't show any symptoms, even though they can cause infertility and other problems, so unprotected sex while you're away should be followed by a checkup when you return home. Insist on a use of a condom to be safe.

The Pill
If you think you'll need this while you are away, see your doctor, a family-planning clinic or your local women's health organisation before you leave. Timing your pill-taking can be tricky if you're crossing time zones, and diarrhoea, vomiting and antibiotics used to treat common infections can all reduce its effectiveness. The pill has also been linked to blood-clot formation, usually in the calf muscles or lungs (especially when you're not moving around a lot), so advice on deep-vein thrombosis is particularly relevant to women. If you're going to be in a high-altitude destination (over 3700m), ask your doctor about alternative contraceptives.

There are over 20 different types of pills, so take a plentiful supply of your medication with you to avoid switching to another brand. In some countries, oral contraceptives may not be readily available.

STAYING SAFE ON THE ROAD

There are some problems that you'll encounter on the road which you can only be immunised against with knowledge and preparation. Most people you meet will be friendly and helpful, but it can pay to be on your guard sometimes and set yourself some basic safety rules.

PERSONAL SECURITY
Not everyone is going to try to rip you off but in crowded, heavily touristed areas such as markets, busy squares, on public transport or even at tourist information centres, pickpockets have been known to operate. You'll probably be most at risk when you first set out because you may not be looking for potential dangers.

Make sure you know where your valuables are at all times, though dividing them between a few different places is always a good idea. If your hostel or hotel looks trustworthy, you can leave some valuables in their safe or in your own locker. Bringing a money belt lets you stow your most precious belongings, usually your passport, travellers cheques and credit cards. The money belt should be worn under your clothing (baggier gear will hide it better, and don't leave straps showing as they can be easily cut) and should never be taken out in public. Save your fumbling for a credit card for the privacy of your hostel room, and take your passport out in advance if you know you'll need it during the day. So what about cash? Carrying a wallet or purse is fine for bigger amounts and another form of ID, so long as it's out of sight. Again, don't go rummaging through this in public places if you can avoid it, and be sure you know where it is when you're in crowded spots. Then there's the 'whip-out' (see p52), which is best for your daily spendings. Some people carry a second wallet with a single form of ID and their daily spendings instead of a whip-out in their pockets. Always keep a little spare cash and a credit card stashed somewhere just in case – this could be your bag back at the hostel if it looks secure.

If you're travelling with a group, you can often make a base camp, where one of you will mind all the bags while the others go to buy tickets or get food. This can be a good technique, but secure your bags to avoid their easy theft – one traveller reported having their bags scooped up at an Indian railway station by enterprising thieves with their own luggage trolley. Also make sure you swap the shifts around in the group, because being the one who always minds the bags sucks.

Vulnerable Spots

Obviously, busy tourist spots will attract pickpockets and some may even work in groups, so avoid being distracted while another member of the gang dips into your pockets. Transport is equally vulnerable, so make sure your bag is looped around your leg on short hops and padlocked down for longer trips, especially on overnight train journeys. The other big danger is when you're drinking. Chances are you'll lose sight of your daypack and some opportunistic local will make the snatch, so keep it under your table (especially in streetside cafés, where a passing motorcycle snatch is possible) and loop your arm or leg through a strap. Just as you would at home, you should avoid lonely and remote areas at night. Public places can be good as there's little chance of violent crime, but don't forget about the pickpockets who love the busy spots. Visit public ATMs whenever possible and be discrete when you type in your PIN.

Make sure you're riding in registered taxis (check a guidebook to your destination for the local situation), and if your driver seems to be heading somewhere remote, make a polite enquiry and think about getting out. Taxi drivers can be saints in some places (especially when you're out late and need to get home fast) and satans in

---

MY FIRST

― ROMAN HOLIDAY ―

As if I wasn't worried enough by my first trip overseas, I had to read the section of my Rome guide-book called 'Dangers & Annoyances'. It clearly told me that the second I got off the train I'd discover 'thieves are very active in the area around Stazione Termini.' In the days leading up to my first international flight, people elaborated on the devious means by which I'd be robbed blind, including Romani women who threw babies at you and the second you caught them the women would cut every bag off you while dipping into your pocket for wallet, travellers cheques, passport and every last stick of gum.

Off the plane I was anticipating robbery. Catching the train in from the airport, I eyed the couple opposite me, convinced they were hardened thieves working this train for chumps who hadn't read the Dangers & Annoyances section. When they pulled out a package I knew it was a trick. I braced myself in case they tried to throw it at me. Instead, it was cheese. They ate for a while and saw me staring so they offered me some. It could be poison or, at the very least, a tranquiliser. But I risked it. And the soft milky taste was worth it.

'Mozzarella di bufala', the man explained. He told me it was from his home town, where he and his wife had just flown back from, so they had plenty. He wasn't a thief, just a man proud of his hometown produce.

The expression 'taken with a grain of salt' is a Roman one. It was used to describe a king who wanted to become immune to poison, so he took small quantities of toxins with just a single grain of salt to make it more palatable. Paranoia should be served with a sack of salt, while kind offerings from strangers generally taste good enough already.

George Dunford is the author of this book.

---

others ('Sir, what about a shortcut via my cousin's bar? You love it!'), so think about getting the mobile number of a good taxi driver when you encounter one.

In the Hostel

There are thousands of different hostels and, frankly, some of them are as secure as a baby's candy. Look for lockable doors and lockers where you can use your own padlock. Big hostels will use lockers that have computerised locks, which are also fine. Some places may have left-luggage areas, which are good for leaving your bag in after you check out, but make sure they're lockable and not generally accessible. Some hostels may even have safes, which are good for valuables so long as they're actually safes and not just a plastic bag under the counter. It won't hurt to ask to see the safe if it sounds dubious.

> ## THE WHIP-OUT

Before you get the wrong idea, the 'whip-out' is that chunk of change you'll carry in your pocket so it's close at hand or easy to whip out. We can't take the credit for this genius, as the Texan author Kinky Friedman coined the expression for the handy money.

Generally, you'll need enough in your whip-out to cover daily expenses such as meals, drinks, admission costs and other little costs. You won't need to dip into your wallet or purse unless it's a really big expense (such as accommodation or transport). If you're going to a museum, have the admission fee in your whip-out so you can pay it easily. Some people go professional with the whip-out and have a money clip for bills, which can be very handy when you change money and are given a huge stack of bills. For Kinky Friedman this was usually the case, as his millionaire best buddy could buy a jet plane out of his whip-out.

Everyday life at the hostel can present chances for thieves. Be sure your room is secure and try to keep the door locked at night (even when it gets hot), as even a charging mobile phone could be too tempting to a passer-by. When you sleep, it can be a good idea to keep your money belt in your pillow case, as even the most out-of-it sleepers will wake up when someone's tugging at their pillow. Make sure your valuables are secure when you go for a shower – take them with you if the room is unsafe. Don't forget that your fellow travellers are just as likely to swipe your valuables as locals.

You should avoid giving your room number to strangers, particularly if you're a solo woman and if you do want to arrange meet-ups with locals, look for public places. If a stranger asks where you're staying, you can be general (in a city with several hostels 'a hostel' is a fine answer, but if there's only one hostel be vaguer), or you can lie outright and tell them later when they've earned your trust.

In Case of Mugging

Muggings are rare, as most theft of valuables is based on sneaky grabs rather than threatening someone with a weapon. In the unlikely event of a mugging, stay cool and give the muggers what they want quickly. Give them the money you have at hand and most muggers will take it and run, but some will ask for your money belt, camera and phone. Give it up, and your insurance (see p31) should cover the loss. If you've got an escape route planned, make a run for it as most muggers won't follow, especially if you shout for help.

Once you're away from your assailant, make for the police station and report the robbery. You'll need some paperwork for the insurance claim and, if you followed the earlier advice about stashing some extra money and credit cards, you'll be okay until you can get replacement cards and passport. Remember to report stolen credit cards as soon as you can, so your mugger won't have too much of a spree.

Scams

Every traveller on the road will warn you about some great scam they claim happened to a guy they ran into in Bangkok or Amsterdam, or was it San Francisco? Some are just good urban myths, but the real ones are based on the fact that most visitors are hugely wealthy relative to locals. Most scams are about money, so if you're careful with yours then you won't be anyone's 'walking ATM'. In a few cases they may be about your personal safety (such as kidnapping scams), though these will often be covered in travel advisories (see Is Your Destination Safe? on p41). Some scams will be about helping a stranger while their accomplice is cutting the bottom out of your daypack. The trick is to remain sceptical enough to stay safe without closing yourself off to good experiences (see My First Roman Holiday boxed text on p51).

You can't make generalisations about scammers: sometimes it's a charming man offering to sell you gems at a bargain price, or it could be a shy kid wanting you to kick a football with them. Most scams revolve around asking you to do something that goes against your common sense, but because that guy is so charming or the kid is so cute you'll find yourself thinking about it. Stick to your safety rules and you'll be fine.

Scams change as quickly as scammers do, but guidebooks will give you the latest and Lonely Planet's **Thorn Tree** (www.lonelyplanet.com/thorntree) is always quick to pick up on scams. Here are a few recent ones:

- **Changing money on the black market** It's always difficult to know what you're getting on the black market. Sometimes the rate will be really bad, sometimes notes will be counterfeit. Our favourite is the fake policeman who just happens to arrive when you hand over your money and he 'confiscates' it.
- **Credit card numbers** With so few people checking your signature and the ease of using someone's credit card number online, credit card fraud is all too easy. Carefully watch your card in restaurants to see that a second bill isn't rung up and check online to see if your balance has any unknown jumps. Be careful when using your credit card online in internet cafés. If it's a good place it's fine, but some places have password-detection software or hardware which will swipe your numbers for use later.
- **Fake police** In Africa, India, Central and South America, official outfits might sometimes fool you into thinking someone is a policeman. They'll demand to see your passport and order you to pay a fee for some fabricated reason. Hang on to your passport and money, and always ask to see ID. If they're the real deal, you can always ask to sort this out at the real police station. In 2007 there was even a fake-police case reported in Sydney (Australia).
- **Gem or carpet deals** These are classic scams where someone will offer you a deal of a lifetime. Either they'll offer to send your recent purchase home or a bargain on gemstones that you could resell for a fortune. Of course, the expensive gems or carpets are worthless or they'll never send you purchase home for you. Another variation is designer clothing that's either fake or stolen.
- **Offers of food & drink from friendly strangers** Whether you're on a bus, in someone's home, in a bar or restaurant, be careful about sharing a drink or a snack with someone you don't know. Travellers can be drugged and their possessions stolen. This can happen pretty much anywhere in the world but seems to be particularly prevalent in the Philippines.
- **Practicing English** You've just met a cute girl or boy at a major tourist attraction and they're keen to practice their English with you. They'll suggest a local café and before you know it, you'll get served with a massive bill. Yep, the attractive English-speaker and the café staff have it all sorted out, so you have to part with a lot of cash for your one drink. Another variation involves an art gallery and a charming young artist.

KEEPING IT LEGAL

Just as you should respect the people you're visiting, when you're in a foreign country you're actually bound by its laws. Your embassy and other authorities can't help you when you break local laws and you could find yourself doing jail time (or worse in countries with capital punishment). High-profile cases have shown that bringing prisoners home can be very difficult – Australians would know of the Bali Nine's sentences for drug smuggling, while Brits would know about Garry Glitter's imprisonment for sex offences.

The best protection is to do some research about the country you're visiting (reading a guidebook will usually make it clear). Even if locals are experimenting with drugs, that doesn't necessarily mean they're legal, and foreigners are usually more visible so getting caught is more likely.

Sex & Drugs

Tourist haunts seem to attract people selling drugs and you can get sick of people trailing after you offering 'Ecstasy, coke, marijuana, whatever you want'. But in some countries where drugs seem easy to come by, they may actually be illegal. Using drugs overseas can often mean getting mixes that vary in quality from lethally pure to throat-lozenge placebos ('Man, I was so high last night and it weirdly cleared up my cough.'). The real danger is that you never know what you get. You'll also be in a stressful environment, so panic attacks and anxiety are more likely side effects. With HIV infection rates higher in many destinations than at home, intravenous drug use is even more risky overseas. And if you're using Larium as an antimalarial, you'll need to be careful of side effects as Larium itself can be a mind-altering drug.

Another concern with drugs is trafficking. No matter how much you're offered to 'just carry one package', it's never worth it and customs people mean it when they ask 'Did you pack that bag yourself?', so you'll wear any penalties for carrying drugs. Don't carry a package for anyone unless you know exactly what's in it (including stuffed toys and wrapped gifts) and keep an eye on your bag at airports. Finally, before you get involved with the drugs industry (even as a customer), consider the impact on local communities as local people get caught up in a lucrative but illegal and dangerous black market.

Safe sex is even more important when you're overseas because of the higher infection rates of HIV (in Africa it's an epidemic that claimed 1.6 million lives in 2007) and other sexually transmitted diseases (STDs; also called STIs for 'sexually transmitted infections'). Not only are infection rates higher, often due to lack of safe-sex education, but medical resources will be limited. Simply put: use a condom. Rubber will break down in heat though, so store condoms deep in your pack and check for holes before using them.

GLOBAL ISSUES

After a browse of the headlines you could be left wondering if it's even safe to go outside your front door. But the news does give you the world's worst. You should plan your itinerary around the best and safest. You may not be able to do anything about some issues such as natural disasters, but being aware of the risks is the best preparation you can have. After reviewing a few travel advisories (see p41), you might reconsider your itinerary, but you should definitely keep an eye on current events for potential dangers.

Natural Disasters

Hurricane Katrina and the Boxing Day tsunami were two tragic events that made many people rethink their travel plans. Realistically though, both these events were freaks of nature that had little warning – is there any way you can prepare for a natural disaster? Even 'safe' destinations, such as New Zealand with its several active volcanoes, are vulnerable to geothermal activity, but people still flock there in the thousands.

Most travel advisories warn of impending natural disasters. Watching the news will also keep you aware of the latest developments. In the event of a natural disaster, your embassy will track down travellers, and local authorities will be aided by international Non-Governmental Organisations (NGOs). To get more information (and possibly make yourself a little paranoid) about what to do in a blackout and similar situations, check out **Centers for Disease Control and Protection** disaster pages (www.bt.cdc.gov/disasters).

Terrorism & Political Unrest

Just as disasters are ruled by natural forces, terrorism and political unrest are huge events rooted in history and social systems beyond a traveller's control. Reading up on the history of your destination can be useful, as you'll develop an understanding of the political situation and the likelihood of a revolution or clash of religious groups. A guidebook can also tell you more about regions where political unrest could be a particular problem – Sri Lanka, for example, has dangerous pockets where the Tamil Tigers are staging a civil war, but other areas see little trouble. Travel advisories (see Is Your Destination Safe? on p41) are good indicators of what may happen in a country. You should, of course, avoid any political activity when you're overseas, including political marches or rallies as they can become violent.

Terrorism has become even more unpredictable with a global campaign waged by organisations such as the Islamic militant group Al-Qaeda, which has been active in New York, London, Madrid and Istanbul. Obviously, increased security in airports has reduced the dangers, but if you see any suspicious activity you should report it to airport authorities or police. Some travel advisories warn about threats of terrorism, so if you can get a regular alert for your destination it will inform your choices.

GET PACKING

Everyone will have advice on what you should pack for your trip. Some people swear by sarongs (handy for wearing or making an emergency tent) while others need to bring their hairdryer and personal salon. It really just depends on your own comfort level, but it's universally agreed that travelling light is the best policy.

CHOOSING YOUR BAG

BACKPACKS

This is definitely the most practical way to carry stuff, even if you're not constantly on the move. It's worth paying a little more when it comes to a backpack, because it will be your constant companion and home for most of your trip. There are all sorts of snazzy designs, but your main concern should be comfort and that it sits easily on your spine.

This is not a last-minute purchase. Buy your backpack six weeks in advance, pack it and take an experimental walk of your neighbourhood for at least an hour (get used to the stares of people as well, because backpackers are pretty conspicuous). It's much better to work out before you go if it doesn't fit or if there's a manufacturing fault. Definitely keep the receipt in case it doesn't work out.

Travel Packs

With a zip that runs around the sides and top of your pack, this is the preferred option of serious backpackers. The zip lets you open your bag completely for when your last pair of clean underpants is buried at the bottom, and you can open it to make sure everything is in there. It's easy to pack and unpack (and you'll do this often).

Good travel packs come with features that push the price up but are worth it. A zippered flap that will cover your harness is handy for flights. A detachable shoulder strap and side handles are also really useful when you need to pass your bag up to a porter or carry it other than on your back. You'd be surprised how biased some hotels can be against backpacks – 'transforming' it into a large soft suitcase by zipping up the harness and using the carry handles often fools a snooty concierge.

Your zips need to be able to lock together and some bags come with a combination lock, though a padlock from a hardware store will do. Make sure your backpack has good back support, because you'll be wearing it for at least an hour most days. Most backpacks have good internal frames that are better than rigid external ones. Another handy feature is a bottom compartment, so you can roll up a sleeping bag or separate dirty laundry from clean.

And then there's the detachable day pack – another piece of baggage that will be your best friend by the end of your journey. These little beauties zip onto the front of your bag when you need to lug all your gear, or they can be worn on your front (it feels like being in a suit of armour) when you need to quickly pull out your passport in a train station. But wait, there's more! The day pack unzips, so you can carry it around separately and leave your big bag safely back in a locker at the hostel. They're usually big enough to carry around supplies for a day or even two, if you can pack lightly for a weekender. The downside is they look dorky (two straps and a chunky design make you look like a school kid), but they're more secure than a courier bag.

Top Loaders

The top loader is the backpack your parents might have used to go hiking. It's basically a long tube with access through the top. They're perceived as more watertight, but if you get a good travel pack it should be well sealed for most downpours. Top loaders are for trekking expeditions because they balance well, but they're really difficult to get things out of, especially that last pair of underpants.

Fitting & Fine-Tuning Your Backpack

Having decided which type to go for, now consider:

○ **Fit** All backs are different, so get a pack that suits yours. Try all potential bags on with weight inside (most shops have small weights for this purpose). A good pack will have an adjustable internal frame that can be fitted to the length of your back and you should adjust this to get the perfect fit. Most big brands have male- and female-specific models (basically 'long' and 'short' ones), though tall women

are often best off with the 'male model'.

○ **Size** The short answer is: 65L is big enough. Camping may require a bigger bag, but if you get much more than this, you'll probably overpack.

○ **Strength** Cheaper models probably won't be as strong as a more expensive one. It's not always obvious from examining a backpack how durable it will be. Some materials seem light but are actually much more durable than heavyweight canvas.

○ **Waterproofing** Getting a bag that's water-resistant will cover you when you're caught in the odd shower, but if you're doing water sports, waterproofing is necessary.

Backpacks are priced from around £60/US$90/A$150 to £200/US$300/A$350. We recommend the midrange packs (£80/US$160/A$200 to £120/US$200/A$240) for affordability, comfort and durability. You'll need to factor your pack price into your budget (see p33).

WHEELIE BAGS

You'll see people dragging this 'pet luggage' after them on wheels by the retractable handle. If you're staying in cities, these bags can save your back. Some are hybrid backpacks with soft sides, a detachable day pack and hideaway straps that mean you can wear the bag on your back when needed or zip harnesses away when that concierge is giving you the evil eye.

Investing in a bag with good wheels will make it easier to manoeuvre on cobblestones and other rough terrain. On stairs (and some destinations just don't *do* lifts) they can cause a real jarring on your spine as you lug them up one crunching step at a time.

DAY PACKS

If you get a travel pack, it'll come with a good day pack, but if not, it's worth investing in one. A smaller bag is handy for your guidebook, camera, map, water bottle, medical kit and sun screen, and you can stretch it when you want to stay out for a night somewhere.

If you're doing loads of walking, a strong, well-padded day pack is a worthwhile investment. If you're not a great trekker, a lightweight foldaway day pack is the way to go. Day packs are ideal as carry-on baggage on flights. A day pack will set you back from around £15/US$25/A$30 to £30/US$100/A$120 and is another cost to add to your list (see p33).

COURIER BAGS

These one-strap, over-the-shoulder bags are great for hopping around town, but if you're wearing them by your side for long periods of time they can yank your spine out of shape. They're best for you if you twist them around onto your back, but then they're out of sight which can be insecure. Our final words of warning: one strap is easier for passing thieves to slash.

PACKING

Before you go you'll need to have a dress rehearsal, where you pack everything you think you'll need and see how well it fits in your pack. Chances are it won't, and you'll have to go back and reprioritise. Backpacker gurus reckon you should pack it all, then *halve* what you've got in there. Walk a lap of your neighbourhood with your fully packed bag just to see how it feels. Now you'll definitely feel like leaving behind that hairdryer.

Unless you're going somewhere really remote, it's worth remembering that you'll be able to buy supplies along the way, so if you rule something out you can often buy it later.

PACKING LISTS

Before you jump in and get packing, think a little about your destination. If you're going to a few places you'll need to pack versatile gear, such as clothes that will get you into a club but can also be worn when camping. Overpacking will be annoying when you're on the road, so consider every item on our lists to see what will be really useful and what you might have to post home or, worse, abandon while you're away. We've organised the lists giving what's most important first and the more optional items further down, though depending on your destination some of these items might be just as vital, for example antimalarial nets in Southeast Asia.

Security

○ **Money belt** A money belt is useful – it's the safest way to carry debit or credit cards, travellers cheques,

cash, passport, tickets and other important items. Buy one that can be worn unobtrusively beneath whatever you're wearing, so bum bags are out. The most common types of money belt are worn either around the waist or the neck. They're not easy to get to, but thieves will find them similarly difficult to access. The fabric is important because plastic gets clammy, while leather becomes stinky. Cotton is ideal as it's washable and comfortable. Put the tickets, passport and paperwork in a plastic bag so they don't get damaged by sweat or water. Check out the belt's clasp or attachment.

○ **Padlock & chain** Apart from securing the backpack, padlocks can fasten hostel and train-carriage doors. Chains are used to attach backpacks to bus roof racks or train luggage racks, though they can be heavy.

○ **Waterproof pouch** Take one of these for your documents and money, especially if you're into water sports.

○ **Personal security** Personal alarms, internal door guards, Pacsafe for your backpack (metal grid work which covers your backpack to make it unslashable), and minisafes (attachable to radiators) are all available.

ONE-BAG WONDER

Think you're doing pretty well on the packing front? Check out Doug Dyment (www.onebag .com) who swears by the single-piece-of-luggage rule. He's hard-core in the belief that you can go absolutely anywhere with just a lone piece of carry-on baggage. His lists will make you rethink everything you've brought.

Documents

Make sure all your documents (passport data and visa pages, credit card numbers, travel insurance policy, driving licence, tickets, vaccination certificates etc) are copied before you go. Leave one set of copies with someone at home and take another with you (keeping it separate from the originals). You can also store this information online – your email account works best. You'll need to access your CV if you're looking for work, so make sure it's current as it's tedious to update your CV in a busy Colombian internet café.

ALASKA'S BEAUTIFUL INSIDE PASSAGE (P243).

Sleeping

○ **Alarm clock** Unless you're taking your mobile phone, an alarm is essential for early morning trains, planes and buses. A good loud watch will also do, plus it's more portable.

○ **Sleeping bag** A lightweight sleeping bag is a must if you want to be totally independent and travel around a lot. A sleeping-bag liner can be helpful, either as a sheet in dubious hotels and hostels or to keep your sleeping bag clean.

○ **Torch** A torch will let you find stuff late at night in a dorm, when you're coming in late or leaving early or if the electricity packs it in. It can be handy for exploring caves and ruins. The Maglite is the toughest, but bulbs and batteries run out quickly. LED (light-emitting diodes) torches don't blow bulbs easily and batteries last longer. Unless you're going caving, headsets are just goofy. Your mobile phone may have a torch but check that it's bright enough for nocturnal runs to the bathroom.

○ **Mosquito net** In malaria-prone regions this is crucial. Even cheap hotels provide mosquito nets, but with your own net you can always be sure it's treated with a mosquito killer (permethrin) and has no holes.

○ **Pillow** If you have neck or back problems, a pillow can be a good addition. Types include inflatable head and neck pillows, inflatable neck cushions and compact pillows. Inflatable ones puncture easily, and even compact ones take up room. We recommend that you skip the pillow and nab a pillowcase from home, which you can stuff with clothes instead.

○ **Tea lights** Handy during power cuts, these are safer than regular candles. You can often buy them at your destination.

Eating & Drinking

○ **Water bottle** Water bottles range in size from 500mL to 2L, though we recommend at least 1L for travelling. The collapsible-bladder water bottles take up very little room in your backpack when not in use. You can save money by refilling a standard plastic bottle, but something sturdier will last longer and be more suitable for regularly purifying water.

○ **Cup & cutlery** Your own cup and spoon come in handy and help to avoid catching and spreading germs. Camping stores stock good knife, spoon and fork sets that lock together so they won't rattle around in the bottom of your pack.

○ **Water purification** See p47 for your options.

Health & Hygiene

○ **Toiletries** Most items are widely available – and often cheaper – but take any specialty products or favourite brands with you. Shower gels are better than soap and often do hair as well as body. Pour the large bottles into smaller ones for travelling and look out for concentrated soaps for washing clothes. Biodegradable soaps will reduce your environmental impact.

○ **Towel** Cotton towels take up too much space in your backpack and never fully dry. Instead, choose a travel towel, made from either chamois (works wet and folds down tiny) or microfibre (works dry and packs down small). Microfibre towels are big enough to wrap around you, while chamois ones are generally much smaller.

○ **Tampons or pads** Depending on your destination, these can be hard to find.

○ **Contraception** Condoms are sold in most countries, but the quality can be variable (always check the use-by date) and it's best to come prepared with your own supply. If you use the pill, bring enough to cover your whole trip, as it is difficult to obtain in many countries.

○ **Medical kit** See p43 for details.

○ **Bath plug** Bath plugs are rare commodities in some cheaper accommodation. Double-sided rubber or plastic plugs will fit most plugholes.

○ **Toilet paper** Learn how to use your hand and water in developing countries because toilet paper often blocks sewage systems. Otherwise, take toilet paper but think about how you're going to dispose of it. When you pack it, squash the roll down and put it in a plastic bag. A small packet of tissues can be useful at times when you expected toilet paper but they're all out.

○ **Washing line** A piece of string, or even dental floss, will do the job, but the cheap lines on the market don't require pegs and include suckers and/or hooks to secure them on even the greasiest wall.

○ **Antiseptic wipes** These are handy where clean water is in short supply (eating on the street or on a trek) and there are concerns about hygiene.

Travel Essentials

○ **Address book, travel journal & pens** You'll want these so that you can keep in touch with friends, family and all the people you'll meet. You can save bag space by keeping a blog (see Staying in Touch, p71) though a journal makes an excellent souvenir.

○ **Guidebooks, maps & phrasebooks** Essential for reading up on your destination and knowing what to expect. Consider tearing out unnecessary pages or get someone else to do the tearing by downloading just the chapter you want at Lonely Planet's website (http://shop.lonelyplanet.com/Primary/Product/Pick_and_Mix_Chapters.jsp).

○ **Pocketknife** With a small fruit knife you can make a picnic from a baguette and a block of cheese. The choice of global MacGyvers is the Swiss Army Knife (or good-quality equivalent) with loads of useful tools: scissors, bottle opener (the most useful item), can opener, straight blade and bomb defuser (okay, maybe not the last one). Unless you're camping or hunting, you don't need a huge knife. Don't keep this in your carry-on luggage, or it will be confiscated.

○ **Sewing kit** Needle, thread, a few buttons and safety pins will mend clothing, mosquito net, tent or sunglasses.

○ **Eye wear** Take your glasses (in a hard case) and contact lenses. Sunglasses are indispensable for both comfort and protection. If you wear prescription glasses or contact lenses, take the prescription with you, along with extras such as a case and contact-lens solution. Consider swimming goggles for pools.

○ **Batteries** Bring spares for all your equipment and put new batteries in everything before you depart.

○ **Gaffer tape** Need a belt for your jeans? Got a hole in your tent? Backpack need repairing? The miracle-working gaffer tape saves you in the most unexpected situations.

○ **Lighter/matches** You'll need something to light your campfire, mosquito coils, candles and cigarettes. Don't take your favourite Zippo lighter, as the fuel evaporates in tropical heat.

○ **Earplugs** You'll never regret taking these if you spend a lot of time in cities or take a bus with a driver who thinks he's Brazil's next hottest DJ.

○ **Glue stick** The glue-on stamps and envelopes can be remarkably nonsticky. Glue is also useful for sticking tickets etc into your journal.

○ **Calculator** If your mobile phone does this, forget it. Otherwise, it's good for currency conversions and budgeting.

TIPS

There's no need to take CDs or lots of clothes to places such as Thailand, Vietnam or Bali. It's cheaper and more fun to buy them there.

Clothing

Whatever clothes you take, you'll need versatility, particularly if you're flitting from climate to climate or between hemispheres. For job interviews, pack some presentable clothes but make sure you can wear them elsewhere.

○ **Keeping cool** If you're travelling in hot climates you'll need a lightweight, loose-fitting wardrobe. Cotton will absorb sweat and keep you cool. Synthetics won't get so creased and they dry out quickly, but can get clammy. Take long-sleeved tops for protection from the sun and biting insects and for appropriate wear at religious sites. Take a hat and make sure it protects the back of your neck from sunburn.

o **Keeping warm** Several layers, topped by a good-quality jacket, will give you the versatility you need. Pack some thermal underwear which allows your body to breathe while offering good insulation. A fleece or pile jacket is lighter and less bulky than a thick jumper or sweater. You'll also need a lightweight, breathable, waterproof jacket. If you're travelling in cold extremes, consider the more expensive Gore-Tex mountain jackets. Take some synthetic or merino wool long johns and then wear your usual travel trousers. Don't forget your gloves and hat.

o **Waterproof poncho** Regardless of the weather, take one of these. You can use it to cover yourself and your pack, as a ground sheet or a sun awning.

Footwear

o **Boots/shoes** Unless you're doing lots of trekking, you probably don't need a full-on boot. Midboots are versatile because they give good ankle support and can pack away easily. Some travellers just wear trainers, though they won't be ideal for longer walks. Whatever you choose, nonwaterproof shoes will let your feet breathe better than waterproof ones, which are really only useful if you're going somewhere cold. Just like with a backpack, give your shoes a walk to see how they feel, particularly before you buy them. Most shoes need breaking in, so wear them around for a few weeks before you go.

o **Water-sport sandals** Brands such as Teva and Crocs are good for day-to-day wear in warm climates, even if you're doing a lot of walking. You'll also need to wear them in grubby showers or when rock-hopping near the sea. More expensive pairs will last forever.

Electronics

o **Adaptors** Many countries have different electrical plugs, so bringing an adaptor is vital. Check Lonely Planet's **Destinations** (www.lonelyplanet.com/destinations) for details of your destination's plugs.

o **Digital camera** Get something with at least four megapixels so you can get good-quality images and consider taking spare memory cards and batteries for when you can't find an internet café to upload your photos or recharge. Old-timers will tell you to get an SLR camera, but unless you're serious about photography they might be a little over the top. Lonely Planet's Travel Photography series has excellent tips on buying cameras.

o **Mobile phone** See p74 for the pros and cons of taking your mobile.

o **MP3 player/radio** Good for long bus trips, but getting one with a built-in radio is handy for keeping up on local news and music.

o **GPS device** These are handiest when you're going into the wilderness. Some rental cars come with GPS, so they'll get you through traffic jams and direct you in that annoying voice.

o **Laptops** A laptop can be your MP3 player, internet café and video store, but it can be a very vulnerable possession. Get a chain and lock if you do decide to bring one and look at the lightest models if you're travelling a lot.

TIPS

Roll your clothes instead of folding them when you're packing. Less creases and more space!

Extras

o **Books** Take a book for long journeys and swap it with other travellers on the road.

o **Games** Playing cards, chess and backgammon are universal, so you can always start a conversation with locals and travellers over a game.

o **Camping gear** Only take this if you're really going to use your tent. It's bulky, heavy and really annoying if you don't use it. You may even sell it if you get bored of camping.

o **Gifts** Take a few presents that people won't be able to get in your destination if you're staying with a family or using local guides.

o **Binoculars** Handy for wildlife-spotting.

TAKEOFF

By the time you get through the emotional roller coaster of airport farewells, checking in and security checks, you'll be relieved to be just sitting on a plane. There's nothing too scary about surviving the airport and the flight, but if you know what you're in for you'll be able to arrive fresh and ready to take on your destination.

BEFORE DEPARTURE DAY

On departure day you'll be preparing for some teary farewells and worrying about which in-flight movies to watch, so make sure everything's organised before then. Most of this preparation is fairly straightforward, but you can definitely save yourself some time and hassle by knowing what to expect and by doing a few basic chores.

SORTING YOUR CARRY-ON

Every airline has a slightly different policy about what you can and can't take on the plane, but details are freely available on their website. Usually you're allowed at least one bag which holds between 13lbs/6kg and 15lbs/7kg. You are often allowed a handbag or laptop bag in addition. On domestic flights you may be able to carry more, but on long-haul international flights they limit carry-on luggage harshly to avoid overstuffed lockers and cramming too much under passengers' seats.

You can fit a surprisingly large amount into your carry-on when you need to, but it's a good idea to get it organised before you go so you can sort out what goes in your main luggage (which you'll check in) and what you'll need with you while you're in flight. If you haven't got a bag already, look for one with an external pocket to keep your passport and tickets handy, as well as an internal pocket to keep other items such as your money or travellers cheques more secure.

Recent security crackdowns have changed the rules on taking liquids onto planes, so you won't be able to bring bottled water in your carry-on luggage. Airports have varying policies, but generally only very small amounts (less than 4oz/100mL) of liquids (including medicines, shampoo and suntan lotion) are allowed (see p63). You can always ask flight attendants for water on longer flights and you can pour liquids like hair gel or toothpaste into smaller containers.

Obviously, items such as razors, pocketknives and other sharp items can't be taken on board, so stow them in your check-in luggage, along with larger liquids you might need. Of course, narcotics, firearms, fireworks and pornography can't be imported anywhere without special permits, but look out for quirks related to medications. Greece, for example, considers codeine (common in a lot of painkillers) a narcotic, so check local laws and review your medication before you go.

CARRY-ON ESSENTIALS

What you'll need on a flight depends on you. Prefer watching a movie to reading a book? Scratch the novel from your list. You might also need to add essential medications and make sure they fit the liquids policy (you can't take more than 4oz/100mL of liquid on the plane). Review this list to see what you'll need to add to your own list:

❂ **PASSPORT, TICKETS, INSURANCE PAPERS, ID & MONEY** Keep it handy so it can be easily checked then put away.

❂ **FRAGILE STUFF** Anything that could be easily damaged such as your camera, MP3 player, alarm clock or binoculars.

❂ **BASIC TOILETRIES** Brushing your teeth or putting on some deodorant can freshen you up in the middle of a long flight.

❂ **CLOTHES** Bring clothes to suit your destination but also throw in something warm as flights can get chilly, even with the complimentary blankets supplied.

❂ **EARPLUGS** Useful for that loud snorer you might get stuck next to.

❂ **ENTERTAINMENT** Games, novels, guidebooks, a travel journal or anything else for when the in-flight movie doesn't rate.

❂ **PEN** Useful for filling in immigration and customs forms.

Money

Getting a few bills in the local currency prepares you for any eventuality. Even if you're planning on carrying your money in another way (see p37), local money comes in handy for when the ATM breaks down or your hotel owner doesn't accept your credit card. You can plan ahead by taking enough to get a taxi into town (in case public transport isn't running) and for your first night in a hotel. That way you can go out and find a working ATM or a place to cash travellers cheques in the morning.

DUTY-FREE

Okay, so this is the fun stuff. If you're planning to buy a digital camera, new mobile phone or other electrical appliance before you go, it might be a good idea to get it duty-free. This means you can avoid taxes in your own country (which can be substantial). Usually you'll have to have it sealed and keep your receipt so you can show it to customs officials (see p63), but the savings can be worth the hassle.

You can also buy alcohol and cigarettes duty-free. Most countries have restrictions on how much you can bring into the country. The US, for example, allows 1 quart (0.94L) and a lung-straining 1000 cigarettes, while boozy Australia lets you take in 2.5L (2.6 quarts) but only 250 cigarettes. Check laws for your relevant destination or you may get slugged with duty fees on arrival.

SPECIAL REQUESTS

Airlines can take care of any passenger requests with a little advance notice. In-flight menus often offer kosher, vegan, low-fat and vegetarian options, which must be specified when booking your ticket. If you have oversized luggage, look at how you'll be expected to pack it and think about checking in early to allow time for this.

Special-needs travellers should ring ahead and make sure there are adequate ramps for wheelchairs or facilities for guide dogs available both in the airport and on the plane.

RECONFIRMING YOUR FLIGHT

Even in these days of e-tickets, you'll still need to confirm your flight. It's a simple process of calling the airline at least 72 hours in advance and letting them know you're still coming. It can prevent getting bumped from your flight (see p65) and it can be a good time to mention your dietary preferences or other special needs you might have. You may be given a number when you reconfirm, which comes in handy for getting a refund or a new ticket if something goes pear-shaped. Some airlines let you make a seat selection when you reconfirm, so this can be a good way to nab the window seat.

AIRPORT

There's nothing quite as embarrassing as having your name hailed through the airport as you rush to the gate then stumble onto the plane with everyone staring daggers at you for holding up the flight. Another couple of minutes and the plane could have left without you. Avoid this drama by giving yourself plenty of time to get to the airport. Most international flights advise arriving at least two hours before departure (sometimes three if there's extra security). Some airports have train connections or bus shuttles which can be great, but allow yourself time in case you miss one. If you're going by road allow for traffic jams and other snafus that could delay you. The earlier you arrive the more time you'll have for browsing the duty-free shops.

CHECKING IN

You're in the airport now and looking for your airline's counter to check in your bags and get your boarding pass. Look out for the departures screen which should list your flight and its departure time. It may be delayed, but check in anyway so you can kick back with your boarding pass sans checked-in luggage.

Before you check in your bag, make sure it's got a luggage label on it which lists your name, address, airline and flight number. Sometimes you can grab these labels at the check-in desk, but if they're available out the front you can fill it in as you shuffle through the check-in line. You may also want to check that everything you'll need for the flight is in your carry-on bag and that your passport and ticket info is handy. Tie up any loose straps or dangling ties on your backpack for the baggage handlers. Zipping up all the pockets is a good idea. If you like, you can put a padlock on your backpack's zipper to ensure it can't be tampered with, but the plastic wrap that some airports sell is really just taking advantage of the extremely paranoid flyers.

By the time you get to the check-in desk, you'll be asked for your passport and ticket information. Then comes the moment of truth as you dump your bags on the scales – have you overpacked? Many travellers find that their checked-in luggage is over the weight restrictions, which means you'll have to do a quick reshuffle by possibly putting heavy items such as books

in your carry-on luggage. If you're changing flights or transferring, ask about getting your bag booked all the way through so you don't have to collect it en route. If you haven't spotted the departures board, you can ask what gate your flight leaves from. Your boarding pass may also have the gate number, though information will be updated on departure boards, so keep an eye out for them.

If your bag is okay, you'll be given a luggage receipt and a boarding pass. Depending on when you check in and how well booked the flight is, you may be offered a choice of seats. Window seats are great for the views, but longer legs are best stretched in aisle seats, plus you can pop out to the bathroom or take a walk whenever you like. You can also try for an exit-row seat – these are located near the wing and have a little more leg room, though they're often near the service area so you'll overhear flight attendants gossiping.

3-1-1

The US is stringent when it comes to security, with some of the world's strictest security checks that can add up to half an hour or more to your check-in time. You can speed things up by getting familiar with their 3-1-1 liquids policy (www.tsa.gov/311).

Some airlines will let you speed up the process with online check-in. If you visit your airline's website you can usually see if this is possible (sometimes security messes things up or some tickets may require you to do a standard check-in). With online check-in, you can print out your own boarding pass, generally 24 hours before the flight, and just line up (usually at a shorter queue) to check in your bags.

CUSTOMS & IMMIGRATION

Despite what you may have heard about body-cavity searches or immigration Nazis, inspections for departing passengers are pretty straightforward, especially when you're leaving a country. Your bag will be X-rayed and you will have to walk through a metal detector which may beep if you've left your car keys or phone in your pocket. Things you cannot take on board include weapons, spray cans, explosives, flammable substances (including lighters) and liquids. You may be asked to step to one side and answer a few simple questions ('Are you carrying any explosives?'). If you have a laptop you'll have to unpack it to go through the X-ray and repack it at the other end. It can be a good idea to put your keys, phone and other metal items in your jacket and just take it off and send it through the X-ray machine rather than dropping everything in the plastic tubs provided.

Immigration formalities are similarly brief when leaving your home country. Usually, the inspector will simply look at your passport and wave you through, so ask for a departure stamp if you want a passport souvenir. You may have to fill out a departure card, which has a few simple questions (reasons for leaving the country, flight number etc) and will be submitted upon departure.

Buying Duty-Free

Once you're through customs, you can grab some last-minute duty-free – perhaps gifts for friends or family meeting you at the other end. There's liquor, cigarettes, perfume, beauty products and electronics, but only cigarettes, liquor and possibly electronics are good value (as they are heavily taxed in most countries). You can also do some duty-free shopping on board the plane, though the prices on most airlines are as high as the altitude. Make sure you don't exceed the duty-free allowances of the country to which you're heading (see p62). Once you've got your booty, head for your gate and prepare for a wait until your flight boards.

IN-FLIGHT

The flight itself can be fun: your choice of movies, free food and drink, and maybe even a bit of a nap. Then there are nightmare flights where you get trapped between a snoring granny and a bragging businessman who won't stop telling you about how hard that board meeting rocked. This is the reason earplugs were invented.

STAYING FLUID

Booze flows freely on planes, but drinking too much is never a great idea. Apart from not wanting to arrive in another country half-shickered, you'll find that the plane's cabin is very dry and drinking alcohol will dehydrate you faster. Worse still, your hangover could kick in halfway through the flight, hours before you can get an aspirin from your checked-in bag. Try alternating water and alcohol to keep yourself hydrated.

SLEEP

If you're lucky there might be a spare seat next to you and you can stretch out and get some zeds, but usually you'll have someone next to you slouching over the armrest as they sleep. Sleeping on a plane is like sleeping on a bus, so if you stay relaxed you should get some shuteye. You'll get a pillow and blanket and your seat will recline, but it's nothing like the sleeping pods in first class (and no, they won't let you sneak through that little curtain to use the expensive beds). Flights will try to create an atmosphere like that of your destination, so lights will be dimmed to simulate night and breakfast will be served right before you arrive in the morning of your destination. Try following this new routine to help with jet lag, but if you're too wired to sleep, watch a few in-flight movies or listen to some chill-out music.

Some travellers take sleeping pills, but they may leave you feeling groggy and make negotiating your way to a connecting fight difficult. If you're taking something to help you sleep, make sure you know how long it will last so you can be daisy-fresh when you arrive.

IN-FLIGHT MEALS

Chicken or beef? Despite top chefs consulting on slick menus for airlines, you'll still be offered these basic

---

NOTABLE QUOTABLES
TAKEN FROM LONELY PLANET'S *EXPERIMENTAL TRAVEL*
Hanging around at Heathrow is like staying home from school and spending the entire day in your pyjamas lying on the couch, watching TV and eating ice cream. (I can't think why it isn't more popular!) **– Michael Clerizo**

choices on flights unless you've preorganised a veggo or other special-needs option. Many travellers opt for vegetarian or vegan meals because they believe these are better than regular meals, plus they come out first so you won't have to wait for the trolley to roll past. You can go for Hindu, low-fat or other options depending on your airline – budget airlines usually have fewer options, if they offer meals at all. An airline's origin and destination have some bearing on the type of food served, so if you're flying out of Japan you might get sushi or if you're on an Indian airline you could get a steaming curry and a yogurty lassi to wash it down.

DO THE BUMP

It's almost a rite of passage for travellers to get bumped from the flight they booked onto the next one. Sometimes airlines overbook popular routes (particularly London Heathrow to Sydney) and sometimes a passenger might need to be pushed onto an earlier flight to make a connection. Whatever the reason, being bumped usually means you'll be given the next flight to your destination, which hopefully will be within the next day. If you get bumped (or miss a connecting flight because your flight was late), airlines are very keen to keep you happy, often plying you with free food and drink, access to a members' lounge or even putting you up in a nearby hotel for the night. You might be a little late, but you may also have sampled a five-star buffet or swum a few laps in the hotel pool. Some airlines even offer a cash compensation if you are bumped.

TURBULENCE

Again, the disaster movies have a lot to answer for here, as some turbulence during flights is fairly normal. In some cases you may be asked to return to your seats and food service may be delayed for a while, but this is usually nothing to worry about. Planes can withstand more stress than you'd think, including stormy weather and even the pilot's bad jokes.

TRANSIT BREAKS & STOPOVERS

If you're swapping from one flight to another, most airports have facilities like prayer rooms or cinemas to help you pass lengthy transit breaks. There may be a day room where you can take a snooze or shower. Airports all have restaurants or cafés offering pricey bites, so save yourself for the in-flight meal if you know one is coming. Ask at the airport information counter about facilities which will help you kill time.

If you're staying awhile you might be able to organise a stopover and build in another destination. Even if you just stay for a day it can be a good way to sample a country. Some brave travellers even zip into town if they've got a layover of more than four hours. This is risky, because your flight may leave without you if you get caught in traffic or lost in town. The annoying process of clearing customs and security again, and possibly organising a transit visa make this an unattractive option.

FEAR OF FLYING

Alternatively called 'aerophobia', 'aviatophobia' and 'aviophobia', fear of flying affects one in four people to varying degrees. If you've never flown before you'll experience some fairly normal anxiety, but if you find yourself having pronounced panic attacks or vomiting, it could be a serious fear of flying. If you already know you have a real fear, seeking out a little counselling or doing a course is a good idea.

Here are a few courses, ranging from psychological help to giving you a better idea of how planes work:

○ **Fear Free Flying** (www.fearfreeflying.co.uk)
○ **Fear of Flying Clinic** (www.fofc.com)
○ **Fearless Flyers** (www.fearlessflyers.com.au)
○ **Soar** (www.fearofflying.com) Offers a DVD course.

If you suffer from mild aviophobia, prepare yourself mentally for the flight before boarding and do some breathing exercises or meditation to focus yourself on the positive aspects of the flight. Getting a good seat (see p63) could help and not getting a window seat might make you feel like it's just a boring bus ride. Drowning your fears with alcohol will only add drunkenness to your anxiety. If you feel that you need something to calm your nerves, speak to your doctor beforehand about getting a mild tranquilliser prescribed.

TOUCHDOWN

'Please adjust your tray tables as we are coming in to land' – could there be a sweeter sound? It means you're about to see the first glimpses of your destination. Even if it's just the tarmac at the airport, you'll start to hear people speaking differently and taste the air of somewhere new.

But hold on, there's still a few practicalities to tackle before you can go and explore town. Get out of the airport and check in to your accommodation while the adrenalin is on your side, because once the jet lag hits you'll just feel like crashing.

AIRPORT

Most international airports have a certain sameness: white, official and plenty of duty-free shops. Before you start stocking up on booze, get the practicalities out of the way.

CLEARING IMMIGRATION

For immigration, you need to fill out a disembarkation card and (sometimes) a customs form. Usually, flight attendants will pass these around during your flight. Otherwise, look for them once you touch down – either on a table in the immigration hall, or being handed out by immigration officials.

Have a pen handy, because they're as rare as friendly officials in airports. Most countries ask for the address of a place you'll be staying at (a hostel or hotel address is fine – even one you've just copied from a guidebook). Many cards ask for an occupation, which can be tricky. Keep it as innocuous as possible, especially if your job falls into a 'sensitive' category such as journalist or reporter. If you're on a working holiday visa, the profession you list might be one you'll be excluded from working in, so keep it vague.

You'll hand the disembarkation card over to an immigration officer with your passport. Generally they read it and may ask a few clarifying questions, though sometimes they're just bored and want to know about your holiday plans ('The wife and I always wanted to see the Lake District, actually.')

Possible sources of trouble include not having the necessary visa (although without one, most international airlines will refuse to let you on the plane in the first place), a passport that is due to expire before the visa itself expires, or a passport that is in poor condition.

The customs form is self-explanatory and, unless you are bringing in a video camera, bicycle, laptop computer or other specialised or electronic equipment, you'll probably have nothing to declare. If you have big-ticket items, avoid overestimating the value of your

goods on the form, as it is likely to create hassles when going through customs inspection. Some countries also require you to declare how much currency you are carrying and may have limits on the amount of currency you can take with you when you go.

A few countries may have a health officer who can ask you to show an international health certificate with proof of yellow-fever (and possibly also cholera) vaccination, so have this ready together with your passport.

BAGGAGE COLLECTION

Through immigration? Follow the signs (or exodus of passengers) to the baggage claim. Off-loading is usually not a speedy process, so be prepared to wait at a carousel for a while. In some airports you will be besieged by porters eager to assist you – refuse politely and organise your own trolley if you have a lot of luggage. Baggage loss is rare so relax, and only when everyone else has their bags should you go over to the baggage-claim desk and report it missing. If your bag does go missing, the airline should courier it to you when it's found or even compensate you if it's lost, so you can go out and buy a new wardrobe.

Sometimes as you leave the baggage-collection area, you'll be asked to show your baggage-claim tickets (often attached to your flight ticket), so don't lose these.

CLEARING CUSTOMS

At customs you can often choose between the green line (nothing to declare) and the red line (goods to declare). The green channel means you stroll straight through with the random baggage search to slow you down. The officer will ask you to open your bags, do a quick check and wave you on. Sniffer dogs may also

PART OF THE OLD SILK ROAD, THE PAMIR HIGHWAY, TAJIKISTAN (P299).

mania. Push your way through them to a rank if there is one (as these are often more dependable taxis), and check with a driver how much it will cost (a guidebook should give you an idea of reasonable fares) and that he has a meter to tally the price (rather than the more casual 'special tour price' made up on the spot). In many countries taxis are an easy, if expensive ride into town, but do some research to see if your destination has specific scams or issues.

CHECKING IN

Once you've arrived from the airport, you'll need to find a place to rest your head and stow your bag. Booking ahead for the first night is a good idea, just so you know where you'll be heading and have something to put down on the immigration forms (see p66). If you don't like the place, you can always move the next day.

Depending on when you arrive you may be able to drop your bag and start exploring. If it's late afternoon you'll usually be fine to check in, but if it's much earlier than 2pm few hotels will let you check in. Usually they'll say it's because of cleaning, but often they just don't want guests hanging around. Some hostels have very strict rules and may not even be staffed before 5pm.

TIPS
BY JONATHAN ROYLE

Dress for the occasion – I think people who arrive in a country looking like tramps deserve it if they get put through hoops by the immigration officials.

The solution is left luggage. With terrorism fears on the rise, many organisations are too worried to take left luggage, but there are still a few key spots. Often a train station will have lockers, museums will have cloakrooms where you can check in small items, and hostels will have space for left luggage (provided they're open).

When you can check in, be sure and ask to see the room first. Even if you have a reservation you can still ask for another room. If a place isn't what it's cracked up to be (websites exaggerate the truth, guidebooks date

be used, so never try to bring drugs or other illegal substances into a country.

If you have something to declare, you'll be asked to pay an excess duty on whatever you're bringing in if necessary. They may also rifle through your bags just to see if everything's in order. Body-cavity searches and further questioning are fairly rare if you do the right thing.

GETTING INTO TOWN

Unless you are being met by someone, you'll probably take public transport into town. Some airports have special shuttles that go to certain hostels, which can be a good option if they're going your way.

It will be at least two days before the public transport system makes sense, so make sure you know which stop you need to go to from the airport and where you'll need to get off. Your guidebook will have a section on getting from the airport to the city centre, spelling out your options and what you should expect to pay.

In a few cases (you've got too much luggage, the public transport is bad) you may need to catch a taxi. Airport taxi drivers range from cigarette-smoking nonchalance to in-your-face, I'll-give-you-special-price etc), always allow yourself the option to leave, even if it means a humiliating taxi ride.

COPING WITH JET LAG

There's a whole exciting destination waiting for you, but depending on your flight you might just want to nod off on a park bench somewhere. Even if the dreaded jet lag doesn't get you, you'll probably be disorientated and a little grumpy from the plane ride. Dumping your bags and hitting the town might not be the best idea. Give yourself a little time to adjust, maybe by putting your feet up in your hostel or going to a nearby gallery in case you're exhausted halfway through.

Jet lag hits when you travel by air across more than three time zones (each time zone usually represents a one-hour time difference). Your body functions (such as temperature, pulse rate and digestion) are regulated by internal 24-hour cycles, so the flight will have put them all out of whack. Your body will take time to adjust to the 'new time' at the destination.

Symptoms of jet lag include fatigue, disorientation, insomnia, anxiety, impaired concentration and loss of appetite. These effects will usually be gone within a few days of arrival as your body clock synchronises with the local day and night cycle. Until it does, you may find yourself wide awake in the middle of the night and tired during the day.

Minimise jet lag by:
- Resting before you go.
- Getting a flight that minimises sleep deprivation. By arriving late in the day, you'll be able to go straight to bed and adjust to local time more rapidly.
- Avoiding overeating, especially fatty foods.
- Limiting alcohol consumption on the plane and during your first few days in the country. Instead, drink plenty of noncarbonated drinks such as fruit juice or water.
- Trying to go to bed in the evening at the appropriate time at your destination.

MY FIRST
‒ PASSAGE TO INDIA ‒

I was expecting to come out of the airport doors in Mumbai and disappear in a locust crowd of beggars and taxi drivers. Everyone I knew had told me that my first few minutes would be terrifying. They made it sound as if I would have to fight to keep hold of my luggage, possibly lose an eye.

Instead, when I turned up in Mumbai after midnight, I found the airport all but deserted. I prepaid for a taxi at a booth and easily found my driver, and we set out for the city. Again, I was surprised – where were all the people? Mumbai at night was a city of men and dogs. Men lying in the street, pissing, riding motorbikes, smoking cigarettes – but nothing like the jumbled hordes I'd been led to expect.

All night outside my window there was the soft music of bicycle bells. In the morning, I heard female voices and rushed to the window to see three women in bright saris – fuchsia, turquoise, daffodil – crossing the road.

I'd arrived in the city with a gruesome cold (ironically, the only illness I would suffer in a year of Indian travel) so I spent my first day dazed in bed, watching Bollywood clips on MTV Asia and reading Pico Iyer. When I finally ventured out on the streets, the first person to approach me was a street vendor who tried to sell me a giant dropsical balloon, almost bigger than I was. This made me laugh. 'A smaller balloon?' he countered swiftly. Ah, the real India at last.

Rose Mulready is an online content writer at Lonely Planet. While she was in India, she learnt that if you could find an ocean big enough, you could float Saturn in it.

STAYING IN TOUCH

With the internet covering most of the world, reliable global telephone connections, and postal services throwing millions of packages around the globe every day, modern travellers have no excuses for not letting their mothers know where they're going to be. You can share videos with your friends back home or go old-school by sending a parcel of your laundry home for your parents to do. You might feel like there are so many options you'll be overwhelmed – should you be twittering now or has your blog not been updated for a month?

The best option is to choose a mode of communication and stick to it throughout your trip. That way your parents won't be alarmed when they're not getting phone calls because you'll be updating them on your blog. Before you choose a mode of communication, though, consider your destination. There won't be much uploading of video in a remote village in Malawi, but in teched-up Singapore everyone will be texting on the train. Some web tools let you plot your itinerary for all to see (beware of privacy concerns – see Cyberstalking & Online Scams boxed text on p72), but you can also just give your parents an old-fashioned list of where you'll be when and use a phonecard to call when you get there safely.

A good place to start preparing your communications strategy is at **Lonely Planet Bookings & Services** (www.lonelyplanet.com/bookings/communications .do) for a range of SIM cards, mobile phones, phonecards and VOIP calls.

WEB

Revolutionising the way we travel since the 1990s, the web means you can always be in touch. But you don't want to spend all your time in an internet café or lugging around loads of useless equipment. Choose your preferred method of keeping in touch to suit your destination and have a backup for when the internet café is too expensive or your mobile battery is flat.

EMAIL

Definitely the most common way of keeping in touch is email. Most people already have an email address, but you might need one that can be used via the web or gives you enough memory to store photos. Some web-based email accounts have generous storage capacities and you can use your account as an online vault for storing copies of your CV, scans of your passport and other details. Then if you lose your luggage, your details are as close as the nearest internet café. Look out though, as email services can be mined for information, so be wary of storing bank account details and passwords unless you're sure they're secure. You'll also need to check out how much storage each email account has – most have limits of some kind – though if you're just sending text-based emails you'll be fine.

To set up a web-accessible email address, try one of these providers:

○ **Gmail** (http://mail.google.com/mail) Generous storage capacities.
○ **Hotmail** (http://get.live.com/mail/options) Can be bundled with Windows Messenger and add-ons.
○ **Yahoo Mail** (http://www.yahoomail.com)

It's okay to send out group emails when you're away, which will save you repeating yourself, though your friends might get bored of long rambling generic emails. An alternative might be to start a blog (see below).

INSTANT MESSAGING

If you haven't tried instant messaging (IM), it's like email on speed and more addictive. You download an application that lets you chat in a small screen and customise avatars, and has other features. It's great for quick chats with people on the other side of the world, and many people sit at computers with a minimised IM screen so they can chat while they work. If you get in five different chats at once it can be frantic, and if you're on a slow connection your conversation will be out of synch. Some businesses block IM because they believe it slows productivity and chews up bandwidth.

Get messaging with one of these services:

○ **AIM** (AOL Instant Messenger; http://dashboard.aim .com/aim) Hugely popular US-based IM software.
○ **Google Talk** (www.google.com/talk) Has talk and IM capability so you get two for the price of one.
○ **NET Messenger Service** (MSN; http://webmessenger .msn.com) Soon to be superseded by Windows Live Messenger.
○ **Windows Live Messenger** (http://get.live.com/messenger)
○ **Yahoo Messenger** (http://messenger.yahoo.com)

Note that some of the major web-based email providers, such as Gmail, offer IM functions within your email webpage. This is a good alternative to dedicated IM applications.

BLOGS

Blog originally stood for 'web log', and while you might not be a blogger at home, it can come in handy when you're away. It can act as a diary for you to reminisce over when you get back or to tell your family and friends where you are. You could even build up a cult following and find yourself a star of the blogosphere.

Most blogs have fairly straightforward back ends where you can work out quickly how to publish text, photos or video. They come with tutorials that will get you started and they're usually free for a basic blog (though some have sophisticated add-ons that cost extra).

▶ BLOGGING FOR BUCKS

Making your fortune off a blog is tough, but you can make a little extra beer money if your blog is getting reasonable traffic. Services such as Google Adsense (www.google.com/adsense) plug advertisements into your blog based on your entries, so if you're blogging about Turkey they will include promotions for hotels in Istanbul. They work based on click-through so if your friends click every time they visit, it can help your bank balance.

Another option is to get affiliate programs with sites such as Amazon (www.amazon.com), so if you mention a book in your blog you can send people to a place where they can buy it and you'll get a share. Finally, if you think you're going to be bigger than a rock band, think about getting some merchandise with sites such as Cafe Press (www.cafepress.com), which will slap your logo on a T-shirt, underwear, caps or mugs.

The big downside with a blog is the time taken to update it. If you're in a backwater internet café with a shaky connection and no air-con, it might takes ages to upload images and video. Some bloggers will wait until they find a reliable connection, then post a few blog posts at once.

Here are a few free blogs you can sign up for:

○ **Blogger** (www.blogger.com) A Google-owned favourite which can be tied in to your email account.

- **Tumblr** (www.tumblr.com) Does short posts that mix images, video and sound.
- **Twitter** (http://twitter.com) Microblogging site with one-sentence-up-to-the-second text; ideal for those with short attention spans.
- **Live Journal** (http://www.livejournal.com) Good basic blog provider that includes voice posts and polls.
- **My Trip Journal** (www.mytripjournal.com) Travel-journal site with photo upload and good maps to show your route.

CYBERSTALKING & ONLINE SCAMS

Don't get paranoid, but the information you put online can be used by some shifty characters. Usually it'll just be spam about penis enlargements (regardless of your gender), which can be avoided by having a disposable email address that you use on the road and leave everywhere, as well as a more private one.

In a very few cases, it could mean full-on cyberstalking where someone will use information you post online to track you down. Avoid this by only ever giving vague ideas of where you are to strangers (a city might be okay but an address isn't), and only organise meet-ups in public places.

VOICE OVER INTERNET PROTOCOL (VOIP)
For most people this means Skype, a web-based voice communicator. It works like a phone call but the transmission is via the internet (costs are minimal, if any). You can create an account and start using the service almost immediately. Video calls are also possible.

The main drawback with VOIP is the equipment. Good internet cafés may have headsets (which include built-in headphones and a wrap-around microphone), but many won't and you'll find yourself using a speaker to hear and a mic built into the computer to speak. Making a romantic phone call is excruciating when the technology is bad. Additionally, it can be hard if you don't have a good broadband connection, which causes sound quality to vary. Some travellers carry their own equipment to plug in at an internet café or use their own laptop.

The best service is certainly **Skype** (www.skype.com), whose charges start at €0.017/£0.013/US$0.026/A$0.028 a minute to land lines worldwide. For Mac users, a good alternative is **iChat** (http://www.apple.com/macosx/features/ichat.html), Apple's sexy in-built video IM service. Google also offers their **Google Talk** service (www.google.com/talk).

SOCIAL NETWORKING
Unless you've been living under a rock for the last couple of years, social networking is what everybody and their gran is talking about. It's used to describe several different types of internet-based services which link people into online communities. This has led to some excellent travel communities. Not only will these services keep you in touch with people at home, but they can also introduce you to some new friends in your destination.

Social networking keeps changing, but here are a few services travellers were using at the time of research:
- **Bebo** (www.bebo.com) A European phenomenon with profiles that include photos, friends, blogs, video and more.
- **Facebook** (www.facebook.com) Create a profile and add photos, trip maps, world clocks and more.
- **MySpace** (www.myspace.com) Create a profile to add music, friends and other features.
- **Where Are You Now** (WAYN; www.wayn.com) A map-based social-networking site that tracks countries you've been to so you can swap advice and stories.

As well as these sites, there's a variety of forums and chatrooms on the web that you can use to communicate with people while you're away. Another excellent resource is Couchsurfing (see p104).

PHOTOS, VIDEO & OTHER MEDIA
The sights and sounds of the road deserve their own little places on the web. Here are a few services that can show off your best videos and pictures:
- **Flickr** (www.flickr.com)
- **Lonely Planet TV** (www.lonelyplanet.tv) OK, so this is our service, but if we like your video we could buy it!
- **Photo bucket** (http://photobucket.com) Also does video.
- **Picasa** (http://picasa.google.com)

- **Woophy** (www.woophy.com) Photo-sharing site with great searchable map of images.
- **You Tube** (www.youtube.com) Upload your videos for all to see. There's even a Lonely Planet channel.
- **Zoomr** (www.zooomr.com) Photo-sharing site.

INTERNET CAFÉS

If you're staying in a backpacker area, you'll see these everywhere, but then you can go for miles in a rural area without knowing where you can log in. Some libraries and post offices act as internet cafés, with surprisingly zippy broadband connections. They charge for blocks of time (often from 15 minutes up) and some require registration. Avoid chain stores that lock you into membership cards as it can be difficult to find the next place if you're travelling around. Work out where you can check your email at **Cybercafe** (www.cybercafe.com) or Google your destination and 'internet café'.

WI-FI

Once just reserved for suits, wi-fi is now more affordable for budget travellers. If you bring a laptop, you can find wi-fi hotspots in cafés, hotels, universities and libraries – some free, some free with a cup of coffee and others requiring you to register with a local internet provider. To locate wi-fi hotspots, search these sites:
- **Free Hotspot** (www.free-hotspot.com)
- **Wifi 411** (www.wifi411.com)

PHONE

Even ET knew when it was time to buzz his parents to let them know he was all right, and giving your parents a call *before* you need money is good karma. There are loads of choices for making your call, including VOIP (see p72), phonecards or your mobile phone. Using a hotel phone should be avoided as you get stung for a much higher rate for calls. Texting home can be a good way to keep the bills low, especially if you use a free web-based service such as **Chikka** (www.chikka.com/messenger.html) or **SMSpup** (www.smspup.com), as well as a variety of Facebook applications (see Social Networking, p72).

Making a call is pretty similar no matter where you are. There's a code to dial out of the country plus a country code and the home number without the zero

CHINA'S DEFENSE AGAINST THE MONGOLS, THE GREAT WALL (P198).

in front of the area code. For a full list of country codes head for **International Country Calling Codes** (www.countrycallingcodes.com), which includes reverse-calling instructions for when you really have run out of cash.

Calling reverse (or 'calling collect' as it's called in North America) is slightly more expensive and the operator will ask the person you're calling if they'll accept your call, but it's good for emergencies. To avoid calling in the middle of the night, use **World Time Engine** (http://worldtimeengine.com), which has a handy time chart and a meeting planner, so you can work out times in several time zones at once.

PHONECARDS

Making a call using a phonecard is one of the more flexible methods of phoning home, because you can often use payphones, other landlines or your mobile to ring the access number. Phonecards are available in newsagencies, tobacconists, post offices and 7-Eleven–style minimarkets, with the rates for popular countries on display. Generally, rates are much better than dropping coins in a public phone, though not quite as good as Skype.

When you buy an international phonecard (available in several different amounts) you get a credit card–like piece of plastic with an access number and a hidden code on it. You dial the access number, then punch in the code (to reveal it you might have to scratch away a protective seal), and then dial your number. Usually there are helpful prompts telling you what you'll need to do next. When you're almost out of credit an alarm or voice will let you know and you might have the option to recharge the card.

Another kind of phonecard is the local phonecard which you can insert in payphones just as you would with coins. Make sure you don't accidentally buy a local phonecard when you're after the international variety, or you'll get very bad rates for your international phone call.

Finally, you can organise a phonecard from your phone company back home, which will allow you to dial in to their network (just as you would using an international phonecard) and the call will be added to your bill back home. Parents will often sort you out with one of these cards that can only call their number. See the Directories (Part Four) for details of local phone operators which offer this service.

MOBILE

Taking your mobile (or 'cell' in North America) can be a handy addition to your trip, but it can also rack up a huge bill. Most travellers leave their mobile at home and buy a handset or SIM card in countries where they might be staying for a while. This ensures you have coverage plus you use a pay-as-you-go option to keep a lid on the bill. If you have a phone that's not SIM-locked (ie you can take the SIM card out and swap it easily with another one), you also have the option of taking your handset and buying a local SIM card when you arrive to your destination. That way you can still use your phone's camera, MP3 player, video and any other handy features. Of course, you'll need to pack your charger as well as an adaptor, so with all that weight to lug, it may just be easier to buy a cheap handset when you get there.

Global Roaming

If you really want to take your mobile with you and keep your number back home, and you don't mind being charged huge rates, then global roaming (also called 'international roaming') is the way to go. You'll need to check with your phone company to see if they offer global roaming where you're going and see if your destination has the right GSM network on a website such as **GSM World** (www.gsmworld.com/roaming). You should review your call plan before you go so it suits your new global lifestyle – you'll definitely find it cheaper to text rather than call.

POST

SENDING MAIL

Though old-school, 'snail mail' will be handy when you travel. Sending a postcard can be a good way to let people know you're still alive and sending larger items home will lighten your backpack. In some countries the postal service is unreliable, so if your package has to get there try **DHL** (www.dhl.com), **FedEx** (www.fedex.com) or **UPS** (www.ups.com). You can also look out for shipping agents who'll ship crates of one cubic metre upwards door-to-door – which can be affordable if you share space with friends.

Airmail is best for letters and postcards as it's quick, but if you're sending parcels home, surface mail is cheaper, though slower (it will take months to get home).

RECEIVING MAIL

There are three main ways to get mail on the road: poste restante at post offices in cities, poste restante at American Express offices (which requires Amex membership), or asking for mail to be sent to your accommodation. Most post offices hold poste restante mail for no longer than a month or so before binning it. You can also think about setting up a post office box if you're staying put for a while.

BEING A GOOD TRAVELLER

It's easy enough to make sure your good time isn't making someone else's life tougher if you're aware of the culture you're visiting. Don't limit yourself to the suggestions in this chapter, as ethical considerations should inform all your travel. Volunteering (see p143) is another way you can make a difference to the places you visit, even if you just help out for a few weeks.

RESPECTING LOCAL CULTURES

Confusing, frustrating, surprising and occasionally hilarious, cultural differences occur no matter where you go. Visiting another country means leaving your judgements at the airport and appreciating the difference. It's easy to feel threatened or scared in a new environment, but a bit of research before you go can prepare you for everyday encounters – see the destination chapters (Part Three) for a few ideas about the cultures you'll be visiting. Another good way of helping out a country could be to volunteer there (see p143).

AVOIDING OFFENCE
Every traveller feels stupid and bumbling at some point in their trip. You'll stick out like a sore thumb and everyday things you do will crack locals up. It goes both ways and your best defence is an apology (needless to say, 'sorry' is a must-learn in every language) and a sense of humour. If you can laugh off hocking up phlegm in China's streets or using the wrong hand to eat in India, locals will warm to you as 'that crazy foreigner'.

Dress
Wearing the right clothes is more than fashion, as locals will use your clothes to gauge who you are. Particularly in Muslim and Indian Subcontinent countries, flashing your flesh is a no-no, especially if you're a woman. After years of sexed-up Hollywood movies, Western women have a bad reputation and showing too much skin only confirms stereotypes. In Latin America, even the poorest people look neat and clean, making your catwalk-fashionable slashed-up jeans best left at home.

Hospitality
Make sure you know what is considered polite and what is rude if you are eating and drinking with local people. In some Asian countries sticking your chopsticks in your rice is considered rude, and in Australian pubs putting your glass upside down on the bar was once a challenge for the whole bar to fight. If in doubt, look around to see what locals are doing.

Religion

Being respectful in a place of worship such as a church, mosque or temple is fairly obvious no matter how many photo opportunities there might be. A good start is dressing respectfully – long trousers for men and long skirts or trousers for women. You may need to remove your hat at some temples, while mosques require you to cover your head. At both temples and mosques, remove your shoes. At Hindu temples, remove leather objects such as belts before entering. Don't point at Buddha images, especially with your feet. If you sit in front of a Buddha image, sit with your feet pointing away.

Showing Emotion

Losing it is really uncool – getting angry in Southeast Asia or Japan just makes you look silly and rarely achieves anything. In many parts of the world it is just not on for couples to show any emotion or physical contact towards each other in public, so leave the display of affections at home.

Women

Like it or not, in many countries women travellers are expected to behave in a certain fashion. For example, women are usually not allowed in the main prayer hall of a mosque. In many countries it is also inappropriate for women to drink alone in a bar or restaurant.

Taking Photos

A good shot doesn't need to humiliate someone. Treating locals with respect when taking pictures means asking permission before you start popping a flash at them. Some people may ask you to send them a copy or you can show them the screen to see if they like the image. Some locals even charge money to have their photo taken, which you should probably also honour as they're

---

LONELY PLANETISATION

In Alex Garland's *The Beach*, two jaded travellers meet in Thailand and talk about how Lonely Planet has ruined the country. They reckon guidebooks have plundered every last 'hidden gem' and put a spotlight on some places that would grow better if left in the shade. They finish their chat saying they'd like to beat up the Lonely Planet author who's done all this damage. Not that we'd put our hands in the air for a beating, but we can see where they're coming from.

Following a guidebook will create a tourist trail, and places included in a book attract more visitors overnight. Tourism brings large injections of cash, but it can also bring large amounts of corruption and a dumbing down of an existing culture. Bringing in tourists does mean that there will be more attention on an area and when you go home you'll be able to talk first-hand about what a country is actually like. We try to review places as often as we can to make sure that they're still 'good' (at what they do as well as doing the right thing), but places do escape us. If you think a guidebook is recommending a place or a business that's 'gone bad', send us an email at talk2us@lonelyplanet.com.au. We take all of this feedback seriously and next time an author goes out on the road they'll be given a copy of your email. We think this might even stop our authors from being beaten up.

As a traveller there are plenty of things you can do to help stop the march of globalisation trampling over a place you loved:

○ Support grass-roots charity groups where the results of your donation are clear.

○ Give to beggars when you know it will go to an individual and not a 'beggar pimp' – if in doubt, give food, toys or other readily useable items.

○ Explore off the beaten track, but be respectful of the people and environment you encounter.

○ Be informed about local politics and find ways to benefit local communities, including drinking a local beer or using public transport.

○ Haggle for what's fair, but remember that you'll always pay 'tourist prices' because of the obvious income inequalities.

---

your 'models'. You should also take care around religious structures unless you know it's okay to photograph.

GREEN TOURISM

There's no doubt travel puts a strain on the environment, but there's a lot you can do to look after the planet. Start with offsetting the carbon of your flight and any other transport you'll use (see p93). Lonely Planet's GreenDex in many guidebooks should direct you to businesses that are minimising their environmental impact.

Here are a few handy resources for green travellers:

- **Climate Care** (www.co2.org) A 'carbon trader' with a good calculator to work out your carbon emissions, also planting trees to counter the effects.
- **Responsible Travel** (www.responsibletravel.com) Site selling holidays from companies that fulfil strict responsible-travel criteria.

(see p93)

EASY BEING GREEN

Here are a couple of everyday things you can do to look after your destination's environment:

✪ Refill your water bottle from water dispensers or by purifying water (see p47).
✪ BYO shopping bags so you can refuse plastic bags from shopkeepers.
✪ Show locals that you're getting rid of litter responsibly.
✪ Trekkers should take all disposable waste away with them. Batteries are particularly bad.
✪ Animal-based souvenirs, such as tortoiseshell trinkets, coral jewellery and seashells should be left well alone.
✪ Take public transport, cycle or walk to reduce pollution.

(see p47)

THE RED SEA (P272), JAMMED BETWEEN AFRICA AND THE MIDDLE EAST, IS HOME TO A RICH ARRAY OF FISH AND CORAL.

PILGRIMS FLOCK TO THE GHATS ON THE GANGES RIVER (P225), INDIA, BRINGING OFFERINGS TO MOTHER GANGES TO CLEANSE THEM FROM THEIR SINS.

COMING HOME

CULTURE SHOCK

First up, you have to prepare yourself for the idea that the home you left behind is gone. Your friends will be doing new things, your town will have moved on and even your family might have changed. Depending on how long you've been away, it might just be minor changes such as your mum cleaning up your room or a friend dyeing their hair a different colour, but the longer you've been away the greater the change.

But you've changed as well, probably for the better. Everything you've seen and done has given you a better insight into the world. It's hard to be racist when you've met real people of different cultures on the road and seen their kindness and humanity close up. Travellers look at their homes differently because they've been away, even if you don't notice it at first.

INCOMING

If you know when you're coming home, make preparations. You can send emails out and organise a reunion drink with everyone you know. Some travellers have a party with a data projector flashing through their photos in the background – just don't turn it into a slide-show night, because no-one will be as interested as you are in your photos.

Getting a lift from the airport is a good idea because you'll feel so physically and emotionally exhausted that you'll really appreciate the support (and a hand with the baggage). Don't organise too much for the day you arrive in case you need some time to settle back in.

WHAT'S NEXT?

Getting home is like gradually realising you've got a crack in those rose-tinted glasses. It's perfect for a while, but slowly you'll start getting bored, looking around for the next adventure, the next wild time. And the truth is they probably weren't in your old life – that's why you went away. So after a few days of catching up and cups of tea with family, you'll start asking the question 'So...what's next?'

ITCHY FEET

Like with a good hangover remedy, some veteran travellers will tell you the perfect cure for post-trip blues is more travel. Chances are you won't have enough money to hit the road again. Give yourself a week of catching up on sleep, sorting out your photos and taking it easy. The world will have been spinning fast and you'll need a while for it to slow down. Jet lag can serve as a good excuse while you settle back in.

THE 'REAL' WORLD

So now you're home, it's time to get back into the 'real world', right? Not necessarily. Tony and Maureen Wheeler enjoyed their first trip together so much they started making guidebooks on their kitchen table once they finished. After years of work they transformed that kitchen table into the international guidebook company that produces this book and hundreds of others each year. There's something to be said for making your vacation into a vocation.

Getting your CV in order is probably the first thing to do. Don't forget to put anything you did while you were away on it. Travel doesn't just belong under 'interests', because the ability to get yourself around the world and back again is an achievement in itself. Any work experience in a foreign country is going to look way more impressive than the kid who's only ever worked at the local supermarket.

When it comes to applying for jobs or university courses, think about what you enjoyed while you travelled. You might have studied physics, but if you really enjoyed talking to people when you were away, maybe you should look at more social jobs. A really obvious 'travel' job is to work in the tourism industry by trying out as a travel agent, tour operator or even as a travel photographer. These are all really popular gigs so there'll be lots of competition, but stick at it and let them know you're passionate about travel.

> ## DEAR ME

Don't forget to send yourself a postcard from the road. It sounds weird, but a little reminder of what you were doing or thinking during the last moments of your trip will be a good shot in the arm when you're back in the real world. Ask other friends you've met on the road to send you a few postcards so you feel popular when you check the mail.

CHANGE THE WORLD

Once you've been around the world you'll appreciate your place in it. If you have enough money to go halfway round the world, you're probably much better off than most of the people you've visited. Some travellers stay involved by donating to charities that will help places they've visited. Others go a step further, volunteering (see p143) internationally or locally to make a contribution.

MEMORIES

Looking at a few photos online or reading your own blog can be a good cure for post-travel blues. You'll wonder what you were on most of the time, but a few memories will take you back.

Consider putting some of your memories online (see p72) for friends to flick through, but avoid subjecting them to hours of watching pictures. Digital cameras have resulted in users being able to take thousands of pictures, but many of them won't be that interesting if your viewers weren't there ('That's Danny – he's a really funny guy. I can't remember anything he said but really funny stuff.'). Don't forget video and audio as well, both of which can be great ways for you to remember your trip.

If you're ever travel-sick you can also hit the **Lonely Planet** website (www.lonelyplanet.com), where you can chat in the Thorn Tree forum with other travellers or browse stories about your favourite destination. There are loads of other chatrooms out there.

Another good idea can be to read some letters that you sent to family or friends. They can be a nice reminder of being away.

PART TWO

TAILORING YOUR TRIP

THE COLOURFUL MASSKARA FESTIVAL (P215), HELD EACH OCTOBER IN BACOLOD, NEGROS, PHILIPPINES, IS A TIME TO SMILE AND CELEBRATE.

WHO WITH?

So you picture yourself, luggage in hand, gazing into the distance of the open road. What do you see? Are you the enigmatic loner, roaming the earth? Or do you have your own entourage, rocking your own international travel party? There are advantages and disadvantages to travelling with or without companions, and even the most social people like to be alone sometimes.

SOLO

Ask any seasoned traveller and they'll tell you that the *best* way to travel is on your own. You never have to ask anyone what they want to do, your plan is always the most popular one and you never have to take anyone else's feelings into account. You won't have to compromise if your travel companions want to hit the art galleries while you'd rather be lying on the beach.

When you're on your own you tend to make more of an effort to meet new people. You start itching for conversation so you become more approachable. But there will be times when travelling solo will feel lonely and you have to expect that. When that happens, make a call, send an email, write in your journal. You'll find you're actually having a better time than you thought when you start talking about it. Plus you can always join other travellers for group fun such as skydiving or

a guided hike, then go your own way afterwards.

Getting sick when you're travelling alone can be a serious bummer. You have to look after yourself and make sound judgements about the seriousness of your condition. Are you too ill to travel? Should you see a doctor? These are questions that are much easier to answer with the help of someone else.

SOLO WOMEN

If you're a woman travelling solo, it's worth doing some cultural research before you head off. Whatever your destination, it's important to establish the status of women in local society, their cultural expectations and how they behave. In some cultures, drinking in bars (particularly on your own), smoking, wearing make-up and showing too much flesh (often quite modest by Western standards) may give the wrong signals to the local male population. Changing the way you dress and behave will not only protect you from harassment but also show respect to the people of your host country. A fake wedding ring and the line 'I'm waiting for my husband' can sometimes help as well.

If you're on your own, you'll find that people are more likely to offer you hospitality because you are perceived as much less threatening than a man alone (these people have obviously never seen women hurling chairs and throwing punches on the *Jerry Springer Show*). You're also perceived as more vulnerable and people might fall over themselves to offer assistance. In some countries you can even take advantage of separate carriages, waiting rooms and queues for women.

Realistically, depending on where you travel, you probably will get hassled. It's often pretty harmless – young men wanting to accompany you down the street to practice their English – but always pay attention to your common sense and instinct. If you start to feel uncomfortable in a situation, get out, and never put up with any invasive behaviour. Check the Health & Safety chapter (p50) for tips on staying out of trouble.

You can also visit the Women Travellers branch of the **Thorn Tree** (www.lonelyplanet.com/thorntree) or check out the Women Travelers' Tips section of About.com's **Student Travel** site (http://studenttravel. about.com), which includes taxi tips and some slightly overzealous advice on pepper spray (it may be illegal in some destinations you visit).

FRIENDS

Sharing a travel adventure with a good buddy can double the fun and halve the expenses. You can get twin rooms and have someone to share taxi and rental-car bills with, not to mention split the odd meal with. And there's the bonus of having someone to reflect on all those awesome travel moments with ('Is it just me or is London Eye really just a pumped-up Ferris wheel?'). When you get home you'll also have someone to help you with the post-travel blues by saying 'Remember when…'.

Of course there are pros and cons to travelling with company. So before you book that twin room in St Petersburg, ask yourself if there's anything that has

FAMOUSLY BIG BREAKS AT BELLS BEACH, AUSTRALIA (P183).

always annoyed you about your travel partner. Are they cranky in the morning? Tight with the cash? Overly fond of the soundtrack to *Hairspray the Musical?* These traits can be charming in small doses and completely annoying in large, 24/7 doses. Even 'best friends forever' will need a break from each other so allow for a bit of 'own time'.

Travelling with a group of friends can be a lot of fun. It's often not as intense as the one-on-one scenario, but it does make it more difficult to make decisions that are going to suit everybody. Avoid this problem by breaking away from the group for a little while. If you set up a policy of letting people in the group do their own thing, then it will be easier further down the track. If things don't work out with the group, you might decide to take your Eurail ticket in another direction

> ## NOTABLE QUOTABLES
> **TAKEN FROM LONELY PLANET'S *THE KINDNESS OF STRANGERS***
> At one point during the [Cuban] trip, we gave a ride to a young woman who we learned was a huge fan of Michael Bolton. We promised to send her all the Michael Bolton swag we could get our hands on in the US, and eventually we did. That was something within our power, our comprehension, something we could fit within our schedules. **– Dave Eggers**

while the rest of your gang heads to Paris. Just hook up again later.

Sharing a trip with a friend or a group can save you money, but it's best if you're all quite evenly matched financially – you don't want to be the one quaffing Pinot Grigio while everybody else looks on in envy as they try to string out their cup of instant coffee. If you do have a little more travel cash, be prepared to pay for the odd drink or meal, but don't be left stuck with the bill all the time.

RELATIONSHIPS

If you're in a relationship, hitting the road together can be great – both romantically and financially. While two people can't travel as cheaply as one, depending on the destination they can travel as cheaply as one-and-a-half. It will also be a good test on how you get along under stressful situations and you might see new sides of your partner.

You'll spend much more time in each other's company than you normally do and you won't have the usual support network of friends to bitch and moan to. Giving each other some space is always a good idea and if your partner wants to watch a movie while you're on safari, that's cool. Everyone sees a destination differently.

Being in a couple will mean you are less likely to make new friends – there's not the same drive to go out and meet new people, and other people might not find you so approachable. So be open and friendly rather than insular and you'll meet lots of fellow travellers regardless of your relationship status.

Another issue to consider is money. On the road, more couples argue about every baht, rouble and złoty than anything else, so it's advisable to discuss your budget carefully. If you decide to have a joint cash pot, it's a good idea to allocate a certain amount each week for both of you to spend on whatever you want.

RELATIONSHIPS ON THE ROAD

While you may have left your home town happily single, you'll probably collide with that crazy little thing called love on the road. Who doesn't want to forget all the regular, boring bits of your home life and instead be in

GOING MY WAY

So you've decided your pilgrimage to the Toaster Museum can wait no longer. Only problem is you don't know anyone who is quite as excited about bread burning as you are – how can toast not float their boat? There's always someone out there who wants to join you on even the kookiest missions. So how do you find a like-minded travel pal (preferably without a string of convictions)? This can be an adventure in itself. There are any number of websites set up for matching travellers, but you can search for friends for the road on these sites:

✪ **CONNECTING SOLO TRAVELLERS NETWORK (www.cstn.org)** A good way to meet travelling Canadians of all ages; has a registration fee, though browsing is free.

✪ **THORN TREE (www.lonelyplanet.com /thorntree)** Check the Travel Companions branch and post your own to find a friend.

✪ **TRAVEL CHUMS (www.travelchums.com)** Offers a member profile so you can check out potential chums.

Some websites can descend into sleazy hook-ups so make sure you're clear about your expectations upfront and check out your potential friends for the road by meeting up for a drink first. Another great way to bump into travellers before you go is at travel talks in bookshops or at local travel expos, so keep an eye out.

an exciting new city with a fascinating (and irresistible) local love? And while geography might get the better of these relationships when return ticket calls, it's still one of the best parts of the travel experience and makes for the juiciest travel journals.

Be sure to read up on local issues before hooking up with a local, so you understand the culture you're getting involved with. Safe sex is always advised (see p53), but it's particularly important when you're overseas.

MEETING OTHER TRAVELLERS

You'll meet the most interesting people on the road. They'll fill you in on good places to stay at and cool things to check out, plus they make great friends and travel companions. Never underestimate the travellers' grapevine; it's one of the most powerful and up-to-date sources of information in the world.

Sometimes, though, you'll find yourself on the flip side where you meet travellers who do nothing but whine about local food, the weather or the mouth-breather they had to share a dorm with. Or you meet someone who appears to be laid-back and amusing, only to find out later that they're about as fun as a declined credit card and they've attached themselves to you like superglue. Developing an escape plan is easy enough. Just change your plans a little – leave a place before they do, or stay on a bit longer when they're heading off. And unless you've really hit it off with a new travel bud, don't go signing up for any share-a-tent tours or treks into the middle of nowhere with someone you've just met.

ON TOUR

If kicking off your big trip on your own with no safety net really doesn't appeal to you, an organised tour might be a good idea. They're a good way of meeting like-minded travellers and take the intimidation out of first-time travel. You'll still feel like an independent traveller but your tickets, accommodation, food and adventure activities will be sorted and you'll travel on a prearranged route in a group with a leader or guide. Tours can be a good alternative to going it alone in culturally intimidating places such as Africa or China – you'll still get to see the place but your culture shock will be cushioned. Check the individual destination chapters (see Part Three) for some sample tour companies, or the Transport Options chapter which lists some international tour operators (see p96). Another good option are hop-on/hop-off buses (see p96), where you're sure to strike up conversations with fellow travellers.

MY FIRST
⁓ FRIENDS EPISODE ⁓

I was idly chatting with my old buddy Linda about how cool it would be to go to New York together and before I knew it, we were stowing our carry-on luggage in the overhead and splitting iPod headphones pumping what we decided would be the signature tune of our trip: Poison's 'Nothing But a Good Time'. Travelling with Linda was a blast. She was always there to laugh with, share a meal or room with, and lean on when I'd overdone it on the local brew.

But it wasn't always a smooth ride. We were spending more time together than you would normally, often 24/7, so patience wore thin sometimes. Much to Linda's chagrin, I snored – she videoed the digital alarm clock showing some ungodly hour then panned to me snoring like a trucker. And much to my disappointment, she got sick while we were away so I was left to explore the city solo while she shivered and hallucinated for three days, which was fine but it stopped me going to areas where I would've felt safer if I wasn't on my own. But we still had great fun and had been friends for so long that I had the freedom to say I wanted to check out the art galleries and the minutiae of department-store cosmetics – something that would've bored her senseless – while she headed off to East Village in search of rare Duran Duran on vinyl. I felt like travelling with Linda was the best of both worlds – time together yutzing it up, and time apart communing with the city on our own terms.

Jane Ormond spends her days writing content for Lonely Planet's web properties, but New York is her spiritual home.

TRANSPORT OPTIONS

As the old saying goes, a journey of 1000 miles starts with a single security check. No matter where you're going, you're bound to spend time waiting for a train or lining up for tickets or sitting next to someone who just won't shut up. Getting from A to B can be downright boring sometimes, but it's worth it.

Mixing up your transport options can become an exciting bonus to your trip. Try cycling your way from Amsterdam (Netherlands) to Bruges (Belgium) with regular stops for local brews, or sit back and watch the vista wash by on a high-speed *shinkasen* (bullet train) from Tokyo to Kyoto. Look out for ways to keep your options open, as once you get on the road you'll hear about new places you'll want to go to and fall in with friends who might be going in different directions.

AIR

As close as we can currently get to teleportation, flying from one country to another is the zippiest way around the globe. Long waits in airports only build the excitement of getting on the plane (find out more about first-time flights on p61) and being transported from one culture to another. With budget flights and round-the-world (RTW) tickets everyone's a part of the jet set, hopping on a plane at Angkor Wat and watching the sun set over the Grand Canyon with lunch from a hawker stall in Singapore. There's a million destinations on the menu when you're flying.

E-tickets (electronic tickets) have made air travel much easier with quick check-ins and no paper to lose. The internet has created literally hundreds of places to buy your ticket (see p30 for more info), so this chapter aims to help you work out which air ticket will suit you. A RTW ticket represents the best deal, particularly if you're coming from Australasia where return flights to European and Northern American destinations are on a par with a well-priced RTW. The blossoming of hundreds of budget carriers has made it cheaper if you don't mind skipping a meal or taking a tighter seat. Don't forget to get your frequent-flyer points (see p92).

No matter which airline ticket you choose, prices will increase in high season. High seasons are different for each destination, but they're generally clustered around ideal weather (often summer, but for ski destinations it's winter) and school or public holidays. The lead-up to Christmas is hectic even in countries where Christmas isn't celebrated, as millions of people are heading home to be with families. Checking out low-season options can be good for the wallet, but if you are flying in high season you'll definitely have plenty of travel companions and the destination should be at its best.

SAMPLE ROUND-THE-WORLD TICKETS

FARE	PROVIDER	MAJOR AIRLINES	MAX DISTANCE	FARES BY DISTANCE
Oneworld Explorer	One World (www.oneworld.com)	American Airlines British Airways Cathay Pacific Finnair Iberia Lan Chile Qantas	Unlimited; based on continents.	NA – but extra sectors can be bought.
Global Explorer	One World (www.oneworld.com)	American Airlines British Airways Cathay Pacific Finnair Iberia Lan Chile Qantas	39,000 miles/62,760km	Based on three fare levels and seasonality; so you can buy: 29,000 miles/46,670km for £2105/US$4199/A$4556; 34,000 miles/54,720km for £2506/US$4999/A$5423; 39,000 miles/62,760km for £2707/US$5399/A$5857.
Round The World	Sky Team (www.skyteam.com)	Aeroflot Aeroméxico Air France Alitalia China Southern Airlines Continental Airlines Delta KLM Korean Air	39,000 miles/62,760km (can be increased for a fee)	39,000 miles/62,760km for £2785/US$5511/A$5819. Shorter-distance tickets available.
Round The World	Star Alliance (www.staralliance.com)	Air Canada Air China Air New Zealand Asiana Airlines BMI Lufthansa Scandinavian Airlines Singapore Airlines South African Airways Thai United Airlines US Airways	39,000 miles/62,760km	Up to 29,000 miles/46,760km for £1493/US$2977/A$3229; up to 34,000 miles/54,720km for £1746/US$3483/A$3779; up to 39,000 miles/62,760km for £2038/US$4063/A$4409.
Great Escapade (UK-departure only)	Great Escapade (www.thegreatescapade.com)	Air New Zealand Singapore Airlines	29,000 miles/46,670km	Up to 49,085km for £75; up to 51,500km for £145; up to 53,915km for £215.
World Discovery (UK-departure only)	British Airways/Qantas (through travel agents)	Air Pacific British Airways Qantas	29,000 miles/46,670km	Up to 29,000 miles/46,760km from £865.
World Discovery Plus (UK-departure only)	British Airways/Qantas (through travel agents)	Air Pacific British Airways Cathay Pacific Qantas	29,000 miles/46,670km	Up to 29,000 miles/46,760km from £865.

MAX STOPS	GOOD FOR	BAD FOR	REROUTE FEES	COST RANGE (NOT INCLUDING TAXES)	SAMPLE ROUTE
Unlimited but restrictions within continents. No more than four flight sectors in each of Europe and Middle East, Africa, Asia, South America, and six flight sectors in North America. Extra sectors can be purchased per continent.	Everywhere – if you want to see it all, this is the fare – price goes up based on the number of continents travelled to, but must count Europe as the first continent.	NA	£62/US$125/A$135 for destination changes, but unlimited date/time changes	£1389–1929/ US$3900–5300/ A$3479–4759	Madrid-New York-Chicago-Dallas-São Paulo-Santiago de Chile-Auckland-Sydney-Cairns-Tokyo-Hong Kong-Johannesburg-Cape Town-London-Zürich-Madrid
10 stops with 29,000 miles/46,670 km; 15 stops with 34,000 miles/54,720km and up	Everywhere – but limited by stop allowance; max three in each continent on 29,000 miles/ 46,670km or four on 34,000 miles/ 54,720km and up.	NA	£62/US$125/A$135 for destination changes, but unlimited date/time changes	£1179–1979/ US$4199–5399/ A$2799–4489	London-Tehran-Bahrain-Trivandrum overland to Columbo-Bangkok overland to Ho Chi Minh City-Sydney-Port Vila-Nadi-Honolulu-Los Angeles-Denver-London
15 stops	Europe, Asia and America	Africa, Australia and the Pacific	£50/US$100/A$108 per transaction	€2099–3049 (£1655–2405/ US$3325–4827/ A$3600–5249)	Seoul-Rome-Paris-Prague-New York-Atlanta-Lima-Mexico City-Los Angeles-Honolulu-Seoul
Max of 15 but restrictions in certain regions; no more than: five in the US and Canada, three in Japan, five in Europe, five in Australasia, and 15 in Central and South America.	Everywhere	NA	£62/US$125/A$135 per transaction	£1493–2038/ US$2977–4063/ A$3229–4409	Sydney-Bangkok-Hong Kong-Tokyo-Copenhagen-St Petersburg-Vienna-London-Montreal-Toronto-San Francisco-Honolulu-Sydney
Unlimited – max of three stops in New Zealand. Must go RTW.	Asia, New Zealand, USA and Pacific Islands	Australia (domestic flights), Africa, South America	£75 before departure and £50 after departure from the UK	£860–1110 with additional miles available for £130 for 1500 miles	London-Las Vegas-Los Angeles-Pape'ete-Rarotonga-Nadi-Auckland-Brisbane-Singapore-Hong Kong-London
Four free stops in more restricted destinations. Only one stop in Australia and one in New Zealand. Must go RTW.	Southeast Asia, Australia and New Zealand	South America, Australia (domestic flights), Africa	£75 for the first change before departure and £50 after departure from the UK	£865–1065; additional 1500 miles can be purchased for £109 and 3500 miles can be purchased for £219	London-Lima overland to São Paulo-Buenos Aires-Santiago-Auckland-Sydney-Brisbane-Singapore-London
Seven stops with a maximum of three in Australia and three in New Zealand.	South America, Australia, USA and Asia	Africa (South Africa only) and Europe	£50 before and after departure	£865–1394 (includes two fare levels depending on availability)	Edinburgh-Vancouver-San Francisco-Sydney-Cairns-Darwin-Singapore-Edinburgh

ROUND-THE-WORLD (RTW)

Globetrotting really kicked off when airlines began to offer these little babies. Currently RTW tickets are offered by large alliances of airlines who link to each other's routes, so you can get the best of several airlines on one ticket. Various routes are pooled together so you can go around the globe by booking with one airline (which will have links to others through their alliance). Prices increase based on your number of stops (usually between five and 15) and the basic deal doesn't allow backtracking on the same continent. If circumnavigating the globe isn't your thing, you can get a RTW ticket that's based on the miles you travel (usually 20,000 to 40,000, priced depending on how far you want to go), which gives you more freedom but costs a little more. Some agencies offer the option to travel 'surface', meaning you'll fly into one destination in a country (say, Los Angeles) and fly out of another destination in the same country (such as New York). This gives you a good chance to see a country by travelling overland (see p95). Some tickets may include the surface sector as part of your route and include it as a stop (so your ticket will include a train or bus ticket) – do check as there might be extra costs if this is not included. If you have a guidebook it's no problem to sort out an overland trip for yourself once you get to a country, so consider opting out of a travel-agent bundle.

You can book through any airline or travel agent but at the time of writing there were three alliances:

○ **One World** (www.oneworld.com)
○ **Sky Team** (www.skyteam.com)
○ **Star Alliance** (www.staralliance.com)

You can check the rules and regulations of RTW tickets on these sites. They all have maps of their routes, so you can use them as planning tools and work out which alliance can get you where you need to go (see the map on p158–9 for some illustrated routes). All of the above include stops in the big centres such as London, Bangkok, Singapore, Hong Kong and New York, but scan their destinations lists if you're looking for a more obscure spot (which can include Sydney and Canadian destinations). If you go through a travel agent, they'll take this headache away from you. Regardless of which way you book, alliances share frequent-flyer points, so you can get them credited to your airline card of choice if you fly with a partner airline.

Prices for RTW tickets increase depending on how many stops you want and some destinations will be bolted on at a higher cost, but prices start at £700 for a basic flight leaving London and taking in six stops. Australia suffers from limited competition on RTW tickets, so you can expect to pay A$2700 for six stops. US RTW tickets were limited at the time of research, but these routes are opening up to new airlines so prices will come down; you can expect to pay around US$3000 for a six-stop flight. No matter which RTW ticket you choose, make sure the price you're quoted includes airport taxes into the final cost (most good agencies and airlines should be able to show you this upfront).

To compare ticket types at a glance check our RTW Table (p88–9). For advice on how to choose your RTW destinations check the Round-the-World chapter (p156).

CIRCLE FARES

Most travel agents will look at you like you're a plane-spotting freak if you ask for one of these, but circle fares are a lot like RTW tickets. Some circle fares let you fly around a particular region and then complete an itinerary with lots of stops (sometimes forming a rough circle) before returning to your point of departure. They're useful for long-haul trips in countries such as Australia and the US, or in regions such as the Pacific and Europe. These tickets are offered by the same alliances that offer RTW tickets. The popular Circle Pacific fare (taking in much of Asia, the Americas and the Pacific) is a good example of the kind of ticket you can get. It allows you to start in a major city such as Sydney and loop around to Perth, Hong Kong, then New York and Santiago (Chile) before returning to the point of departure in Sydney. This kind of ticket can be a great way to explore a few continents but does have to follow the circle-route path.

OPEN JAW

With this ticket you fly into one destination and out of another. Like the surface-sector option of the RTW ticket, you can enjoy a solid road trip between your two destinations. Flying into Bangkok and out of Singapore allows you to loop through Cambodia, Vietnam and travel

ALTHOUGH THE TIME OF THE MAYA HAS PAST, EVIDENCE OF THEIR ADVANCED CULTURE REMAINS AT THE RUINED CITY OF TIKAL, GUATEMALA (P257).

down the southern gulf of Thailand and into Malaysia before flying out of Singapore. Open-jaw tickets are rarely more expensive than standard return fares. They are also an excellent way of seeing a lot of Europe (fly into London and out of St Petersburg to see most of the continent) or North America (in through Canada, out through Peru), particularly when using budget airlines to zip around other parts of a continent.

RETURN TICKET

Most travellers go with a return ticket, the solid workhorse of the ticketing stable. The basic proposition is that you fly from your home destination to another place and then fly back from your place of entry. Within this structure there's lots of room to explore. Many travellers get a return ticket with their return date a year

after leaving. From there they can either come home after a year or pay a small fee to stretch the return date out even longer. Some cheaper tickets don't allow for any flexibility, so check conditions before shelling out your hard-earned cash.

ONE WAY

Designed for the directionless, one-way tickets are ideal if you don't know where you'll be going next. They usually cost significantly more than half the price of a return ticket (sometimes more) so some travellers invest in a return ticket just in case. Some destinations have grumpy customs officials that won't let you in unless you have an ongoing ticket, but if you can show you have sufficient funds to support yourself for the length of your stay and still buy a ticket out, it's usually okay.

BUDGET AIRLINES

Cheap and cheerful or budget blues – it depends on your comfort levels. Budget airlines or no-frills carriers have made it more affordable for everyone to travel by offering flights that only give the bare minimum. You might not have a comfy seat that reclines and you'll have to skip a meal and the in-flight movie, but the savings can be worth it. Some airlines offer meals or DVD players for an extra fee, so beat the hidden costs by packing your own snacks and bringing your own entertainment (an MP3 player can be handy to block out noisy passengers). Some budget operators save on costs by using secondary airports such as Stansted or Luton instead of Heathrow for London, or Westchester instead of La Guardia or JFK for New York. While you may save on the flight cost, you may have to travel longer to get there, so check your destination to avoid expensive taxi fares.

For lists of low-cost providers, check the Getting There section in the destination chapters of this book (see Part Three). To search for other budget airlines, head to **Attitude Travel** (www.attitudetravel.com/lowcostairlines), which will give you heaps of options.

AIR PASSES

Another secret of the travel industry, air passes can be great if you're exploring a large country (such as Australia, Brazil or India) or a region (eg Europe or North America) in depth. Travel agents are usually in the know though you can check airline alliances (see p90) and with individual airlines. The catch with air passes is that they're often not available from within a country, which means you have to buy them before you go.

An air pass works much like a Eurail ticket (see p95-6), with various packages available based on how many flights you'd like over a certain period of time. The more flights and the longer you want to explore, the higher the price. Depending on where you go there will be a system of zones (the US is divided into six while Australia is divided into three). A basic North American itinerary could run New York–Boston–Toronto–Miami–San Francisco–New York and cost just over £500/US$1000/A$1100, while a European route could run London–Vienna–Budapest–Rome–Madrid–Paris–London and cost as little as £345/US$675/

A$735. While you'll need to lock in the route when you book your ticket, you only need to lock in the first destination date, leaving the others open. Some tickets also include an inbound flight.

Air passes are great if you know your route, but if you're not sure exactly where you want to go, they might not be right for you. They're much cheaper than a series of one-way flights though these days budget flights can be just as cheap, so shop around before you book.

COURIERS

Ever seen that episode of *The Simpsons* where Bart becomes an air courier to get home from a botched road trip? It's probably a slight exaggeration of the job description when Bart is called on to deliver a kidney to Amsterdam, but basically as an air courier you'll be expected to deliver parcels for multinational corporations in exchange for a cheap ticket. It's great if you like to travel ultralight as you'll be allowed only your carry-on luggage and that's it.

You'll be on a tight schedule as courier tickets are locked into exact dates and you might have to return to do another job, sometimes as soon as within two weeks. Only major routes have courier flights, so you might not be able to get exactly where you need to go on the first flight. With new technology ('Just email it to Brussels.') and international couriers such as FedEx serving most of the world, courier jobs are drying up. Budget airlines can also be cheaper than a courier discount.

Still interested? Here are a few agencies that accept wannabe couriers:

○ **Courier Travel** (www.couriertravel.org) A US agency specialising in flights between the US and Asia with a registration fee of £20/US$40/A$43.50 through PayPal.
○ **International Association of Air Travel Couriers** (IAATC; www.courier.org) They sign up wannabe couriers for around £25/US$50/A$55 from anywhere in the world.

FREQUENT-FLYER PROGRAMS

Most airlines offer frequent-flyer programs (also called 'air miles' in the UK and Canada), where you accumulate points for every flight which are redeemable for flights and often goods and services

Wanna buy a cheap ticket? While there are some great deals out there, there are also some big cons and a few problems best avoided. If it really does sound too good to be true, it probably is.

❂ **BACK-TO-FRONT TICKETS** These tickets are return fares purchased in your destination city, rather than your home city. For example, if you are living in Sydney (where tickets are relatively expensive) and you want to fly to London (where tickets are cheaper), theoretically you could buy a ticket by phone using your credit card and get a friend to mail it to you in Sydney. The only catch is that airline computers will know that the ticket was issued in London and will probably refuse to honour it. Be careful that you don't fall foul of these back-to-front rules when purchasing plane tickets on the web.

❂ **SECOND-HAND TICKETS** Usually, second-hand tickets are advertised on hostel noticeboards or in newspapers, when somebody purchased a return ticket or one with multiple stopovers, and wants to sell a couple of unused portions of the ticket. Prices will be rock bottom, but these tickets are worthless unless the name on the ticket matches the name on the passport of the person checking in. Don't listen to deals where they'll check you in with their passport, then give you their ticket and the boarding pass. When immigration officials see that your boarding pass and passport don't match, you'll have some explaining to do and won't be allowed to board the flight.

---

too. You can also get points from hotel chains, rental-car companies and other travel-related traders. If you make a major long-haul flight (between Europe and Australia, for example) you'll probably accumulate enough points for a short domestic flight, which will come in handy on your trip, especially if you can use points on affiliate airlines.

Some frequent-flyer programs require you to pay a small fee to join, though many are free. You'll definitely want to join the frequent-flyer program of the company that will fly you over a great distance, but signing up for a few can be rewarding. Some banks offer frequent-flyer points on credit card purchases and other transactions, so check these partner programs when you sign up.

Every program has different rules about how soon your points will expire and how you can use them, so read the fine print for the best deal. Most programs allow you to keep points for five years and you'll only be credited with points after you've made a flight. Quote your frequent-flyer number when you're booking and you should be able to see a note about your frequent-flyer points on your boarding pass. When you redeem your points your 'reward flight' will be limited to certain times (Christmas will be difficult) and may book out before a paid flight.

Some airlines also allow access to their airport lounges to frequent flyers – these are great places to put your feet up and drink endless cups of coffee.

You'll receive a frequent-flyer card, but generally the number is more important than the card (as you'll need it to book on the web and with travel agents), so make a note of it somewhere handy.

CARBON TRADING

With an average return flight from London to New York producing 1.57 tonnes of CO_2, there's no doubt your flight will have a heavy impact on the environment. But there's a lot you can do about it. Many airlines offer carbon-trading options on most flights, where you can offset the damage your flight will do by spending a few extra dollars. But are they doing enough? Look closely at the measures behind an airline's carbon-trading policy and you might want to do more. If you want to calculate how much carbon your next flight will emit, check out the air travel CO_2 calculator at **Climate Care** (www.climatecare.org), which will tell you how much CO_2 your flight will produce and give you options for offsetting them. Check the Directories for information on local carbon traders.

If you want a slow-paced trip, prepare for the high seas. Ship life will give you plenty of time to think between your destinations and can be a little cheaper. If you want speed, though, flying is your best option, because a journey of hours by air will take days by sea. For info on getting a job on a yacht see the boxed text on p129, and see p128 for information on working on cruise ships.

FERRIES

If you're looking at doing some island-hopping, ferries will become your favourite travel companion. If you're travelling independently, you can take a bike or car on a ferry for a little more on your fare and have an eco-friendly way to explore your destination. On longer routes ferries double as seaborne bars or casinos, often because they can dodge local laws – the Calais–Dover ferry between the UK and France is notorious for boozy Brits buying up big. It can be a great party if your stomach can handle shots *and* the shifting seas.

Several ferry lines offer passes which give you unlimited travel over limited period of time. If you can organise your travel well, passes are a great way to explore the islands, but if you skimp and get a week to explore Scotland's Outer Hebrides, they might blur together like a big night on the whisky.

Some destinations are better served than others by their ferry services (Europe, for example), but you can find out more about common ferry routes in the destination chapters (see Part Three). For a comprehensive list of ferry companies, head to **Interferry** (www.interferry.com), which lists members of this official ferry organisation.

FREIGHTERS

Freighters sound tough, but they're actually fairly cruisey. If you want to take it slow and hop off at a few ports along the way, a freighter might be just the ticket. Unlike a cruise, they're limited in passenger numbers so there's rarely more than a dozen passengers aboard. Most freighters offer a cruise package, so you'll stop at several ports and see the seaside of a country (some port towns can be very grungy).

There's no need to work on deck as you can pay for a room that's fitted out a lot like a midrange hotel room complete, with TV/DVD and a kitchenette in the better rooms. Fares are calculated by the day and are around €75 to €90 per day (£56/US$110/A$120 to £68/US$135/A$145). You'll need to be organised and cashed up if you want to take a freighter, because you'll have to make a deposit of a quarter of the total when booking, with the remainder due at least a month before you sail. Of course, it's not the quickest trip with a transatlantic crossing taking at least 10 days, and with some return cruises stopping at several ports taking up to 70 days. Another downside is that retirees are fond of taking freighter cruises, but you can always hide in your cabin and prepare for the next port.

The following services can book freighter trips:
- **Freighter Cruises** (www.freightercruises.com) Offers several freighter cruises and has a members' newsletter.
- **Freighter Travel** (www.freightertravel.com.au) Sails between Australia, Europe and the Americas.
- **Freighter World** (www.freighterworld.com) Books berths on freighter ships globally.
- **TravLtips** (www.travltips.com) Membership-based organisation that offers freighter and cruise passage from North America.

CRUISE SHIPS

An old-school luxury cruise is probably not what you're after if you're on a budget. Aside from being pricey, they have a reputation for attracting older travellers, which is great if you want to bump into your grandma's bridge club on holiday. At least that's the stereotype. In truth, there are lots of different cruises to suit different lifestyles and age groups. Destinations such as Antarctica and Arctic are best experienced on a cruise with its long slow approach. Working on a cruise ship is another way to get around and get paid at the same time (see p128).

To book a cruise, try these big providers:
- **Cruise Authority** (www.the-cruise-authority.com) US-based booking agent that covers many companies.
- **Orient Lines** (www.orientlines.com) Does cruises to Europe, Antarctica and Africa.
- **P&O Cruises** (www.pocruises.com) One of the biggest cruise companies with local branches.

Whether it's the essential road trip racing to Las Vegas or the slow mosey of a camel ride to Samarkand, travelling overland is the best way to really see a country. Getting the bus or hopping on a train are great ways to get someone else to do the driving, so you can lie back and watch the scenery pass you by. Jetting around a country will be quicker and sometimes cheaper, but if you want to watch Italy gradually morphing into Switzerland or see New York's frantic metropolis slowly fade into countryside, taking a train is definitely the way to go. It may cost a little more than a budget flight, but you'll be free to take your time, especially if you hire a car.

You can find out more about specific overland trips by heading to the destination chapters (see Part Three).

RAIL

The idea of catching a train might sound like a throwback to travel a 100 years ago. On a state-of-the-art train network such as Japan's famous *shinkasen* (bullet train) or France's *Train à Grande Vitesse* (TGV) trains, however, train travel can be zippy and affordable. Someone else will be doing the driving, plus with many train stations centrally located you'll be dropped right into the centre of town. Train travel is always safer than juggling a road atlas as you drive on foreign streets, so you'll arrive stress-free. If you're concerned about the environment, trains represent the most energy-efficient way of travelling.

In India you'll be riding trains packed with locals and in South America you might be sharing space with the livestock as well, so comfort can be difficult. Choosing a better class (see below) can sometimes get you out of 'cattle class'. If you're moving around a lot in one country or region, you should look at passes such as the Eurail ticket (see p95) that's been helping transport travellers for decades.

Some train journeys are destinations in themselves. The Trans-Mongolian railway traces the slow changes of cultures and oscillating vistas from Beijing to Moscow. The northern route, the Trans-Siberian, is even more dramatic as it climbs through freezing temperatures and summery steppes. Other great journeys include Australia's Ghan, a desert trip that weaves its way to Uluru (Ayers Rock) in the country's red centre, or the run from China to Tibet that rises gradually to help travellers avoid altitude sickness.

Use some common sense when travelling on trains. Solo travellers should avoid travelling at night. All travellers should consider ways to secure their baggage, particularly if they're sleeping on trains.

Classes

All train services offer a variety of classes, from first-class sleepers which provide your own compartment to single seats in crowded economy class. Consider how far you'll be going as you might be okay in economy for an hour or two. In some destinations (India, for example) air conditioning could be essential and you may want to pay a little more for a cooler trip. Higher classes often book out, so you'll need to reserve your seat in advance, though even lower classes can be packed. If you're sitting in the wrong class, a grumpy conductor will eventually catch up with you, so take the hassle out of the trip by sitting in your allocated seat.

Tourist-class tickets often cost more but are usually the most comfortable for travellers. In China a tourist-class ticket can include an air-conditioned waiting room, so while you'll pay a little more for these tickets, they can often be worth it.

Timetables

Getting a timetable in advance will help with your planning, but all timetables will date so picking one up when you arrive can be very helpful. One of the better timetables is the huge **Thomas Cook timetable** (www.thomascooktimetables.com), which has a European timetable for around £15/US$29.50/A$32 and a world timetable for £13/US$25.50/A$28. Another good resource is **The Man in Seat 61** (www.seat61.com), which does a sweep of the globe's train services with suggested routes and links to local sights. It's particularly strong in Europe as it is the passionate project of a former British Rail employee.

Eurail & Other Passes

If you want a flexible way to see a country or a region, you should definitely prepurchase a rail pass. Passes are usually valid for a limited time (seven, 14, 21 and

28 days are common) and allow either hop-on/hop-off options for unlimited travel (which means you'll be frantically trying to see as much as you can) or a certain number of trips. Prices increase based on the amount of flexibility you're after. Passes are generally only available to foreigners and you'll need to buy them before you travel (often they're not available in-country).

Popular passes include:

○ **Amtrak** (www.amtrak.com) Offers a 15- or 30-day pass that starts from around £200/US$400/A$435 and gets pricier in peak periods (May to August and December to January). They also offer the North American Pass, a 30-day pass that includes Canada, starting at £360/US$710/A$770. You'll need to collect your pass from a US station when you arrive.

○ **BritRail** (www.britrail.com) Various passes covering England, Scotland and Ireland available to non-Brits, starting at US$410/A$450 for all three countries, with a monthly pass that gives you five days of travel. Check individual trips as the pass may not be the best value, although it does include some ferries.

○ **Eurail** (www.eurail.com) The granddaddy of all passes is available only to non-Europeans and must also be purchased in advance. It starts at 15 days (from US$485/A$570) to three months (from US$1360/A$1610), depending on how many days you want to travel. The passes allow travel to most European countries (except Britain) and include some ferries.

○ **Indra pass** (www.indianrail.gov.in/intert.html) This pass starts at half a day £29/US$57/A$61 and goes up to 90 days £540/US$1060/A$1150. Passes are available through Indian Airlines, Air India and other agents listed on the website. You can also buy them from travel agents in Delhi, Mumbai, Calcutta and Chennai.

BUS

Buses get a bad rap, particularly in the US. Sure, they can be slow (the cross-country route in the US takes at least 70 hours) and can get delayed in traffic, but they're budget-friendly and better for the environment than driving a car. At least with a bus you'll be sharing the carbon burn with your fellow passengers. Good bus journeys can even come with a movie screening, while bad ones come with an old woman who keeps falling asleep on your shoulder and an entertainment system that blares Cantopop. But you'll get into conversations with local people and fellow travellers and, much like on trains, you'll get to see the country glide by. Because buses are so common, timetables are harder to pin down than for trains. Check out local bus providers for the latest details.

Tour buses

If you need a little more support, taking a tour bus can be a good option. You'll get to see the big sights with knowledgeable guides, and fellow travellers can make for good company. And if you're worried about costs, these trips will present you with a clear price that usually includes accommodation and meals. The downside can be that you'll be locked into an itinerary which might not suit you. Your fellow tourists often make or break the trip so look for a tour company that suits you.

Here are a few good tour options:

○ **Contiki Holidays for 18-35's** (www.contiki.com) Specialist in European, North American and Australian tours from three to 48 days.

○ **Top Deck Travel Ltd** (www.topdecktravel.co.uk) Offering trips to Europe and Africa.

○ **Trafalgar Tours** (www.trafalgar.com) A global provider with tours of the US, Europe, China, Russia, Australia and New Zealand.

Hop-On/Hop-Off Buses

More flexible than a tour bus, these buses are geared towards backpackers, so you'll be delivered to a network of hostels and definitely have plenty of new friends to explore your next destination with. Routes usually follow circuits so if you start in London, you'll be dropped back there at the end. You can stay at any stop as long as you like (as long as your pass is still valid) and there are often optional side routes. Passes generally run for a limited time (a month can be a good length of time, but longer options are available) and some include add-on tours that can be good ways of getting to distant places when you don't have your own wheels. Hop-on/hop-off buses are popular on backpacker trails, so if you're looking for a place of your own, you might need to break away by hiring a car or cycling.

Check the destination chapters (see Part Three) for details on local hop-on/hop-off options.

CAR & MOTORBIKE

They may be big polluters and are terrible in traffic, but your own wheels are convenient. Taking a motorbike across the sludgy back roads of Cambodia or hiring a car for a romantic weekend away in Paris (with plenty of room for bulging shopping bags) will make your trip a lot more fun. It's budgetary insanity to take your own vehicle, so you'll usually have two options: buying a vehicle when you arrive or hiring one when you need it.

Whatever you do, make sure you sort out a licence that's going to work in your destination country and be sure to brush up on local laws. Common road signs and which side of the road to drive on are just some of the things you'll need to know before you hit the asphalt. Make sure your license is valid in the country you'll be driving through (see p98).

Just as with air travel, you can look at carbon-trading options (see p77) to reduce the impact of your car or

TRANSPORT YOURSELF AROUND THE WORLD
BY JESS WHITE, TRAVELLER, UK

○ **TUT-TUT FOR TUK-TUKS (THAILAND)** Tuk-tuks are ubiquitous in Thailand and especially so in Bangkok, where they are increasingly more of a tourist trap (rip-off) than a genuine transport option. Stick to the Skytrain, river ferries or taxis when in Bangkok – although the introduction of tuk-tuks in Brighton (UK) has added a cheap transport option to the city's overpriced taxis.

○ **GOING LOCO IN A COCO (CUBA)** Like the tuk-tuks, Cuba's coco-taxis are basically motorbikes with additional and often dubious passenger seating. However much the thought of entrusting your safety to an enclosed back seat made of coconut fibre scares you, it's a cheap way to get around and costs less than the much cooler, genuine 1920s American taxi cars.

○ **VAPORETTOS IN VENICE (VENICE)** If you have any money left over after the extortionate costs of overnighting in Venice, you could spend the same again on a gondola, but a much cheaper way to get around is to use the vaporetto. Basically the Venetian water-bus service, vaporettos are quick, frequent and network across the whole of the city.

○ **HOP ONTO A FERRY (GREECE)** Island-hopping in Greece is still a fantastic way to spend a whole summer on the cheap. Don't be put off by the sometimes confusing number of ferry routes and operators – sunning yourself on the deck during a four-hour crossing is a surprisingly relaxing way to travel. For journeys at night, however, it's worth paying extra for a cabin.

○ **LONG-TAILING AROUND KO PHI PHI (THAILAND)** Post-tsunami tourism is picking up in Thailand's islands, and if you are on a smaller one, such as the gorgeous Ko Phi Phi, you may find that the only way to get around is by long-tail boat. Travelling by longtail is the essence of laid-back boho luxury, but the captive tourist market means it can be surprisingly expensive.

○ **GO BY GREYHOUND (USA)** The USA is such a big place that the only sensible way to travel around it is by plane, but the best way to really see it is by Greyhound. Using this extensive bus network means you get to see the sort of places usually found in road-trip movies, while meeting a variety of usually friendly (and usually American) fellow travellers.

○ **TAKE THE TRAM (STOCKHOLM)** If you have a burning desire to travel by tram, there are many places you can visit to do so, such as San Francisco and many European cities. However, the most underrated of these has to be Stockholm, a beautiful city built on a number of islands with a transport system that encompasses the metro, ferry, bus and old-world trams.

THE QUINTESSENTIAL CUBAN EXPERIENCE: THE INDESCRIBABLE MIX OF COLOUR, MUSIC AND JOIE DE VIVRE IN HAVANA, CUBA (P243).

motorbike on the environment. The companies quoted under air travel can also offset your vehicle's emissions.

Licenses

If you've got a valid license at home, then you're halfway to driving in another country. Get an International Driving Permit (IDP) to act as a translation of your license – if you are stopped and asked for your license, you'll need to show traffic cops a copy of both. The IDP will only cover the type of licence you have, so if you don't have a motorcycle license, you won't be qualified to drive one just because you're in another country. In practice, many travellers ride mopeds and light motorcycles, particularly in Southeast Asia.

IDPs are available from your local automobile association or car club; check your section of the Directories (Part Four) for details.

Hire Cars

Hiring a car is a flexible way of getting the freedom of a car without the hassles of worrying about its maintenance. With your own car, you'll be able to stop when you want, plan your own route and go at your own speed. Hire costs will be based on a daily rate with the essential insurance costing extra. If you don't get insurance, an accident could really ruin your trip with huge costs and a tangle of paperwork, and that's if no-one gets hurt.

Most rentals are all-inclusive, but beware of mileage charges where you'll be charged if you exceed a certain amount of miles or kilometres. You can often pay more to drop your car off at a different destination to your point of origin, but work out if this is going to be cheaper. You'll also be stung with an additional fee if the car isn't returned with a full tank of petrol and if there are any unpaid parking fines or damages (they'll do a check when you leave and when you bring it back).

Some global hire companies include:

- **Avis** (www.avis.com)
- **Budget** (www.budget.com)
- **Europcar** (www.europcar.com)
- **Hertz** (www.hertz.com)
- **Thrifty** (www.thrifty.com)

Look out for smaller local operators who offer older vehicles at better rates.

Buying

If you're in it for the long haul, then buying a car or motorbike of your own can be a good idea. Generally, a stay of a several months where you'll be regularly travelling is the best way to get value out of your car, but it can also be good to have the freedom to get away when you want.

With rising fuel costs and parking fees to factor in, it will definitely be cheaper to use public transport for everyday travel. Then there's the environmental concern of your own gas guzzler – some cities such as London have introduced hefty fees to discourage bringing your car into the city, and other cities have introduced large car-free zones.

Still keen to buy a vehicle? Buying a smaller vehicle will increase your fuel efficiency and minimise your pollution impact, so make sure you get the right car for your needs. You can often find cars advertised in hostels, in local classifieds and in used-car lots. There are several online forums that sell cars in specific countries, and Lonely Planet's **Thorn Tree** (www.lonelyplanet.com/thorntree) has a separate branch for selling cars with good deals, particularly for Australia, North America and the UK. If you're in one of the big backpacker hangouts (London and Sydney, for example), you can often buy a car from a traveller who's just made a trip in the car and is about to leave the country.

Once you've found a car, give it a good inspection, preferably by an experienced mechanic. Some countries have automobile associations which will inspect cars for a fee, but at other places you might just get a test drive and a look under the hood, and you'll have to make a decision on the spot. Make sure you give it a thorough lookover, particularly if you're buying a car from another traveller which may have some high numbers on the odometer. If you're not mechanically minded, bring along someone who is.

Ridesharing

If you have an empty car going on a long journey, getting someone along for the ride makes sense for the environment as well as helping with the petrol money. If you're the passenger getting a lift, it will mean a bargain trip and maybe making some good friends on the way. Sort out the deal before you go. Some questions to consider include:

- Are you paying for all the petrol or going halves?
- How much luggage can you bring?
- Will you need to stay overnight on the way and will you need a tent or extra cash for a room?
- Can you bring your iPod packed with great trucking songs?

Unfortunately, there's no easy test for 'best friends forever' versus axe murderers, so be sure and check out a ride before you're trapped in a car with someone for several hours on a cross-country trip. A 'getting to know you' coffee or drink can be a good idea even if it's just to discuss what music you'll be listening to on the 12-hour drive up Australia's east coast. If you don't like the person who's offering you the ride, don't go. Solo women should be particularly careful and you may only feel comfortable travelling with couples or other women.

Ridesharing is most common in massive regions that have big traveller populations, such as North America, Australasia and Europe. Finding a ride is often fairly easy if you're on a busy travel route or in a backpacker hangout (such as Prague, London, Sydney or Amsterdam). You can start by casting an eye over a hostel noticeboard, and if no-one seems to be going your way, put up an ad yourself. There are plenty of services online that offer ridesharing, including:

- **eRideshare** (www.erideshare.com) North American rideshare outfit with free registration.
- **NeedARide.com.au** (www.needaride.com.au) Good for lifts in Australia with a straightforward login that gives you access to ride databases.

- **Share Your ride** (www.shareyourride.net) The US, Canada and Australia are served by this registration-driven portal.
- **Thorn Tree** (www.lonelyplanet.com/thorntree) Lonely Planet's own bulletin board with postings under specific countries – especially good for out-of-the-way spots.

Most of these services have long disclaimers about how they take no responsibility for the rides they offer, which is all the more reason to make sure you feel comfortable about who you're going to get a ride with.

Driveaway Cars

This budget alternative to hiring a car is common in the US and works best when you want to drive on a long-haul trip that's a popular route, such as New York to Los Angeles. Basically, you'll drive someone else's car (often for a dealer or manufacturer, so the car could be brand-new) across the country. You'll need to be over 21, have a couple of references and a deposit (at least US$300) to reassure everyone you're not going to steal the car. The time and date of the delivery will be specified and you'll have a maximum mileage, so there won't be much room for detours or going at your own speed. The company usually pays for insurance and you'll pay for all the petrol.

Finding a driveaway company can be as easy as skimming through a phone book under the entries 'Automotive Transport' and 'Driveaway Companies' (phone a week or two before you want to travel), or try **Driveaway USA** (www.driveawayusa.com).

Hitching

Hitchhiking is never entirely safe (ever seen *Wolf Creek* or *The Hitcher*?) and isn't really advisable, especially with better alternatives such as ridesharing. Warnings about checking out who you're riding with are crucial with hitching, and often you'll have to make a split-second decision based on what someone's car looks like. Not only is hitching risky, it can also be tedious waiting in the rain for the next ride.

Still, some young travellers are thumbing their way around the world for its affordability and ease. If you're keen to find out more, check out **Digi Hitch** (www .digihitch.com), an online community of hitchers with stories and tips.

BICYCLE

Cyclists the world over will tell you (sometimes as if they're members of a cult): four wheels bad, two wheels good. If you've ever eased around the windmills and green countryside of the Netherlands or chimed your bell as you power past another cyclist on the Tour de France route, you'll know what they're talking about. Not only is it clean and green, it's fairly easy to maintain a basic bike and buying a bike is much easier than the paperwork and hassle of a car.

You can rent bikes almost everywhere and some hostels may even have free bikes. The quality of rental bikes may not be great and maintenance is a job that's low on the list of most hostel owners, but they'll be okay for short cycles around town. If you're after a better-quality bike, head for a local bike shop which will have shining mountain bikes and hybrids maintained by bike techs. They can also be good sources of advice on good trails and trips. In remoter parts of the world spare parts will be limited so stocking up on spare inner tubes and basic tools will be useful.

If you're thinking about some serious treks, you'll want to bring your own bike. Most airlines will charge you extra to bring your bike and you'll want to pack it carefully (probably by pulling it apart).

Once you've got a bike you'll need to obey local traffic laws, including those about wearing a helmet and drink riding. On short trips you can often take a bike on a train or bus, sometimes with a ticket for your bike but often for free. On long-haul trips you'll need to pack your bike away in a luggage carriage.

ACCOMMODATION

Whether it's just a place to stow your backpack or a cosy home base, working out where you'll sleep is big part of planning. If you don't like where you're staying – too noisy, too far from the major sights in town or too cockroach-infested – don't forget you can always move on. Even if you're doing it all on the cheap, budget for a few splurges in a pricier place for when you want to relax a little or ditch the hostel crowd.

As a guide, you can check the costs table in the relevant destination chapter in Part Three to do rough calculations.

If you want to book some or all of the accommodation online beforehand, there are plenty of websites that can help you do just that, often at a discount. Also try **Lonely Planet's Hotels & Hostels** (http://hotels .lonelyplanet.com).

HOSTELS

Staying in a hostel is a rite of passage for most travellers and, with facilities geared towards low or no budgets, plenty of fellow travellers and proximity to major sights, it's no wonder. Don't expect too many frills or room service because you get what you pay for at a youth hostel.

The deal is fairly straightforward: you get a bunk and a locker in a shared dormitory for a cheap rate. Some hostels charge less if there are more beds in a dorm, if you don't mind sleeping in a larger dorm with others. They also offer single and double rooms at rates that are usually slightly cheaper than at a budget hotel. There are common bathrooms (usually separate for men and women), kitchens and lounge areas that everyone can use. Some better hostels might add extras such as a café for when you can't face another home-made pasta, internet access and sometimes luxury facilities such as swimming pools, saunas, free surfboards or bicycles. Guidebooks will give you an idea of the good places and fellow travellers will quickly tell you if the next place you're booked into is shitty, but standards are generally high, particularly in busy cities.

Because hostels are backpacker epicentres, you'll meet lots of other people who are interested in the same things as you are. You'll soon have friends to visit sights with, and if you're staying in hostels in the same area for a while you'll bump into the same people again ('Hey, aren't you the guy who stole my towel in Khao San Rd?'). Some hostels have party reputations organising barbecues, talent contests or DJs in their on-site bars, or brilliant links to the local tourism industry so they can organise discount tours or activities. There will be times when you get exhausted, and the sound of 10 of your roommates rolling in drunk at 3am will not be conducive to a good night's sleep. For these times we recommend splashing out to stay in a B&B or hotel.

Look out also for hidden extras when you're staying at a hostel, with some owners thinking it's cool to charge extra for linen, car parking, showers and oxygen. It's not, and there's often a place nearby where 'extras' will be part of the price.

As well as the dependable **Hostelling International** network (HI; www.hihostels.com, see p40) there are often independent hostels which can be better or worse. The HI network has standards that their hostels comply to, while independents don't. Don't be shy of independents, but if places aren't included in your guidebook, it's usually for a reason.

HOTELS

Budget travellers usually recoil from hotels, but sometimes the only place to stay in town might be a hotel, and when the hostel stops being fun a hotel can make a good escape route. If there's two of you, twin or double rooms can be quite affordable in a basic hotel. You'll get a room of your own and a variety of other perks depending on how much you want to pay. A good midrange hotel room will have a small TV, tea- and coffee-making facilities and a bar fridge.

Beware of the in-room minibar, which usually has a budget-crushing mark-up on everything (even a Coke). Some hotels will have restaurants and may include breakfast in your room rate, though you can always grab a cheaper bite at a local café to negotiate a few dollars off your room rate. A top-end hotel will have a

ONE OF THE MODERN WONDERS OF DUBAI, UAE (P281), THE BURJ AL ARAB, RESEMBLING A BOAT SAIL, IS A LUXURY HOTEL BUILT ON AN ARTIFICIAL ISLAND

gym, excellent restaurant and/or bar and a few other opportunities to damage someone else's credit card ('The casino chips are on me!').

GUESTHOUSES & B&BS

Short for 'bed and breakfast' (because that's exactly what they offer), B&Bs are common in Australasia, North America and the UK, while guesthouses (also called *pensions* in Spain and Italy) are common in Europe. With a few regional variations (Scots will almost force a hot breakfast of blood sausage despite protestations) they offer the same service. As private businesses, they can have the homey feel of staying at your favourite aunty's or they can be kitschy nightmares of porcelain kittens and teddy bears, depending on the owners. Pricewise they offer a good compromise between hostels and hotels, plus you'll often find friendly owners keen to offer sightseeing tips.

You'll get a room of your own which will have limited furnishings, and breakfast is in a common dining room so you'll get a chance to meet a few of the other guests. B&Bs are often used by older travellers so they'll usually be fairly quiet, and loud music or drunken 3am returns could raise the eyebrows of the owners as they bring you your toast the next morning.

CAMPING

Budget options don't come much better than this. In many parts of the world you'll just need to find enough ground to lay out your tent and you've got your night's accommodation. The only catch is that in many places pitching your tent will be illegal and fines will make it a less-than-budget experience.

Even if you have to fork out for a camping ground, this is still the cheapest option, and there'll be the bonus of facilities such as toilets, barbecue areas and possibly even laundries. National parks, hostels and caravan parks will all let you put a tent up for little cost.

LIVING IN

There's no better way to get to know a culture than to live and work among its people. You can expect to learn more of a language and make lifelong friends. Some hospitality jobs (see p126) will include board as part of the wage – which will usually be at the pub or guesthouse you're employed in. While the savings are great, you may find that living and working in the same place can be too much, especially if your employers are insane.

> ## SPECIAL SLEEPS

Before you bunk down in another youth hostel look out for some of these more intriguing options:

✪ **ENTER THE RYOKAN** Sleep like a samurai at a Japanese ryokan, which are designed to look like the original roadside hotels with the Zen simplicity of tatami mats, sliding rice-paper doors and futon beds. These old-school Japanese guesthouses are most common in Kyoto.

✪ **ROCKING THE RIAD** Morocco's traditional palaces could put you up for a night with their oasis-like interior gardens and stark white walls. Marrakesh and Essaouira are the best places to start at, but they're common across the country.

✪ **TAKING YOUR CAPSULE** What is with Japan and kooky accommodation? These supermodern spots are minicapsules snug enough for a drunken salaryman to sleep off his hangover. Tokyo and Osaka have some of the best.

✪ **YURT FLIRT** Camping out in Mongolia or Central Asia often means getting your yurt on. These are huge tents with intricate wooden frames drawn together in a crown but can be packed up to be lugged away on a camel or horse.

A lot about 'living in' depends on who you'll be living with, from delightful hippies who'll bake fresh bread for you to people who don't realise they're not your parents and give you curfews. Be sure to check them out with a phone call before agreeing to stay, particularly if they're in remote areas.

COUCHSURFING

Ever stayed on a mate's couch after a few too many? What if you had thousands of mates living all around the world whenever you needed them? Good news is you can have access to a worldwide network of couches offered by fellow travellers who are happy to put you up for the night. Couchsurfers register their details on the site and are free to search for available couch space, local guides or just people to share a drink with.

You can create a MySpace-like profile at Couchsurfing (www.couchsurfing.org), which details how you'd like to be involved though it's usually expected you'll offer a couch if you're going to use someone else's. Once you're registered you can start searching for couches. How do you know your potential host isn't a lunatic? There are peer reviews from people who've visited before, which you can review before visiting. You'll build up similar comments as you surf around. Couchsurfing, of course, is short-term only and it just isn't cool to outstay your welcome.

Two similar organisations are Hospitality Club (www.hospitalityclub.org) and Global Freeloaders (http:// globalfreeloaders.com).

HOMESTAYS
These are great opportunities to live with hosts who may require you to work or study. It can be as simple as staying with friends, or it can be part of a formal program including language classes.

Here are a few organisations that offer homestays:

○ **Homestay Web** (www.homestayweb.com) A large site that requires registration and lists homestays around the world.
○ **Village Homestays** (www.villagehomestays.com) A grass-roots organisation that has places in villages in Thailand, South Africa and Fiji.

FARMSTAYS
These are ideal if you want to get out of the city and soak up the rustic lifestyle. Prices start at budget rates and you can reduce them with work around the farm. Hosts will advertise a private room and who they would prefer (some specify women, couples or students), and you can apply for a place in most parts of the world. Farmstays can include courses and training in everyday chores, so you may come home with a trade.

A few organisations that offer farmstays include:

○ **Farmstays International** (www.farmstays.org) A service that includes Canada, Australia, New Zealand and several South American countries; prices include language courses and start with an eight-week option for €4,000 (£3000/US$6100/A$6600).
○ **Willing Workers on Organic Farms** (WWOOF; www .wwoof.org) Work in exchange for your food and board at this global network of organic farms; membership starts at £15.00/A$55. Farm lists are offered, costs vary.

THE ADVENTURE TRAIL

Like the sound of having only a rubber tube between you and the wildest rivers Belize can serve up as you drift through a dark cave? Or perhaps hiking through the rugged volcanic wonderland of the Tongariro Crossing (New Zealand) just waiting for an eruption? You don't go halfway round the world to sit inside, so when you're planning your trip mix in a little adrenaline, sprinkle liberally with the great outdoors and wash the whole thing down with a shot of danger to make an adventurous meal out of your trip. If you're stuck for ideas, check out **Year of Adventures** (www .yearofadventures.com).

Hiking in a national park can give you a peak at the wildlife. Try strolling through Australia's Flinders Ranges to spot emus and kangaroos or romping with orang-utans in the thick jungles of Sumatra (Indonesia). Sometimes the scenery itself can be more than spectacular, such as China's Tiger Leaping Gorge where you walk beside a raging river then climb up to jagged peaks. Another favourite is the barren beauty of the Namib Desert (Namibia), broken only by the oasis of Sossusvlei. Or you can get another perspective while floating above it all by hang-gliding over the Zambezi river and Victoria Falls from Livingstone (Zambia). You don't need to be a complete fitness freak for cheerful strolls such as the Cinque Terre (Italy) or easy day walks in the Rocky Mountains (USA).

Even if you start out not knowing how, you can surf the swells in Bali and go from learner to legend, or do a PADI-approved (Professional Association of Diving Instructors) course in Turkey, which will have you mastering life beneath the waves. And you can hire equipment so when you're ready to take on the big waves of Indo

CHRISTIAN ASLUND / LONELY PLANET IMAGES

HITTING THE BLACK RUNS OF THE ALPS (P168).

AS WELL AS HOT MUD POOLS, ROTORUA, NEW ZEALAND, HAS NEARBY RIVERS FOR WHITE-WATER RAFTING (P183), SUCH AS TUTEA'S FALLS, OKERE RIVER.

TOP FIVE ADVENTURES

✪ **STROLLING THE SERENGETI (TANZANIA)** Africa's most famous park that seethes with migrating wildebeests and a few other beasties.

✪ **NATURE CALLS AT ANGEL FALLS (VENEZUELA)** The thundering waters of the world's highest waterfall will stir something in you.

✪ **BULLISH MARKET IN PAMPLONA (SPAIN)** A stampede of bulls coming at you for three heart-stopping minutes.

✪ **TAKING MACHU PICCHU (PERU)** Hike the Inca trail and finish at this massive monument to a lost civilisation.

✪ **CHUUK LAGOON'S UNDERWATER MUSEUM (MICRONESIA)** Explore WWII wrecks crusted with stunning corals.

(that's pro-speak for Indonesia), you can hop on a plane without going over your carry-on limit.

Just getting to some places can be an adventure in itself. This includes the dry-throated camel trek through Xinjiang in China as you trace the old Silk Road, or pumping your thighs cycling from Baños to Puyo (Ecuador) with jaw-dropping views of the upper Amazon basin. Throw in a tent and you can dawdle and stop anywhere you can drive a tent peg into the ground.

While the big wildernesses of Africa, Australasia and North America might seem like the most obvious places to look for outdoor action, other destinations will surprise you – try tackling Japan's North Alps or paddling a kayak on Poland's Lake Serwy.

Think it's all been done? Adrenaline junkies are always looking for something new to rappel off, drive a crampon into or bungee jump off. Try volcano boarding off Mt Yasur in Vanuatu where you'll carve up the marble-like pumice of an active volcano. Skydiving and bungee jumping weren't enough so they're always looking for new thrills in Rotorua (New Zealand) and at the moment it's zorbing – getting locked into a giant plastic sphere that rolls down a hill – without any brakes.

For more specifics on activities, see the individual destination chapters in Part Three.

HECK OUT THE DINOSAUR FOSSILS IN THE TÉNÉRÉ DESERT (SEE P272), SAHARA, NIGER, REMNANTS OF ITS PREHISTORIC TROPICAL-RAINFOREST PAST.

WITH BORAT NOWHERE TO BE SEEN, THE TIAN SHAN RANGES (SEE P299), KAZAKHSTAN, MAKE A BEAUTIFUL AND SERENE WINTER ESCAPE.

TRY SOME SNORKELLING OR DIVING IN HAWAI'I (P244), HOME TO ALL SORTS OF UNDERWATER WONDERS SUCH AS MOLOKINI, A SUNKEN VOLCANIC CRATER

NEW ZEALAND, HOME TO ALL MANNER OF WEIRD AND WONDERFUL EXTREME SPORTS (SEE P184) – AND SOME OLD FAVES LIKE BUNGEE JUMPING TOO.

CARNAVAL (P260), RIO DE JANEIRO, IS ONE OF THE MOST HAPPENING PARTIES IN THE WORLD, WHERE BLOCOS OF COSTUMED PEOPLE PARADE THE STREETS.

THE FESTIVAL CIRCUIT

The riotous clatter of drums at a street party, the serene meditations in a temple in honour of the gods or the 'kerang' of a rock gig taking it to volume 11 – festivals come in many forms. Some travellers plan their whole trip around the festival circuit, attending gigs such as the UK's Glastonbury and the USA's Burning Man in the Northern Hemisphere before heading south to party down in Rio's epic Carnaval or catching the Big Day Out gigs in Australia or New Zealand. You can plan a route around festivals by getting a copy of Lonely Planet's *Year of Festivals*. Alternatively, you can just show up and see what parties you can join, but be warned that festival-going is a mission not to be accepted lightly. Hotels book out months in advance, tickets go on sale up to six months before and hardcore attendees start working on outfits as soon as last year's festival ends.

But it's not all wild dancing and sampling local brews. Religious festivals are about proving you're devout through elaborate rituals – such as Ramadan, the Muslim festival practiced in many countries that requires fasting during daylight hours. After 70 days of fasting, food is savoured at the Eid al-Adha, Ramadan's official end. The end of Buddhist fasting, Vassa, sees Asian monks leave monasteries with alms bowls and the release of banana-leaf boats at river festivals.

Days of fasting could explain some local crankiness, so realising that festivals can impact peoples' daily lives helps in showing respect.

Religious festivals aren't all about abstinence though. At Turkey's Mevlâna Festival and Egypt's Moulid of Sayyed Ahmed al-Badawi, Sufi Muslims attempt to attain oneness with God by chanting and dancing into a trance. In Haiti the voodoo Fete Gede involves

SIMON GREENWOOD / LONELY PLANET IMAGES

GET MESSY AT LA TOMATINA (P169) IN BUÑOL, SPAIN.

A COLOURFUL HOKO FLOAT, WITH THE REQUISITE TRADITIONAL TAPESTRIES, DURING A RAINSTORM IN THE GION MATSURI (SEE P200), KYOTO, JAPAN.

ELEPHANT FESTIVAL IN JAIPUR, RAJASTHAN, INDIA, HELD IN THE LEAD UP TO HOLI (SEE P230), IS A GREAT TIME TO WATCH A MATCH OF ELEPHANT POLO.

MYSTERIOUS MASKED PARTIERS ARE A COMMON SIGHT DURING THE VENICE CARNEVALE (SEE P168), ITALY.

DRAGON BOAT RACES ARE HELD THROUGHOUT HONG KONG TO CELEBRATE THE ANNUAL TUEN NG OR DRAGON BOAT FESTIVAL (P200).

a visit to the cemetery to dance with the dead, and Mexico's Día de los Muertos (Day of the Dead) sees candlelight meals for the recently departed placed on flower-covered altars. Macabre marzipan shaped into skeleton, skulls and other emo themes are relished by kids.

Of course, there are big bashes such as Germany's techno-throbbing Love Parade, Sydney's simply fabulous Gay and Lesbian Mardi Gras and London's Notting Hill Carnival. Special mention must go to Rio's Carnaval, which kicks off with streetside *bandas* (bands), each party having its own fancy dress code. The event climaxes with a massive street parade and much drinking and debauchery. California's Burning Man is a community art project on a grand scale with a five-mile camp that gathers to sculpt,

dance, topless-cycle and eventually incinerate an enormous human effigy.

Not weird enough? Head for Turkey's Camel Wrestling festival where the ships of the desert spar to shove each other out of the ring. Looking for something tougher than an eyebrow ring? The Hindu Thaipusam festival in Malaysia and India sees body piercing taken to the next level with some participants dragging offerings of milk jugs by hooks buried into their skin. Pyromaniacs converge on the Shetland Islands for Up Helly Aa, where wannabe Vikings toss burning torches on a longship they've spent a year building, then spend the night drinking and dancing as it burns.

For more specifics on festivals, see the individual destination chapters in Part Three.

JOBS

Work may be the 'curse of the drinking classes', as Oscar Wilde quipped, but sooner or later you'll need to top up your wallet to keep going to the bar. Getting a job while you're overseas can be a great way to build your CV – working internationally always impresses potential employers, plus it can be a good way to sample a couple of jobs to see if it's a career you want to pursue when you get back home. Like a holiday romance, if a job overseas doesn't work out you can always move on with no hard feelings. Plus there's seasonal and casual work that's ideal for commitment-phobes and because the expectation from employers is that you'll only work for a while before moving on to explore more of the world.

Getting the right mix between travel and work is the key. You don't want to go half way around the world to be stuck in an office in New York or be trapped waiting tables 24/7 in a Pacific island paradise. Some travellers keep a tight budget when they're working to save up for a big trip, while others hop away for weekends to break up their working weekdays – this is particularly easy from London with more than 30 countries accessible by budget flight.

This chapter looks at a few of the common traveller jobs, from fruit picking to freelancing. There are tips on what you'll need to do most of these jobs and what you should bring with you to help the job hunt. Working out the visa situation is tricky – it changes too quickly and you should look online for the latest information, but information here was correct at the time of research. If you're looking for work as a nanny or on a summer camp, see Working With Kids (p133), and if you're keen to teach English see Teaching English (p138). If you're looking for a deeper way to experience a culture and give something back to the communities you'll be visiting, perhaps volunteering is for you (see p143).

The best thing about the holiday job is that it will feel more exciting just because you'll be doing it in another country. Even washing dishes in Lisbon will get you inside a Portuguese kitchen and a whole culinary culture – you can learn how to make *alcatra* (beef roasted in red wine and garlic) and enjoy a few after-work drinks with genuine locals. Long nights working as a door bitch in a Moscow club might seem dull, but you'll be talking to people every day (great for learning local slang) and you'll get to hear local bands and DJs that you never would have access to back home. When you do finally return, your stories about jobs – the good, the bad and the ugly – will be much better than some of the postcard moments other travellers had.

READY TO WORK?

Before you hit the road you should do some research about your destination and look at how likely it is that you'll be able to find work, not to mention check out local pay rates. There's not much use in showing up at a place where the exchange rate is terrible and you're competing in a market with high unemployment. Many countries have a minimum wage, and if you surf a few local job sites you can often find how much specific jobs will pay. This will be invaluable when a potential employer says 'But this is what I pay everyone.'

Language is another good piece of knowledge to take with you. If English is your only language, you'll need to focus on English-speaking countries. English is an international language but without the local lingo you might be limited in the kinds of jobs you can do. If you have a smattering of the spoken local language, you might be able to get by in basic jobs and maybe even work in hospitality. If you're looking at office jobs, you'll need to have some developed language skills, particularly with written language. Interviews will be near impossible if you can't speak the same language as your potential boss, so consider language lessons if you're heading to destinations such as China, France or parts of Africa.

VISAS, TAX & RED TAPE

No matter where you want to work, you'll need to sort out a visa. Working without one is illegal and you can be deported for 'working black', as it's often called. Australia, Canada, New Zealand and the UK all share working holiday visas, which mean that people aged 18 to 30 can travel between these countries and work up to 12 months. In the past the US has been very difficult to secure work in, but Australia's 'special relationship' with the US has meant that these two countries have recently set up the snappily named Student Work and Travel pilot program, which lets young people swap between countries more easily to work, holiday and study.

If you're from the UK, the J1 visa is your best hope of getting into the 'land of the free'. This visa requires sponsorship from a company, so big companies, nanny or au pair agencies and cultural exchange groups can organise sponsorship. For citizens of the US, options are more limited. There are trial reciprocal arrangements with Australia, but other than that Americans will be relying on sponsorship, so arrangements such as internships or cultural exchanges can be a good option. See the Directories chapter in Part Four for relevant visa sites.

Taxes are another issue for working internationally. Whatever country you're working in, you'll contribute to its taxation system. This tax will often be taken directly from your salary unless you're working in an illegal 'cash in hand' job. Just like working without a visa, getting caught not paying tax can come with tough penalties for travellers, though many industries such as hospitality still rely on this method.

Of course, if you've paid too much tax (which is common if you're working for less than the full financial year), you might be able to get some of your tax back. Check the sites below for details on this, or cut through the red tape by using a service such as **Tax Back** (www .taxback.com) or **Global Tax Back** (www.globaltaxback .co.uk).

Here are some sites that will give you more specific information about tax in the countries you might visit:

- **UK Inland Revenue** (www.inlandrevenue.gov.uk) Click on 'Individuals & Employees' then 'Non Residents' to find out about reclaiming tax.
- **Department of Work & Pensions** (www.dwp.gov .uk) Get a national insurance number here to work in the UK.
- **Australian Taxation Office** (www.ato.gov.au) Click on 'Individuals' then 'Non-residents' for FAQs; get your Tax File Number (TFN) here.
- **New Zealand Inland Revenue Department** (www .ird.govt.nz) New Zealand's tax laws made simple.
- **Inland Revenue Service** (www.irs.gov) US tax authority which issues essential social security cards and explains federal tax.
- **Canada Revenue Agency** (www.ccra-adrc.gc.ca) Apply for your Social Insurance Number (SIN) and find out more about Canada's tax system.
- **European Job Mobility Portal** (www.europa.eu.int/ eures) Has information about most countries in the EU.
- **Tax Sites** (www.taxsites.com/international.html) Has information on tax laws in most countries.

LOOKING FOR WORK

With CVs to write, application letters to send and then interviews (sometimes a few rounds), applying for jobs is never easy, but it's worth it when you get that first pay cheque, especially after you've had a couple of months of the bank balance dribbling away during travel.

The first step is to get you curriculum vitae (CV, also called a 'résumé') in order. Simply put, this is a round-up of your relevant work history (no need to put baby-sitting if you're going for an accounting job), but more importantly, it markets yourself to potential employers. Think carefully about what to include and how to represent yourself in the best light. You should try to summarise your work experience and include job titles, dates and tasks you did in each position, plus any training you have or awards you may have won or memberships of clubs or societies. Some people include hobbies though these are fairly optional. If you're not sure whether the information belongs in your CV, ask yourself how it will help you get the job. The web is filled with tips and advice on writing a good CV, and many employment agencies and job sites offer good formats for CVs, which can be handy to get the hang of local terms and ideas. A good basic site is **CV Tips** (www.cvtips.com).

You'll need to bring an electronic version of your CV with you and it's good to have a hard-copy version too (though it might get mangled in your bag). A better idea is to bring a soft copy on a USB key or

ET TO KNOW THE LOCALS BY WORKING IN ONE OF THE NEW AND FUNKY BARS IN ALMATY (P299), KAZAKHSTAN.

email it to yourself. The advantage of having a soft copy is that you can customise it to a specific job in an internet café, then print out a few copies when you need it. Depending on where you are, many employers will want you to apply by email, but hard copy is always handy for face-to-face interviews and written applications.

A hostel noticeboard can be a good place to start looking for jobs and cafés will often advertise for wait staff with signs in their windows. Here are a few useful job sites:

- **Backdoor Jobs** (www.backdoorjobs.com) An unfortunately named site that has adventure and alternative options in the US and beyond.
- **Careerbuilder** (www.careerbuilder.com) A US site.
- **Escape Artist** (www.escapeartist.com) Huge US site that includes global jobs and a free online newsletter.
- **Hot recruit** (www.hotrecruit.com) A UK recruitment site listing global jobs.
- **Job bank USA** (www.jobbankusa.com) A US job site with searches by job, state and city.
- **Job Ware** (www.jobware.com) Searches for international jobs.
- **Jobs Abroad** (www.jobsabroad.com) Good US job site, with subsites Intern Abroad and Study Abroad.
- **Monster** (www.monster.com) A truly global company which has offices in the UK, USA, Canada and most European and Asian countries. Register and create a digital CV and contact job experts.
- **Nixers.com** (www.nixers.com) An Irish site that's good for Ireland but has global reach.
- **Pay Away** (www.payaway.co.uk) An excellent UK website with jobs advice, an email newsletter and jobs bulletin board.
- **Seek** (www.seek.com) Job site with ads for Australia, New Zealand and the UK.
- **Start Next Week** (www.startnextweek.com.au) An Australian job site.
- **Undutchables** (www.undutchables.nl) Netherlands-based site with jobs and advice especially for multilingual people.
- **Yahoo! Hotjobs** (http://hotjobs.yahoo.com) A good global site that's strong on North America and has articles on job hunting.

Most jobs will require you to write application letters and sit an interview. Your application letter should describe why you're the best person for the job and point to relevant experience you might have mentioned in your CV. Often the 'letter' is an email with your CV attached. If you're lucky enough to get an interview, it means they liked what they saw in the letter and want to see if you'll be a good 'fit' for the job. Interviews are also a chance for you to see if this is the kind of place you'd like to work in. For more tips on application letters, you can talk to careers counsellors at school or university, or check job sites which offer sound advice.

TYPES OF WORK

Once your CV is in order, you can start thinking about what type of work you want. You might want to consider how long you want to work for and whether you want to sample a career while you're away. Some of the jobs you do while you're travelling might not end up on your CV, but will get you the very necessary cash to stay on the move. Other jobs can be a way into an industry or even be something that will have an interviewer saying 'Ah, I see you've worked in an art gallery in New York, that's going to come in handy in curating.' If you're looking to build your career, an internship (see below) might be just the ticket. Otherwise you might want the low commitment of fruit picking, labouring work or even occasionally strutting onto a film set (see p128).

INTERNSHIPS & WORK PLACEMENTS

So you're serious about going overseas and working in a job that will help your future career? Depending on where you go, these roles are variously called internships (North America), work placements (UK and Europe) or work experience (Australia and New Zealand). Whatever you dub them, internships can be a great way to break into an industry and employers are always impressed by overseas work experience. Internships are often confused with volunteering (see p143), but internships are more tightly tied up with careers, while volunteering (which can also lead to a career) aims to help the country you're visiting.

What to Expect

Completing an internship is the best way to get an idea of what an industry is really like from the inside. Management, finance, commerce, law and publishing are just some of the industries that have internship programs, though you can ask any organisation if they take interns. Few organisations will turn down free labour, especially if you have some skills. Most organisations, though not all, will pay you a small salary or allowance, and the more selective ones may even pay for your travel costs and accommodation.

You'll actually be doing work that you'd do if you had a full-time position. Some of your coworkers might not have the right idea of what an intern does and may ask you to get the coffee, do the photocopying or even wash their cars. It's important to set some ground rules and ask about what the job entails when you're being interviewed for an internship. You can expect to be doing a certain amount of chores (so some photocopying might be okay), but you should also look to do a few higher-level tasks (such as helping out with a marketing plan at a publishing company) and possibly even completing a research paper or report about your time with the organisation.

The length of the job varies depending on the organisation. In North America summer internship lasts for two months, while in Europe paid interns are called *stagiaires*, with programs lasting up to five months. Longer positions may even run for a year. There's a chance that your internship may lead to an ongoing job, but if it doesn't you're always free to keep on travelling.

What You'll Need

Like with most jobs you'll need a visa, but your employer will usually sort this out for you by acting as a sponsor (you'll still have some paperwork to fill out though). If your employer can't help out with a visa, there's a large industry around setting up visas for interns, but if you stick with reputable outfits such as **British Universities North America Club** (BUNAC; www.bunac.org), you can usually get a visa for a small fee. Most agencies will ask for an application fee, which will be used to cover your paperwork and possibly pay for your fare, so you'll need to have some savings behind you.

Obviously, if you're studying in a country with a language other than English, you'll need to speak that language and probably be able to read and write it. While English may be the international language of business, you'll find that local business likes to speak its own language, and you'll miss out on a lot of office gossip if you don't have the linguistic skills. Some programs require you to be a university student and you'll apply for internships within your field of study. Others will put you through a rigorous selection program of testing or video-conferencing interviews, but it's worth it.

Finding Internships & Work Placements

If you like the direct approach, many companies or organisations advertise on their sites for interns. Try googling a couple of multinational organisations in your industry and look into their jobs pages. This can be a bit hit-and-miss, plus you may not have the support services of an agency behind you.

Here are a few examples of larger organisations that offer internships:

- **Council of Europe** (www.coe.int) Dig down to Traineeship Opportunities to get the dirt on working in European politics for this large organisation.
- **Deloitte** (www.deloitte.com) Offers graduate and student placements in finance and business industries across the globe.
- **European Commission** (www.europa.eu.int/comm/stages) For European nationals, with a few additional 'stages' for non-Europeans, to intern in various government organisations; you need to be a university student with skills in at least one language other than English.
- **European Parliament** (www.europarl.eu.int) Look for 'Traineeships' on this site that has opportunities for EU students in journalism and languages, with paid and unpaid options.
- **Google** (www.google.com.au/support/jobs) Hit 'Students' to find out about internships at one of the web's biggest players.
- **Guggenheim Museum** (www.guggenheim.org) Navigate your way to 'Education/Get Involved' to get experience at one of these museums in Venice, New York, Bilbao (Spain) or Berlin.
- **IBM** (www.ibm.com) Search for 'internships' on this massive site to find several information technology internships and graduate opportunities.
- **PricewaterhouseCoopers** (PwC; www.pwcglobal.com) This leading management consultancy offers summer and long-term internships at its offices around the world, with preuniversity options as well as graduate programs.

Several good books can point you in the right direction for other intern opportunities, including the *Internship Bible* (Princeton Review), *Peterson's Internships* (Peterson's Internships) and *Vault Guide to Top Internships* (Vault Career Library), which all list several agencies in the US that offer regular international intern programs.

By far the best way to organise an internship is to go through an agency that will organise visas and check that your potential employer is on the level. Some of these organisations charge registration or application fees – some only charge on a successful placement, others ask for a small fee upfront. These organisations can take a lot of the headaches out of finding a placement, but if you're looking at a small or unknown organisation, do your research and look around for good word of mouth on the web. You could post a thread on the **Thorn Tree** (www.lonelyplanet.com/thorntree) to see if anyone else has had a good or bad experience.

The US is definitely the place for internships, with several opportunities open to international applicants. Here are a few websites with placements in the US:

- **Association for International Practical Training** (AIPT; www.aipt.org) Does work placements in the US with a focus on getting visas.
- **Camp Counsellors USA** (CCUSA; www.ccusa.com) Primarily about camp staff (see p137), but also has a good traineeship program that helps with placement paperwork.
- **CDS International** (www.cdsintl.org) Offers a Professional Development Program for career-related internships with paperwork and some support.
- **InterExchange** (www.interexchange.org) Sponsors training placements with prearranged placements or support if you want to find your own.
- **Internship Programs** (www.internshipprograms.com) US internship search engine that requires (free) registration.
- **Internships.com** (www.internships.com) Publishes guides to US internships, broken down by city or subject.

Look in the Directories chapter for opportunities only available to people from your country, but here are a few that are open to all.

- **Intern Abroad** (www.internabroad.com) Part of a larger Jobs Abroad group with intern positions worldwide.
- **Intern Jobs** (www.internjobs.com) Member of the AboutJobs.com group, with a huge database of internships worldwide and registration so they match you to internships.
- **International Association for Students of Economics and Management** (AIESEC; www.aiesec.org) The world's largest student organisation does graduate internships with online registration (for a fee).
- **International Association for the Exchange of Students for Technical Experience** (IAESTE; www.iaeste.org) Provides engineering and industrial placements overseas for more than 300,000 students.
- **International Jobs** (www.internationaljobs.org) Publishes listings of internships worldwide and offers a subscription newsletter of the latest opportunities.
- **Internships Australia** (www.internships.com.au) A good gateway to Australian internships for international visitors; has a small placement fee.
- **IST Plus** (www.istplus.com) Offers internships in the US and Australia for postsecondary students.
- **Kiwi Internships** (www.kiwi-internships.com) Organises custom-made internships and work-experience programs in New Zealand with an environmental focus.
- **KPMG** (www.kpmgcareers.com/globalcareers) Head for your local site for vacation, cadetship and work-placement opportunities at this accounting firm.
- **Monash Professional** (www.monashprofessional.com.au) An Australian university's link to local internships, with an application fee.
- **Mountbatten Internship Programs** (www.mountbatten.org) Has programs in New York, London and India.
- **Office of the United Nations High Commissioner for Human Rights** (OHCHR; www.ohchr.org/english) Head for About Us/Internship if you've got a degree that relates to human rights and fluency in a second language.
- **Travel Tree** (www.traveltree.co.uk) Includes a search option for paid internships.

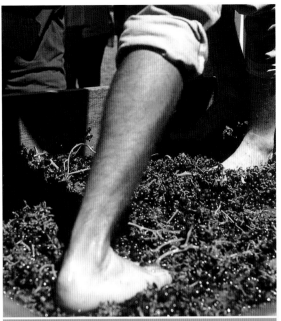

PICK FRUIT IN THE BAROSSA VALLEY, SOUTH AUSTRALIA (P183).

Finally, a lot of job websites also list internships and work placements. Try searching local branches of international job sites, especially of countries you may be visiting.

TEMPING

The term 'temp' was first used in the 1930s to mean 'temporary worker'. Today temps represent more than 10% of the total workforce. Some workplaces are so dependent on temps that they almost couldn't run without them. If you're looking for work as a temp, you're bound to find a job if you have the right skills. Most big companies use temp agencies to fill short- to medium-term vacancies while staff are off sick, on maternity leave, or taking a holiday. Temp agencies are also used when a company is having a busy period such as Christmas, or when they're launching a new product line.

What to Expect

Mostly you'll be working in an office from nine to five doing basic tasks such as replying to emails, answering phones, filing or data entry. Simply put, it's often not very exciting, but you can rely on a pay cheque at the end of the week. Money generally starts at £7 (US$13.70/A$15) an hour in the UK, US$10 (£5/A$11) an hour in America

○ **ARTIST'S MODEL, HONG KONG (HONG KONG)** I was in a pool changing my pose every three minutes. The teacher goes around the room explaining to the students how best to draw the monstrosity in front of them. Work paid for a week in Thailand.

○ **SMURF, NOUMEA (NEW CALEDONIA)** I helped sand down the boat for a friend of the hostel owner. It was blue and after a day, so was I. Walking home, a boy yelled out *Schtroumpf!* which I learnt later means 'smurf'.

○ **SALESMAN, IRKUTSK (MOSCOW)** On the Trans-Siberian, Chinese vendors were selling clothes, cameras, toys and such from the windows to Russians on the platform. A guy in my compartment sold my shoes without asking, and gave me the roubles with a very big smile.

○ **PAN PIPIST, VIENNA (VIENNA)** Miming along to a CD of Andean music, wearing a poncho and breaking out in hoots in time with my fellow performers: a pleasant day as a stand-in for a friend from the hostel.

○ **LADDER HOLDER, VICENZA (VENICE)** A friend's family got me a job in Vicenza as a painter's assistant. For a week, I held the ladder while he painted a hotel. Passers-by ribbed me in Italian. The word *pazzo* (fool) was often uttered.

○ **DEAD BODY, TOKYO (TOKYO)** Lying under playground equipment with a head covered in fake blood, I practised zazen meditation and realised I would never be a star on Japanese TV.

○ **SANTA, LAGOS (NIGERIA)** Christmas in Africa is fun. A recently met friend got me a job as a Santa for his company's family Christmas party. They only paid me in beer, but the thrills on the kids' faces with my real white beard were worth the effort.

○ **MEDICAL EXPERIMENT, MELBOURNE (MELBOURNE)** Signed up as a subject in a drug test for treatment for a socially communicable disease. Clean bed for a week, no need to keep food in my backpack in case of dormitory thieves. Came out with a wad of dollars and slightly green nipples.

www.lonelyplanet.com

and A$18 (£8.50/USD$16.50) an hour in Australia, with higher rates for legal staff or other specialised skills such as experience with accounting software, web-publishing skills or touch-typing. The IT industry usually commands higher salaries, particularly if you have programming skills, though even working on a help desk can pay well.

You'll be employed directly by an agency which will pay you a week in arrears, so don't count on the first pay cheque to pay the rent. You may also have to invoice the temp agency or fill out a timesheet. Placements can be very brief (a day), or an ongoing role that you could stay in for years. Your fellow temps will often be travellers but could also be locals working their way through university or paying the rent while they do another 'side project' (aspiring actors and artists often take temp jobs to finance themselves in between their other work).

Some travellers alternate between temp contracts and travelling, particularly in places such as London or Sydney, where you'll find plenty of work. While many people find temp work a little dull, the ability to quit at short notice ('Sorry I won't be in today – I'm in Amsterdam') does suit the travel lifestyle. While some travellers find it difficult to break the mould of being 'just a temp', others have turned a temp job into a career. You may also get some useful training in a temp job which will help you get a better job next time around.

What You'll Need

You'll need an up-to-date CV to start looking for temp work, and having at least one set of business clothes will be useful for interviews. Getting through your first week with one outfit is difficult ('Hasn't that new temp been wearing the same skirt since Monday?'), so your first pay cheque will be spent on expanding wardrobe options.

Any skills you can bring to an agency will help them find you a better temp job, so typing courses, software training and general communication courses will all come in handy. Bring along copies of qualifications you have as temp agencies may ask to see them. Having a few referees at home could also be useful.

Finding Temp Work

The best place to start looking for work is a temp agency. Most big cities have scores of them and some specialise in certain industries, such as IT, accounting, law, medicine or general office administration. Most temp agencies advertise in local newspapers, though you can often find them with a simple internet search. When you sign up with a temp agency they may get you to complete tests to gauge your typing speed, ability with various software packages, spelling and grammar, and resistance to boring, repetitive tasks. An agency will often interview you before they start to send you out to interviews with employers.

These global companies will get your temp job hunt started:

- **Adecco** (www.adecco.com) This international recruitment agency has more than 5000 offices in 62 countries and specialises in temp and permanent jobs in business, education, engineering, health and construction.
- **Drake Employment** (www.drakeintl.com) Drake has offices in the UK, USA, Canada, Australia, New Zealand, South Africa, Hong Kong, Singapore, Malaysia and Switzerland and covers most professions.
- **Hays Personnel** (www.hays.com) This leading recruitment agency specialises in office, IT, education, engineering and construction jobs and has offices in the UK, Europe, Canada and Australia. You can register and do a virtual interview over the web.
- **Kelly Services** (www.kellyservices.com) Has offices in the UK, Europe, the US, Canada, Asia, Australia and New Zealand. There are temp and permanent office, technical, engineering, IT and education jobs around the world.
- **Manpower Services** (www.manpower.com) This international agency offers temp and permanent jobs and has offices in the US, Canada, Latin America, Europe, the UK and Asia.
- **Reed Executive PLC** (www.reed.com) Another multinational recruitment agency, with hundreds of offices in the UK, Europe, Canada, South Africa, Australia and New Zealand. Reed specialises in temporary and permanent office, engineering and construction jobs.
- **TMP/Hudson Global Resources** (www.hudson resourcing.com) TMP/Hudson has 101 offices in 28 countries and offers mainly permanent and contract jobs. Staff can provide visa advice and conduct interviews on behalf of overseas companies.

FREELANCING

Some people will tell you freelancing is just a fancy word for unemployment, because you have to find your own work. Occasionally you'll be lucky enough to score a longer contract which will give you some security. Freelancing is common in journalism, design, web development and translating, so if you have the skills to pay the bills, this may be for you.

YOU SUCK AT WEB DESIGN

This hilarious podcast (www.yousuckatweb design.com) gives an insight into what it is like to be a freelance graphic designer – from pitching for jobs to the near hand-to-hand combat of getting people to pay you on time.

What to Expect

When you're a freelancer there's no such thing as too hungover mornings. If you don't work, you don't get paid. It can be difficult for your bank account, which will be on a roller-coaster ride that will probably make your bank manager more than a little queasy – mention words like 'overdraft' or 'loan' to see what they had for breakfast. The upside is that you can choose the jobs you want to work on and say no to the ones that look dull (then later say yes to them when you need the money).

EXPLORE THE UNIQUE MIX OF THE MODERN AND THE ANTIQUE IN THE HISTORICAL METROPOLIS OF DAMASCUS, SYRIA (P281).

Depending on the industry, you'll generally work to deadlines set by clients and have to work hard to meet their needs if you want to work for them again. Clients are the best and the worst of the job, so you should only pitch for jobs that involve working with the good people.

Rates of pay are always difficult to work out, as you'll often be pitching and including a price estimate in your pitch or quote. Most freelancers start out charging low rates so they can develop a portfolio of their work. The only problem is that it can be hard to get a client to pay you more if they're used to the 'bargain' rates. Start out with a realistic price, ask colleagues what they'd charge or look at professional associations for some rough indications. Work out an hourly rate, then roughly calculate how long a project will take, to give a rough quote. In journalism there are usually per-word rates for articles, but you can expect more for photographs.

What You'll Need

If you have skills (bring along any qualifications and portfolios you might have to prove it) in any of the big freelance areas, you're halfway there. You can do the work, but how do you find work? Getting some business cards will come in handy, though these days you might need to think about getting a website to market your work (especially if you're a web designer). You'll need an email address that you can check on the road so potential clients can contact you while you're away (or even before you get there). Even if you're a little shy, you'll need to be able to 'sell yourself' by talking about jobs you've done in the past and what you can do on this job.

Becoming a member of a local association can be useful. Here are a few journalist associations which can give you advice on rates, contracts and where to find work in a destination you're visiting:

- **Media and Entertainment Alliance** (www.alliance.org.au) Australia's professional organisation for journalists, actors, cartoonists and entertainers.
- **National Union of Journalists – UK** (NUJ; www.nuj.org.uk) UK union for journos.
- **National Writers Union** (www.nwu.org) US union for writers and journalists.

Journalism is the most obvious freelance gig, especially if you've got a few stories from your recent travels that could make feature stories. Joining one of the above associations also means you'll get a press card in the country you're visiting and helps open doors to all sorts of events.

Translating is another skill you can use almost anywhere, with translating into English becoming more important as businesses look to global markets. Teaching is also a skill you can freelance almost anywhere in the world (see p138).

As a freelancer, you'll technically need a work permit though if you're working for clients back home then this won't be necessary. You'll still have to pay tax on these earnings as your friendly neighbourhood tax agent has an international reach.

Finding Freelance Work

You'll need to go out and get work, because work rarely calls up asking for you. In journalism you'll need to pitch your story to the travel editor of a relevant section of a newspaper or magazine, and if you're a web developer you'll need to be able to meet clients, assess their tech needs and then give them a quote of how long it will take to do the job. Finding markets for journalism can be as simple as flipping through a local newsstand or writing down a few email addresses in a library. If you have contacts back home, you can email them stories so you might like to write down a few editors' email addresses before you go. Lonely Planet's *Travel Writing*

NOTABLE QUOTABLES
TAKEN FROM LONELY PLANET'S *BY THE SEAT OF MY PANTS*

I had flown to Prague at the last minute to write a piece for a music magazine. An up-and-coming British band happened to be playing in town, and I'd been asked to cover it. I'd said yes straightaway – this would be my first chance to see Prague, and the trip would include several hours where I'd have nothing to do. I could see the sights, get a feel for the place, go to the gig and go home. I'd be meeting the photographer in a couple of hours, in the centre of Prague. But that was only if I made it that far.

I'd been told I'd be picked up by a local driver called Honza, a friend-of-a-friend of the man who usually picked people up – and here he still was, still holding his Uzi 9mm, still grinning. I grinned back. Now we were just two men, in a small white car, grinning at each other – one of them armed.

'You want Uzi 9mm?' he asked.

'I'm fine for Uzi 9mm's,' I said, quite honestly. I could only hope that by offering me an Uzi 9mm, Honza wasn't also challenging me to a duel.

'I mean, to hold?' he said. 'You want hold gun?'

He was looking at me with what seemed to be real hope in his eyes. I didn't quite know what to say. I didn't really want to hold the gun, but being British, I didn't want to not hold it either, in case by not holding this man's gun I in any way made him feel uncomfortable or offended. As a well-raised Briton, I find it increasingly difficult to refuse anybody anything they might want whatsoever. This is also, incidentally, why I tend to avoid the gay nightclub scene.

'Okay then,' I said, slowly. 'I will hold the gun.'

He passed it to me, his face aglow, and I held it for a moment. It was heavy and metal. That's all I can tell you. I was, it seems, never destined to be a reviewer for *Guns 'n' Ammo*.

– Danny Wallace

---

can be a useful resource, with good advice on how to write an article as well as how to pitch.

Finding work in areas such as IT can involve looking for tenders or ads for upcoming projects, which you can do with a good base of local contacts. Many web designers and IT professionals fund their travels by registering with temp agencies who can hook them up with longer-term contracts. You can take your name off the books to go travelling and then sign back on when you're ready to return (or when the money runs out).

Here are a few useful resources for journalists and other freelancers looking for work:

- **All Freelance Work** (www.allfreelancework.com) Site with ideas on freelancing and a directory of work.
- **Aquarius Net** (www.aquarius.net) Long-running agency with translating jobs worldwide.
- **Freelance.com** (www.freelance.com) A US site for freelance IT professionals; requires (free) registration.
- **Freelance.Net** (www.freelancers.net) A UK site with international listing for IT professionals.
- **Freelance Writing** (www.freelancewriting.com) Portal for information on freelance writing.
- **Go Freelance** (www.freelanceworkexchange.com) US site with media, web-design and programming jobs; site use requires registration.
- **Graphic Define Magazine** (www.graphicdefine.org) A US magazine for freelance graphic designers.
- **ProZ.com** (www.proz.com) Site with extensive jobs message board for freelance translators.
- **Suite 101** (http://selfemployment.suite101.com) Guide to self-employment for writers, designers and entrepreneurs.
- **Translation Directory** (www.translationdirectory .com) Portal for freelance translators with jobs and dictionaries.

TOURISM & HOSPITALITY

Getting a start in hospitality isn't just about liking a drink, though it's probably the only industry where you'll get paid to hang out in a bar or club. A lot of employers start hiring in summer to tackle the seasonal thirst, though Christmas is another peak time for bartenders, waiting staff and hotel workers. Working in hospitality may not be all that glamorous (try being the only sober person in a bar full of drunks), but you can always find work wherever people are raising a glass or enjoying food. In fact, resorts in exotic Caribbean islands and bars in the sunny Greek islands get busy with tourists and need experienced bartenders more than dreary pubs in your home town do, so top holiday spots are often the place to look for work.

What to Expect

Jobs in hospitality are busy and social. If you don't like talking to people and the idea of reciting a menu to a lunch-time crowd isn't your thing, hospitality may not be for you. The job will give you more confidence though, as you learn to chat with regulars and develop skills in cheerful conversation.

Shifts get busiest for waiting staff around meal times and for drinking in the evenings, with weekends flat out for both. Short shifts are usually four hours and can run as long as eight or 10 hours with a lunch and dinner break. This will eat into your social life, as most of the nights people want to go out will be the nights you'll be called in to work (practice saying 'No, I can't tonight. I'm working.' because you'll need it). Pay is generally the bottom of the scale, though tips can supplement your take-home wage, especially in the US where tipping can be a competitive sport. Some jobs, especially in UK pubs, might be live-in jobs, where you'll get a small salary but your room and board will be covered – though you might be over pub grub after a while. A shorter-term option is to look for work at an event which will usually only last for a day or a week.

You may also be able to find work in your hostel which will often involve doing a shift on the front desk, helping change sheets, general cleaning and possibly some cooking. These jobs are often in exchange for accommodation so the pay package won't be brilliant, but you will get an instant peer group and the perks of the hostel such as free internet or a better room.

Your fellow hospitality workers are usually a cheery bunch who are in the job for a good time, not a long time, so you'll have a ready crew for after-work debriefing (okay, it's really just drinking but we wanted it to sound professional). Work is often easy-come easy-go, so if you're not enjoying it you can often get out in a hurry.

YOUR FIRST RESORT

Like the sound of mixing drinks to the sound of waves swishing in the background, or taking a lunch-time dip in the resort's lagoon? Or perhaps you'd prefer a quick slalom down the slopes before the dinner shift? Resort jobs can get you to some of the oddest locations on someone else's dime. You could be a rock-climbing instructor, mixing cocktails or just looking after a family chalet, and while the work will be demanding you'll still get to enjoy a bit of the lush life.

Here are a few sites that can get you resort-side before you can say 'Pass me a piña colada':

- **BIG PLANET PLACEMENTS** (www.bigplanetplacements.com) Has global gigs in the ski industry.
- **CLUB MED JOBS** (www.clubmedjobs.com) With more than 120 holiday villages around the world this organisation takes on thousands of resort staff ranging from hospitality to outdoor instructors.
- **COOL WORKS** (www.coolworks.com) Lists seasonal, resort and sporting jobs worldwide.
- **FREE RADICALS** (www.freeradicals.co.uk) Recruits for ski resorts all over Europe and America.
- **LEISURE OPPORTUNITIES** (www.leisureopportunities.co.uk) Good for leisure jobs in the UK and Europe.
- **NATIVES** (www.natives.co.uk) Online recruitment agency with listings of ski and resort work year-round.
- **RESORT JOBS** (www.resortjobs.com) An AboutJobs.com subsite listing resort opportunities worldwide.
- **SKI CONNECTION** (www.skiconnection.co.uk) Huge database of ski jobs worldwide.
- **THEME PARK JOBS** (www.themeparkjobs.com) Search engine for US theme parks that could have you operating a Ferris wheel; includes an email newsletter.
- **VOOVS** (www.voovs.com) Excellent ski site with listings of current ski and seasonal jobs around the world.

What You'll Need

The job won't be too mentally taxing but physically you'll be running back and forth from the kitchen, stacking tables and lugging fresh kegs to the cellar, so fitness will definitely come in handy. Having the gift of the gab will be useful too, though there are some sullen bartenders and downright uninterested waiting staff out there. Being 'switched on' is something a lot of bosses look for, which usually means being quick on your feet, not 'standing around gossiping', and having an eye on the customer, which means you can anticipate their needs in a spookily psychic way ('How did you know I needed a refill?' 'Just doing my job!' [salutes customer]).

You may also need 'black and whites', the uniform of waiting staff around the world. This usually consists of a white (sometimes black in swanky places) dress shirt and a good pair of dress trousers or a skirt. Experience is useful (though not essential as some places will train you), so if you can work in a bar at home or do some catering work, it will come in handy when you're in that first interview. Often hospitality staff work their way up a ladder and get better paid as they work in more prestigious places, so a more sophisticated restaurant or stylish bar will take more experienced staff. Start at more basic places if you have no experience. Doing a course in bartending or hospitality will come in handy, especially for making tricky cocktails, and in some cases a course can be a requirement. In Australia, for example, many employers require you to complete a Responsible Service of Alcohol (RSA) course, a six-hour course about when to stop serving customers who have had a little too much.

Here are a few providers of hospitality courses:
- **Alseasons** (www.alseasons.com.au) An Australian company offering RSA courses and more.
- **Australian School of Bartending** (www.bartending.com.au) Offers RSA qualifications and more advanced courses.

- **Nationwide Training Company** (NTC; www.nation widetrainingcompany.com) UK organisation offering hospitality courses.
- **RDI** (www.rdi.co.uk) A UK organisation with distance-learning courses in hospitality.

You can also get work as an instructor in the tourism industry if you've got some training – see Those Who Can't (p154) for more information on courses that can get you trained up as an outdoor activities instructor.

Finding Hospitality Work

The easiest way to find work in hospitality may be to look up from your breakfast plate to see a local café's wanted ad. Signs in windows are universal, though it's equally popular to walk into a restaurant with your CV and ask to speak to the manager – avoid meal times to get their full attention. You can also try word of mouth by asking travellers who've found work or by checking a hostel noticeboard. Hostels themselves often employ staff, so you can ask if there's work when you check in.

The following agencies specialise in hospitality jobs:
- **Alseasons** (www.alseasonsagency.com) Recruitment agency in Australia that provides work for working holiday–makers at certain times of year.
- **Berkeley Scott** (www.berkeley-scott.co.uk) A UK recruitment agency for temporary hospitality, leisure and office jobs.
- **Caterer** (www.caterer.com) Huge catering website with worldwide jobs.
- **HelpExchange.net** (www.helpx.net) Lists host families, farms, hotels and B&Bs in Europe, Australasia and North America that provide free accommodation and food in exchange for unpaid labour.
- **Hostels.com** (www.hostels.com) Lists jobs available in hostels for the upcoming seasons around the world.
- **Restaurant & Catering Australia** (www.restaurant cater.asn.au) Australian professional association with lists of course providers.
- **Wine and Hospitality Jobs** (www.wineandhospitality jobs.com) Large US hospitality recruitment site.

Finally, special events can be a good source of work. You could find yourself staffing a vegan burger van at a music festival or passing around the champagne at the races. You'll need to contact the events themselves at least three months in advance to lock in a job at most big events.

WORKING ON A CRUISE SHIP

Most travellers plug into the cruise scene by working for the mix of free transport, free accommodation, tax-free

> ## EXTRA, EXTRA!

If you want to give acting a try, work near celebrities, or even if you just like the sound of a free meal, being an extra could be for you. The pay isn't great, but you'll only be expected to stand around and possibly move through shots. Some agencies ask for 'headshots' (portrait pictures of you) and acting classes, while others just need to fill another suit of armour in a massive battle sequence. You should be wary of casting calls for dancers (which can turn out to be exotic), but if you register with a reputable agency you can expect to get paid to stand around. Some agencies may charge a registration fee (in Hollywood it's usually US$25) but beware of agencies that want to charge you to get some modelling shots of you (which will often cost a lot more). Pay isn't great but you will be fed, get to wear a costume and maybe even get to pause the DVD to show everyone your scene ('See! I rollerblade behind Jack Nicholson's shoulder...now!').

Start your web search here:

✪ BACKSTAGE (www.backstage.com) A US-based site that posts casting calls and features more tips on getting into 'serious' acting.

✪ SCREEN ACTORS GUILD (www.sag.org) US actors' union that protects rights of actors and can give you tips on casting calls.

✪ STAGEPOOL (www.stagepool.eu) A German-based agency that charges around €10 for registration and promises jobs on the continent.

salaries and perhaps the odd tipple of duty-free booze. With bigger ships having a small army of 1000-plus staff, there's bound to be a vacancy. Some of the best gigs on a cruise ship are as entertainers with a packed bill every night featuring singers, musicians and dancers. If you have stage fright, there are plenty of other jobs as a cruise ship is like a town that needs gym instructors, sales assistants, waiting staff, cooks, cleaners, masseurs and admin staff. Staff are drawn from around the world, so you'll be part of a multicultural crew who'll be good friends to travel with afterwards.

What to Expect

Top jobs pay anything from £20,000/US$40,000/A$43,000 per annum upwards, but most jobs pay as little as £10,000/US$24,000/A$26,000. If you're in hospitality, you'll get less, but your income will be supplemented by tips. The work itself is demanding with 50-hour weeks common and cruise guests who assume you're always on call. You'll generally sign on for a season which usually lasts five to six months, though it's possible to sign on again for another season once you've finished.

In 2002 the charity War on Want and the International Transport Workers' Federation wrote a report called **Sweatships** (downloadable from www.waronwant .org), highlighting that cruise ships employ people from developing nations to do more menial jobs. So there are ethical concerns to working on board a cruise ship.

What You'll Need

Whatever job you try out for, you'll need a passport that will be valid while you're working aboard a ship. Some international outfits might require a police check, just so they know you'll be trustworthy once you're on the high seas. Others require you to complete a medical check-up once they've decided you're right for the job.

Any experience you can bring to a job will be useful, even if you're just going for hospitality or retail positions. Obviously, jobs as entertainers will require some experience on stage and a few headshots will come in handy, but if you're looking at a job as a masseur, gym instructor or medical staff, a qualification is a must.

Finding Cruise-Ship Work

If you're looking for more information on working for cruise ships, check these links:

○ **Cruiseman** (www.cruiseman.com/cruiseshipjobs .htm) A US-based site with a search engine for cruises and good job advice.

READY STEADY CREW

Crewing on a yacht can be a good way to work your route. You'll have to be fit and some skippers look for sailing experience, but you'll also need a passport with at least a year left on it to sail into most countries. Meeting your skipper beforehand is a good idea to get a sense of what it would be like to be around them all the time. Women should look out for crusty old sea dogs who are looking for more than just workmates. Make sure you're comfortable and have enough money to get a ticket home if things don't work out. With the right skipper, though, you can learn new skills and have a blast.

Begin your job search with these sites:

✪ **CREW SEEKERS INTERNATIONAL (www.crewseekers.net)** Looks for crew (including cooks and waiting staff) across the world.

✪ **SAILNET (www.sailnet.com)** Check their 'Classifieds' for jobs or leave your own post to find a yacht where you want to go.

✪ **SUNSAIL (www.sunsail.com)** Employs around 1700 assorted staff on its yacht and beach resorts around the world. There are opportunities for qualified sailors, sailing instructors and general resort support staff, mostly in the Mediterranean.

✪ **THE FLOAT PLAN (www.floatplan.com)** Hit 'Crew Wanted' for no-fuss ads for crew and staff.

- **Cruise Community** (www.cruise-community.com) Has links to big cruise companies.
- **Cruise Staff** (www.cruisestaff.com.au) Recruits from Australia and New Zealand.

FRUIT PICKING & FARM WORK

Rolling up your sleeves on a farm is a good option if you want to see the countryside and dodge the big city. Work is usually seasonal and extremely casual, so if you're looking for a no-strings-attached gig, this might be for you. There's no need for previous experience so it's a job that almost anyone can fall into. Any place that has agriculture usually needs hands to pick the crops, so you can expect to find work reasonably easily.

What to Expect

The expression 'back-breaking labour' was probably coined by someone who'd spent an afternoon pulling turnips from the dry ground. Picking fruit and vegetables is hard work and you'll need to be fit to do it. Chances are you'll be doing the same repetitive tasks so you will get bored and working with an MP3 player will make it more bearable. Fruit ripens fast so farmers are keen to get it to market quickly. This means you'll be required to work hard, with very early starts (some travellers have reported 5am) and often six days a week. But you won't be working for long with the average fruit picking season lasting only six weeks.

You can expect to meet plenty of other travellers who'll be doing this job to make some more cash. Many travellers enjoy the social life with a real 'work hard, party harder' feel. Some travellers just enjoy the break from the city. Better jobs will pay by the hour, but many pay based on how much you pick or harvest. About half of fruit-picking jobs involve climbing ladders, though grapes and other low fruit are okay if you suffer from vertigo. Some farms will include a bunkhouse with your own shower block, others will let you camp on their property for free. When a farm wants to charge you rent or other costs, work out if you'll be able to make enough money to make it worth your while – while there are only a few crooked farmers, you might not make much money if you have to travel to a distant place to work for a few

weeks. Some farms may be so remote that you won't get too much nightlife, unless you bring your own. If you're interested in farmstays, including Willing Workers on Organic Farms (or WWOOFing), check the Accommodation chapter (see p104).

As well as picking fruit, there are jobs for packing fruit, driving tractors, crushing grapes and a hundred other tasks. If you play your cards right a farmer may even need you in the off-season to help out with fencing, trimming trees, crop-dusting or other farm-maintenance tasks.

HARVEST SEASONS

UK
- apples and pears – August to October
- hops – August to October
- soft fruit – June to October
- vegetables – May to October

FRANCE
- apples and pears – July to October
- grapes – September to October
- olives – November to December
- soft fruit – May to September
- vegetables – July to October

SOUTHERN MEDITERRANEAN
- apples and pears – June to October
- grapes – June to October
- olives – November to April
- oranges – November to April

AUSTRALIA
- apples and pears – January to September
- bananas – July to August
- grapes – January to March
- soft fruit – August to December
- vegetables – year-round

NEW ZEALAND
- apples – January to May
- grapes – January to April
- kiwi fruit – May to July
- soft fruit – November to December
- vegetables – July to October

What You'll Need

You won't need any special skills to pick fruit, but if you have some good, sturdy shoes and sun-protecting clothing, it will help. A tent can be handy on some properties – check for second-hand camping gear on hostel noticeboards or local camping stores rather than lugging it from home.

Finding Work

Harvesting usually kicks off when the crop is ripe, with farmers advertising in advance for many jobs. Some farmers even advertise in hostels and backpacker magazines to get travellers. Check the Harvest Seasons table on p130 to get an idea of when you could pick fruit in a few destinations.

If you want to get really organised here are a few websites that advertise fruit-picking jobs:

○ **Anywork Anywhere** (www.anyworkanywhere.com) A worldwide job board with fruit picking at its core.
○ **Appellation Contrôlée** (APCON; www.apcon.nl) Popular Dutch organisation that places workers on the grape harvest in France.
○ **Fruitfuljobs.com** (www.fruitfuljobs.com) This is a recruitment service for UK soft-fruit industry.
○ **Jobsearch Australia – Harvest Trail** (https://jobsearch.gov.au/harvesttrail) Government website which tells you what's growing where and when.
○ **Picking Jobs** (www.pickingjobs.com) Global site specialising in fruit picking around the world, including the US, Canada and South Africa.
○ **Seasonal Work New Zealand** (www.seasonalwork.co.nz) New Zealand's first stop for fruit-picking jobs.
○ **Work In New Zealand** (www.workinnz.co.nz) Fruit-picking jobs in Hawkes Bay, New Zealand .
○ **Willing Workers on Organic Farms** (WWOOF; www.wwoof.org) Join this international group to work (for six hours a day) on organic farms almost anywhere in the world.

CONSTRUCTION WORK

If fruit picking wasn't tough enough for you, then working on a building site should really exhaust you. You'll need to be physically fit, and having a few building-related skills will help your pay package. The construction industry relies on contractors, so short-term building work is easy to find in most countries. It can also pay well, particularly if you have experience working with heavy machinery. There are openings around the world for labourers, steelworkers, heavy-vehicle drivers, electricians, plumbers, bricklayers, roofers and carpenters.

Going through an established recruitment agency will get you most jobs, though (as with hospitality) word of mouth can also get you a start. Construction is a heavily unionised industry so joining a local union can be a good way to start your job search. Building work can range from completely unskilled jobs such as labouring, to highly skilled jobs such as plumbing or structural engineering. As well as big construction sites, many small businesses take on unskilled labourers for short-term projects such as site clearing.

Useful resources for anyone thinking about building or construction work include:

○ **Builder's Planet** (www.buildersplanet.com) Worldwide resources for working in construction; check their Job Bank.
○ **Construction Jobs** (www.constructionjobs.com) US site with lots of job listings, with registration and CV posting.
○ **Constructor.co.uk** (www.constructor.co.uk) Good construction and civil-engineering site with lots of UK jobs.
○ **Grunt Labour Services** (www.gruntlabour.com) Australian site with good listings.
○ **Hill McGlynn** (www.hillmcglynn.com.au) Has offices in the UK, Middle East and Australia with jobs worldwide.

ALTHOUGH PROMINENTLY HINDU, NEPAL IS HOME TO SACRED BUDDHIST SITES SUCH AS THE TEMPLE AT SWAYAMBHUNATH IN KATHMANDU (P225).

WORKING WITH KIDS

Families can be the key to a culture. Short of being adopted yourself, looking after someone else's family is the closest you can get to becoming a part of a family. Not only will you live in their home, but you'll get to go on family outings and develop real relationships with local people. Plus you'll learn a language through the kind of deep immersion that's impossible in any foreign language course.

Okay, now the downsides. If you don't like changing nappies and making 'goo goo' noises, you're definitely going to be looking for work with older kids. Prepare yourself for some bad behaviour, because even the sweetest-natured kids can throw tantrums as soon as their parents slip out the door. If you have younger siblings, you've probably seen this act before, but it's more intense when you're responsible. The job can vary from child to child so if you've got a real little 'darling', your job will be very hard. Sometimes kids may be responding to problems in their environment such as moving towns, parental divorce or school bullies, so you might feel out of your pedagogical depth.

That said, it can be very rewarding to see kids you've been looking after improve their grades or develop better social skills. Some travellers who start out as au pairs catch the bug and go into teaching. You'll certainly learn better ways to look after pesky younger siblings.

Before you go you should try to get some experience looking after kids. You can start with basic baby-sitting, then look for work at a local nursery or after-school care. This will help you work out if you actually like looking after kids, but will also push your application up a little higher in the pile (North American camp organisations are very keen on previous experience).

AU PAIRS & NANNIES

There's more to looking after kids than *The Nanny Diaries*, but working in New York for a wealthy family is a nice dream to start with. Called 'au pairs' in Europe and 'nannies' in the US and elsewhere, there's no shortage of work for this profession, with more mothers choosing to continue their careers and have a family at the same time. In Australia childcare centres are a popular option with parents, so you might start looking for work there. Men are slowly appearing in this field, but many employers still look for young women.

WHAT TO EXPECT

Often this job will mean living in with a family, though some nannies do live elsewhere and come in while the parents are at work. If you're living in, you'll have free accommodation, but some families will want you to be always on call. You should discuss this with a potential employer and ask about having regular days off (usually weekends, which will be good for sightseeing). Many parents will want to spend time with their kids when they get home, so you may have your evenings free. If it's not made clear in the job description, you should have a conversation with your potential family about the amount of time you'll be expected to work and what kind of chores you'll be doing. In a live-in job you can expect to work a minimum of 25 hours a week, though some families may ask for two nights per week of baby-sitting, which pays a little more. Most positions will be for a limited time, usually a year, so you should allow for some travel after your trip.

Au pairs in Europe may even be encouraged to attend language classes, which brings another great dimension to the job. If you score one of these positions you can expect time off to attend classes. Families generally prefer nonsmokers (even if they smoke themselves) as they're concerned about their kids' health and habits.

Some agencies will hook you up with casual work if you only want to do a couple of days' work and live in a place of your own.

Pay

If you're looking to make millions, then we suggest inheriting money, because nannying doesn't pay brilliantly. Families often pay 'pocket money' rates with the understanding that they're providing board and food. If you're travelling with the family, you may not even be paid as your employers will buy you a ticket and accommodation.

According to the **British Au Pair Agencies Association** (www.bapaa.org.uk), you should generally start at around £60 a week plus board for 25 hours a week, though with more qualifications or additional

---

MY FIRST

– GREAT EXPECTATIONS –

The letter arrived from Massachusetts sealing my plans for the summer. Fran explained in glowing detail what I could expect as a nanny for their Hannah, a bright and vivacious five-year-old who would learn to swim that summer with the aid of her nanny. Their 'bathed in sunshine' New England–style house, with family-heirloom furniture and native hardwood floors, was set on half an acre next to a babbling stream in the heart of the Berkshires.

High school finished, my mother and I set off on the two-day road trip to Massachusetts and rocked up to the 'mansion' to discover it looked more like a derelict trailer-park home with a porch for shoes, shovels and rusty gardening equipment. It was too late to drive off. The inside of the house was homey enough and the heirloom furniture was more like uncoordinated op-shop bargains and the hardwood floors were beyond repair.

Payment hadn't been discussed in advance, but given the humble weekly wage they were offering I assumed I'd have weekends and some weeknights off. Instead, I was allowed one day off per week. No wonder I was more interested in going windsurfing than teaching Hannah to swim. In retrospect though, it was a good thing to put on my CV even though she pretty much taught herself.

Despite feeling deceived and increasingly hemmed in with all my baby-sitting tasks, which began when Hannah woke up and ended after she went to bed around 8pm, I did manage to have a very good time and even squeezed in a summer romance with the sailing champion of the boat club. Fran didn't approve as I was no longer available to hang out with her in the evenings to smoke cigarettes on her concrete doorstep.

The Berkshires were absolutely beautiful, and the people I met are still in my photo albums. Would I do it again, knowing what I know now? Absolutely – but this time I'd ask more specific questions about what was expected of me.

Born in Canada, Janine Gray works in communications and dabbles in documentary-making.

---

hours you can expect more. In the States, live-in nannies working five days a week for 30 hours can expect to start on US$160 to US$200 per week for live-in roles, but again, more qualifications will increase the salary.

Work

It's worth bearing in mind that 'au pair' means 'on an equal footing', so you should be treated like a member of the family rather than a slave. You should talk to your family about what the job will entail, ideally at an interview, and work out if this is the right fit for you.

Generally, your duties should be based around the children, with a few extra helping-out tasks such as cleaning or shopping to be negotiated with your family. Some tasks you will do could include:

- Waking the children and getting them dressed.
- Preparing breakfast.
- Clearing up the children's rooms.
- Washing dishes or loading and unloading the dishwasher.
- Tidying away toys from every corner of the house.
- Collecting the children from school.
- Grocery-shopping.
- Playing with the children.
- Helping to prepare the children's meals.
- Bathing the children and putting them to bed.
- Sweeping up and vacuuming.
- Ironing the children's clothes.
- Accompanying the family on outings or holidays.

Generally, families are pretty reasonable, but if your family starts expecting you to cook for dinner parties or wash the car without any discussion, you should think about leaving.

WHAT YOU'LL NEED

You'll need to sort out a visa before you go, though many agencies will help you organise a visa. The US and UK have special nanny visas that you can apply for so long as you're 18 to 25, single, with no kids of your own. Generally the visas will require a commitment of two months to a year from both the family and you.

Generally, you'll need to pay for travel to your host so choosing a country that's cheaply accessible is a good idea. Experience in working with children will come in handy (higher-end agencies ask for 200 hours of documented experience which can be baby-sitting), plus you'll need to be able to supply character references (usually from people who'll say you're trustworthy and responsible). Some nannies complete courses or other training to prepare them, though this isn't essential.

NANNY SCAM

In 2006 a web scam suckered several potential nannies and families out of a lot of cash. The most common scam was a bogus US family who claimed to be living in Nigeria or Kenya and needed a nanny for their children. Stories ranged from a chemical-engineer father to a fashion-designer mother. Several emails were exchanged with potential nannies and it all seemed genuine. Then the nannies were asked to send a fee or deposit via Western Union or a travellers cheque – only a small amount. A small amount over a few thousand people adds up enough to make a worthwhile scam.

A more audacious scammer sends nannies an advance cheque, then announces before the phoney cheque clears that the scammer's family have all been killed in a car accident and that they need you to send back the amount (using your own legitimate cheque, of course).

Using a nanny agency avoids these problems though the odd scammer has tried to use a nanny agency as well – good agencies even list the names of scammers. You should beware anyone who offers a too-good-to-be-true deal, and be careful sending money in advance.

FINDING WORK

The best way to find work is through an agency which will look after paperwork and vet families that seem difficult. You might also have some success looking on noticeboards in hostels or on job websites. You could also try childcare centres, particularly in Australia where nannies are less common.

Signing up with an agency takes a lot of hassle out of looking for work. Some agencies charge a fee, but ideally only when they place you with a family. This means you can register with several agencies and only pay the one that finds you work. Several agencies allow you to register online and create a profile detailing your experience and what you will and won't do.

Some good places to start include:

○ **Almondbury Au Pair & Nanny Agency** (www.aupair-agency.com; www.nanny-agency.com) This site places people in Europe and the US.
○ **A-One Au Pairs & Nannies** (www.aupairsetc.co.uk) Recruits nannies and au pairs for southern England.
○ **Au Pair Association** (www.iapa.org) This international organisation has good links to member agencies in most European countries and the US.
○ **Au Pair in America** (www.aupairamerica.co.uk) A British-based organisation that finds work in the US.
○ **Au Pairs International** (www.aupairsinternational.com) A Denmark-based agency that places au pairs throughout Scandinavia.
○ **Au Pair World** (www.aupair-world.net) A global organisation that requires registration and lets you search for families and post your CV online.
○ **Go Au Pair** (www.goaupair.com) A good organisation for finding au pair work in the US.
○ **Great Au Pair** (www.greataupair.com) Places nannies worldwide with online interviews where you can chat to families before you start.
○ **Peek-a-boo Childcare** (www.peekaboochildcare.com) A UK-based organisation that offers work in Europe and the US, plus courses in first aid.

DESPITE BEING FROWNED UPON BY THE STATE, THE FESTIVITIES OF THE COLOURFUL CUBAN CARNIVAL (P245) PERSIST.

- **Quick Help** (www.quickhelp.co.uk) Offers shorter-term and casual work as well as regular live-in jobs in the UK.
- **Union Française des Associations Au Pair** (UFAAP; www.ufaap.org) Includes several French organisations and a search-by-region function for work anywhere in France.

CAMP COUNSELLORS

Summer camp is as American as apple pie, with over 12,000 camps across the US imprisoning…err, entertaining children from six to 16 for periods between one and eight weeks over summer. You can expect to be very busy as you'll be both supervising the kids and getting them into hiking, water sports, basketball, horseback riding, crafts, music and several other activities. The days are long, but it can be surprisingly fun, plus there are a few weeks to sightsee when camp finishes.

In Europe there's a camp job called 'courier' which often involves working with children but frequently with a whole family too. You'll generally be working closely with guests, doing everything from cleaning their tents to acting as a guide to the local area. You'll be on call during the day or the evening in case guests need help, and you get additional training in first aid for emergencies.

Most camps will ask you to pay for flights, application fees, insurance and other costs, or they will be deducted from your salary, so do the sums before you sign up to see which deals work out best. You'll also have to live the clean life as there's no smoking or drinking at the camp – save all that up for your trip after camp.

The best time to look for camp jobs is autumn though camps recruit year-round. If you have specialist skills, such as working with special-needs children or teaching an activity, you might qualify as a specialist counsellor which gets your paid a little more.

FINDING WORK
Although camps are most popular in the US, it's also possible to find jobs elsewhere, with the UK offering some good opportunities. Here are a few organisations to kick-start your job search:

- **Acorn Adventure** (www.acorn-jobs.co.uk) A UK adventure-holiday company with 300 jobs across Europe; includes a training course and activity-training options.
- **American Camp Association** (www.acacamps.org) Useful for finding camps in specific states.
- **Barracudas** (www.barracudas.co.uk) A UK outfit specialising in day camps, with teaching and training qualifications an advantage.
- **British Universities North America Club** (BUNAC; www.bunac.org) A UK-based organisation that runs nine- to 12-week camps in the US.
- **Camp America** (www.campamerica.com.au) A huge organisation that looks for Aussies and Kiwis to work on camps.
- **Camp Counsellors USA** (CCUSA; www.ccusa.com) Offers camp jobs in the US, Croatia, Russia and Canada.
- **Club Med** (www.clubmed-jobs.com) This global hotel consortium takes camp counsellors and others to look after kids.
- **Holidaybreak** (www.holidaybreakjobs.com) Owner of the Eurocamp and Keycamp holiday companies, which employ over 2000 staff in Europe with training provided.
- **Kids Klub** (www.kidsklub.co.uk) A UK outfit that runs summer programs.
- **Kingswood Group** (www.kingswoodjobs.co.uk) Does camps in the UK with a need for activity instructors and general staff plus qualifications in teaching climbing, archery or lifeguarding.
- **PGL Travel** (www.pgl.co.uk) UK provider of camps that offer some outdoor training for instructors; jobs run from one to six weeks in Europe.
- **Village Camps** (www.villagecamps.com) Has jobs for camp staff (including hospitality and counsellors) across Europe.

TEACHING ENGLISH

If you're reading this, you're probably one of the 309 million people in the world who have English as their first language. Don't get too excited though, because English actually comes in third, after Mandarin Chinese and Spanish, for native speakers. You've probably been taking your mother tongue for granted, but it's actually complicated (ever tried explaining the difference between 'there', 'their' and 'they're' to a classroom full of snickering non-English-speakers?) and very difficult to learn, particularly if you have a non-Romance language background (those that aren't based on Latin, such as English, Italian or Spanish). Fortunately, this means that English-language teaching is always in demand.

TEFL WATCH

This US-based blog (www.teflwatch.org) keeps an eye on TEFL courses and jobs around the world. It's a good read if you're interested in becoming a teacher and it's an ideal place to read the goss on a language school you might be thinking of signing up to.

Not only is it portable (you might need a textbook and a few hand-outs, but these can just be PDFs on a USB drive), but English-teaching is needed everywhere. Even in English-speaking countries new arrivals, including everyone from refugees to businesspeople, are keen to learn the lingo. Plus you'll get to meet local people and give them a skill that they'll have all their lives. This is a sure-fire way to make friends.

WHAT TO EXPECT

Your teaching experience will depend on your class. You could be teaching one-on-one with a wealthy kid in Tokyo or you could be standing in front of a class of adults in a Brazilian village. Teaching one student can be easy and you'll get to know a single student better than a whole class, while a class has more difficult dynamics – who's getting on with whom, who's throwing paper planes at you and a hundred other challenges.

The good news is that teaching can pay very well, depending on where you are. A better school in Japan or Korea, for example, could pay £18,000/US$35,000/A$40,000 a year, while teaching in South America will be more like volunteering with an allowance of £1000/US$2000/A$2250 for the year. Schools usually help out with your accommodation (either subsidising or helping find cheap local apartments) and flight costs so your expenses will be limited while you're teaching, though it could be tough to save up for a huge trip after teaching. Most schools are fairly clear on rates of pay and conditions on their websites. Your fellow teachers are bound to be from several different countries as schools recruit from around the world, which will be helpful when you're couchsurfing (see p104) your way around the world later.

Most schools will keep you pretty busy with four- or five-day weeks, plus there may be opportunities for extra tutoring. Preparing lessons is more time-consuming than you think though, and you should allow at least as much time to prepare a class as you'll be teaching. If you're marking written assignments (which is rare if you're doing a speaking-only class), this will also take up time. In a good school you may already have a curriculum to teach, complete with detailed lesson plans and exercises; in a bad one you may find yourself with a pile of faded Charles Dickens' books and a blackboard.

Outside the school, you'll often have a support network of other teachers to go out and drown your sorrows with or team up with for weekend escapes. Many schools will employ you for a year, so once

you're finished it might be a good time to explore the rest of the country as you'll have developed better language skills yourself.

WHAT YOU'LL NEED

Before you start milking this cash cow, you'll need to know if you can teach. Some people fear public speaking more than death, while others feel most comfortable in front of a crowd. You'll have some experience of this from school, but you might like to try teaching in another environment. Because English is everywhere, there are often opportunities to practice teaching in your own home town. You can start by doing some basic conversation with non-English-speaking neighbours or friends, then graduate to helping out a migrant resource centre or refugee group. Not only will this give you a taste, but it will also give you some experience to impress English-teaching schools.

There are several qualifications offered in teaching English which will help your job search. In the US, Canada and Australia, the qualification is called Teaching English as a Second Language (TESL), while

---

MY FIRST
~ ENGLISH PATIENTS ~

It started abruptly. While working at a crappy job in Adelaide, I occasionally surfed teacher websites, more out of curiosity than actual intent. Then there was an interesting job ad for a small school in central Japan, so I shot off an application. Eighteen days later I landed in Nagoya International Airport, pondering the question, 'Do I even like kids?'

No, it turned out to be more like a passion and I spent a year there teaching kindergarten and primary-school kids. Teaching, I quickly discovered, was a great skill to combine with travel; it allowed me to keep my expenses way down while getting a really rich experience of the culture. Who better to show you around town than one of your own students? And no classroom was the same. In Japan the well-built classrooms were warm enough for me to teach wearing shorts and a T-shirt, unusual in such a formal country. In China, my classroom was only a few degrees above freezing level and my teaching attire was more like snow gear. In Russia I taught summer school and had no classroom at all, instead teaching the kids in the open air.

There was no shortage of challenges. For China, the oddity came in the first lesson, where my school wanted me to randomly assign 'English names' to each of my new students. It's remarkable how quickly you run out of names when required to produce them on the spot – my classes had far too many Johns, Bobs and Maggies that year. In Japan I somehow always seemed to find myself at the local karaoke bar at 3am with locals pleading me to butcher yet another Billy Joel classic.

Adam Stanford works as Lonely Planet's marketing analyst and sometimes hums 'Piano Man'.

START ANY TIME It takes a month and £1000/US$2000/A$2250 to qualify. Unqualified travellers sometimes pick up teaching work, but the pay is lower, the opportunities fewer and the teaching worse. If you want to dip a toe in the water before you decide, enrol in a weekend teaching course.

GO ANYWHERE You can go to almost any place where people don't speak English. Fancy learning to tango in Buenos Aires, going diving in Thailand, volunteering in an African village? Register on the job websites, start looking, say your goodbyes and pack!

LEARN A LANGUAGE Learning another language is much easier when you live in that country, but easier still when you are teaching English to speakers of that language. If you teach at an institute, you may well be offered free local-language classes yourself.

EXPAND YOUR ADDRESS BOOK Teaching English is a great way to make local friends, get social invitations, learn about your host culture and practice their language. Even if the language is too difficult to learn completely, you will earn yourself Brownie points for trying.

ENJOY THE REWARDS It is nice to know that you have helped someone develop a skill they may use and benefit from forever. Learning English, the global language for business, is seen in so many countries as being the passport to a new and better life.

MEET OTHER TEACHERS Unless you are in the middle of nowhere, there will likely be other English teachers from all over the world who can help you settle. If teaching English is a big life change for you, their often similar stories will inspire you and remind you why you're doing it.

BE THE ONLY ONE If you are in the middle of nowhere, with no colleagues around, you will probably feel like a local celebrity! You will have the pleasure of knowing your experience is unique, and you can pat yourself on the back for your sense of adventure.

DEVELOP CONFIDENCE Teaching in front of a class can stretch your confidence and transferable skills. See yourself as a comic, actor, world leader? Classes can be as interesting as you make them, so your creative juices can be employed to the full to help the students learn.

FALL IN LUURVE... You might meet the love of your life in a classroom (assuming you are teaching adults, and you and your love are not wooing each other on school grounds). I won't go on about this, because it could be frowned upon and it never happened to me!

CHANGE YOUR LIFE The whole experience can help you reassess what you want in life and give you the fresh outlook to go get it. Indeed, the memories will leave a smile on your face when you remember them one day as you sit in that great waiting room for the sky.

in the UK it's called Teaching English as a Foreign Language (TEFL; pronounced 'teffle' by those in the know). In the UK, Ireland and New Zealand, courses can also be called Teaching English for Speakers of Other Languages (TESOL). Courses vary in length and the clout they carry with employers, but it seems pretty obvious that a cheap 'learn everything in an hour' course won't be that useful unless you've already got a general teaching qualification.

Not surprisingly, the most respected courses come from the UK, as many people still see it as the cradle of the English language. The Certificate in English

Language Teaching to Adults (CELTA) is a widely respected qualification administered by the University of Cambridge. There's an explosion of bogus places (often with suspiciously self-important titles such as Mr Cambridge's Anglification Institute), so check for centres that offer the real deal on the **University of Cambridge** website (www.cambridgeesol.org). Another well-regarded course is Certificate in Teaching English to Speakers of Other Languages (CertTESOL) offered by **Trinity College London** (www.trinitycollege.co.uk). Good courses usually take three to four months full-time and can be done part-time over a year.

Elsewhere in the world, there are local organisations (see the Directories chapter relevant to you in Part Four) and good web resources which offer their own version of these courses. Some courses even come with a job offer at the end, because they have links to schools around the world.

Here are a few global providers:

○ **Cactus Language** (www.cactusteachers.com) Offers language courses worldwide; also has an admissions service for internationally recognised TEFL/TESOL certificate courses.
○ **ICAL Online TESOL/TEFL Training** (www.icalweb .com) An online course (£135/US$265/A$280) that includes video lessons and a Facebook group to gossip with other students.
○ **International House London** (www.ihlondon.co.uk) Offers good 'distance education' modules to prepare you for CELTA courses.
○ **International Teacher Training Organisation** (IITO; www.teflcertificatecourses.com) A network of teacher-training groups that offer online training and placement after successful completion.
○ **i-to-i** (www.onlinetefl.com) An online TEFL course (from £220/US$430/A$475) that uses video and audio; popular with volunteers; has a placement program.
○ **TEFL Online** (www.teflonline.com) A solid online provider with a video-based course costing €230 (£160/US$315/A$390).

Of course, you'll also need to sort out a visa, though many schools will organise this for you. Some schools will also ask for either general teaching experience or up to 200 hours of English-teaching experience.

FINDING WORK

Many travellers find work through an established school, which will sort out most of the details for you. Schools prefer a TEFL/TESL qualification and some may even be looking for university graduates.

ESL TEACHER-TALK PODCAST

This monthly podcast (www.eslteachertalk.com) gives tips for teachers and would-be teachers.

SCHOOLS & ORGANISATIONS OFFERING WORK

○ **Berlitz** (www.berlitz.com) A huge international employer with more that 400 schools worldwide. Teacher-training available.
○ **Cactus Language** (www.cactusteachers.com) Offers jobs and subsidised courses.
○ **China Education Exchange** (www.china educationexchange.org) Approved by the People's Republic of China, this program offers teaching jobs to university graduates and includes accommodation.
○ **China TEFL Network** (www.chinatefl.com) An agency that links Chinese schools with foreign teachers.
○ **ECC Foreign Language Institutes of Japan** (www .japanbound.com) A Japanese agency that requires no formal TEFL/TESOL qualifications. Requires a minimum one-year commitment.
○ **English First** (EF; www.englishfirst.com) An international school offering work in China, Indonesia, Russia and occasionally other countries such as Thailand, Vietnam, Malaysia and Saudi Arabia.
○ **Europa Pages** (www.europa-pages.com) A list of schools in Europe.
○ **Japan Exchange and Teaching Programme** (JET; www.jetprogramme.org) One of the best opportu-nities in Japan. Recruits university graduates.
○ **Marcus Evans Linguarama** (www.linguarama.com) Language schools in Western Europe.
○ **YBM Education** (www.ybmecc.co.kr) Runs a series of schools across Korea with placements of one year for university graduates.

If you have an ESL (English as a Second Language) teaching qualification and you're confident about finding work yourself, there's no shortage of places that have listings.

Top websites for teaching jobs:

○ **Ajarn** (www.ajarn.com) A site with jobs in Thailand.

○ **Dave's ESL Cafe** (www.eslcafe.com) Dave Sperling's long-running ESL site has jobs listings, teaching advice and teachers' forums.

○ **EFL Web** (www.eflweb.com) Good TEFL site for beginners with advice on teaching, TEFL courses and job vacancies.

○ **EL Gazette** (www.elgazette.com) Online TEFL magazine with teaching news and job listings.

○ **ELT News** (www.eltnews.com) Japanese teaching site with job listings and a message board.

○ **ESL Guide** (www.esl-guide.com) US site with world-wide listings of jobs and English-language schools.

○ **Europa Pages** (www.europa-pages.com/jobs) Europe-focused site with information on TEFL courses in Europe and teaching jobs worldwide.

○ **Ohayo Sensei** (www.ohayosensei.com) Bimonthly newsletter for foreign teachers in Japan, with extensive job listings.

○ **Teach in China** (www.teach-in-china.net) Online classifieds site with teaching jobs across China.

○ **Teaching in Japan** (www.teachinginjapan.com) Useful website with information on all aspects of teaching in Japan.

○ **Teach Korea** (www.teachkorea.com) Useful site with job listings and tips about teaching in Korea.

○ **Teachers of English to Speakers of Other Languages** (TESOL; www.tesol.org) International association that offers resources and preparation courses.

○ **TEFL.net** (www.tefl.net) International TEFL site with listings of jobs and courses and a forum for teachers.

○ **TEFL.com** (www.tefl.com) An established jobs site with TEFL job listings worldwide.

○ **TESall.com** (www.tesall.com) A large bulletin board of jobs plus advice and resources.

VOLUNTEERING

So you'd like to save the world? Good news, because volunteering is a way for you to become actively involved in global development. According the US Department of Labor, more than one in four US citizens did some form of volunteer work in their own country in 2007. Getting out into the world though is a long way from organising a cake raffle for your local church, so you need to prepare yourself for a difficult job that probably won't be well paid. But this is your chance to buck the trend by not just thinking globally, but acting globally.

Today many people are motivated to volunteer by a strong desire to 'do good' or to make a meaningful contribution. Some find themselves in a remote African village teaching kids the importance of hygiene, while others help out in a Sri Lankan elephant orphanage. What you want to do depends on your interests and what sort of contribution you want to make. You may not want to make a year-long commitment but decide to just do a few weeks – in which case we suggest you take a volunteering holiday. Volunteering holidays mix a taste of volunteer work with a tour. More hard-core volunteers apply for programs with charities, Non-Governmental Organisations (NGOs) and sending agencies. These organisations require longer commitments, possibly fundraising to send yourself away, and often conduct several rounds of interviews. Somewhere between these two options are organised volunteer programs, which set up almost everything for you.

Whatever you decide to do, it's important to research the organisation you're working for. Sadly, there are a few organisations that are jumping on the 'voluntourism' bandwagon and riding it all the way to the bank. Look for organisations with transparent financial structures and minimal administration costs. NGOs and tourist groups with long track records are a good place to start. If you're wary of an organisation, give a shout out on the **Thorn Tree** (www.lonelyplanet.com/thorntree), where someone may have already had a nightmare trip they'll be keen to warn you about. You can also prepare yourself by picking up a copy of Lonely Planet's *Volunteer: A Traveller's Guide to Making a Difference Around the World,* which profiles over 190 organisations and presents lots of background advice and case studies, with a companion website at www.lonelyplanet.com/volunteer. See p149 for more resources.

VOLUNTEERING HOLIDAYS

Want to do some good and still relax a little? Then this is the option for you. A volunteering holiday might mix working to save the Thai tiger with a tour of northern

✪ **BECAUSE I'M SELFISH** I don't volunteer because it helps people. I volunteer because I enjoy volunteering... it makes me feel good... I mean, if volunteering was as painful as being hit over the head with a frying pan, you wouldn't do it! (Remember that *Friends* episode where Phoebe found it near impossible to do a selfless act?)

✪ **BECAUSE IT 'HELPS' OTHERS** However cynical I've become about volunteering, volunteers have at least done something. If you have made one person's day or one person laugh in a month, then regardless of whether they are now fluent in English or have a new school, it's worth it...because people in developing countries might not have much to smile about. It's better than doing nothing.

✪ **BECAUSE IT TEACHES YOU...** You learn compassion, care, confidence, communication, new skills, that life is harder for other people than you can imagine, (sometimes) a new language, new customs, and you learn to adapt and work with others from all over the world.

✪ **BECAUSE IT TEACHES THEM...** There is more to life than just traditions, cultures, languages... Naive as it is, I hope that if I encourage just one child or adult to reach for the stars (be that earning millions or visiting a new village), then I have helped them LIVE life.

✪ **WOULD I DO IT MORE THAN ONCE?** Absolutely – every time! I made a few children smile...it's better than sitting on the sofa daydreaming...

www.lonelyplanet.com

---

hill villages or a language course, followed by hitting the beach for some well-earned relaxation. Programs usually range from a week to three months and most are tailored to travellers. You'll be expected to pay a donation to the organisation you're working for, to cover the costs. During the holiday part you might be in luxury accommodation, but during the volunteering part you may be staying with local families or in villages, so standards won't be what you're used to at home. For some travellers this mix of volunteering and travelling isn't enough, so they go on to do a longer volunteering stint. You'll get more of an 'insider' experience than your average tourist, though, and you may even make some friends. Experiences range from helping save sea turtles in Costa Rica (with a little surfing thrown in) for Spring Break to working for a month in a school in Tanzania.

Such 'voluntourism' has drawn frowns from some in the development community because they see it as bringing in people for too short a term to make any big changes. Some see it as a disruption to large-scale projects, creating an almost neocolonial culture in some nations. Another perspective is that 'every little bit helps',

and if you've done some research into an organisation and you believe it's making a meaningful contribution, you should help out. The forum on **VolunTourism** (www.voluntourism.org) has great discussions of the benefits of this kind of volunteering.

Check your section of the Directories in Part Four for recommended organisations that combine volunteering and vacationing. The site www.responsibletravel.com has links to small-group and tailor-made volunteering holidays. Many travel agents also offer options called 'meaningful', 'ethical', 'responsible' and 'volunteer' tourism, so check their websites for suggestions.

ORGANISED PROGRAMS

If you're after a longer-term commitment with a solid organisation around you, opt for an organised expedition or placement. These volunteer experiences are backed by a large organisation which has plenty of experience and a good support network. They are often run by gap-year organisations, which cater specifically to under-30-year-olds, but other programs accept volunteers of all ages.

WHAT TO EXPECT

Whatever you expect, volunteering is bound to surprise you. The benefits of a large organisation, though, are that you'll get plenty of support and be working on an existing program that other travellers have participated in. Often the groups will be aimed at 'youths', so there will be plenty of young people around. Generally, if you're placed by a large organisation you can expect to get support such as insurance, visas, accommodation and food included as part of the package. For some volunteers there can be too much structure, too much 'hand-holding', as these programs are designed to take care of everything. You'll usually have to make a solid time commitment (between three months and a year), in which the organisation will have a definite idea of the tasks you'll be completing, so think carefully about the commitment you want to make.

What you'll be doing from day to day is, of course, based on the kind of project you'll be working on. Before you look for an organisation, consider whether you have any useful skills or particular preferences. If you like animals, working in an animal sanctuary is for you, but if you hate being outdoors, don't volunteer for a conservation project that will have you out tagging desert lizards. Community projects can mean educating about HIV risk or teaching English, so before you sign on any dotted lines make sure you have a job description.

Although you'll be paying for this trip, you won't be treated like a hotel guest. Accommodation won't be fancy, as you'll often be living in a developing community where hot water will be uncommon. A room of your own and breakfast in bed are unlikely. You'll probably live with other volunteers, who will give you support and be your travel buddies when you want a diversion, though homestays with locals will give you a chance to rub shoulders with your community.

You won't make a fortune volunteering. Some organisations might give you an allowance that will be relative to local salaries, but if they don't, you'll need to budget for some basic living costs to cover phonecards, airport shuttles and other little expenses (see p35). Allow a little more for travel on weekends or after you've finished your placement.

Finally, you'll need to prepare yourself for the culture shock. Even in a place with a large community of other volunteers, you'll still feel isolated and find that nothing is as easy as it was back home. However, this is a unique experience and no matter where else you travel, you'll never experience a place this deeply.

WHAT YOU'LL NEED

You won't need any special skills or training to get involved, as most of these programs assume you'll be developing skills along the way. Enthusiasm and patience will get you out of most tricky situations. Some organisations will offer information days and other courses to help you adjust to volunteering – all very useful when you're in the field, so allow time for these before you go, but generally there's no special training required.

ETHICAL VOLUNTEERING

If you want to ensure you do more good than harm, there's a lot to weigh up before you decide on volunteering. Ethical Volunteering (www.ethicalvolunteering.org) has top tips on questions to ask an organisation, as well as yourself before signing on.

More practically, most of these organisations will charge a fee for placing volunteers. Some volunteers organise fundraising to collect money to help pay for the costs, while others work summer jobs. Fees vary between organisations and usually depend on how long you're going for and what you'll be doing. Generally, you can expect to pay in the range of £850/US$500/A$650 to £4000/US$5000/A$6000. Costs go towards setting up the programs, but if you're unconvinced by a program you should do some research to see how an organisation spends its money. Very few genuine aid groups have CEOs who drive Porsches.

The beauty of this kind of program is that they will let you know what to bring, give you an idea of immunisations required and help you arrange travel. You may even get a handy checklist of what you'll need to do and when.

FINDING AN ORGANISED PROGRAM

Most of the agencies which offer organised volunteering programs are nationally based, so head to your section of the Directories in Part Four for a list of local organisations. Many of these organisations will offer information days which give you a taste of volunteering.

Here are a few organisations that accept volunteers from anywhere in the world:

○ **AFS Volunteering** (www.afs.org) Find a local office to search through a variety of opportunities, from rebuilding homes in Honduras to working in a Peruvian orphanage.

○ **Cross-Cultural Solutions** (www.crosscultural solutions.org) Offers a variety of internships and placements in 16 regions of the world, including a week-long Insight Abroad for those with short attention spans.

○ **Gap Sports Ltd** (www.gapsports.com) Coach children in a variety of sports in Costa Rica, Ghana and South Africa. There are also non-sports-related opportunities.

○ **Greenforce** (www.greenforce.org) With offices in the US and UK, this group places volunteers in various ecological and conservation programs around the world.

○ **Kwa Madwala** (www.kwamadwalagapyear.com) A South African–based outfit that will have you tracking lions and surviving in the bush.

○ **Student Partnerships Worldwide** (SPW; www.spw. org) Runs health education and community resource building in India, Nepal, South Africa, Tanzania, Uganda, Zambia and Zimbabwe. Their Youth Empowerment Programs present 11 months of personal development in communities.

○ **Volunteer Africa** (www.volunteerafrica.org) A global recruiter that does hands-on community projects which involve physical labour.

MY FIRST

─ BLACK-MARKET VOLUNTEERING ─

Living in Cuba requires jumping through hoops for American citizens. To spend a year volunteering in Havana, I would need permission from two countries, then a plane ticket routed through a third, 'neutral' country, and finally, enough savings to last twelve months on a communist island, where ATMs were obsolete.

Once I collected all the visas, tickets and the tall heap of travellers cheques, I felt the wind at my sails. Little did I know the host country would turn my goodwill boat right around. The last thing Cuba needed was a Yankee volunteer.

A curly haired bureaucrat put it this way: as a non-Cuban, I had zero right to access Cuban institutions, which – thank you very much – were well staffed with Cuba's very own public servants. I would have to quit the Revolution and return home, at once.

Stunned, I felt my lip twitch. Before I could bite it, tears slid down my red cheeks. The amused bureaucrat called my reaction an *aguacero* – a sudden rainstorm. In Cuba, *aguaceros* can dry up as quickly as they fall. I caught my breath, went on a bike ride, then did what one wise Cuban recommended. I went underground.

Catholic nuns ran a few nursing homes outside the capital. Through their mercy, I was allowed to 'help' so long as I kept quiet. After the *aguacero* episode, I trod more carefully on Cuban turf. I did whatever simple tasks – mopping, spoon-feeding, playing dominoes – I was unlikely to screw up.

My public service didn't make much of a dent in Cuba – not, at least, as I'd originally hoped. But I learned that on this communist island, the key was to make no dent at all. If you could get by, despite the rules and strictures, then you'd learned the Cuban way.

Colleen Kinder is the author of Delaying the Real World: a TwentySomething's Guide to Seeking Adventure *(www.delayingtherealworld.com).*

ORANG-UTANS (P215), WHOSE NAME MEANS 'MAN OF THE FOREST', ARE NATIVE TO RAINFORESTS IN SUMATRA (INDONESIA) AND BORNEO (MALAYSIA).

CHARITIES, NGOS & SENDING AGENCIES

If that all sounds too prescriptive and you're looking for an experience that's more grass roots, then you should approach one of the hundreds of charities and NGOs that look for volunteers. These organisations work directly with social problems such as poverty, HIV prevention and disaster relief. If other programs seem to be too far from the issues or too brief, these ones are for you.

Many of these organisations might have international offices in your country, but if they don't, 'sending agencies' are the ticket. These groups match volunteers with smaller organisations using vast networks and reliable international contacts. They are a bit like huge global temping agencies. But unlike temping, working with one of these groups requires loads of enthusiasm and serious dedication on your part, with very little standing around the water cooler.

WHAT TO EXPECT

This will be a tougher volunteering experience than a gap-year organisation trip, with less direct support. You might be sharing a small house with other volunteers in a village, with power from a generator and a diet that will be different from what you're used to. Depending on where you are placed, you may not have other volunteers around you and you may see people from your own country irregularly. On the plus side, you'll get a good grasp of another language and culture, with locals as friends, and work alongside an international crew of volunteers. While there's some overlap with organised volunteering, charities, NGOs and sending agencies will focus on their work and the people they serve first, with your comfort often coming last.

The organisation will help out with visas, medical needs, finding accommodation and other daily needs. Some groups may charge a placement fee, but some are free, provided a volunteer can pay for their own

KIBBUTZNIKS

Political and civil unrest in Israel means that a kibbutz might not be top of the list right now, but these cooperatives are renowned for fostering a sense of community among volunteers. Now if only Israel and Palestine could share that idea...

If you're aged between 18 and 40, you're eligible to volunteer as a kibbutznik in Israel. It's an old-school commune ideal with all the members acting as an assembly to make their own governing rules. Volunteers come from all backgrounds (provided their country of origin has diplomatic relations with Israel) and the average kibbutz has around 600 people living and working on its grounds. There are about 270 of these communities spread throughout the country. The kibbutz movement is nonreligious and pluralistic. While you are living in the community everything is shared with you, but in return you will be expected to work and make a proper contribution to the communal life.

Work is physically arduous and volunteers can be expected to work up to eight hours per day, six days a week. Work is usually in agriculture, tourism and services, though technological work is becoming more common. It's not all hard work, with volunteers welcomed into the social life of the community which can include cinemas, swimming pools and sports teams. The weekend in Israel is Friday and Saturday, while Sunday is a normal working day. Every three weeks volunteers are given an extra day's holiday, which is often used for travelling within the country.

A minimum commitment of two months is expected, but you can live and work in a kibbutz for up to eight months. You can apply all year round and are required to give two weeks' notice. A fee of around £410/US$810/A$870 includes your return flight, accommodation, food, insurance, laundry facilities and pocket money. For more information and current updates, check out the Kibbutzim Site (www.kibbutz .org.il/eng) or the more chatty Kibbutz Volunteer (www.kibbutzvolunteer.com).

flights and accommodation. Some organisations, such as Voluntary Service Overseas (VSO) and Australian Volunteers International (AVI; www. australianvolunteers.com), pay a small allowance that is relative to local wages. You'll be able to live well in-country on this allowance, but you probably won't come home with savings.

Volunteering can be emotionally draining and difficult, so you should make sure that you're *really* into it before you sign up for a year in Botswana or Myanmar. Volunteering in your own country can be a good insight. Try your local **Red Cross** (www.ifrc .org/volunteer; navigate to a local office) or **Oxfam** (www.oxfam.org). These organisations focus on community work in health and other social issues and can offer good preparation. International volunteering organisations will look at your experience as a sign of your commitment and it may push you higher up in their recruitment process.

WHAT YOU'LL NEED

Sending agencies, charities and NGOs are normally small organisations that recruit by word of mouth. Most require between three and six months' notice and have a selection or interview process. Some have a minimum-age restriction and might prefer you to be aged 21 and over, or to have completed a university degree. Others take school leavers, but you'll need to convince the recruiters that you're dedicated to their work and can cope with the challenges. Do some research before you approach an organisation by going deeper than their website – try finding people who've worked for this organisation before or post a question on the **Thorn Tree** (www.lonelyplanet.com/ thorntree).

Some organisations will charge a placement fee or require volunteers to be self-funding. Fees are often a necessary income for a charity group. This can depend on the length of the placement, but at the upper end you shouldn't be paying much more than £2000/US$4000/A$4500. Some volunteers do fundraising or enlist sponsors to help cover the costs before they go.

Your length of time in a placement will vary depending on the organisation – anything from two weeks to two years, though longer commitments are more useful to organisations and the communities you'll be working in.

Some organisations, such as the Peace Corps or AVI (Australian Volunteers International), have a lengthy application process that can include a few rounds of interviews and medical examinations, just to see how serious you are. Some are simple formalities while others have the intensity of a job interview, but the more hoops you have to jump through, the better the organisation (and the reward at the end). Some organisations may have religious motivations, in which case you may need to have 'the faith', while some apparently religious groups don't require you to share their beliefs, and accept that you want to help.

A few organisations look for specific skills or will match your skills to a particular placement, so if you get knocked back you might just need to apply again after you've completed a degree or you have been working for a while. **IESC Geekcorps** (www.geekcorps.org), an IT volunteering organisation, is a good example as they look for people with five years of tech experience and often a foreign-language skill. If you don't have any experience, don't panic. There are organisations that are looking for school leavers, and future employers will respect your volunteering experience.

FINDING A CHARITY, NGO OR SENDING AGENCY

Start by acting locally and head to your section of the Directories for organisations in your own country. Many organisations will hold information days, forums and talks by previous volunteers, so you can get an idea of what an organisation is like. You can also look at the ethics of the organisation – many explain where their money goes on their website.

Here are a few contacts to get you started:

○ **ATD Fourth World** (www.atd-uk.org) Sends volunteers around the world to work in communities for six months.

○ **Casa Guatemala** (www.casa-guatemala.org) Teach or help care for orphaned, abandoned or poverty-stricken children in a children's village on the banks of the Río Dulce.

○ **Charity Guide** (www.charityguide.org/charity/vacation.htm) Links to volunteer programs in the US and Canada that cost from US$50 to US$3000.

○ **Earthwatch Institute** (www.earthwatch.org) An international organisation with ecological expeditions you can join.

○ **International Committee of the Red Cross** (www.icrc.org) Find your local site to check out programs you'll be eligible for with this international humanitarian organisation.

○ **Jesuit Volunteers** (www.jesuitvolunteers.org) Navigate to your own country's site from the US site for placements with this group of committed Christians.

○ **Voluntary Service Organisation** (VSO; www.vso.org.uk) An international agency that recruits EU residents, US and Canadian citizens and a few other nationalities.

USEFUL WEBSITES

○ **Intervol** (www.intervol.org.uk) Offering free registration, this site has lots of information on international volunteering. You can search for opportunities and there's also an 'Ask the Expert' section.

○ **Make Poverty History** (www.makepovertyhistory.org) Keeps you up to date with what's happening with this famous campaign.

○ **Serve Your World** (www.serveyourworld.com) This well-organised guide to international volunteering addresses a variety of relevant topics, from philosophical to practical.

○ **Volunteer Abroad** (www.volunteerabroad.com) NGOs and nonprofit organisations throughout the world upload volunteer opportunities. You can search by region or type of volunteer work and find a wealth of supplementary info and links.

○ **World Service Enquiry** (www.wse.org.uk) Lots of information on international volunteering and development work, including one-on-one advice and a newsletter called *Opportunities Abroad*.

COURSES

Wherever you go, you'll always take your head with you, so doing a little study can make a great souvenir. There are millions of courses you could try: mastering Arabic in Morocco, practicing yoga in a Goan ashram, studying art history in Florence or mastering your very own elephant as a *mahout* (handler) in Thailand. Not only will you come home with impressive skills and party tricks, you'll have a deeper travel experience through learning about your destination's culture. Because courses are usually in small groups, you'll meet other travellers and make some good friends to hit the road with later on.

In addition to this chapter, we've listed a few courses in the destination chapters in Part Three. If you're looking for courses to help you get a job, see Those Who Can't (p154) or head for the Tourism & Hospitality section of the Jobs chapter (p126).

LANGUAGES

A big buzzword in language learning is 'immersion'. Hopefully this won't mean someone drowning you, but rather having the language you're learning around you all the time. Going to a weekly class is a good start, but 'living in' a language is hard to beat. Everyday you'll have a chance to practice and see how the language relates to a culture, plus you'll pick up all the slang and cursing they won't teach you in class. If you already speak a language, going overseas to do a course will help make you fluent and introduce you to locals. Most courses offer advanced options and some may even team them with cultural studies such as dance or cookery. Ideally they'll also offer a homestay or au pair work (see p133).

You can try getting started before you go with a short course at your local community college or polytechnic, which will come in handy no matter where you travel.

GENERAL LANGUAGE ORGANISATIONS
There are several groups that offer language programs, which are great chances to learn and travel. Shop around as prices vary, but here are a few places to start.

○ **AmeriSpan** (www.amerispan.com) Began with Latin American programs and now does language immersion for Spanish, Italian, German, French, Portuguese, Arabic, Japanese, Chinese and Russian.

○ **Bridge-Linguatec Language Services** (www.bridge linguatec.com) Offers in-country opportunities (as well as US-based courses) to learn Spanish in Brazil, Argentina or Chile.

- **Cactus Language** (www.cactuslanguage.com) Offers tailor-made language holidays worldwide, combining courses with activities such as salsa dancing, diving, cooking and volunteer work; languages include most Western European languages, Chinese, Japanese, Greek, Russian and Turkish.
- **CESA Languages Abroad** (www.cesalanguages .com) In-country courses in Chinese, Japanese, Latin American Spanish, Arabic, Russian and Western European languages.
- **EF International Language Schools** (www.ef.com) Provides courses in Chinese, French, German, Italian, Russian and Spanish, sometimes teamed with Teaching English as a Foreign Language (TEFL) courses and/or au pair placements.
- **IST Plus** (www.istplus.com) Offers international work and language opportunities in China, Thailand, Canada, Australia and New Zealand.
- **Language Courses Abroad** (www.languagesabroad .co.uk) Offers language courses, volunteer and work-experience programs in Chinese, Arabic, Japanese, Russian and several other European languages. Also has homestay and courses in cookery or dance.
- **Language Studies International** (LSI; www.lsi.edu) Provides language courses and work-experience programs in Chinese, French, German, Italian, Japanese, Russian and Spanish.
- **OISE Intensive Language Schools** (www.oise.com) Offers intensive language training, teaching and can include homestays in Heidelberg (Germany), Madrid (Spain) and Paris (France).
- **STA Travel** (www.statravel.com) Navigate to language courses on this travel-agent website that offers live-in courses and other options in several countries.

ARABIC
- **Arabic Language Institute** (www.aucegypt.edu) In Cairo (Egypt), this organisation offers serious Arabic instruction.
- **DMG Arabophon** (www.arabicstudy.com) Offers month-long intensive courses set in romantic Fez (Morocco).
- **University of Jordan Language Center** (www.ju .edu.jo) In the Jordanian capital of Amman, there are two-month courses on offer.

CHINESE
- **Allied Gateway** (www.mystudyinchina.com) Offers language courses at Chinese universities, which can include martial arts, cooking and traditional medicine.
- **Mandarin Rocks** (www.mandarinrocks.com) Shanghai-based language school with different course options including a summer camp for under 25-year-olds.
- **Taipei Language Institute** (TLI; www.tli.com.tw) With five centres in Taiwan, you can transfer between them to see more of the country while you study; also has centres in mainland China, Tokyo and New York.

FRENCH
- **BLS Bordeaux** (www.bls-frenchcourses.com) Offers classes in Bordeaux, Biarritz and Toulon.
- **ELFE Paris** (www.elfe-paris.com) Set in a mansion near the Arc de Triomphe, courses can include culture classes.
- **France Langue** (www.france-langue.fr) Runs courses in Nice and Paris.
- **LSC Language Studies Canada** (www.lsc-canada .com) Runs courses in Montreal.
- **Vis-à-Vis** (www.visavis.org) Offers courses in Belgium, Canada and France, with homestays and student flats arranged.

GERMAN
- **Actilingua Academy** (www.actilingua.com) Situated in central Vienna. Courses for beginners start once a month, while intermediate-level courses start weekly.
- **Colón Language Center** (www.colon.de) This long-standing Hamburg school starts with beginners' courses and ranges to advanced.
- **GLS Sprachenzentrum Berlin** (www.german -courses.com) Runs regular courses in Berlin.
- **Goethe Institut** (www.goethe.de) This worldwide organisation promotes German language and culture, with institutes all over Germany.

GREEK
- **The Athens Centre** (www.athenscentre.gr) One of the leading places to study Greek, with regular classes and a summer school.

If you didn't get enough of school in your own country, what about an exchange program? It might sound crazy to go across the world to study, but some travellers look at international study as a way of expanding their CV and getting experience of the wider world. Some qualifications seem to be worth more than others, so with experience at a prestigious British school or an Ivy League qualification in the US you could be flooded with job offers when you get home. Other courses may not fit within your home country's educational system, so check before you go if a course will be accredited in your country.

Exchanges are offered by secondary and tertiary schools and often last for a year. Some involve staying with host families while other involve dormitories or finding your own digs. Some programs have selection criteria and look for 'future leaders', while other (generally self-funding) programs have few requirements.

Here are a few organisations for exchange, though you might find your university, college or school has regular programs:

○ **AFS** (American Field Service; www.afs.org) An international organisation (not just for Americans) that offers high-school and university exchanges.

○ **DAAD GERMAN ACADEMIC EXCHANGE SERVICE** (www.daad.de/en/index.html) University study in Germany.

○ **INTERNATIONAL ASSOCIATION FOR THE EXCHANGE OF STUDENTS FOR TECHNICAL EXPERIENCE** (www.iaeste.org) Offers opportunities to secondary students interested in technical work.

○ **INTERNATIONAL EXCHANGE PROGRAMS** (www.iep.org.au) For Australians and New Zealanders.

○ **ITALIAN CULTURAL INSTITUTE** (www.italcult.net) Click on 'English' and find scholarships and exchanges in your home country.

ITALIAN

○ **Istituto Italiano, Centro di Lingua e Cultura** (www.istitutoitaliano.com) Ten minutes' walk from the Colosseum, beginners' courses start monthly and other courses each Monday.

○ **Linguadue** (www.linguadue.com) Classes are held in a beautiful Art Nouveau building in the centre of town; most courses start weekly. The school has its own garden.

○ **Linguaviva** (www.linguaviva.it) Housed in a 19th-century building, close to the main railway station; most classes start any Monday. You can also study cookery, art history and fine art along with your language course.

JAPANESE

○ **WorldLink Education** (www.wle-japan.com) The school is in the heart of Tokyo. Most classes start each Monday throughout the year, but some have a specified start date. There are also Japanese art, culture and cooking workshops.

RUSSIAN

○ **Liden & Denz Language Centre** (www.lidenz.ru) Situated in the heart of beautiful St Petersburg; most courses start twice a month. There is also a Liden & Denz Language school in Moscow.

SPANISH & LATIN AMERICAN SPANISH

Latin American Spanish has evolved so far from its European parent that the language you learn in Mexico will be very different to the language of Spain, and vice versa. Studying one will help you with the other, but find out which one you're learning in advance by asking if it's Castillian Spanish or Latin American Spanish.

○ **Academia Tica** (www.academiatica.com) One of Costa Rica's oldest schools; they offer courses for various levels.

- **ABC Language Center** (http://abccollege.es) Overlooking Barcelona (Spain), this school has excellent beginner's classes.
- **Don Quijote** (www.donquijote.org) This well-regarded international organisation offers courses in both Spain and Latin America, with homestay and student flats.
- **Estudio Internacional Sampere** (www.sampere .com) This large school offers courses in several spots in Spain plus Cuenca in Ecuador.
- **Excel Spanish Language Center** (www.excel-spanish languageprograms-peru.org) Courses at several locations in Peru can be combined with volunteering.
- **Latin Immersion** (www.latinimmersion.com) Based in Chile, with schools in Peru and Argentina.
- **Malaca Instituto** (www.malacainstituto.com) An upmarket option in Spain that can include cooking and dance courses.
- **Solexico** (www.solexico.com) This Mexican institute has two schools in Oaxaca and Playa del Carmen teaching year-round.
- **Spanish Abroad** (www.spanishabroad.com) Offers programs with language schools across Latin America and Spain, including specialised classes for professionals and cultural add-ons.

CULTURE

Whether it's whipping up a green curry or busting out your best flamenco moves, there's no better way to impress the folks back home than showing off the skills you 'picked up' while you were away. These are just a few ideas and you can usually find more in a guidebook.

ART & CRAFT
- **Art History Abroad** (www.arthistoryabroad.com) Runs year-long trips to Italy that look at the masterpieces of European art.
- **Art Workshops in Guatemala** (www.artguat.org) An art program that includes backstrap-weaving, beading, painting and Mayan culture lessons.
- **Centro Dedalo Arte** (www.dedaloarte.org) An international association running residential courses in all media (sculpture, painting, frescoes and more).

- **Chinese Culture Club** (www.chinesecultureclub.org) Beijing-based organisation with classes in Chinese opera, calligraphy, mah jong and more.
- **Istituto di Moda Burgo** (www.imb.it) Fashion and design school with several options in Italy's fashion capital of Milan.
- **Scuola Orafa Ambrosiana** (www.scuolaorafa ambrosiana.com) Famous goldsmith school teaching jewellery-making in central Milan (Italy).
- **The Verrocchio Arts Centre** (www.verrocchio.co.uk) A residential art school with fine-art courses running for 16 weeks.

COOKING
- **Apicius The Culinary Institute of Florence** (www .apicius.it) Florence's first-rate cooking school with everything you need to know about pasta, wine and more.
- **Casa Luna Cooking School** (www.casalunabali.com) Lessons in making Balinese grub worthy of paradise.
- **Chiang Mai Thai Cookery School** (www.thai cookeryschool.com) Great school for Thai curries and other dishes.
- **Hoa Sua** (www.hoasua.com) Simple Vietnamese cookery in Hanoi with proceeds going to disadvantaged youth.
- **Mexican Home Cooking School** (www.mexican homecooking.com) Hands-on courses that can have you cooking up colonial cuisine in Tlaxcala (Mexico) and can include accommodation.
- **Rhode School of Cuisine** (www.rhodeschoolof cuisine.com) Courses in France, Italy and Morocco.
- **Tasting Places** (www.tastingplaces.com) Cookery holidays in UK, France, Italy, Thailand, Spain and Greece, including a stint in Gordon Ramsay's restaurant.

FILM
- **The Film School** (www.filmschool.org.nz) Cheap option in New Zealand in a school that has a good international reputation in TV and film.
- **New York Film Academy** (www.nyfa.com) Has short practical courses on screenwriting, acting, film-making, editing and production.
- **Sydney Film Base** (www.sydneyfilmbase.com.au) Offers short courses for would-be directors.

MUSIC & DANCE

o **Carmen de las Cuevas** (www.carmencuevas.com) Based in Granada (Spain), they run flamenco courses.

o **Kala Academy** (www.kalaacademy.org) Goa's most prestigious cultural group offers courses in traditional Indian dance and singing.

o **Kusun Study Tour to Ghana** (www.ghanadrumschool.com) Play with Ghana's virtuoso drummers, dancers and singers in these limited tours.

o **Unitango** (www.unitango.com) Offers tango classes in Buenos Aires (Argentina).

YOGA & WELLNESS

o **Lek Chaiya** (www.nervetouch.com) Chiang Mai's legendary Thai massage class that's similar to acupressure with fragrant herbs.

o **Morarji Desai National Institute of Yoga** (www.yogamdniy.com) This Delhi (India) centre offers pranayama and hatha yoga along with meditation.

o **Purple Valley Yoga Centre** (www.yogagoa.com) Long-established school in Goa (India) offers drop-in classes and longer programs in Ashtanga, hatha and pranayama yoga, plus meditation.

SPORTS & OUTDOORS

If all these options sound a bit too slow for you, you're after activities. Check the Adventure Trail chapter (p105) for more ideas on injecting adrenaline into your travels. Try these on for size:

o **Aussie Surf Adventures** (www.surfadventures.com.au) Does surf lessons in Australia from Sydney to Byron Bay.

o **Fairtex Muay Thai Fitness Camp** (www.muaythaifairtex.com) Upmarket Thai boxing school that starts with half-day spars and ranges to week-long arse-kickings.

o **Leconfield Jackaroo and Jillaroo School** (www.leconfieldjackaroo.com) Learn how to work an Australian outback property and ride horses.

o **Plas y Brenin** (www.pyb.co.uk) A mountaineering centre based in Wales, with trainer courses available.

o **Southern African Wildlife College** (www.wildlifecollege.org.za) A course in bush skills and conservation in South Africa.

o **Thai Elephant Conservation Center** (www.changthai.com) Offers one- to 10-day *mahout* (elephant handler) training courses near Chang Mai (Thailand).

THOSE WHO CAN'T...

If just learning an outdoor skill isn't enough for you, you could always do an instructor course, which may give you the qualifications to work your way around the world. Outdoor instructor jobs are often easy to come by, especially in popular holiday destinations, and some courses can even direct you to jobs. Professional Association of Diving Instructors (PADI; www.padi.com; navigate your way to 'Teach Diving', then find your home country) training qualifications mean you can teach diving in Thailand, the Maldives or another resort destination. If you'd rather play it cool and carve up the world's white stuff, try a snowsport-instructors group in your home country. Check 'Your First Resort' (see p127) for details and tips on where to find ski-resort jobs.

☉ AUSTRALIAN PROFESSIONAL SNOWSPORT INSTRUCTORS (www.apsi.net.au) Offers courses in snowboarding (Nordic and downhill).

☉ BRITISH ASSOCIATION OF SNOWSPORT INSTRUCTORS (www.basi.org.uk) Offers accredited courses that travel well.

☉ FLYING FISH (www.flyingfishonline.com) Skiing courses with branches in Australia, the UK and US, plus lessons in sailing and kitesurfing.

☉ PROFESSIONAL SKI INSTRUCTORS OF AMERICA (www.psia.org) Courses and certificates obtainable through their academy.

WHERE TO GO?

ROUND-THE-WORLD

Think you can take on those slowcoaches from *The Amazing Race*? In this jet age, Phileas Fogg's 80-day circumnavigation is looking pretty slow, so your version of the trip around the world will be much faster. Chances are you'll be switching between planes, trains, automobiles, camels and tuk-tuks to get around the world any way you can. For more information on globetrotting, go to Transport Options (p87), particularly the section on getting a round-the-world (RTW) ticket (see p90). If you're going around the world you'll be hopscotching through countries and skipping over borders, so this chapter will tell you a little more about factors that affect planning such as climate and hassle-free border crossing.

PLANNING YOUR ROUTE

The most exciting part of any trip is when you spread out the maps, break the spines of those guidebooks and start planning your global adventure. Using a RTW ticket (see p90) is the best way to touch down on several continents, but how will you work out your route? With one of these tickets you'll need to lock in your destinations before you head off around the world…even if you're going to be flexible about timing.

CREATING AN ITINERARY

Personal decisions should always come first when you're planning your route. Start with a list of your 'must-sees' then prioritise 'would-like-to-sees' and 'would-like-but-can-drops', down to 'really-don't-cares' and 'no-friggin'-ways'. Your 'must-sees' can be based around needing to visit family or places you've waited your whole life to see. You can get a better idea of other priorities (including big festivals and the best weather) by checking the destination chapters in Part Three. You might also like to think about balancing your trip so there's some downtime mixed in with the partying. There's no better cure for a hangover than spending two weeks on a beach in Thailand.

From here you'll need to search for a ticket that covers all your 'must-sees' and work out how many of your other priorities the ticket takes in – check the fares table in Transport (see p88–9) for an easy comparison. You might have to drop a few of your choices or take side trips via an add-on flight or overland trip. If your RTW ticket drops you in Sydney, for example, you could get a budget flight to Darwin before heading south to see Uluru, then loop back to Sydney via the wineries around Adelaide. Try to work out how long you want to stay in each place including side trips, so you can look at getting visas (see p27) for the right length of time.

Sounds too complicated? A travel agent can take some of the grunt work out by sorting out a RTW ticket for you.

The basic RTW loop includes London–Singapore–Sydney–Los Angeles (LA). More complex (and pricier) routes could look like this:

○ Singapore–Sydney–Christchurch–Wellington–Auckland–Rarotonga–Papeete (Tahiti)–LA–London
○ LA–New York–London–Cape Town–Johannesburg–Perth–Melbourne–Brisbane
○ London–Helsinki–Bangkok–Singapore–Cairns–Sydney–Auckland–Santiago–Lima–Buenos Aires–London

You might also like to plan a few 'surface sectors' by going overland to explore places in depth. It can be the legendary road trip, a camel ride or a long hike. We've listed some popular surface sectors here.

○ **Africa** Nairobi (Kenya) and Johannesburg (South Africa); Johannesburg and Cape Town (South Africa)
○ **Asia** Bangkok (Thailand) and Singapore; Bangkok and Bali (Indonesia); Beijing and Hong Kong (China)
○ **Australia and New Zealand** Sydney and Melbourne (Australia); Perth and Brisbane (Australia); Cairns and Sydney or Melbourne (Australia); Adelaide and Darwin (Australia); Auckland and Christchurch (New Zealand)
○ **The Indian Subcontinent** Delhi and Mumbai (India); Delhi and Kathmandu (Nepal)
○ **North America** LA and New York (USA); San Francisco and LA (USA); Vancouver and Toronto (Canada)
○ **South America** Rio de Janeiro (Brazil) and Buenos Aires (Argentina); Quito (Ecuador) and La Paz (Bolivia); Lima (Peru) and Santiago (Chile)

CLIMATE

Hitting your destination at its sweetest time means working out the weather and making sure you get there in the right season. Each hemisphere has different seasons, with the northern hemisphere enjoying spring from March to May, summer from June to August, with autumn running September to November and winter sinking in from December until February. In the southern hemisphere summer runs from December to February, autumn March to June, winter June to August and spring September to December.

Not surprisingly, many travellers opt for summer and spring, when the days are long and the temperatures warm in many destinations, so each hemisphere is popular during these seasons. Days get longer in summer the closer you get to the poles, so places in northern Scandinavia experience the 'midnight sun' where the sun is partying for most if not all of the night. This is balanced in the depths of winter with the 'midday dark', when Scandinavians look to sunbeds to supplement their lack of solar rays.

As well as checking the When to Go sections of the destination chapters, you can look up some of these sites that give average temperatures in several world destinations:

○ **Intellicast** (www.intellicast.com/Global) Includes excellent weather maps and active storm tracking.
○ **World Climate** (www.worldclimate.com)
○ **World Travel Guide** (www.worldtravelguide.net)
○ **Yahoo Weather** (http://weather.yahoo.com)

Wet, Dry & Hurricane Seasons

Different regions experience very different weather systems. The simplest pair are the Artic (in the extreme north of the world) and Antarctic (in the south) regions which both suffer long winters and very short summers.

At the other end of the extreme are the tropics, the broad band that surrounds the equator (roughly between the latitudes of 23°30'N and 23°30'S, if you want to get technical) and includes Africa, India, South America as well as southern parts of the US, northern areas of Australia and much of Southeast Asia. Travel in the tropics is ruled by the rain belt which rages through the southern hemisphere from October to March, creating the wet season. Expect rain almost every day with brief intense showers in the afternoon. It's still hot though, and some tourists call this 'the green season' because plant life loves the mix of rain and heat (and so do mosquitoes). At the same time the northern hemisphere experiences the dry season, when there isn't so much rain and it can be a good time to travel. The northern hemisphere gets its dose of the wet season from April to September, when it's better then

ARCTIC OCEAN

KARA
SEA

LAPTEV
SEA

EAST SIBERIAN SEA

CHUKCHI
SEA

BARENTS
SEA

FINLAND

St Petersburg
THE HERMITAGE

BERING
SEA

BALTIC
STATES

penhagen

ICELAND | BELARUS

rague

UKRAINE

Vienna

ROMANIA

THE
BALKANS
GREECE
☆THE
ACROPOLIS

TURKEY

THE
CAUCASUS

UZBEKISTAN
TURKMENISTAN

KAZAKHSTAN

MONGOLIA

RUSSIA

NORTH
PACIFIC
OCEAN

SEA
OF
OKHOTSK

NEAN SEA
PYRAMIDS
OF GIZA ☆

SYRIA
JORDAN
YA   EGYPT

IRAQ IRAN

Tehran

Bahrain

SAUDI
ARABIA

UAE

TAJIKISTAN
KYRGYZSTAN

AFGHANISTAN

PAKISTAN

NEPAL BHUTAN

TAJ MAHAL ☆

INDIA

BANGLADESH

Jammu &
Kashmir

CHINA

SEOUL
SOUTH
KOREA

JAPAN

Seoul

Tokyo

HAD

CENTRAL
AFRICAN
REPUBLIC

SUDAN

ERITREA YEMEN

ETHIOPIA

OMAN

ARABIAN
SEA

Trivandrum
Colombo SRI
LANKA

Bangkok

MYANMAR LAOS

TIGER
LEAPING
GORGE ☆

HALONG BAY ☆

THAILAND VIETNAM
ANGKOR WAT ☆

KO PHI PHI

Hong Kong

PHILIPPINES

Northern Mariana
Islands (US)

Guam
(US)

Honolulu

Hawai'i
(US)

DEMOCRATIC
REPUBLIC OF
CONGO
(ZAIRE)

UGANDA
KENYA

☆ MT KILIMANJARO
TANZANIA
SEYCHELLES

SOMALIA

PALAU

MALDIVES

Singapore

MALAYSIA

INDONESIA

MICRONESIA

MARSHALL
ISLANDS

KIRIBATI

EQUATOR

NAURU

TUVALU

Tokelau
(NZ)

American
Samoa
(US)

OLA
ZAMBIA MALAWI
MOZAMBIQUE
BIA ZIMBABWE
BOTSWANA

COMOROS

MADAGASCAR

MAURITIUS
Reunion
(Fr.)

INDIAN
OCEAN

EAST
TIMOR

Darwin

Cairns

PAPUA
NEW
GUINEA

SOLOMON
ISLANDS

GREAT
BARRIER
REEF ☆

VANUATU

SAMOA

Port Vila
New Caledonia
(Fr.)

FIJI

Nadi

TONGA **Rarotonga**

SOUTH
PACIFIC
OCEAN

SOUTH
AFRICA

Johannesburg

Brisbane

AUSTRALIA

Sydney

Auckland

Prince Edward
Island (S. Afr.)

French Southern &
Antarctic Islands
(Fr.)

Heard Island &
McDonald Islands
(Aust.)

TASMAN
SEA

NEW
ZEALAND

ROTORUA ☆

SOUTHERN OCEAN

THE PRACTICAL GRANARIES IN TIRELI VILLAGE, MALI, BELIE THE RICH ANIMIST SPIRITUAL TRADITIONS OF THEIR DOGON OWNERS (P272).

travelling in the southern hemisphere's dry season.

Between the tropics and the Arctic is the northern temperate zone and to the south of the tropics lies the southern temperate zone, which typically have four seasons each year though they can be struck by unpredictable weather.

Another season that will affect your travel plans is the hurricane season, when there are…well, hurricanes. The Atlantic hurricane season stirs in the Atlantic Ocean during the northern-hemisphere summer and autumn and affects countries around the North Atlantic Ocean, Caribbean Sea and Gulf of Mexico. The Pacific hurricane works its way around the Pacific Ocean (including the southwest coast of the US and Mexico) from May to November. Hurricane season doesn't mean there will be a violent storm rolling through the area at these times – in fact, many nations never see hurricanes during this season. See Health & Safety (p41) for local travel advisories on the situation.

BORDER CROSSINGS & CUSTOMS

Even with all the bureaucracy of customs regulations, crossing borders should be relatively simple, so long as you're doing the right thing (see p53). Most countries have limits on how much alcohol and cigarettes you can bring in (see p62) and quarantine laws about not taking out animal products or local art treasures. In certain parts of Africa and the Middle East you may only take out small amounts of local money unless you enjoy filling out lengthy declaration forms. Obviously, drugs and firearms are off limits when leaving or entering a country.

Provided you've got all that sorted, the process should be a matter of a customs official looking at your passport and possibly stamping it on entry and exit. You may be asked a few questions on entry, such as where you'll be staying, but leaving a country is usually fairly straightforward. Two notable exceptions are Cuba and Israel. If you get your passport stamped in Israel, it may prevent you from entering Syria, Lebanon and countries on the Arabian Peninsula. The alternative is to ask customs officials to stamp a separate piece of paper that they'll attach to your passport. The US has a strict embargo imposed on Cuba, which includes limiting the number of its citizens it will allow to visit (limiting them to zero if possible), and even foreigners will find it difficult to get there from the US without special permission from the US Treasury Department. For non-US citizens this means you can't fly from the US to Cuba, but US citizens have the additional complication of what to do with their passports. Simply put, Cuban authorities will stamp a piece of paper rather than your passport, which could create some hassles on the way home. Closed borders are typical when diplomatic relations break down between countries, so check travel advisories (see p41) for the latest.

EUROPE

WHY EUROPE?

With more than 30 countries packed into this continent, each European culture has become dynamic and unique to distinguish itself from its neighbour. The European Union (EU) has thrown a lasso around most of them to create a powerful trading bloc that is unified in name but diverse in its traditions. Many travellers come to the area to explore the 'living museums' of fairy-tale Prague or classic Athens and Rome, while others come for the party life of smoky Amsterdam, hedonistic Ibiza or techno-pulsing Berlin. With budget flights and reliable public transport, it's possible to hopscotch between countries so quickly that they blur into one another. Slow down to spot the differences between Slovenia and Slovakia, or Latvia and Lithuania.

You've probably heard of the big-name destinations – London, Paris, Rome, Barcelona – but swilling a pint in a corner pub, devouring your éclair in a café, refuelling with coffee in a little-known piazza or tasting tapas after a night of drinking will really let you feel like these 'brand names' are your own. Always popular, Europe has a particularly busy calendar from June to August, and if you don't like the crowds try on some of our Roads Less Travelled (p190)

ITINERARIES

Getting around in Europe is relatively easy as most countries have good public transport. If you'll be travelling around by train, consider buying the **Thomas Cook rail timetable** (www.thomascookpublishing.com) and getting a **Eurail pass** (see p207). Get on the bus with **Eurolines** (www.eurolines.com), which runs coaches to most Western European capitals. Look out for deals from budget airlines (see p194).

EUROPEAN VACATION

You'll see most of Western Europe on this tour. Touch down in **London** and settle in by hitting the legendary clubs and markets. Then you can hop over to **Dublin** to sample pubs and traditional Irish *craic* (good times), double back to London and catch the Eurostar across to **Paris** to cop an Eiffel and grin at Mona. You can head north to **Antwerp** for some amazing beer, then on to **Amsterdam** if you'd like something stronger… Keep cruising along the Rhine and spend a few days playing in **Berlin's** nightlife. **Vienna** beckons with its classical music riches, then head west to **Zürich** and the Alps for awesome skiing, or views if you want to save some cash. Chill out amid the canals of **Venice** before kicking on to **Florence** with all its historic charm. The

EUROPE

GREENLAND
SEA

Faxaflói

⭐REYKJAVÍK

ICELAND

NORWEGIAN
SEA

TRONDH...

**Faeroe
Islands
(DENMARK)**

**Shetland
Islands
(UK)**

**SOGNE-
FJORDEN**

NORWA

BERGEN

OSLO⭐

Scotland

**Northern
Ireland**   ⭐EDINBURGH

⭐BELFAST

DENMARK

COPENHAGEN

IRELAND⭐   Irish
DUBLIN⭐   Sea

**UNITED
KINGDOM**

NORTH
SEA

Wales   **England**

**THE
NETHERLANDS**

HAMB...

LONDON⭐
LONDON EYE

ATLANTIC
OCEAN

ANTWERP

⭐AMSTERDAM

BEF...

BELGIUM

GERMANY

LUXEMBOURG⭐

PARIS⭐   **LUXEMBOURG**

PRA...

FRANCE

ZÜRICH

BERN⭐

SWITZERLAND

AUST...

SLOV...

Bay of
Biscay

VENICE

**GUGGENHEIM
MUSEUM**☆

SAN SEBASTIÁN   BAYONNE

NICE

PORTUGAL

MADRID⭐

ANDORRA

MARSEILLE

PISA

FLORE...

**Corsica
(FRANCE)**

ITA...

LISBON⭐

SPAIN

BARCELONA

ROME⭐

**The
Algarve**⭐
FARO

SEVILLE   CÓRDOBA

VALENCIA

**Balearic
Islands
(SPAIN)**

**Sardinia
(ITALY)**

TARIFA   GRANADA
MÁLAGA

MEDITERRANEAN
SEA

TYRRHENI...
SEA

**Madeira
(PORTUGAL)**

**Canary
Islands
(SPAIN)**

MOROCCO

ALGERIA

TUNISIA

MA...

☆ HIGHLIGHTS

- –o– European Vacation
- –o– Mediterranean Meander
- –o– Northern Lights
- ✈ Air   🚃 Train
- ⛴ Boat   🚴 Cycle

THE MAJESTIC SOGNEFJORDEN (SEE P166), CARVED OUT OF THE MOUNTAINS BY GLACIERS, IS THE LARGEST FJORD IN NORWAY.

BIG BEN AT THE PALACE OF WESTMINSTER ON THE RIVER THAMES, AS SEEN FROM EUROPE'S TALLEST FERRIS WHEEL, THE LONDON EYE (SEE P166).

HE DANCING HOUSE, ALSO KNOWN AS FRED AND GINGER, CODESIGNED BY ARCHITECT FRANK GEHRY, IN PRAGUE, CZECH REPUBLIC.

Eternal City, **Rome**, is next with the Colosseum and the Vatican – spend a day exploring each. Ferry across to **Athens** and then explore an island such as **Rhodes**. Head back to the south of France and Mediterranean towns like **Nice** to relax. Continue on to **Barcelona's** late-night carousing before heading to the Moorish towns of the south such as **Granada**. Finish up with laid-back **Lisbon**, toasting the continent with a glass of local port.

MEDITERRANEAN MEANDER

Finish off your education with a look at Europe's classic sites. Hop across the channel from **London** and take in the poetry of **Paris** before heading southwest to **Bayonne**. Cross over into Spain's Basque country with a visit to **San Sebastián** and travel south to **Madrid**. Catch a train from Madrid to **Lisbon** and continue south to **Faro** and the **Algarve**. Make your way east to **Seville**, before checking out **Tarifa** and **Málaga** on the coast. From there continue on to **Granada**, **Córdoba** and **Valencia** before hitting **Barcelona**. Cut back into France and visit **Marseille** and **Nice** before stepping into Italy. No Italian tour would be complete without a visit to **Pisa**, **Florence** and **Rome**. Reach Greece by boat from **Brindisi** (Italy), check out **Athens** and spend the last leg relaxing in the Greek islands.

NORTHERN LIGHTS

From **London** zip over to **Amsterdam** to check out its coffee-shop scene, then strike out for Scandinavia on this arctic adventure. Head to **Hamburg** (Germany) to see a big port town at work, then ferry across to beautiful **Copenhagen** (Denmark). Continue north to **Stockholm** (Sweden) to cruise the city's **Gamla Stan** (Old Town) on a series of islands before veering west to **Oslo** (Norway) to explore its Viking Ship Museum. Take the train to **Bergen** and then wend your way north to **Trondheim** and the spectacular **Arctic Circle**. Bus north to **Nordkapp**, Europe's most northerly point before returning south through **Rovaniemi** (Finland), where there are husky rides and snowball fights to be had. Continue south through **Tampere**, dubbed the 'Manchester of Finland' for its wild nightlife and postindustrial cityscape. Finally, snuggle up in **Helsinki**, the austere capital, before catching a flight out.

WHAT TO DO?

HIGHLIGHTS

o Gawking from the **London Eye** (UK) at the best views of the Olympic city.

o Oohing and aahing at **Aya Sofya** (Turkey), Istanbul's grandest church that has survived for thousands of years.

o Romancing **Paris** (France) amid the Gothic cathedrals, winding streets and sophisticated cafés.

o Dreaming up your own fairy tale in the cobbled streets and medieval squares of **Tallinn** (Estonia).

o Fancying yourself as a medieval noble while you stroll by merchant stalls on the Ponte Vecchio to take in **Florence's** soaring Duomo (Italy).

o Mixing Gaudí and gaudy in **Barcelona** (Spain) with the city's architecture and street life.

o Gliding past **Sognefjorden** (Norway), Europe's longest, deepest and most impressive fjord.

o Marvelling at the **Acropolis** (Athens, Greece), one of the greatest surviving monuments of a classic civilisation.

o Puzzling over the **Guggenheim Museum** (Bilbao, Spain), a postmodern symphony in stainless steel housing a ground-breaking gallery.

o Sailing into **Dubrovnik** (Croatia) and seeing the crystal waters of the Adriatic lapping at the ancient walled city.

GET ACTIVE

Europeans love scaling mountains or hopping on their mountain bikes for cycling weekends. Skiing is a popular way to get rid of the winter blues, though it can be pricey.

Walking & Mountaineering

From country strolls in Ireland to mountaineering in Italy's Dolomites, Europe has unlimited options to get out there and wander. The Alps and Dolomites offer the greatest variety for mountaineers, while trekkers may opt for Spain's national parks or France's rolling countryside (try the Pyrenees for remote villages). Alternatively, escape the crowds by heading to the Carpathian Mountains (Romania), the High Tatras mountains (Slovakia), Sardinia (Italy) and Bulgaria.

ONTE VECCHIO, WITH MYRIAD MERCHANT STALLS AND FAMOUS DUOMO, IS A CHARMING PITSTOP WHEN CYCLING THROUGH FLORENCE, ITALY (P166).

For long-distance walkers there are a number of transcontinental routes, known as Gran Recorrido (GR) in Spain and France. The most popular trek is the Camino de Santiago pilgrim's route, which starts in France and ends in Santiago de Compostela (Spain). Northern Italy's Cinque Terra is a gentler walk through five coastal towns in a region known for its history, food and wine.

Via Ferrata (www.viaferrata.org) is a high-adrenalin cross between walking and mountaineering, popular in southern France, Switzerland and Italy. You're roped up to climb using steel rungs and preattached cables.

Cycling & Mountain-Biking

Europe is a cyclist's paradise. Cities such as Amsterdam, Copenhagen and Berlin are flat enough for anyone to ride around, while mountain-bikers pump their calf muscles through the Alps and pannier-laden tourists breeze through southern France. Among the best cycling regions (with huge cycle-path networks) are the Netherlands, the Belgian Ardennes, Scandinavia, the west of Ireland, the upper reaches of the Danube in southern Germany, and Provence and the Dordogne (France).

As foot passengers you won't be charged extra for taking a bike on most ferries and trains – just look for the bike symbol on the timetable. This makes cycling an attractive option in Europe's pricier regions such as Scandinavia and some of central Europe, where transport and accommodation costs can easily be cut with two wheels and a tent. Hassle-free bike hire is common throughout Europe and in bike-friendly Copenhagen you can rent one for free.

THE ANCIENT WALLS OF DUBROVNIK (P166), CROATIA, ON THE ADRIATIC.

Skiing & Snowboarding

With global warming creeping in, you'll be lucky if the ski season runs from December to late March, with January and February the busiest months. The French Alps are the best and most popular ski destination in Europe. Well-known resorts include Chamonix (France), Interlaken (Switzerland) and Val d'Aosta (Italy). The best skiing in the Pyrenees can be found at Soldeu-El Tarter and Pas de la Casa-Grau Roig in eastern Andorra. These are among the most affordable ski resorts in Europe in terms of equipment hire, lift passes, accommodation and après-ski. There are cheaper (though more limited) options opening up in Bulgaria, Romania, Slovakia, the Czech Republic and Poland. One of the most attractive Alpine resorts for snowboarders is the Stubai Glacier, which is south of Innsbruck in Austria.

Cross-country skiing is very popular in Scandinavia and the Alps, while snowshoeing (a great alternative to winter walking) is also possible – these activities are more popular from February to April.

Water Sports & Diving

There are some good surf breaks on the Atlantic coasts of southern France, Portugal and Spain. There are even passable waves in the UK's Cornwall and Newquay. Tarifa (Spain) is one of the best windsurfing locations in Europe.

Canoeing and kayaking is possible on rivers and lakes across Europe and sea kayaking around the Greek islands and Scandinavia is popular. More extreme white-water rafting can be found in the Alps, Norway, the Pyrenees, Slovenia and Turkey.

Great sailing locations include the Greek and Balearic Islands, Croatia, southern France, Ireland and Turkey. Look out for crewing along the Côte d'Azur (France) and Europe's wealthier sailing centres.

There are dive centres all around the Mediterranean. Croatia, Malta and the Balearic Islands are particularly recommended along with Turkey and Greece if you want to dive among antiquities.

FESTIVALS

Europe likes to party whenever it can, but many events warm themselves up around the good weather, so June to August are busy. Here are a few favourites:

- **Venice Carnevale** (Italy) Held in the 10 days leading up to Ash Wednesday (January/February). Venetians don masks and costumes for a continuous street party.
- **St Patrick's Day** (Ireland; www.stpatricksday.ie) March's excuse for drinks, parades and revelry in the name of Ireland's patron saint.
- **Las Fallas** (Spain) Week-long party in Valencia held in mid-March with all-night drinking, dancing and fireworks.
- **Glastonbury** (England; www.glastonburyfestivals.co .uk) UK's biggest music festival rocks out in late June.
- **Roskilde** (Denmark; www.roskilde-festival.dk) Grungy Danish music festival with alternate vibe, held in June or July.
- **Athens Festival** (Greece) A feast of opera, ballet and classical music lasting from mid-June to November. Other Greek festivals take place at Easter (March/April).
- **Bastille Day** (France) 14 July is a national holiday and celebrations take place across the country but the biggest celebration is in Paris (check out the fireworks at the Eiffel Tower).
- **Baltica** International Folk Festival (Estonia, Latvia and Lithuania) Week-long celebration of Baltic music, dance and parades, held in mid-July.

- **Exit Festival** (Serbia; www.exitfest.org) Europe's hippest music festival with stages in a hilltop fortress overlooking the Danube River, held during July.
- **Castle Party** (Poland; www.castleparty.com) July's annual Goth music festival in a spooky old castle.
- **Il Palio** (Italy) An extraordinary horse race held in the main piazza of Siena on 2 July and 16 August. Get to it if you can.
- **Festival of Avignon** (France) Held between early July and early August featuring some 300 shows of music, drama and dance. There's also a fringe festival.
- **Edinburgh Fringe Festival** (Scotland; www.edfringe .com) Heckle the world's best comedy and stroke your chin at intriguing arts every August.
- **Tomatina** (Spain; www.latomatina.es) In August, the tiny town of Buñol breaks into a massive food fight with overripe tomatoes.
- **Love Parade** (Germany; www.loveparade.de) Once Berlin's festival, now shared by several cities, this August parade-cum-party is a gay fiesta with plenty of techno and house.
- **Notting Hill Carnival** (London; www.londoncarnival .co.uk) London's African-Caribbean community takes to the street in August for one of the world's largest street parties.
- **World Air Guitar Championships** (Finland; www.air guitarworldchampionships.com) Big hair and windmill solos rule at Finland's hilarious September event.
- **Cannabis Cup** (the Netherlands; www.cannabiscup .com) Held in November; 'judges' gather to sample and rate the best weed and listen to some mellow tunes.
- **Hogmanay** (Scotland; www.edinburghshogmanay .org) Sing out the old year with Scotland's biggest knees-up replete with whisky, haggis and dancing.

PARTY SCENE

There are never enough nights to enjoy Europe's many party places so you'll have to be selective. The rave is still on in Ibiza, though it's pretty crowded and you might be better off looking for another Balearic island for hedonism. The Greek islands attract an older crowd in summer, but can be good for chilling out. Amsterdam's coffee-shop scene has brought on many hazy nights after ordering a 'green' option, while Prague has become a centre for neo-Bohemians who like an arty party.

MY FIRST
~ FRANKFURTER ~

When I stepped out of Frankfurt airport as a young, naive backpacker on my first 'big trip' overseas, I noticed a couple of people dressed as clowns. In the underground train station I saw two more clowns drinking from large bottles of beer. Sitting opposite me on the train was another clown having an animated conversation with a court jester. I had no idea what was going on. My first thought was that because Europe is a season ahead in fashion this was the latest look and everyone would be dressing like clowns in the Australian winter. It was no laughing matter, though. When a rather intoxicated clown gave me a big bear hug I started to get a little freaked.

By the time I hit the streets after checking into my hotel most of the clown population in Frankfurt seemed to be rolling drunk, which meant there were a lot of very happy clowns. I saw them collapsed in doorways and throwing up in gutters. I even saw two clowns on the riverbank trying to make little clowns.

When I finally got the courage to ask someone what was going on, I found out that the Germans weren't clown fetishists after all. It was actually part of an ancient festival called Fasching and, as well as dressing up, people danced, sang and drank massive steins of beer for three days straight.

I ended up having the most marvellous time and, by midnight of my first day in Europe, I had three clowns, an ape and a nun as my new best friends.

English-born Brian Thacker is the bestselling author of Rule No.5: No Sex on the Bus *and several other crack- ing travel books including* I'm Not Eating Any of That Foreign Muck *and* Where's Wallis? *His latest book is* Sleeping Around *and it will be out in early 2009.*

DINERS AT BALIKCI SABAHATTIN FISH RESTAURANT IN SULTANHAMET, ISTANBUL, HAVE THE FAMED AYA SOFYA (P166) AS A PERFECT BACKDROP.

Berlin's Love Parade highlights the local techno scene that rarely finishes before 6am, while Edinburgh's Hogmanay is one of the best ways to ring in the New Year. There are a few surprise packages such as Belgrade, Serbia's all-night barge-party capital, and Madrid, where *madrileños* don't end the night until it's dead under their dancing heels after all-night flamenco and salsa.

ROADS LESS TRAVELLED

There are still pockets of Europe where you won't be pushed aside by tour groups, and even just visiting in winter can help beat the crowds. If you steer clear of Prague, Eastern Europe still feels undiscovered – try sailing down the Dalmatian coast (Croatia) or making the pilgrimage to Rila Monastery (Bulgaria).

If your wallet can handle it, Scandinavia has rugged wilderness such as Norway's spectacular fjords, or

sophisticated cities including Copenhagen. Billed as the 'next big thing', the Baltics are ideal for finding your own haunts such as medieval Estonia and historic Lithuania.

OTHER ACTIVITIES

Learning a little of the language will definitely get you points with locals and make it easier to make friends without having to draw diagrams or resorting to a lot of pointing (try working out sign language for 'No, I will not sleep with you!' in a hurry). Here are a few places to get a grasp of the basics:

○ **Alliance Française** (www.alliancefr.org) Global network of French language and culture schools.
○ **Goethe Institut** (www.goethe.de) Learn German in over 70 countries.
○ **Instituto Cervantes** (www.cervantes.es) Mostly in Spanish, so click on your own language for a PDF

guide, or click on 'IC en el Mundo', then choose a city where you can study Spanish.

WORKING

If you've got yourself a visa (for more details see p67) then working in Europe couldn't be easier. Many travellers work in the UK so there's an excellent network of services there to support you. These include magazines such as the backpacker-stalwart **TNT** (www.tntmagazine.com) and **The Loot** (www.loot.com), a newspaper with job and flat classifieds. Jobs in hospitality, temping, nannying, au pair work and seasonal fruit picking are all popular with travellers though there are limitless possibilities.

Outside the UK, the EU could see you cleaning chalets (and hitting the slopes on your days off) in the French Alps, picking grapes in France (and doing a little 'quality-control' on the wine) or pouring ouzo in a bar on the Greek islands. British travellers can work most places as they're a member nation of the EU, but other nationalities will have to jump through some seriously difficult hoops to get work legally. Many jobs (particularly hospitality and looking after kids) can come with board and lodging, which will save your euros. Busking is legal in many European cities (though there are exceptions in parts of Austria and Switzerland, for example, and you require a permit to perform in London) if you can perform for your supper.

Here are a few sites to get your hunt for work started:

- ○ **Eurojobs** (www.eurojobs.com) A huge free-to-access jobs board.
- ○ **iAgora** (www.iagora.com/iwork) Specialises in entry-level jobs and internships – mostly for free, with some subscription-based.
- ○ **Jobs in Europe** (www.jobs-in-europe.net) Links to hundreds of organisations looking to employ both non-Europeans (with the correct work permits) and Europeans.
- ○ **Jobs in the Alps** (www.jobs-in-the-alps.com) Mainly service jobs, eg chambermaids, bar staff and porters. Some language skills required.
- ○ **Monster** (www.monster.com) Good international site that's particularly strong in Europe.
- ○ **Natives** (www.natives.co.uk) Summer and winter resort jobs and various tips.

- ○ **Picking Jobs** (www.pickingjobs.com) Includes some tourism jobs too.
- ○ **Season Workers** (www.seasonworkers.com) Best for ski-resort work and summer jobs, though it has English-teaching jobs and courses.

WHEN TO GO?

Summer is definitely the time to hit Europe. That's when the bright sunshine hits the Eiffel Tower turning it into a set from a romance film, Rome basks in lazy warmth and even grim old England shines. Unfortunately, everyone knows how good Europe is at this time of year, so it will be crowded. Even Europeans know how good it is and many take extended summer holidays in August in big cities such as Paris and Barcelona. Others shut up shop to head off to their holiday houses.

Winters in southern Europe are mild so Andalucía, the Greek islands, Malta, the Canary Islands and Cyprus are good places to get a winter tan, but in Scandinavia and northern UK you can expect very short grey days, often with snow. Spring and autumn may be a little wetter, but they can be good times to visit out of season.

WHAT TO EXPECT?

LOCALS & OTHER TRAVELLERS

Europeans are a diverse bunch. Just look at the different ways they enjoy a night out: the Portuguese go out to *beber como uma esponja* (drink like a sponge) while the French get so drunk they're *bourrés comme un cochon* (full as a pig) but the poor old Danes complain of hangovers as at have *tømmermaend* (to have the carpenters in – usually drilling and hammering!). Usually you can get to know Europeans over a drink in a pub, taverna or café. You can strike up a conversation about football (ie soccer, though beware you're not backing the wrong team) or the freakishness of the popular annual music show, the Eurovision Song Contest.

Western and Eastern Europe have a Christian tradition evident in impressive architecture and common laws. Each country has its own interpretations, though, so Greek Orthodox worshippers aren't the same as French Catholics, British Anglicans or German Lutherans. There's a smattering of Islam in Eastern Europe and

Turkey is a Muslim nation, so be respectful of customs such as avoiding alcohol (yep, there are exceptions to almost every rule in this diversity) and not dressing scantily. Suave metropolises such as Barcelona, Milan or Paris give way to rural villages where locals still ride donkeys and make their own wine, but the overriding rule is to respect the people you're visiting. A church frequently visited by tourists could also be a weekly place of worship, a market photo opportunity could block a thoroughfare as well as offend locals, and siesta time is never a good time to try busking. Common sense and taking your cues from the locals are definitely the way to go.

Tourist crowds from across the world tend to hit popular spots such as Paris and London. The UK has long been a second home for many Antipodeans and Canadians, who use it as a base to work in before exploring continental Europe and the rest of the world. The support network in London is so good that you might get bored and want to head for other parts of the UK. You'll meet intrepid Americans, though with limited work visas they may be on shorter trips and want to zip around Europe in a hurry.

If you're looking for other people to travel with, there are backpacker hang-outs in London, Barcelona, Amsterdam, Berlin and Prague, with hostels always the top spots to hook up with other travellers.

FOOD

Table for one? Europe will tuck a napkin into your shirt and have you gobbling down its celebrated regional grub before you know it. Italian and French cuisine have conquered the world, but tasting a rich tomato sauce slapped on a pizza crust in Naples, where the famous pie was born, or slurping down bouillabaisse in Marseille, are quintessential food experiences.

Spain and Portugal are catching up on the culinary giants with tapas, cured *jamón* (ham) and juicy sardines grilled to deliciousness. There are also low points – Scandinavians are a little too fond of pickled herrings, and vegetarians struggle in Eastern Europe where you'll have a hard time explaining to waiters that pork wurst isn't a vegetable – but your plate will be piled high in most smorgasbords (avoid the rollmops though – they're code for more herrings).

There's no shortage of beverages, either, with Britain's recent return to real ale, the psychedelic absinthe popular in France, Switzerland and the Czech Republic, and Italy's and France's wines which are too precious to export. Scotland's distilleries make whisky so good it's mystically called *uisce beatha* (the breath of life). Whatever you do don't try to outdrink locals on ouzo (Greece), raki (Turkey) or Jägermeister (Germany) – all powerful spirits that will make you thankful for Europe's excellent coffee the next morning. Can we order another double espresso over here, please?

LANGUAGE

While some countries might like to pretend differently (*bonjour*, France!), English is a widely understood second language in much of Europe. In Scandinavia and the Netherlands most people will be happy to speak English, but elsewhere you'll get better results if you kick off a conversation in the local language. Learning a few basic words in French, German and Spanish is ideal for travellers around the Continent.

Speaking English louder or losing your temper over miscommunications are only going to make you look stupid. In Eastern Europe you'll definitely need a phrasebook as English is uncommon and can be difficult to understand when it is spoken, though the thickly accented Scottish or Irish English could also leave you shrugging your shoulders in parts of the UK.

COMMUNICATION

Europe is plugged in to new technology. Most of Europe uses the GSM 900 mobile network, which is good news for Australians and New Zealanders who also use this network (meaning you may be able to use your phone in Europe – check with your mobile company if they offer global roaming), but not for North Americans. GSM 1900/900 phones work in some countries, but you may be better off to rent or buy a pay-as-you-go phone.

Internet cafés are common in most of Western Europe and almost as common in Eastern Europe. There's wi-fi in some hotels and cafés, particularly in the west, and you can often get access in libraries (often for free) and hostels.

SAMPLE COSTS

	UNITED KINGDOM (POUND, £)	FRANCE (EURO, €)	FINLAND (EURO, €)	CZECH REPUBLIC (CZECH CROWN, Kč)
HOSTEL/ BUDGET ROOM	£10–30 US$19.50–58.50 A$21.50–64	€15–50 £11.50–38 US$22–73.50 A$24–80.50	€12–25 £9–19 US$17.50–37 A$19–40	Kč300–1000 £9–30 US$17.50–58 A$19–63.50
CHEAP RESTAURANT MEAL	£3–10 US$6–19.50 A$6.50–21.50	€4–15 £4–11.50 US$6–22 A$6.50–24	€4–6 £3–4.50 US$6–9 A$6.50–9.50	Kč 60–150 £2–4.50 US$3.50–9 A$4–9.50
1L BOTTLE OF WATER	£0.50 US$1 A$1	€0.50 £0.50 US$0.75 A$0.80	€3 £2.50 US$4.50 A$5	Kč 30 £1 US$2 A$2
SOUVENIR T-SHIRT	£10 US$20 A$21.50	€10 £7.50 US$15 A$16	€20 £15 US$30 A$32	Kč300 £9 US$17.50 A$19
BOTTLE OF BEER	£2.50 US$5 A$5.50	€4 £3.75 US$6 A$6.50	€5 £3.75 US$7.50 A$8	Kč35 £1 US$2 A$2.25
STREET SNACK	Fish and chips £4 US$8 A$8.50	Filled baguette €4.50 £3.50 US$6.50 A$7.25	Hamburger €4.50 £3.50 US$6.50 A$7.25	Goulash Kč100 £3 US$6 A$6.50
1L PETROL	£0.80 US$1.50 A$1.70	€1.30 £1 US$2 A$2.00	€1.30 £1 US$2 A$2	Kč30 £0.90 US$1.75 A$2

HEALTH

All up, Europe is in pretty good shape. Poor diet in parts of Scandinavia, Eastern Europe and even the UK (Scotland invented the deep-fried Mars bar!) may mean you'll have to hit the vitamins, but there are few required shots or vaccinations.

HIV and sexually transmitted diseases (STDs) are on the rise in Europe (use a condom) and a typhoid vaccination is also recommended for some southeastern countries. Tuberculosis is becoming more common, especially in the east, and there's the odd case of rabies. Tick-borne encephalitis (TBE) can occur in most forest and rural areas of Europe, especially in Austria, Germany, Hungary and the Czech Republic. Consider a vaccination against this disease if you're in the woods between May and September or if you are doing some extensive hiking.

Consult the Health chapter (p134) and seek professional medical advice for more travel-health information.

🐗 URBAN MYTHS – STENDHAL SYNDROME

Here's one we're not sure about. In 1817 French writer Marie-Henri Beyle (better known by his pen name Stendhal) visited Florence and was so overwhelmed by all the art and beauty he saw that he became physically sick. His art attack became known as Stendhal Syndrome.

In 1979 psychiatrist Dr Graziella Magherini observed racing heart rates, nausea and dizziness in patients visiting Italy and named the symptoms 'Stendhal Syndrome'. Similar effects have since been observed in Japanese visitors to the French capital, leading to the coining of the term 'Paris Syndrome', which is estimated to have a dozen cases a year. There have been no fatalities or trips to emergency wards as a result of either syndrome, but if you start to feel overwhelmed by the art, take a seat and drink some fluids.

The affliction has appeared in a film, *La Sindrome di Stendhal* (1996) and played a role in US author Chuck Palahniuk's novel *Diary*, but the greatest tribute comes from the culturally rich Paris–Venice route, which Italy's rail company has renamed 'Stendhal' in honour of the awestruck original.

ISSUES

Scoring a visa in Europe is generally pretty simple as most nations have signed up to the Schengen Agreement. This piece of diplomatic genius allows US, Australian, New Zealand and Canadian citizens to skip over most of Western Europe and Scandinavia's borders with ease and a valid passport. EU citizens (including the UK) will usually get no more than a bored eye from local customs officials and a wave through. Once you start heading over to Eastern Europe, however, you'll find yourself in a whole tangle of visas. Many countries (Romania, Albania, Macedonia and Moldova at the time of writing) don't allow you to get a visa on arrival, so you'll need to plan ahead and may need to send your passport off to a local consulate.

Border guards, police, train conductors and other low-level bureaucrats in Eastern Europe may ask you for a bribe to oil their creaking bureaucratic machines, but more common are rip-offs, scams and petty thefts in popular tourist destinations. Tourist areas and routes are often targeted, so keep your wits about you, know where your money, passport and credit cards are, and you should be okay. See Health & Safety (p134) for more tips.

Recently, several tourist spots including London, Madrid and Istanbul, have been hit in bombings by terrorist groups. Bombings like this are difficult to predict or avoid, though they sometimes target state interests such as banks or embassies. Staying away from the Iraqi border in Turkey is advised due to continued conflict. Check travel advisories for more information. In parts of Croatia, Bosnia and Hercegovina and around Kosovo unexploded land mines remain a problem. The bordering areas of Serbia and Kosovo have ongoing civil unrest. Sarajevo's **Mine Action Centre** (www.bhmac.org) has valuable mine-awareness information.

GETTING THERE

Air travel is surprisingly affordable in Europe thanks to the competition of several budget carriers, but rail and ferry transport are also superefficient.

AIR

Most travellers begin their European trip by flying into one of London's airports (Heathrow and Gatwick are closest to London, but Luton and Stansted are also options). Currently there are direct flights between big-name European destinations such as Paris, Frankfurt, Milan, Amsterdam, and Zürich, but with new agreements between the US and Europe (called the Open Skies Agreement) there'll be more competition and more direct flights by the time you read this. Most countries in Europe have their own national airline, but the bigger ones include:

- **Air France** (www.airfrance.com)
- **British Airways** (www.ba.com)
- **KLM** (www.klm.com)

○ **Lufthansa** (www.lufthansa.com)
○ **Swiss International Air Lines** (www.swiss.com)

Flexible 'open-jaw' tickets (flying into one city and out of another) are a good option if you're planning to do some overland travel while in Europe. Budget airlines (see p144) also mean that it's cheaper to hop between European destinations.

There's just over a hundred budget carriers jetting around Europe and beyond, but here are a few of the more popular ones:
○ **Aer Lingus** (www.aerlingus.com) A low-cost carrier flying from Dublin, Shannon and Cork to destinations throughout Europe.
○ **Air Berlin** (www.airberlin.com) Operates a wide network of flights from Germany to destinations around Europe.
○ **BMI Baby** (www.bmibaby.com) UK-based airline that makes child's play (and prices) of flights to Europe.
○ **Easyjet** (www.easyjet.com) Another good budget outfit flying out of the UK with destinations around Europe, particularly winter-busting trips to Spain.
○ **Helvetic** (www.helvetic.com) Flies to Eastern European destinations from its hub in Zürich.
○ **Iceland Express** (www.icelandexpress.com) Offers cheap tickets to Reykjavík from various airports.
○ **OpenSkies** (www.flyopenskies.com) A spin-off of British Airways that makes budget flights between Europe and the US.
○ **Ryanair** (www.ryanair.com) Flying from London's Stansted to several European destinations.
○ **SkyEurope Airlines** (www.skyeurope.com) A Slovakian airline with flights from to Budapest, Košice, Kraków, Warsaw and Bratislava.
○ **TUIfly** (www.tuifly.com) Flies to several European routes from its German hub in Hanover.
○ **Wizz Air** (www.wizzair.com) Central European budget operator that connects Budapest, Katowice and Warsaw with the rest of Europe.

SEA & OVERLAND

There are numerous sea-travel options for crossing from the UK into France, Belgium, the Netherlands and Scandinavia. Calais in France is one of the busiest ports and a main gateway into Europe. If you're not sure which ferry service is available where, **Ferry Lines** (www.ferrylines.com) can give you an overview of Europe.

The most popular route is between the UK and the Continent. Here's a handy list of passenger ferries with routes from the UK:
○ **Brittany Ferries** (www.brittany-ferries.com) Connects Britain, Spain and France.
○ **DFDS Seaways** (www.dfdsseaways.com) Sails between the UK and Scandinavia.
○ **P&O Ferries** (www.poferries.com) Plies the waters between Britain, France, the Netherlands and Spain.
○ **Sea France** (www.seafrance.fr) Runs from Dover to Calais.
○ **SpeedFerries.com** (www.speedferries.com) Ferry from Dover to Boulogne.
○ **Stena Line** (www.stenaline.com) Links Britain and Ireland, Scandinavia and the Netherlands.

For a quicker trip catch the **Eurostar train** (www.eurostar.com) from London to the heart of Paris, Avignon (France), Brussels, Lille or several French ski resorts. It is also possible to get into Europe from Central and Eastern Asia, though it takes at least eight days to do so. Railway routes include the Trans-Siberian, Trans-Mongolian, Trans-Manchurian and Trans-Kazakhstan. For more information see the chapter on Russia, Central Asia and the Caucasus (p122). Many visitors to Europe get a **Eurail pass** (www.eurail.com), a budget train ticket that allows you several trips over a limited time period; it's only an option for non-Europeans though (see p145).

SPECIALIST TOUR OPERATORS

There are hundreds of tour operators running specialist activity and sightseeing tours in Europe. A few European specialists include:
○ **Busabout** (www.busabout.com) A hop-on/hop-off tour operator with maximum flexibility.
○ **Contiki Holidays** (www.contiki.com) Offers group trips across Europe for between three and 48 days.
○ **Radical Travel** (www.radicaltravel.com) Parent company for Shamrock (Irish) and Haggis (Scotland) tour groups that specialise in budget tours.
○ **Top Deck Travel Ltd** (www.topdecktravel.co.uk) Offers double-decker adventures, plus a few short trips to festivals.

BEYOND EUROPE

Classic overland routes from Europe include journeys across Russia on the Trans-Siberian Railway (see p123), from Gibraltar to Morocco and on to the rest of Africa, or from Denmark and Iceland on to Greenland. Iraq and Syria aren't recommended while travelling from Turkey to Iran, and routes from Istanbul to Cairo are fantastic ways into Egypt.

FURTHER INFORMATION

WEBSITES

- **The Backpacker's Ultimate Guide** (www.bugeurope .com) A good resource with country-by-country transport advice and hostel reviews.
- **Budget Traveller's Guide to Sleeping in Airports** (www.sleepinginairports.net) Funny and useful resource for backpackers flying stand-by.
- **Europa** (http://europa.eu.int/index_en.htm) Gateway site for the European Union.
- **Guide for Europe** (www.guideforeurope.com) Backpackers guide to Europe including hostel reviews.
- **Hostel World** (www.hostelworld.com) Handy for other travellers' views on hostels.
- **Jobs in Europe** (www.jobs-in-europe.net) Includes links to job websites and agencies in Europe.
- **The Man in Seat 61** (www.seat61.com) A personal site that covers transport in Europe (including itineraries to get you anywhere) and beyond.
- **Money Saving Expert** (www.moneysavingexpert .com) Tips on the UK's best travel deals.

BOOKS

- *Neither Here Nor There* (Bill Bryson) Wander the continent with this famed US author for comedic company.
- *Rule No. 5: No Sex on the Bus* (Brian Thacker) Follow the misadventures of a bus-tour leader wandering through Europe. See also p190
- *On the Shores of the Mediterranean* (Eric Newby) Lap up the sun, sand and strife with this travel-writing veteran.
- *Through the Embers of Chaos: Balkan Journeys* (Dervla Murphy) Details a sobering bicycle ride through the Balkans.
- *Driving Over Lemons* (Chris Stewart) A no-bullshit drive through Andalucía with plenty of chuckles.
- *Rite of Passage: Tales of Backpacking 'round Europe* (Lisa Johnson, ed) Lonely Planet's home-brewed stories of backpacking misadventures.
- *Almost French* (Sarah Turnbull) Live the romantic (and not so romantic) life of a young woman in France.

FILMS

- *L'Auberge espagnole* (*The Spanish Apartment/ Euro Pudding*, 2002) A slightly uptight French guy shares a pan-European student house in wild Barcelona.
- *Bend It Like Beckham* (2002) An Anglo-Indian girl takes on her dream of playing professional football.
- *Paris, je t'aime* (2006) Twenty film-makers compose this love letter to the city of love and cliché.
- *Musta Jää* (*Black Ice,* 2008) A Finnish psychological thriller that will keep you on the edge of your seat from start to finish.
- *Before Sunrise* (1995) The classic Eurail love story where an American falls for a French girl and they spend the night in Vienna.
- *Good Bye Lenin!* (2003) Dissatisfied Berliners pretend the wall never fell...with quirky comedic results.
- *Volver* (2006) Penélope Cruz shines in Pedro Almodóvar's tale of Spanish family, murder and redemption.

AUSTRALIA, NEW ZEALAND & THE PACIFIC

WHY AUSTRALIA, NEW ZEALAND & THE PACIFIC?

Beach to bush to bungee – is there anything Australasia doesn't offer? If you're up for awesome snowboarding or spooky rafting through caves, New Zealand can deliver. Australia can serve up the icons: expanses of outback, wavelike Sydney Opera House, and then there's climbing to the top of the Big Coat Hanger (Sydney Harbour Bridge). If you're feeling crowded, find your very own Pacific paradise lost in a dazzling sea fringed with coral.

There are well-worn flight paths between Sydney and the world, so in Australia and New Zealand locals won't be surprised by the sight of a backpacker. There are definitely hubs of action: you'll always be able to find party people in Byron Bay, Sydney, Cairns, Rotorua, Auckland or Queenstown. These places have populations of backpackers, so activities will be geared towards your budget and there'll be ample short-term jobs if you need to top up the budget. Plus with Australia and New Zealand having British heritage, language and culture shouldn't be a problem.

The downside is you might feel like you're a little too much on the beaten track. But if you want some more intrepid travel, head for the Aussie outback or discover the Pacific. In the vast Pacific Ocean you'll choose between Polynesia (from the Greek for 'many islands'), Melanesia ('black islands') and Micronesia ('small islands'), with a heady cocktail of cultures to keep you guessing. Pack some flexibility and cultural sensitivity with the sun cream as Islanders come from very different backgrounds. Wherever you choose to go, Australasia won't let you down.

ITINERARIES

Most travellers opt for the big sites of Australia and New Zealand by arriving through Sydney or Auckland. Try wandering out into the Pacific if you want to dodge other travellers.

OZ–NZ: THE WORKS
Start out in **Sydney** (everyone does) then take the hippie trip to **Byron Bay** and onto **Cairns**, then **Townsville**. Head west into the Red Centre for destinations including **Alice Springs** and **Uluru**. Dogleg north for **Darwin** then go west for a pretty pit stop at **Kununurra** or the getaway mecca of **Broome**. Sweep out to **Ningaloo Reef** or down to **Monkey Mia** before heading further down to **Perth**. Prepare for one sunburnt arm if you're driving across the **Nullarbor**

AUSTRALIA–NEW ZEALAND–THE PACIFIC

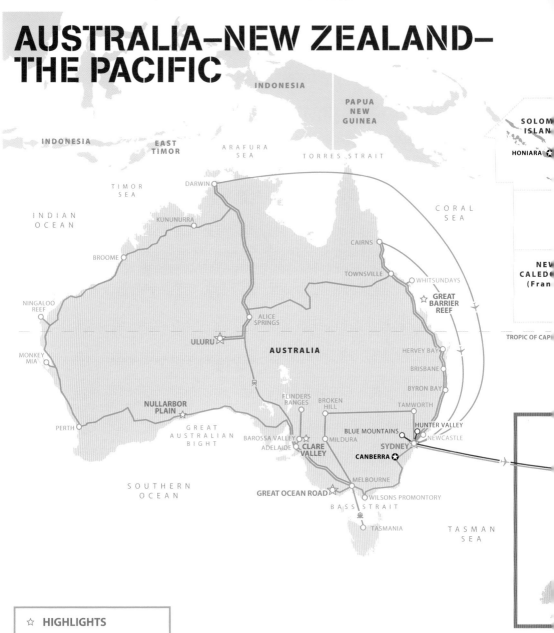

INDONESIA

PAPUA NEW GUINEA

SOLOMON ISLAN

HONIARA ✪

INDONESIA

EAST TIMOR

ARAFURA SEA

TORRES STRAIT

TIMOR SEA

DARWIN

CORAL SEA

INDIAN OCEAN

KUNUNURRA

BROOME

CAIRNS

TOWNSVILLE   WHITSUNDAYS

NINGALOO REEF

ALICE SPRINGS

☆ GREAT BARRIER REEF

NEW CALEDO (Fran

MONKEY MIA

ULURU ☆

AUSTRALIA

TROPIC OF CAP

HERVEY BAY

BRISBANE

BYRON BAY

NULLARBOR PLAIN ☆

FLINDERS RANGES

BROKEN HILL

TAMWORTH

PERTH

GREAT AUSTRALIAN BIGHT

BAROSSA VALLEY   MILDURA

ADELAIDE   CLARE VALLEY

BLUE MOUNTAINS

HUNTER VALLEY

NEWCASTLE

SYDNEY ☆

CANBERRA ✪

SOUTHERN OCEAN

MELBOURNE

GREAT OCEAN ROAD ☆   WILSONS PROMONTORY

BASS STRAIT

TASMANIA

TASMAN SEA

HIGHLIGHTS

☆ HIGHLIGHTS
–○– Oz–NZ: The Works
–○– Comprehensive Kiwi
–○– All Over Australia
–○– Pan-Pacific Championship
✈ Air   🚃 Train
⚓ Boat   🚲 Cycle

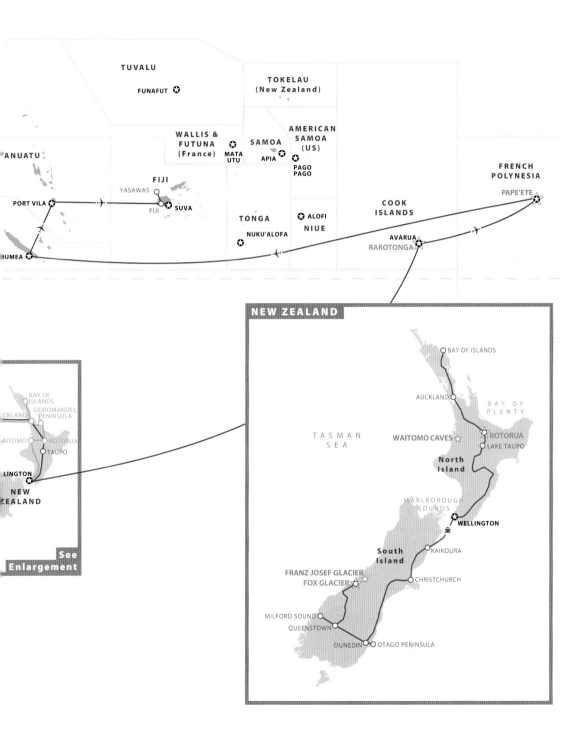

CHECK OUT THE KOALAS, THE CUTE COUSINS OF THOSE HORRIBLE DROP BEARS (SEE P189), AT MELBOURNE'S HEALESVILLE SANCTUARY (SEE P186).

STAYING IN BUNGALOWS IN THE BEAUTIFUL BLUE WATERS OF TAHITI (SEE P183) – FUN FOR EVERYONE EXCEPT SLEEPWALKERS.

JET BOATING, WHITE-WATER RAFTING AND BUNGEE JUMPING ALL TAKE PLACE AT SHOTOVER RIVER (SEE P185), NEAR QUEENSTOWN IN NEW ZEALAND.

Plain to **Adelaide**. If you have time, do a side trip up to the boozy **Barossa Valley** or the ochre-coloured **Flinders Ranges**.

Crack on to **Melbourne** via the **Great Ocean Road**. Consider a trip south to **Tasmania** – best done by ferry – if you have a bit of time up your sleeve. Back in Melbourne, take the coastal route north via **Wilsons Promontory**, through coastal spots such as **Narooma** or bushy **Jervis Bay**. Detour to **Canberra** before hitting the big smoke of Sydney again.

From here it's a plane ride over to New Zealand's **Auckland**, where you can take time out with a snorkel around **Goat Island**, then rip over to the **Bay of Islands** to see where the Treaty of **Waitangi** was signed. Double back south and make for the forests of the **Coromandel Peninsula** before hitting **Rotorua**, the backpacker hub. Head west for **Waitomo** with its impressive caves, then dawdle your way down to **Wellington** taking in **Lake Taupo** or the Art Deco town of **Napier**. From the New Zealand capital catch a ferry across to **Blenheim**, then wander around the stunning bays of **Abel Tasman National Park**. Ease down the west coast with stops for the layered rocks of **Punakaiki** and the jade polishing in **Hokitikia** before getting your pick of **Franz Josef and Fox Glaciers**, magnificent trips if you don't mind the cold. Depending on your budget, you can continue down to **Queenstown** for more outdoor fun or double back to fly out of **Wellington**.

COMPREHENSIVE KIWI

See New Zealand top to bottom, by starting in **Auckland** and heading up to the **Bay of Islands** to juggle surfboards, kayaks and scuba gear in this outdoorsy spot. Double back to **Auckland**, then make for **Rotorua** for volcanic bubble and gush before heading further to **Lake Taupo**. It's time for café culture in **Wellington** or beeline for the **Beehive** (national parliament).

From here catch the ferry across the Cook Strait to the South Island and some whale-watching in **Kaikoura**. Cathedrals are the go in **Christchurch**, but for more fauna make for **Otago Peninsula**. Head back into town at **Dunedin** before taking the side road down to **Milford Sound** then looping back to **Queenstown**, another outdoorsy spot. Either head north for **Franz Josef and Fox Glaciers** or fly out of here.

ALL OVER AUSTRALIA

Make the east-coast run from **Sydney** first by taking in renaissance **Newcastle**, fire-twirling **Byron Bay** and on to **Brisbane** and whale-watching in **Hervey Bay**. If your budget can stretch, head for the blissful **Whitsundays** and onto tropical **Cairns**.

Fly back to Sydney and work a little to power the next leg. Head south for summer by taking on the outback with a trip out via country-music capital **Tamworth** and onto the deserty mining outpost of **Broken Hill**. You could head southwest to **Adelaide** if you like a long drive or take the trip down to artsy **Melbourne** with a stop for a paddle-boat ride in **Mildura**.

After you've sipped all the coffee you can handle in **Melbourne**, head west to **Adelaide** and soak up the key wine regions: the **Barossa and Clare Valleys**. Head north into the Red Centre by taking the Ghan railway all the way to **Uluru** and **Alice Springs**. Finish up in **Darwin** and fly back to **Sydney** or out to Southeast Asia.

PAN-PACIFIC CHAMPIONSHIP

Start your race in **Sydney**, possibly with a job to recharge the credit card, or with side trips to the **Blue Mountains** or up to the **Hunter Valley** for a wine tasting or twenty. From here hop on a plane across to **Auckland** to experience its vibrant Polynesian culture. Explore the North Island (**Rotorua**, **Taupo**, even **Wellington**) before shipping out to **Rarotonga** for classic coconut tree–lined lagoons.

When you've had all the sun you can stand, hop over to **Pape'ete**, the vibrant capital of French Polynesia via **Avarua**. If you're still fancying Frenchy fun, make the trip over to **Noumea** in New Caledonia, then onto **Port Vila** in Vanuatu for a kava session. Make for **Fiji**, a regional hub that will allow you to catch a boat out to the **Yasawas** or head home.

WHAT TO DO?

HIGHLIGHTS

○ Glamming up in the beach-blessed and icon-endowed **Sydney** (Australia), the region's unofficial capital.
○ Diving the polychromatic coral of the **Great Barrier Reef** (Australia) that sparkles with rare fish.

URU (AYERS ROCK), THE DUSTY RED HEART OF AUSTRALIA, IS SACRED TO LOCAL ABORIGINAL PEOPLES.

○ Koala-spotting in the bush or cutting the curl of top beaches along the **Great Ocean Road** (Australia).

○ Saluting the outback's red heart at **Uluru** (Ayers Rock, Australia).

○ Booze-cruising Australia's top wineries in the **Barossa Valley** (Australia).

○ Enjoying a *hangi* with Maori or soak in percolating mud pools in **Rotorua** (New Zealand).

○ Playing it cool at **Franz Josef and Fox Glaciers** (New Zealand) as ice floes tumble before you.

○ Black-water rafting through eerie glow-worm-lit **Waitomo Caves** (New Zealand).

○ Biting into **Rarotonga** (Cook Islands), a chilled-out slice of heaven just a plane hop from New Zealand.

○ Fusing cosmopolitan French chic and Pacific paradise beach-bumming at **Pape'ete** (Tahiti).

GET ACTIVE

Australasia is one massive playground. If you're not busy bungee jumping in New Zealand, you'll be bush walking or surfing Australia's sweetest beaches. National parks are the best places to find activities.

Surfing & Windsurfing

Awesome beaches make surfers travel here from across the globe; there are waves that make grown waxheads weep. Best of all, anywhere there's a swell, a surf school will be there renting out all the gear and giving a few hours' instruction to get you up on a board.

Surf culture is deeply rooted in Australia, with classic breaks all along the coast at Bells Beach (Victoria), Byron Bay (New South Wales), Margaret River (Western Australia) and Fleurieu (South Australia). Geraldton

FOX GLACIER (P183), NEW ZEALAND, FLOWS DOWN TO LUSH RAINFOREST.

(Western Australia) is a blustery windsurfing mecca. The Pacific islands have great surfing destinations such as American Samoa, the Cook Islands, Guam, Tonga, French Polynesia and Fiji. Pacific Islanders make decent money in summer by renting out cheap beach huts and gear to surfers.

New Zealand surfers wear wetsuits all year round, particularly so on the South Island, but if you don't mind zipping up there's always somewhere to bust out the board. There are awesome breaks at Ragland (including the famous Waikato break), Marlborough Sounds and even around Wellington.

Extreme Sports

New Zealand shreds the biscuit and washes it down with a draught of pure adrenaline when it comes to fear-enhanced activities, but Australia tries to keep up. New Zealand is famous for bungee jumping in Queenstown, Hanmer Springs, Taupo and Auckland, and jet-boating at Queenstown and the Bay of Islands, but there's also zorbing (the Kiwi-invented sport of rolling down a slope in a giant transparent ball) and blowkarting (another New Zealand innovation that has you 'sailing' on land in a custom-built cart). In Australia bungee jumping

is popular on the Gold Coast which, along with Byron Bay and Townsville, also makes an awesome spot for parachuting. Then there's paragliding on thermal winds at spots such as Rainbow Beach (Australia), Bright (Australia) and Taupo (New Zealand). If all that hasn't got your heart racing, try kiteboarding, a combination of surfing and paragliding usually practiced at windy spots such as Newcastle (Australia), Melbourne (Australia) and the Bay of Islands (New Zealand). Thrill-seekers in New Zealand have been known to go river sledging in the waters around Queenstown and Wanaka. Then there's cave rafting, riding a tube through the dark caverns around Waitomo, Westport and Greymouth. But only in Sydney can you have the buzz of climbing the Harbour Bridge and seeing the whole city spread out beneath you.

Diving & Snorkelling

Divers are in for a real treat in the Pacific Ocean with its clear waters, unique marine life, impressive wrecks and heaps of places to grab a snorkel and explore. Most travellers float over Queensland's Great Barrier Reef, but there are impressive dives at South Australia's shipwreck-strewn Kangaroo Island, and at Esperance, Rottnest Island, Ningaloo Reef and Carnarvon, all in Western Australia. There are plenty of places where you can learn to dive and rent gear, so beginners won't miss the fun. New Zealand's best aqua action is around Bay of Islands Maritime Park, Hauraki Gulf Maritime Park, Great Barrier Island, Goat Island or Marlborough Sounds.

Diving among the Pacific islands' stunning coral, jaw-dropping drop-offs and the undersea museum of WWII wrecks make it a highlight for divers the world over. Operators vary greatly in this area – from a bloke with a boat to fully qualified PADI masters – so check the credentials before you climb aboard. Rarotonga (Cook Islands), French Polynesia, Tonga and New Caledonia are all popular spots for diving. Don't forget tiny islands such as the Federated States of Micronesia, Guam and the Marshall Islands, which are less crowded and have coral-encrusted wrecks.

Cycling & Mountain-Biking

Spin two wheels through Australasia and you'll see the region at a good pace. The light traffic and good bike tracks make for enjoyable riding throughout. Smaller Pacific islands can be crossed without changing gears, never mind hiring a car. Coastal routes – the east coast in Australia and around the North Island in New Zealand – can be scenic pedalling for beginners. The more adventurous take on longer trips, such as the Otago Central Rail Trail (following an old rail line through the gold region), and the experienced can try heading out from Alice Springs along the Todd River. If all that sounds a bit tame you can hurtle down rough roads on a mountain bike – many wilderness areas have good trails, including Australia's Blue and Snowy Mountains and New Zealand's Queen Charlotte Track.

Both Australia and New Zealand offer easy cycling – relatively flat, with plenty of camp sites or other cheap accommodation. Renting is affordable, though it's also cheap to buy a bike when you arrive if you plan on doing a lot of cycling. While laws in the Pacific are pretty forgiving, Australia and New Zealand both slap fines on cyclists for not wearing helmets and for riding under the influence of alcohol.

Kayaking, Rafting & Other Water Sports

Surrounded by expanses of ocean and often blessed with calm conditions, the Pacific islands are a great spot for sea kayaking. Countries such as Fiji, Tonga, New Caledonia and Samoa rent out kayaks and sometimes offer multiday trips. Papua New Guinea's turbulent mountain rivers offer some extreme kayaking opportunities.

Australia's best white-water rafting trips are probably on the upper Murray and Nymboida Rivers in New South Wales and Tully River in Queensland. There's great canoeing in Katherine Gorge in Nitmiluk National Park (Northern Territory), the Ord and Blackwood Rivers (Western Australia), Murray River National Park (South Australia) and the Franklin River (Tasmania).

New Zealand's best rafting is on Rangitata River, but the Shotover and Kawarau Rivers are both strong contenders for the title. Sea kayaking at the Bay of Islands, Marlborough Sound, Abel Tasman National Park, Milford Sound and Coromandel offers slower-paced enjoyment.

Or you can slow it down on a cruise yacht. Sailing cities such as Auckland (the so-called City of Sails), Sydney and Hobart, as well as Vava'u (Tonga) and Fiji, are all good places to get shanghaied as a crew member. There are also sailing cruises from spots which take in impressive vistas, including Cairns (Queensland), the Bay of Islands (New Zealand) and Dunedin (New Zealand).

Trekking & Mountaineering

Whether it's bush walking (in Australia) or tramping (in New Zealand), it's easy to explore the wilderness on foot. While many of the Pacific islands are too small to offer really challenging walks, Papua New Guinea has a network of trails (including the infamous Kokoda Trail) that take several days.

Australia and New Zealand offer better opportunities to stretch your legs. Tiny Tasmania, in Australia, boasts the magnificent Overland Track (plus plenty of other walks in Cradle Mountain–Lake St Clair National Park), while South Australia has the impressive Mawson Trail in the Flinders Ranges. The Blue and Snowy Mountains both have well-trafficked trails, but less-beaten tracks include Western Australia's Bibbulmun Track and central Australia's challenging Larapinta Trail.

Many of these regions also offer fantastic rock climbing; don't forget to check out Mt Arapiles and the high country around Mt Buffalo (Victoria), Warrumbungle National Park (New South Wales), the Hazards (Tasmania) and Karijini National Park (Western Australia). The best places for caving in New Zealand are around Auckland, Wellington and Waitomo (which offers a spectacular 100m abseil into the Lost World cave).

New Zealand is crisscrossed with thousands of kilometres of marked tracks, many serviced by well-maintained huts. The South Island has wonderful walking trails through majestic national parks, including the Abel Tasman Coastal, Heaphy, Milford and Kepler Tracks. The North Island offers the Tongariro Northern Circuit and Whanganui Journey. The walking season follows the good weather from January to March, but tracks are useable any time from April to November. Mt Cook has New Zealand's most outstanding mountaineering and climbing areas; others are Mt Aspiring National Park, Lake Taupo and Fjordland.

RAROTONGA (SEE P183), THE MOST POPULOUS OF THE COOK ISLANDS, IS SURROUNDED BY A SHALLOW, CALM LAGOON – IDEAL FOR A BATH.

Skiing & Snowboarding

From June to November, New Zealand boasts the best downhill skiing in the southern hemisphere, particularly on the South Island around Queenstown, Wanaka and Arthur's Pass. The North Island, while blessed with slightly fewer slopes, offers the chance to ski on volcanoes – both Mt Ruapehu and Mt Taranaki are popular resorts. Australia's ski slopes are limited to New South Wales and Victoria, with resorts at Thredbo and Perisher in New South Wales' Snowy Mountains, and Falls Creek, Mt Hotham and Mt Buller in Victoria, all of which have brief seasons from mid-June to early September.

WILDLIFE

Outside Africa there are few places where the wildlife is as unique and as accessible as in Australasia. The marsupials (kangaroos, koalas and wombats) are a must-see and you can find them at zoos and parks such as Sydney's Taronga Park or Melbourne's Healesville Sanctuary, or try to spot them in the wild on Kangaroo Island. Migrating whales pass Australia's southern shores between May and November. Popular whale-watching spots include Warrnambool (Victoria), Head of Bight (South Australia), Albany (Western Australia), and Hervey Bay and Fraser Island in Queensland. Dolphins are ubiquitous and can be seen year-round along the Australian east coast (Jervis Bay, Port Stephens, Byron Bay) and Western Australia (Bunbury, Rockingham, Esperance, Monkey Mia).

Kaikoura on New Zealand's South Island is the centre for marine mammal–watching, with dolphins and seals swimming year-round, while sperm whales are visible from October to August. Whakatane, Paihia and Tau are other good spots to experience swimming with dolphins in New Zealand. Look out for kiwis, the cute flightless national bird, at sanctuaries and parks across the country.

FESTIVALS

There's no shortage of festivals, sporting events and general partying in Australasia. Here's just a sample of what you can get up to:

○ **Festival of Sydney** (Australia; www.sydneyfestival.org.au) The metropolis' high-art showcase, with open-air concerts, street theatre and fireworks in January.

○ **World Buskers Festival** (New Zealand; www.worldbuskersfestival.com) See the streets of Christchurch alive in January as international performers have their eyes on the trophy.

○ **Big Day Out** (Australia and New Zealand; www.bigdayout.com) A hard-rocking, roving music festival in late January in several Australian cities and Auckland.

○ **Summer City Program** (New Zealand) A fabulous series of festivals in and around Wellington in January/February.

○ **Rugby Sevens Tournaments** (Fiji, Samoa and the Cook Islands) A massive Pacific rugby competition (January/March) that includes much dancing, feasting and celebrating as well as the odd game of rugby.

○ **Pasifika Festival** (New Zealand) An explosion of Polynesian partying, from traditional dancing to hip-hop, on the streets of Auckland in March.

○ **Marlborough Wine Festival** (New Zealand) Gives you the chance to gobble great quantities of gourmet food and booze in mid-February in Blenheim.

○ **International Festival of the Arts** (New Zealand; www.nzfestival.nzpost.co.nz) Brings an entire month of national and international culture to Wellington in February (even-numbered years only).

○ **Gay & Lesbian Mardi Gras** (Australia; www.mardigras.org.au) Sydney's outlandish celebration in February/March. Melbourne's **Midsumma Festival** (www.midsumma.org.au) in January/February is also big.

○ **Golden Shears Sheepshearing Contest** (New Zealand) A must for lovers of sheep, scat and sweat, held in Masterton during March.

○ **Womadelaide** (Australia; www.womadelaide.com.au) A celebration of world music and global rhythms that wakes up normally sleepy Adelaide in March or April.

○ **Henley-on-Todd Regatta** (Australia; www.henleyontodd.com.au) Alice Spring's unusual boat race 'run' on a dry river bed in September.

○ **Festival of Pacific Arts** (Pacific islands; http://pacartsas.com) A celebration of rare arts, crafts, dance and song held in October every four years (the next is 2012).

○ **Hawaiki Nui Va'a** (French Polynesia) Massive canoe race between the islands of Huahine, Rai'atea, Taha'a and Bora Bora in October.

○ **Melbourne Cup** (Australia; www.melbournecup.com) The country-stopping horse race held on the first Tuesday in November.

○ **Schoolies Week** (Australia; www.schooliesweek.qld.gov.au) A debauched end-of-school party for Australian high-school students that occurs from mid-November to mid-December, usually around Queensland's Gold Coast.

Christian festivals are a big deal in the south Pacific, so if you're around for Christmas or Easter, prepare for much merriment.

PARTY SCENE

There's no shortage of party places throughout Australasia. Melbourne is known for its backstreet bars around the city, St Kilda and Fitzroy, while Sydney has more of a pub culture with promising pockets in Kings Cross and Glebe. Check out Melbourne's **ThreeThousand** (www.threethousand.com.au) and Sydney's **TwoThousand** (www.twothousand.com.au) subcultural guides to get the juice on the latest bars.

Auckland's K Rd and Ponsonby are the epicentres of nightlife, but you can seek out a few other places in Vulcan Lane including the hard-rocking dive, Papa Jack's Voodoo Lounge. Live music has always been big in Wellington, and you can find no shortage of backpacker drinks specials in Rotorua, Taupo and Queenstown.

ROADS LESS TRAVELLED

Luckily, there's plenty of Australasia to go round so if you're looking to get away from it all, there's always somewhere. In Australia you can head over to Perth, the western capital that isn't visited by many Australians because of its isolation. For accessible outback drives, head for Broken Hill with its streets named after minerals and characters in every pub, or make a beeline for Coober Pedy, South Australia's underground opal capital.

In New Zealand you can find plenty of space on the South Island, from the hippy hang-out of Golden Bay to the wildlife wonders of Otago Peninsula. There are even spectacular places that weren't used as sets for *Lord of the Rings*, including Doubtful Sound and the bird haven of Stewart Island.

Your best bet for escapes, though, is the Pacific islands; from far-flung Easter Island to the Cook Islands, there's a hidden paradise waiting to be discovered.

WORKING

Getting a job can be a great way to extend your stay. If you're lucky enough to get a working holiday visa (see p116), you can easily and legally find work in Australia and/or New Zealand. Many travellers use Australia and New Zealand as a place to work and jobs don't have to be a drudge – there are opportunities in ski resorts (you can sample the slopes on your day off) and in the outback as a jackeroo or jillaroo. In French Polynesia you could mix drinks poolside at a resort. You might not find a career, but the skills and experiences you'll acquire will be some of the best souvenirs.

Employment prospects in Australasia are usually good, with plenty of casual work on offer, including fruit picking and work in the hospitality industry (see p126). Hostels are often good places to start your job hunt, with many travellers finding other jobs on notice boards. If you have some basic computer skills, temping in office jobs is another option; several temp agencies find employment specifically for working-visa holders (see p121). While the working holiday visa prevents you from working in your professional field (though this is difficult to police), you can gain good career-building experience by volunteering (see p143).

Employment in the Pacific is trickier. You could try working in a resort – many recruit activities trainers and hospitality staff from Australia, New Zealand, the UK and the US.

WHEN TO GO?

When isn't a good time to go to Australasia? Southern Australia and New Zealand's South Island are not at their best in winter, but temperatures still compare favourably with the UK or North America. Overall, spring (September to October) and autumn (April to May) are probably the best times to travel – the weather is reasonably mild everywhere and spring brings out the outback's wild flowers. Some parts of the outback will be extremely hot from November to February, so you may want to plan around these unbearable temperatures.

The wet seasons in far-northern Queensland, around Darwin (November to December and April to May) and Papua New Guinea (December to March) can make travel difficult, with dirt roads often closed in Papua New Guinea. Heading into the Pacific during shoulder seasons (October and May) will reward you with smaller crowds and lower prices. Christmas is difficult everywhere, with many expat islanders returning home – flights can be booked out months in advance.

WHAT TO EXPECT?

LOCALS & OTHER TRAVELLERS

You certainly won't be lonely in most parts of Australasia, as wandering Canadians, backpacking South Africans and working-holiday Brits have established a trail across the region.

Locals in Australia and New Zealand are products of multicultural societies, with many citizens coming from Europe and the Middle East during the post-WWII wave of immigration. Polynesian migration to New Zealand is common, with the indigenous Maori population numbering over 500,000. Australia's Aboriginals number around 380,000, with their culture enduring throughout the country.

Aussies and Kiwis have a famously 'blokey' culture that worships 'footy' players and other sporting heroes. They still occasionally describe Brits as 'Poms' (allegedly from POME, Prisoner of Mother England) and Americans as 'Yanks', but it's really little more than harmless teasing. Both countries have a sporting and cultural rivalry, and the worst thing you can do to a Kiwi is mistake them for an Aussie, so listen out for the telltale New Zealand accent that pronounces 'i' as 'u', providing many 'fush and chups' jokes. Kiwis, for their part, refer to Australia as the 'Western Island' and make merciless jokes about their rugby and netball superiority. Both countries are famously laid-back with a mutual love of the beach and the outdoors that has many of them living for the weekends.

Diversity is the only rule among Pacific islanders. Many islands have European colonial histories that brought Christianity with it. After WWII many islands gained independence from European colonial masters (notably not New Caledonia, which remains administratively part of France), but religion is still a strong influence. Holiday islands such as Tahiti are usually fairly relaxed, but more conservative islands such as Tonga frown on nakedness. The family continues to be important, and traces of the 'big man' culture of strong leaders rather than consultative democracies remain in islands such as Fiji and the Solomons. Rugby is played by many islanders and runs a close second to church in terms of devotion.

FOOD

An abundance of fresh seafood and produce means that Australasia can boast some good eating. New Zealand is known for organic produce, dairy goods and some damn fine wines. Some visitors base itineraries around wine regions such as Marlborough, Hawkes Bay or the aptly named Bay of Plenty. Australia has good grapes in the Barossa, Clare, Yarra and Hunter Valleys, though their reputation for beer is borne out by thirst-quenching lagers and some boutique breweries.

Dining in Sydney and Melbourne serves up some of the world's best with Greek, Vietnamese, Italian and Thai cuisine all filling plates. Auckland is similarly cosmopolitan, including the flavours of the Pacific, making it one of the best places to sample Polynesian food. Sadly, many of the Pacific islands are moving away from traditional foods as arable land disappears and globalisation sees the rise of tinned food. Still, you can find Maori-style *hangi*, which is mutton, pork or lamb baked underground – ideally using volcanic heat!

LANGUAGE

English is spoken throughout Australasia, though sometimes with impenetrably thick accents. Both Australian and New Zealand English notoriously abbreviate many words, so you can expect to eat brekky (breakfast) after a night of slapping mozzies (mosquitoes) and downing tinnies (cans of beer). Fortunately, in both countries you can get out of most scrapes by calling someone 'mate' (friend or buddy). For insider's slang and Aboriginal languages, Lonely Planet's *Australian Language & Culture* guide should have you bunging another shrimp on the barbie in no time.

New Zealand has two official languages: English and Maori, which are both taught in schools, so even *Pakehas* (non-Maori New Zealanders) use a little Maori in their daily conversation. You'll probably only need English, though learning Maori will make your trip more interesting and you'll come home with an authentic souvenir.

The South Pacific has a confusing mass of languages, but most islanders also speak either French or English. Unless you're having an extended stay, you probably won't need to learn any more of the Pacific languages than those covered in Lonely Planet's *South Pacific* phrasebook (which also covers Maori).

COMMUNICATION

Broadband and wi-fi, pay-as-you-go mobile phones and cheap phonecards are widely available in Australia and New Zealand's bigger cities. Travellers with laptops, PDAs and other portable devices usually have

URBAN MYTHS – DROP BEARS

There's nothing Australasians love more than to pull your leg, especially about the dangerous (and entirely made-up) predators of their countries. When the coals of a barbecue begin to fade, a crazed uncle will usually warn younger kids about the dangers of drop bears. The fictional beastie is (depending on the insanity of the storyteller) either a rare carnivorous koala, a genetically modified or nuclear-mutated marsupial or a very lost polar bear. Allegedly the drop bear will pounce from gumtrees that people camp under, though the danger of falling branches is the real threat. Drop bears make a cameo on Family Guy, when Peter is pounced on by one after he pokes a crocodile.

Bunyips and yowies (southern hemisphere Bigfoot) are other Australian inventions used to scare tourists and explain bumps in the night.

no problems uploading photos and videos even in internet cafés, though some will require dial-up levels of patience.

The Pacific is less teched up but you'll be able to check your email on most islands, and mobile-phone networks are improving.

HEALTH

Despite exaggerated reports of sharks, snakes, and other scary critters (see p189), Australia and New Zealand are generally very safe and free of health risks. A few cases of mosquito-borne diseases (such as dengue fever, Ross River fever, malaria and Murray

SAMPLE COSTS

	AUSTRALIA (AUSTRALIAN DOLLAR, A$)	NEW ZEALAND (NEW ZEALAND DOLLAR, NZ$)	FIJI (FIJIAN DOLLAR, F$)	COOK ISLANDS (NEW ZEALAND DOLLAR, NZ$)
HOSTEL/ BUDGET ROOM	A$20–60 £9.50–28 US$18.50–55	NZ$15–60 £6–24 US$12–47 A$13–52	F$18–45 £6–15 US$12–30 A$13–32	NZ$20–75 £8–30 US$16–60 A$17–65
CHEAP RESTAURANT MEAL	A$10–15 £4.75–7 US$9–13.75	NZ$7–15 £3–6 US$6–12 A$6–13	F$10–18 £3.50–6 US$6.50–12 A$7–13	NZ$5–10 £2–4 US$4–8 A$4.50–9
1L BOTTLE OF WATER	A$3 £1.40 US$2.75	NZ$2.50 £1 US$2 A$2.25	F$2 £0.70 US$1.30 A$1.50	NZ$3.50 £1.50 US$2.75 A$3
SOUVENIR T-SHIRT	A$30 £14 US$27.50	NZ$20 £8 US$16 A$17	F$20 £7 US$13 A$14.50	NZ$20 £8 US$16 A$17
BOTTLE OF BEER	A$3 £1.40 US$2.75	NZ$3.50 £1.50 US$2.75 A$3	F$4 £1.50 US$2.75 A$3	NZ$5 £2 US$4 A$4.50
STREET SNACK	Kebab A$7 £3.28 US$6.40	Meat pie NZ$3.00 £1.22 US$2.38 A$2.60	Samosa F$8 £2.71 US$5.28 A$5.77	*Ika mata* (raw fish in coconut cream) NZ$8 £3.25 US$6.50 A$7
1L PETROL	A$1.40 £0.65 US$1.25	NZ$1.80 £0.75 US$1.50 A$1.60	F$1.50 £0.50 US$1 A$1	NZ$1.90 £0.75 US$1.50 A$1.75

Valley encephalitis) have been reported in northern Australia. You can get amoebic meningitis from bathing in New Zealand's geothermal pools, and a few unclean lakes and rivers have been known to transmit giardia. Parts of the Pacific are prone to mosquito-borne diseases, so check with a doctor for vaccinations beforehand and take precautions when visiting.

The weather poses the greatest risk to health in the region. The sun can be fierce, especially if you're not used to it, so heat exhaustion, dehydration and sunburn pose a constant threat. Most Aussies pack sunscreen and a bottle of water with them before facing summer days, and sun hats are compulsory. With the expanding hole in the ozone layer above much of Australia and New Zealand, skin cancer is an all-too-real threat, and you can burn in as little as six minutes in some places. In New Zealand, exposure and hypothermia are dangers for unprepared trekkers at high altitude.

For more travel-health information consult the Health & Safety chapter (p41) and seek professional medical advice.

ISSUES

Despite spooky films such as *Wolf Creek,* Australasia remains a relatively safe destination. In Australia and New Zealand there are few health risks (and world-class medical facilities if something does happen) and serious crime is limited. If you're unlucky, the worst you'll encounter is a swiped purse in a market or a less-than-scrupulous hostel owner overcharging you.

In the Pacific there are more complex social problems that could mean you should give some places a miss. Papua New Guinea, Solomon Islands, East Timor and Fiji have all recently had periods of civil unrest, leading to tarnished reputations with tourists. Other areas, such as Tuvalu and Kiribati, have been impacted by rising tides that have reduced their land and crop-growing areas – that's global warming creating environmental refugees of many locals. The Australian government has a website dedicated to travel warnings (www.smartraveller.gov.au) that gives sound advice on the region.

GETTING THERE

AIR

Flying is definitely the most popular way into the region. With a round-the-world (RTW) ticket you can grab a couple of stopovers, though even basic return fares will offer stopovers in South America, the Middle East and, more commonly, Asia. More than one stopover is possible with some airlines (see p90 for details), and some offer more open-jaw ticket options and general flexibility on this route than on others.

The main international hubs are Sydney, Melbourne, Perth and Auckland, though some airlines offer connections into Brisbane, Darwin, Wellington, Hobart, Cairns, Canberra and Adelaide. In the South Pacific, Nadi (Fiji), Pape'ete (French Polynesia) and Apia (Samoa) are regular stopovers for jets coming from the US (Air New Zealand flights from Los Angeles stop in a number of South Pacific islands), but many South Pacific destinations are serviced via Sydney or Auckland.

Most major airlines (Qantas, British Airways, Singapore Airlines, Cathay Pacific, Emirates, Malaysian Airlines, Royal Brunei, Korean Airlines, Thai Airways and Air New Zealand) fly into the area, but the region is opening up more with budget carriers (Jetstar, Virgin Blue, Tiger, Kiwijet and more every day). It's worth shopping around and even planning on buying a budget flight to Asia while you're in Australia or New Zealand.

SEA & OVERLAND

After a real challenge? Heading to Australasia by land should give you plenty of kicks. From Europe you'll pass through the Middle East and Southeast Asia on what was once called the 'hippie trail', partly because of the easy narcotics that were said to be available to travellers in the 1960s (maybe even your parents!). There are no ferries linking Southeast Asia to Australia, so crewing a yacht or hitching a ride on a cargo boat are the only options.

Coming from the US can be a great tour through Pacific life as you island-hop your way from Hawaii or Easter Island. Boat transport between islands is often by small operators and can be difficult to coordinate, but relax and have another daiquiri and the boats will come.

BEYOND AUSTRALIA, NEW ZEALAND & THE PACIFIC

Leaving already? Flights to Asia are particularly cheap with budget airlines appearing everywhere, and flights to Africa, South America and North America from Australia and New Zealand are all reasonably priced. It's definitely cheaper, however, to use a RTW ticket from your home country to travel on to these countries. You can also extend Pacific island–hopping from major destinations such as New Caledonia, Samoa and Fiji to Hawaii or Easter Island, which also make great gateways into North or South America. Again, a RTW ticket is handy for this, but you can organise individual hops.

With a one-way ticket to Australia you can go on some brilliant overland trips to get back home. You could head to East Timor and fly to Indonesia (there are no ferries linking the two countries) to follow the old 'hippie trail'. Or head north to China and take the Trans-Mongolian railway from Beijing to Moscow. With a few stops in the Pacific, you can take a wandering route to North or South America.

FURTHER INFORMATION

WEBSITES
For the lowdown on specific countries, check out Destinations on Lonely Planet's website (lonelyplanet.com). These websites will help you with planning:

- **aboriginalaustralia.com** (www.aboriginalaustralia.com) Aboriginal-owned, community-run website covering culture, art and tourism.
- **Australia Online** (www.australiaonline.com.au) Information on accommodation, tours and activities.
- **BUG** (www.bugpacific.com; www.bugaustralia.com) Two sites from backpacking pros that cover Australia, New Zealand and the Pacific.
- **Department of Conservation** (www.doc.govt.nz) New Zealand Department of Conservation site with news and information about parks and conservation.
- **Department of the Environment, Water, Heritage and the Arts** (www.deh.gov.au/parks) The portal for Australia's national parks.

- **New Zealand Travel guide** (www.destination-nz.com) Plenty of links to other sites with a special 'on a budget' take on New Zealand.
- **PacificIslands.com** (www.pacificislands.com) Useful travel information on the Pacific.
- **Pacific Magazine** (www.pacificmagazine.net) Website for the Pacific's top magazine with news and more.
- **Pacific Regional Environment Programme** (www.sidsnet.org/pacific/sprep) Detailed information on environmental issues in the Pacific.
- **Study in Australia** (www.studyinaustralia.gov.au) A government site with the lowdown on courses and universities.
- **Study in New Zealand** (www.studyingnewzealand.com) All the news on Kiwi courses and universities.

BOOKS
- *Sean & David's Long Drive* (Sean Condon) The tale of two ill-equipped urban Australians faced with the vastness of their own country.
- *Down Under/In a Sunburnt Country* (Bill Bryson) America's funniest traveller hilariously carves up Australia.
- *The Other Side of the Frontier* (Henry Reynold) A fascinating and frightening Aboriginal view of Australia's colonisation.
- *Where We Once Belonged* (Sia Fiegel) A gripping account of a Samoan girl's rite of passage.
- *Tu* (Patricia Grace) Follows a Maori battalion through WWII.

FILMS
- *Ten Canoes* (2006) A stunning retelling of an Aboriginal legend in the remote Arnhem Land.
- *Whale Rider* (2002) A young girl asserts her identity among the male-dominated Maori.
- *Australia* (2008) Director Baz Luhrmann's big-budget homecoming about the romance between a stockman and an aristocrat.
- *Sione's Wedding* (2006) Four Samoans living in Auckland try to sort out their friend's hilariously messed-up wedding.
- *The Disappearing Tuvalu* (2005) A documentary exploring the Pacific's inconvenient truth about rising water levels flooding islands.

NORTHEAST ASIA

Dominated by the massiveness of China, smaller destinations such as Japan, Hong Kong, Mongolia, Korea, Taiwan and Tibet could easily get lost down the back of the couch of Northeast Asia. But these other countries have no problem finding a place on the world stage thanks to karaoke, karate, *kimchi*, kabuki, Kyoto – and that's just the 'k's.

China has long been the bully of the region with human-rights issues that stretch way back before Tiananmen Square in 1989, but with the 2008 Olympics the world decided to kiss and make up with one of its heftiest superpowers. If you think China is all the same, you may need to explore the country more – there's the ancient Buddhist culture of Tibet, horse-mad Mongols in the north, and Uighur folks in the west who have more in common with Borat than Beijing.

Quirky Japan offers cultural surprises from anime to Zen, and the capital Tokyo is an up-to-the-second technopolis where even the most traditional geisha has a laptop, a mobile phone and a device that hasn't even been invented where we're from.

With all the script characters and intense culture, some travellers to Northeast Asia feel isolated. The Japanese *gaijin* (foreigner) and Chinese *laowai* (foreigner) are both labels worn with embarrassment by many. But if you pick up a bit of language and learn to read a few characters, you'll get a head start with locals. The region will reward your efforts too with its incredible diversity. You could wake up in a Japanese capsule hotel and go to bed in a Mongolian yurt, start the day with dim sum in Hong Kong and finish it with Uighur kebabs.

ITINERARIES

If you're serious about exploring the region, you'll definitely wander through China. Well-known gateways such as Hong Kong and Tokyo are getting strong competition from Beijing, Shanghai and even Macau, as more tourists want to discover their own routes.

THE WHOLE SHEBANG

Here's a route that will give you a little of everything Northeast Asia has to offer, but hurry up as you can't stay anywhere too long! Kick off in **Tokyo**, drift south to check out traditional **Kyoto**. Now ferry from western **Honshu** to **Busan** in South Korea where there are enough palaces, temples and nightlife to keep you busy for a week. Call into **Seoul** to get a feel for the capital, then from **Incheon** ferry to **Tianjin**, an old town in China worth exploring for its antiques. From here slide over to **Beijing** to wonder at the **Forbidden City** and

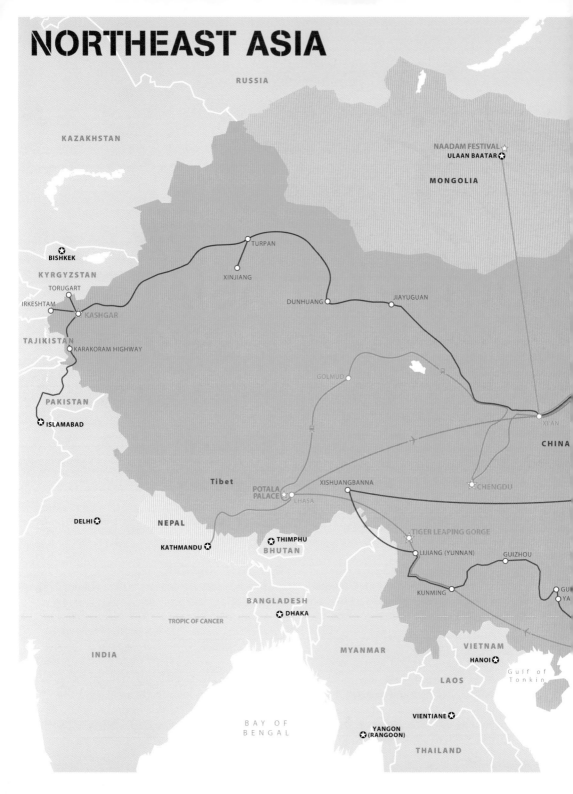

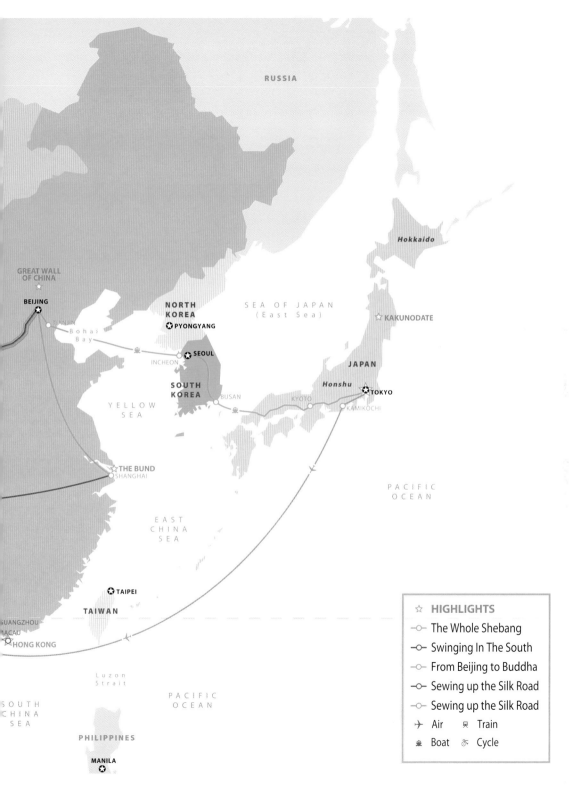

RUSSIA

Hokkaido

GREAT WALL
OF CHINA
☆

★ BEIJING

TIANJIN
B o h a i
B a y

NORTH
KOREA
✪ PYONGYANG

SEA OF JAPAN
(East Sea)

☆ KAKUNODATE

✪ SEOUL

INCHEON

JAPAN

Honshu
✪ TOKYO

KYOTO

SOUTH
KOREA

BUSAN

KAMIKOCHI

YELLOW
SEA

☆ THE BUND
SHANGHAI

PACIFIC
OCEAN

EAST
CHINA
SEA

✪ TAIPEI

TAIWAN

GUANGZHOU
MACAU
✪ HONG KONG

*Luzon
Strait*

PACIFIC
OCEAN

SOUTH
CHINA
SEA

PHILIPPINES

✪ MANILA

☆ HIGHLIGHTS
—○— The Whole Shebang
—○— Swinging In The South
—○— From Beijing to Buddha
—○— Sewing up the Silk Road
—○— Sewing up the Silk Road
✈ Air   🚃 Train
🚢 Boat   🚲 Cycle

WITH THE MOST SKYSCRAPERS IN THE WORLD, THE CITY OF HONG KONG IS SPECTACULAR, ESPECIALLY AS SEEN FROM VICTORIA PEAK (SEE P198).

THE REMOTE WIND CLOUD DANCING WITH NOW-DORMANT MT FUJI (SEE P199), JAPAN, IS EVOCATIVE OF THE MOUNTAIN'S VOLCANIC HISTORY.

RY SOAKING UP THE ATMOSPHERE OF BUSTLING CITY LIFE IN CHINA'S CAPITAL, BEIJING (SEE P198).

see a section of the **Great Wall**. Wander over to **Xi'an** to see the terracotta warriors before heading north to **Ulaan Baatar** for some horse trekking in **Mongolia**. Backtrack to **Beijing** to fly out or onto **Shanghai**, the artsy, cosmopolitan second-largest city of China.

SWINGING IN THE SOUTH

Spend a few days shopping in **Hong Kong** before hopping over to casino capital **Macau**. With your winnings, hit the mainland in **Guangzhou**, where you could spend a few nights in the city before heading on to **Guilin** with its stark karst scenery. A boat trip around **Yangshou** is the serenest way to view the limestone peaks from their best vantage points. You can hang out with China's minority peoples in **Guizhou** or press on to **Kunming** (where you can also branch south into Vietnam). From here stop in at **Lijiang**, a maze of cobbled streets and gushing canals that's one of the most visited spots in **Yunnan**. Take time out for a few treks in the verdant **Xishuangbanna** region before heading up to **Shanghai** for your last leg.

FROM BEIJING TO BUDDHA

Touch down in **Beijing**, where you can soak up the atmosphere of China's capital. From here catch a train out to **Xi'an** to meet the terracotta warriors or hop on the plane direct to **Chengdu** if pandas are your thing. Then take the spectacular train route to Lhasa overnighting in **Golmud**. After a glorious train ride, you'll find yourself in **Lhasa**, the Buddhist heartland that has overland trips across the Himalaya to **Kathmandu** (Nepal).

SEWING UP THE SILK ROAD

Follow the Silk Road from **Beijing** by stopping in at **Xi'an** to gawk at the terracotta warriors, then stop at the end-of-the-world fort at **Jiayuguan** before calling in at the cave grottos of **Dunhuang**. Next stop is the grim deserts of **Xinjiang**. Stop off at backpacker-friendly **Turpan** before taking the train on to medieval **Kashgar**, a Central Asian city of Turkic-speaking Uighurs that buzzes with the world's greatest bazaar. From here exciting options include heading over the **Irkeshtam** or **Torugart** mountain passes into Central Asia or down the **Karakoram Highway** to Pakistan.

WILD WILD EAST

From **Tokyo** start off with a few warm-up strolls, such as **Kamikochi**, an excellent base for hikes up the 3180m **Yari-ga-take**. Now you're ready to take on China. Fly over to **Kunming** and make for **Tiger Leaping Gorge**, one of the world's deepest gorges complete with dramatic cliffs and waterfalls. There are other hikes around **Yunnan** including the spectacular rice terraces of **Yuanyang**, so take your time before heading west to Tibet, where the altitude change will mean you'll have to take it easy for a couple of days around **Lhasa** before a *kora* (pilgrimage circuit of a holy site) around **Drepung Monastery**. Not exhausted yet? Make the impressive four- to five-day hike from **Ganden Monastery** to **Samye Monastery** with the aid of some good guides. If you've still got some energy fly back to **Xi'an** and take on **Hua Shan**, one of five sacred Taoist mountains. From Hua Shan head back to **Beijing** for a lie-down.

WHAT TO DO?

HIGHLIGHTS

- Balancing on the **Great Wall** (China) and imagining all the other tourists are invading Mongol hordes.
- Meditating amid yak-butter lamps and chanting monks in Lhasa's **Potala Palace** (Tibet), the bruised heart of Tibetan culture.
- Sharpening your swords at **Kakunodate** (Japan) among its 17th-century samurai houses.
- Dressing up with kooky cosplay gangs or hop on a bullet train out of **Tokyo** (Japan).
- Playing paparazzi with pandas at **Chengdu** (China).
- Chasing **Tiger Leaping Gorge** (China) from the depths of the Jinsha River to the peaks of Haba Shan.
- Asserting your inner warrior with horse racing, wrestling or archery at **Naadam Festival** (Mongolia).
- Haggling yourself hoarse at **Kashgar** (China), a Central Asian city with the world's wildest market.
- Strolling Shanghai's **The Bund** (China) for a glimpse of the former European occupation.
- Seeing all of Hong Kong (China) as though the city were a toy town arrayed beneath **Victoria Peak**.

WOLONG NATURE RESERVE (P200), SICHUAN PROVINCE, CHINA, PROVIDES A SAFE HOME FOR THE HIGHLY ENDANGERED GIANT PANDA.

GET ACTIVE

Japan, Korea and Taiwan love their outdoor activities, and although China has incredible scope for adventure sports, much of this is DIY at the moment.

Trekking & Mountaineering

Scaling sacred mountains provides both a spiritual and health high in Northeast Asia. The trek up Mt Fuji (3776m) is the must-do overnight pilgrimage. Treks up one of China's sacred mountains – Emei Shan, Huang Shan or Tai Shan – wind up thousands of stone steps to a network of Buddhist monasteries linked by mountain paths. With thousands of Chinese on the roads, you won't be a lonely pilgrim.

Elsewhere there's classic, accessible walking, particularly in the mountains of Japan, South Korea and Taiwan. Many routes have camp sites and mountain huts. You can also try these: Japanese Alps on Honshū

and in the heart of Hokkaido; Songnisan and Seoraksan National Parks in South Korea and Yangmingshan National Park in Taiwan.

The most exciting vertical terrain lies in the huge Himalayan peaks of western China and Tibet (where you can just about get away with DIY trekking). The remote mountains of western Sichuan offer challenging treks and horse treks, but lodges or trekking agencies are difficult to find. Other spectacular hikes include the alpine valleys of Jiuzhaigou (Sichuan), Tiger Leaping Gorge and the jungles of Xishuangbanna (both in Yunnan).

Cycling & Mountain-Biking

Biking is *the* way to explore China – it's environmentally sound and plenty of locals will pass you cheerfully chiming their bells. Most towns hire out clunky bikes with a few places offering mountain bikes for rural exploration. Cycling around the wondrous peaks of Yangshuo is one of China's real highlights, while the physically demanding run from Lhasa to Kathmandu is one of the world's great mountain-biking routes.

The mountains of Japan, South Korea and Taiwan also offer numerous mountain-bike trails. Japan's back roads, especially in the coastal regions, are particularly popular with cycling tourists.

Skiing & Snowboarding

South Korea has some reasonable skiing, and Japan has more than 300 ski resorts which get some great powder from December to April. In Japan powder hounds head for Niseko, Shiga Kōgen or Nozawa Onsen (which offers skiing and some warming hot springs afterwards). Cross-country skiing is also very popular and often cheaper. Skiing in China is possible but nothing to write home about.

Other Activities

There's good scuba diving around the Japanese islands of Okinawa and Yaeyama; Jejudo in South Korea (a volcanic island and home of female pearl divers); and Kenting and the Penghu Islands in Taiwan (the cheapest place to learn).

Saddle up for horse riding across the steppes of Mongolia, plus there are cheap multiday horse treks around Songpan (China). Camel rides are popular in inner Mongolia and the deserts around Dunhuang (China).

WILDLIFE

The animal celebrities of the region are definitely the ultracute pandas, who have turned China's Wolong Nature Reserve into their dressing room and stage. China's other wildlife is less spectacular, unless you're heading into the northwest to spot reindeer, moose or the rare Manchurian tiger. You'll be able to see the odd small mammal such as squirrels and badgers in wilderness areas, with monkeys very common – especially macaques who are known to intimidate hikers into handing over their picnics at Emei Shan in China.

Sneaky macaques even found their way over to Japan, where they hang around areas such as Honshū, Shikoku and Kyūshū. You may even spot Japan's only

carnivores – two species of bear, though hopefully not while camping. Korea's hikers have been known to spot the Siberian tiger, though it's more common to see chipmunks or squirrels.

FESTIVALS

The region's fascinating festivals are a varied and unusual mix:

o **Tsagaan Sar** (White Month; Mongolia) Merriment held in January and February that features the best booze and food.

o **Chinese New Year** (China, Korea and Taiwan) Usually falling in January or February, this huge festival is the reason fireworks were invented, plus there's traditional culture and merriment.

o **Yah-Yah Matsuri** (Owase, Japan) An argument contest at the beginning of February with competitors screaming samurai chants.

o **Sapporo Snow Festival** (Japan; www.snowfes.com/english) Held in February. Expect ice sculptures and illumination of the park's winter landscapes.

o **Losar** (Tibet) A colourful new-year festival of drama, pilgrimage and dressing up, held in February/March.

o **Hanami** (Japan) A celebration of the first plum, peach and cherry blossoms from February to April, with park picnics and the odd sip of sake.

o **Water-Splashing Festival** (China) Held at Xishuangbanna in Yunnan around mid-April, this is a giant water fight in the name of washing away the dirt of the old year.

o **Dragon Boat Festival** (Hong Kong) Honours the poet Qu Yuan with boat races and lively festivities in June.

o **Naadam** (Mongolia) Showcases Mongolia's nomadic roots (namely horse racing, archery and wrestling) across the country on 11 and 12 July.

o **Gion Matsuri** (Japan) Commemorating a 9th-century request to the gods for an end to the plague sweeping Kyoto; an incredible parade of massive human-dragged floats on 17 July.

o **O-Bon** (Japan) The Buddhist Festival of the Dead taking place in July and August with dazzling lanterns hung everywhere.

o **Chusoek (Harvest Moon) Festival** (Korea) People return to their family homes in September to pay homage to their ancestors.

- **Birthday of Confucius** (China) Celebrated on 28 September with a giant festival in Qufu (Shandong province), where the great sage was born and where he died.

ROADS LESS TRAVELLED

To escape the throngs, seek out the pockets of China with fewer tourists, such as traditional villages including Chuandixia just outside Beijing, or head for Anhui province which has several tranquil spots including Hongcun, Xidi, Nanping, Guanlu and Yuliang. Countries off the backpacker trail, such as Taiwan and Korea, are good places to score some tranquillity.

WORKING

Go east, young man/woman! China's economic growth has brought with it more opportunities, especially if you're interested in teaching English. You'll need a working visa and some Mandarin Chinese would be useful, though you can also improve your chances by studying a TEFL/TESOL course (see p138). You can start your job search at sites such as **ChinaJob.com** (www .chinajob.com) and **ChinaOnline** (www.chinaonline .cn.com). For English-teaching jobs, try **Dave's ESL Cafe** (http://eslcafe.com) which has regular openings.

Japan is also looking for English-language teachers, and having a university degree will get you ahead of the crowd. It can be expensive to set up in Japan, but once you're earning yen it can be reasonably affordable. The Japan Exchange Teaching (JET, see p141) is a good place to start. Bartending, hostessing and even modelling are all possibilities in Japan, Korea and Taiwan. Taiwan offers several good language opportunities, which you can start to explore at **ESL Island** (www.eslisland.com).

WHEN TO GO?

Stretching from sub-Siberian Mongolia down past the Tropic of Cancer, Northeast Asia straddles the four seasons though you'll find more extreme weather in the north and south. The northern hemisphere enjoys summer from June to September, though the humidity can be sweatily unpleasant in high summer. That's also when Japan, southeast China and South Korea are hit by the odd typhoon. Taking on the Silk Road during the sizzling temperatures of August is really only for heat freaks.

Spring and autumn (when the foliage is spectacular and skies are clear) are the best times to travel in China, though you have to be prepared for any weather at this time. In Mongolia and north of the Great Wall of China it gets incredibly cold in winter (how's minus 40°C for ya?), while the central Yangzi River valley experiences fiercely hot temperatures during long, hot summers – the only time it's unlikely to rain in central China. Summer is also the best time to visit Tibet, the mountains of western Sichuan and Mongolia, though the days can be hot in the Gobi Desert. South China is sweet year-round, though some travellers opt for winter because temperatures are cool but not prohibitively cold and the crowds of tourists are absent.

Japan has the most diverse climate in the region (thanks to the length of the archipelago and high mountains down its spine), which means it can be snowing in northern Hokkaido and positively balmy in southern, subtropical Okinawa. Western Japan receives a large amount of precipitation in winter, while the Pacific side is cold but less snowy. If you're travelling in summer or winter, try to focus on coastal and southern areas, which are more temperate than inland.

WHAT TO EXPECT?

LOCALS & OTHER TRAVELLERS

China has a large community of American and British businesspeople called 'expats' (or 'expatriates' – people who live away from their home country), who flock to big cities, especially in the former British colony and financial centre of Hong Kong. There's a backpacker pocket in China's south around Yangshuo and in Yunnan, but otherwise foreigners are a novelty. Travellers are much more common in Japan, South Korea and Taiwan, where locals are used to seeing American tourists and the odd European. Seoul and Tokyo have large English-speaking expat communities.

Northeast Asians themselves are a diverse people with complex etiquette and religious beliefs. A few helpful generalisations will get you through most conversations. Directness is uncommon. People often tell you what they think you want to hear, especially in China, where a smile doesn't necessarily indicate

✪ **SHE IS A ROCK STAR.** Self-conscious? You're out of luck. In China, you will be photographed, sketched, and sniffed at by children. If the attention gets old, simply imagine that you're a celebrity. A rock star. And you're simply *huge* in China.

✪ **SHE CAN SKIP THE GYM FOR A WHILE.** Because a few weeks of squatting over hole-in-the-floor toilets will give you the thighs of a James Bond vixen. Just remember: a successful vixen always carries her own toilet paper.

✪ **SHE ONLY THOUGHT SHE WAS JADED.** Even everyday life in China is foreign enough to fascinate: pharmacy employees starting their day with a dance; t'ai chi with swords and fans; that lane-by-lane dance you do to cross the enormous road; 'Edelweiss' in Chinese; wrigglies on sticks…

✪ **SHE'S GRATEFUL THAT SHE PACKED SOME GOOD NOVELS.** Because the bookshops in Chinese airports are all business, featuring such titles as *Forty-Nine Habits Related to Success and Failure*, *Do Business So Simple*, and the enchantingly cryptic *Things That Build Up the Relation and Do Correctly*.

✪ **SHE IS AT PEACE WITH THE BACKGROUND MUSIC.** Copious, lusty, soulful spitting abounds; embrace cultural difference and get used to it. The ubiquitous guttural 'chhh' and the heartfelt 'ptoo!' that follows it… Really, it's no worse than blowing your nose. Just don't look too closely.

✪ **SHE CAN ENJOY INTERPLANETARY TRAVEL WITHOUT LEAVING EARTH.** Shanghai is Jupiter and Saturn and the setting of every science-fiction story ever written – all cones and improbable spheres, extreme planes and swooping roofs. It's the 24th century as imagined by the 12th – baffling, strange and very beautiful.

✪ **SHE ENJOYS A GOOD FOOT RUB. ALSO BLISSFUL IGNORANCE.** If there's a red light outside the foot-massage place, do know that feet are not the only body parts massaged there. Though truth be told, one might not realise this until much later, long after one has received a rather decent and well-priced foot rub.

✪ **SHE WRITES LEFT-HANDED AND AMAZES MANY.** Chinese children are made to write with their right hand in school, so if you're a lefty, you qualify as a sort of medical oddity; folks will gather round, enthralled. Just smile, keep writing and imagine yourself all doll-like and inscrutable.

✪ **SHE KNOWS WHEN TO PROFFER AN ORANGE.** Carry snacks to share with the locals who will offer you food, hand you their babies (but beware those bare bottoms!), and approach you with awkward but genuine curiosity. Enjoy these encounters; all you need is an open mind…and a bag of oranges.

✪ **SHE MAKES A LITTLE MANDARIN GO A VERY LONG WAY.** *Mei guanxi* means 'no problem, it doesn't matter, no worries' and it's not a bad mantra for your trip. Taxi driver lost? Camera stolen? Charged three times as much as the locals? *Mei guanxi*. Eventually, you'll even begin to believe it!

www.lonelyplanet.com

happiness – sometimes just embarrassment or worry. Just as in Southeast Asia (see p217), maintaining 'face' is crucial throughout the region. Try not to make anyone back down directly or look stupid if something goes awry. Smiling negotiation is the best method; direct confrontation is a last resort.

Japanese people are generally extremely friendly and courteous, shy and hospitable (there's even a tourist system of evening home visits). The Japanese are most forgiving of social gaffes but long-term residents complain that it's difficult to get beyond being treated as a *gaijin* (foreigner).

China has only been 'open' to foreigners for 20 years, so many people have a curious or suspicious attitude to travellers, especially in remote areas. Chinese people will stare unashamedly at hairy, big-nosed foreigners, and travellers often tire of the endless cries of *laowai* (foreigner) which is usually followed by giggles – and then there's the constant battle against overcharging for foreigners.

FOOD

If you're used to Chinese takeaways or sushi at home, then Northeast Asia will blow your taste buds away. The fiery flavours of China's Sichuan cuisine leave many grabbing for a jug of water, Peking duck is justifiably

SAMPLE COSTS

	CHINA (YUAN, Y)	HONG KONG (HONG KONG DOLLARS, HK$)	JAPAN (YEN, ¥)
HOSTEL/ BUDGET ROOM	Y180–250 £13–16 US$25–35 A$28.50–40	HK$200–850 £13–55 US$26–110 A$29–125	¥2800–3850 £13.25–18.50 US$26–36 A$30–41
CHEAP RESTAURANT MEAL	Y7–35 £0.50–2.45 US$1–5 A$1.10–5.50	HK$10–50 £0.65–3.25 US$1.30–6.50 A$1.50–7.25	¥550–880 £2.60–4.20 US$5–8.25 A$6–9.50
1L BOTTLE OF WATER	Y2 £0.15 US$0.20 A$0.25	HK$8.50 £0.50 US$1 A$1.25	¥120 £0.60 US$1 A$1.30
SOUVENIR T-SHIRT	Y25 £1.75 US$3.50 A$4	HK$35 £2.25 US$4.50 A$5	¥1500 £7 US$14 A$15.50
BOTTLE OF BEER	Y2–10 £0.15–0.70 US$0.25–1.40 A$0.30–1.60	HK$40 £2.60 US$5 A$6	¥300 £1.50 US$3 A$3.25
STREET SNACK	Lamb kebab Y2 £0.15 US$0.25 A$0.30	Bowl of wonton HK$18 £1.20 US$2.30 A$2.50	Bowl of ramen ¥400 £1.90 US$3.75 A$4.25
1L PETROL	Y3 £0.20 US$0.40 A$0.50	HK$12 £0.80 US$1.50 A$1.75	¥140 £0.65 US$1.30 A$1.50

famous but the authentic wood-fired flavour only tastes this good in Beijing, and Hong Kong's celebrated dim sum or *yum cha* (Chinese snacks taken with tea) just keep coming on trolleys heavy with goodies you'd never see in Chinatown back home.

Japanese restaurants often specialise in one dish, so you'll be able to discover your favourite *yakitori* (skewers of grilled meat and vegetables) or *sushi-ya* (top-shelf tuna or squid sushi). Korean cuisine is all about seafood and pickled vegetables. The kapow of *kimchi* (pickled cabbage) is a flavour you won't forget in a hurry.

LANGUAGE

You can get by with English in Japan, South Korea, Taiwan and Hong Kong, but in mainland China it's mostly a language for students and businesspeople. China is a tongue-tangling mix of languages and dialects. Mandarin (Putonghua) is the official language, though Cantonese is dominant in the south and in Hong Kong. Then there are at least half a dozen other Chinese languages, as well as minority languages, ranging from Turkic to Thai. Confused yet?

There is an increasing number of signs with English letters (particularly in post-Olympics Beijing) accompanying local script, but you'll definitely need to understand a few characters in Mandarin to get around. Many travellers take a course before they go or have an audio lesson on their iPod, but look for courses that include a written booklet as well.

By contrast, the Japanese and Korean languages are fairly uniform across their respective countries, with only a few obscure dialects in rural areas. Korea has adopted a new method of Romanising the Korean language and introduced a few new spellings. You may see some old spellings knocking around.

COMMUNICATION

Unless you're in Mongolia or rural China, you're likely to get good mobile-phone coverage and internet access. Japan and larger cities in China will also have wi-fi, often at competitive rates.

EACH YEAR VISITORS FLOCK TO SAPPORO, JAPAN, TO SEE THE GIGANTIC ICE SCULPTURES AND SNOW STATUES AT THE ANNUAL SNOW FESTIVAL (P200).

HEALTH

Plan ahead for the artillery of needles you'll need for visiting China. Dengue fever and Japanese encephalitis occasionally occur in Taiwan and are present in rural China, which is also a huge reservoir of hepatitis B and various forms of flu. Schistosomiasis (bilharziasis) and typhoid are present in the central Yangzi River basin.

You may have the odd out-of-stomach experience when trying new food in China and Mongolia, though travellers rarely have problems in Japan or Korea.

Blood banks in Northeast Asia don't stock Rh-negative blood. Consult the Health & Safety chapter (p41) and seek professional medical advice for more travel-health information.

ISSUES

China's human-rights record has long been a worry, though the 2008 Olympics put pressure on the country to clean up its act. The occupation of Tibet remains a sticking point, but there is also continuing repression of the ethnic Uighur Muslim minority in Xinjiang province.

China's economic progress has come at considerable cost, with pollution of air and water at levels that can cause discomfort for some travellers. The World Bank reckons China had 16 of the world's 20 most polluted cities in 2007, so you may need to acclimatise to the air quality when you arrive.

Foreigners face travel restrictions in Tibet, and you'll probably have to take some kind of tour just to get to Lhasa. Towns and monasteries off the beaten track require travel permits that you can only get when booking a tour, but most of the major sights are visitable without much hassle.

Japan is relatively crime-free though the government has recently introduced a control system requiring all foreigners to be fingerprinted and photographed – all in the name of terrorism prevention.

GETTING THERE

AIR

Most big airlines offer direct flights into Northeast Asian hubs, including Beijing, Shanghai, Hong Kong, Seoul, Taipei, Tokyo and Osaka. If you're flying into Hong Kong,

Macau or Osaka, then these budget carriers might be an option:

- **Air Asia** (www.airasia.com)
- **Jetstar** (www.jetstar.com)
- **Oasis Hong Kong** (www.oasishongkong.com)
- **Tiger Airways** (www.tigerairways.com)
- **Viva Macau** (www.flyvivamacau.com)

It's no problem getting open-jaw tickets into the region, plus Beijing, Hong Kong and Tokyo crop up on most RTW tickets (see p90). Stopovers to the latter two, plus Osaka and occasionally Seoul, are possible on some tickets into Sydney (Australia) with carriers such as Japan Airlines and Korea Air.

Northeast Asian routes are highly competitive and there's usually a wide choice of fares. European airlines such as KLM, Air France and Lufthansa were offering cheap student fares to Northeast Asia at the time of writing. British Airways, Air China, Cathay Pacific, and Gulf Air also turn out cheap deals.

SEA & OVERLAND

Although there's plenty of sea transport between the countries in Northeast Asia, there are only three sea links out of the region, namely the ferries from Vladivostok (the terminus of the Trans-Siberian railway) to Fushiki in Japan and Sokcho in South Korea, or the much shorter run from Korsakov (Sakhalin Island, Russia) to Wakkanai (Hokkaido, Japan).

You can cross overland from China to Vietnam, Laos, Nepal, Pakistan, Kyrgyzstan, Kazakhstan and Mongolia. Train routes lead in from Mongolia, Kazakhstan and Vietnam. There are fantastically scenic high road passes to Pakistan and Kyrgyzstan in the far west. You can't cross into Afghanistan, Bhutan or India by land.

SPECIALIST TOUR OPERATORS

- **Haiwei Trails** (www.haiweitrails.com) US-British company that operates out of Lijiang (Yunnan province).
- **Karakorum Expeditions** (www.gomongolia.com) Foreign-run company based in Mongolia.
- **Khampa Caravan** (www.khampacaravan.com) Overland trips from Yunnan to places including Tibet. The company emphasises sustainable tourism and supporting local communities.

- **Koryo Group** (www.koryogroup.com) North Korea specialists.
- **Wild China** (www.wildchina.com) Professionally run adventurous trips to China's most interesting regions.

BEYOND NORTHEAST ASIA

The Far East is much easier to get to nowadays than when Marco Polo dragged himself over from Europe. Flights out of the region's hubs can take you anywhere in the world reasonably cheaply. Heading overland on the Trans-Mongolian or Trans-Siberian railways will take you on one of the world's great train journeys.

Then there's the mind-blowing possibility of crossing into Nepal from Tibet and following the old overland 'hippie trail' from Kathmandu back through Iran and the Middle East. Travellers are also hopping across the border into Vietnam, Laos or Myanmar and heading on to Australasia. Circle Pacific airfares (see p90) will let you explore the great ocean's islands and it won't cost the earth.

FURTHER INFORMATION

WEBSITES
- **China Backpacker** (www.chinabackpacker.com) A site with information about hiking and trekking in China.
- **China the Beautiful** (www.chinapage.com) Covers Chinese art, poetry and language.
- **China Travel** (www.cnta.com/lyen) The portal of the China National Tourism Administration.
- **Discover Hong Kong** (www.discoverhongkong.com) Hong Kong's tourist association website.
- **Gaijin Pot** (www.gaijinpot.com) Jobs in Japan and general travel tips.
- **Japan Travel Information** (www.japantravelinfo.com) Portal of the Japan National Tourist Board.
- **Life in Korea** (www.lifeinkorea.com) A busy but brilliant guide to living and travelling in Korea.
- **Outdoor Japan** (www.outdoorjapan.com) A light overview of the outdoor activities available in Japan.
- **Taiwanderful** (www.taiwanderful.net) A good hub for information on Taiwan.
- **Tibet Online** (www.tibet.org) Examines Tibet's tragic occupation and repression.

- **Tour2Korea** (www.tour2korea.com) Stacks of Korean travel information and links.

BOOKS
- *Trespassers on the Roof of the World* (Peter Hopkirk) Recreates European explorers' early attempts to enter forbidden Tibet.
- *Fire Under Snow: Testimony of a Tibetan Prisoner* (Palden Gyatso) A moving autobiography recounting the life of a Buddhist monk imprisoned for 33 years.
- *Riding the Iron Rooster* (Paul Theroux) The travel veteran rides China's trains to meet its characters and conductors.
- *Speed Tribes* (Karl Taro Greenfield) A racy foray into the drug-peddling, computer-hacking underworld of Japan's disaffected youth.
- *Memoirs of a Geisha* (Arthur Golden) The modern classic that looks into the life of one of Japan's oddest professions.
- *The Noodle Maker* (Ma Jian) Stories of a professional blood donor from inside China's complex present.

FILMS
- *Lust, Caution* (2007) Taiwanese-born director Ang Lee tells an espionage tale set in WWII Shanghai.
- *Hero* (2002) A blockbuster where a single man takes on three assassins who are scheming to kill one of China's greatest warlords.
- *Kung Fu Hustle* (2004) A beat-them-up parody of martial-arts movies set in the gangster world of 1930s Shanghai.
- *Lost in Translation* (2003) Two Americans find themselves isolated in contemporary Tokyo and form a possibly creepy bond.
- *Ringu* (The Ring; 1998) This eerie Japanese horror film is about a video that sucks in viewers and has killer overdue fees. Remade into English.

SOUTHEAST ASIA

Ringing rickshaw bells, chanting monks and rumbling curried bellies – Southeast Asia is a jumble of convenience and inefficiency, spirituality and consumerism. Twenty-first century megacities such as Thailand's Bangkok and Malaysia's Kuala Lumpur exist alongside the postcolonial capitals of Vientiane (Laos) and Phnom Penh (Cambodia), both of which are slowly recovering from their turbulent histories.

Most visitors to Southeast Asia come for the wow-worthy beaches, occasionally dipping into jungle safaris or sampling the rich history of temples such as Angkor Wat (Cambodia) or Borobudur (Indonesia).

While there are loads of other travellers, you don't have to travel far to find 'undiscovered' Southeast Asia. The beaten path isn't very wide. Within the confines of even the most touristy towns are streets where only the locals go.

Some areas in this region have internal problems that may make travel unadvisable (see p41) at the time of research and you should check travel advisories before heading out, but many more countries have stable governments.

Wherever you decide to rest your pack, you'll join an illustrious list of Southeast Asian pilgrims, from Indian merchants, Chinese mandarins, European colonisers and modern globetrotters.

ITINERARIES

Most trips start from Bangkok, because the metropolis is central and usually has cheap inbound flights, but you can customise these trips to your own plans. Spend a few more days on the beach, go wild in the club scene or take a few extra days for a riverboat cruise – the choice is yours.

BEACH BUMMING

Get to **Bangkok**. When you're over Khao San Rd, hop on a bus south and do some beach bumming in the Gulf of Thailand. From the mainland town of **Surat Thani** you can choose between boats to resorty **Ko Samui**, hammock-friendly **Ko Pha-Ngan** or dive-paradise **Ko Tao**. After you've had your fill, step over to the Andaman beaches in upscale **Phuket**, where there's magnificent **Ko Phi Phi**, rock-climbing haven **Krabi** and navel-gazing retreat **Ko Lanta**. If you're after a secluded spot, try **Ko Tarutao National Marine Park**.

When you're done with Thailand, traverse the border into Malaysia at Satun and beeline for family-friendly **Pulau Langkawi** or continue by boat to **Georgetown**, a spicy port city. Bus from Butterworth to Kota Bharu, the gateway to the jungle islands of **Pulau Perhentian**. Chase the coastline south to Mersing and pop into beach

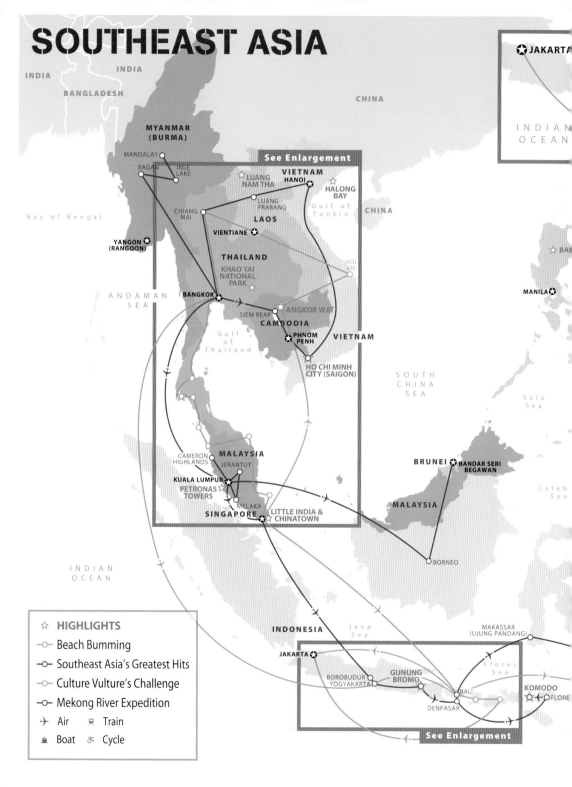

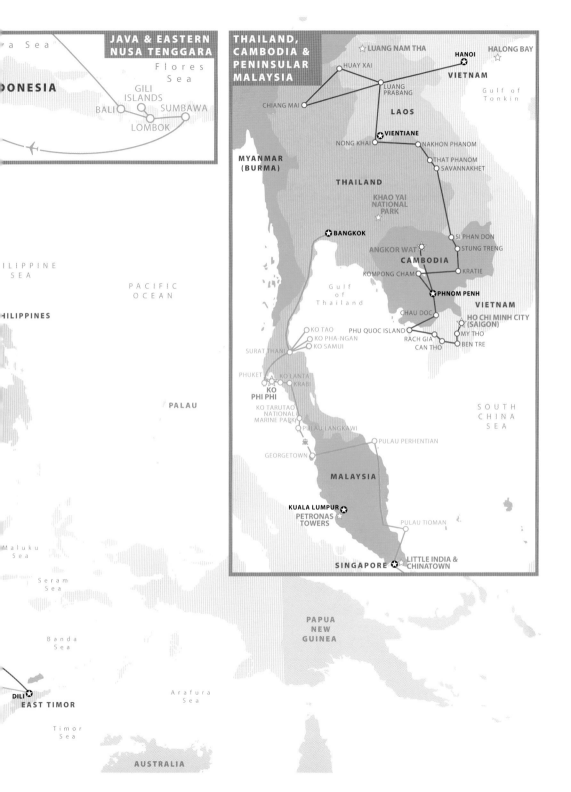

BEYOND THE METROPOLISES OF SOUTHEAST ASIA, TRADITIONAL COUNTRY LIFE CONTINUES, EVIDENCED BY CENTURIES-OLD FARMING TECHNIQUES.

ASY-SYAKIRIN MOSQUE AND THE PETRONAS TOWERS (SEE P214), KUALA LUMPUR, MALAYSIA, WHICH ARE AMONG THE WORLD'S TALLEST SKYSCRAPER

INDONESIA IS RENOWNED FOR ITS BEAUTIFUL BEACHES AND GREAT SURF LOCATIONS (P214), SUCH AS BINGIN, BALI, INDONESIA.

villages such as **Pulau Tioman** before taking a sand-shaking shower and hitting the town in **Singapore**. If your tan still needs topping up, fly to **Bali**, the sun-worshipping temple of the backpacker trail. Take a break from the crowds in **Lombok**, then ferry to **Gili Islands** for snorkelling among the brilliant reefs or catch the curl with surfing **Sumbawa**. Head back to **Jakarta** before you get sunstroke and fly out.

SOUTHEAST ASIA'S GREATEST HITS

Pack your MP3 player with travelling music in **Bangkok's** markets, then fly over to **Siem Reap** for a spin of Angkor's top temples. Take the bus south to **Phnom Penh**, the colonial capital that still has a faded charm. March to the communist beat in **Ho Chi Minh City**, though the city is playing catch-up capitalism these days. Navigate your way through the leafy boulevards of **Hanoi** before skipping the tracks over to **Luang Prabang**, Laos' temple epicentre. Fast-forward to **Chiang Mai** in Thailand, a cool pocket in the tropics, where you can hit pause for a while before heading back to **Bangkok**. From here you can choose the Myanmar playlist: the ruins of **Bagan**, the floating gardens and island monasteries of **Inle Lake**, and mysterious **Mandalay**; or fly straight to **Kuala Lumpur**.

Malaysia is at your fingertips, so decide if you'd like to take a bus to the hill station of Tanah Rata in the **Cameron Highlands** or head further on to the historic

A MOTORCYCLE CROSSING OF THIS BRIDGE OVER NAM SONG RIVER, LAOS, IS NOT FOR THE FAINT HEARTED.

port of **Melaka** then on to **Jerantut**, where long-tail boats dip into the rainforests of Taman Negara. Rewind back to **Kuala Lumpur** and fly on to **Borneo** through **Bandar Seri Begawan**, Brunei's capital, or skip to up-tempo **Singapore** which pulses to Indian, Malay and Chinese beats. Tune into Javanese heritage in **Yogyakarta** and go slack-jawed at **Borobudur**, the giant stupa that tops traveller's must-see charts. Next it's **Gunung Bromo**, an active volcano, before jetting over to **Denpasar** to chill out in **Bali** or soak up the sun in **Kuta**. Mix it up with Balinese culture in **Ubud**. Head back to Denpasar then take a flight to the stunning landscape of **Flores** before touring **Komodo**, the stomping ground of the namesake mini-Godzilla.

Reverse to Denpasar, then get into the rhythms of Sulawesi's capital **Makassar** before getting down to **Dili** in East Timor and on to Australia or Papua New Guinea. Alternatively, swing back to Singapore and take off to your next destination.

CULTURE VULTURE'S CHALLENGE

Begin in **Singapore** with a scramble through Little India, Chinatown, Malay-based Kampung Glam and the colonial area of Clarke Quay. This should whet your appetite for a deeper look into Asia's different cultures. Wing your way over to **Angkor Wat** (via Siem Reap) to admire the ancient temples, then head up to Vietnam's **Hoi An**, a living museum of a trading town turned colony.

Contrast this with a trip to **Vientiane** (Laos) to see traditional wood houses with colonial mansions and modern concrete monstrosities. Head up to **Chiang Mai**, famed for its moated old city that held off Burmese invaders more than 700 years ago. From here there are tours to Hill Tribe communities that have remained unchanged for decades. Backtrack to **Bangkok** and hop on a cheap flight over to **Yogyakarta**, the base for heading onto **Borobudur**, a Buddhist monument in the middle of the world's largest Islamic population. By now, you've earned a break so unwind in **Bali** before heading on via **Jakarta** or **Dili**.

MEKONG RIVER EXPEDITION

The Mekong River is known as the Father of Waters and it works hard throughout this region as a highway, marketplace and habitat. Swim upstream from Vietnam's flat delta to Thailand's hilly interior with a start in bustling **Ho Chi Minh City**. Catch a bus to **My Tho**, the gateway to the Mekong Delta. Charter a boat to rural **Ben Tre** and bus to the floating markets of **Can Tho**. Take a bus to **Rach Gia**, the jumping-off point to tranquil **Phu Quoc Island**, a good detour if you need to chillax.

Back on the mainland, catch a bus to **Chau Doc**, before floating into Cambodia at the Kaam Samnor–Vinh Xuong border crossing, all the way to the faded gentility of **Phnom Penh**. You could side-trip to **Angkor Wat** from here or stick with the river by bussing to **Kompong Cham** and speedboat to **Kratie**, home of the rare freshwater dolphin. Continue by boat north through the rocky rapids to **Stung Treng**, a transfer point into Laos via the Voen Kham border crossing and the 4000 river islands of **Si Phan Don**. Get a bus to **Savannakhet**, a border crossing into Thailand at Mukdahan.

Twist with the river's crook to the quiet hamlets of **That Phanom** and **Nakhon Phanom** to charming **Nong Khai**, another crossing point into Laos at Vientiane. Hop on a bus to bewitching **Luang Prabang**. Stick with the watery route northwest to **Huay Xai** to bust another border into northern Thailand, then continue south to **Chiang Mai**. Many travellers head east to **Hanoi**, continuing this journey on to Kunming in China's Yunnan Province (see p198).

WHAT TO DO?

HIGHLIGHTS

○ Discovering your top temple at **Angkor Wat** (Cambodia), vestige of the mighty Khmer empire.
○ Wandering between rice terraces carved out of the lush volcanic slopes of **Banaue** (Philippines).
○ Cruising between humpbacked limestone mountains rearing out of a sapphire sea in **Ko Phi Phi** (Thailand).
○ Grazing your way through **Little India** and **Chinatown** (Singapore) on street snacks and hawker treats in the great grub capital.
○ Exploring the remnants of the American War by day and partying in **Ho Chi Minh City's** (Vietnam) backpacker zone by night.

- Testing your vertigo at **Petronas Towers** (Malaysia), one of the world's tallest skyscrapers.
- Ecotrekking in the picturesque hill country around **Luang Nam Tha** (Laos).
- Bird-watching, waterfall paddling and trekking 'til you drop at **Khao Yai National Park** (Thailand).
- Meeting the world's biggest lizards in eponymous **Komodo** (Indonesia).
- Navigating an old-school junk through the karst peaks of **Halong Bay** (Vietnam).

GET ACTIVE

Activities in Southeast Asia are all about the water or heading into the jungle to discover tough terrain or rare beasties. Whatever you do, search for qualified operators who are going to do the right thing by you and the environment.

Diving, Rafting & Other Water Sports

Gin-clear waters and dazzling coral reefs make Southeast Asia a must for aquaholics. Thailand owns the diving crown, thanks to its accessibility and budget-friendly PADI-certificate courses, particularly on the east-coast island of Ko Tao. From Phuket, on the west coast, live-aboard trips go to the uninhabited Similan Islands. Indonesia gets second prize with Bali offering a variety of dives and live-aboard plunges around Komodo and Flores. If you're after a little fauna with your aqua, the seas around Sulawesi abound with sharks and turtles. The Philippines also has a wealth of underwater action around Boracay, Alona Beach (Panglao Island, off the coast of Bohol), Puerto Princesa (Palawan) and the island of Apo.

The rivers of Southeast Asia are curved and cut perfectly for white-water rafting. Good spots include Java's Suyugai Citarak (Citarak River), bordering Gunung Halimun National Park near Bogor, and Bali. There's also kayaking and tubing on the white-water rivers around Vang Vieng (Laos). For a change of pace, rafting trips on large bamboo 'house rafts' drift down a number of rivers in northern Thailand around Pai, Fang and Tha Ton.

Surfing

If you've ever seen a surf movie with thundering waves and drool-worthy breaks, it was probably filmed in Indonesia, one of the world's wildest surf destinations. Top spots include the Bukit Peninsula in Bali, Java's G-Land (Grajagan on the southeastern tip), Pulau Nias in northern Sumatra and the Nusa Tenggara islands. Windsurfing is possible in the southern resorts of Bali. Elsewhere, the breaks off Siargao Island (Philippines) reach Hawaiian heights between October and May. Kuta in Bali is a famous spot, but there's surf right along the south coast of the inner islands – from Sumatra through to Sumbawa, and Sumba across to Papua. Pulau Nias, off the coast of Sumatra, is another beloved place.

Trekking

Like the sound of scaling volcanoes or visiting minority hill-tribe villages? Then it could be that Southeast Asia is the place for you. In Indonesia, you can trek Sumatra's volcanic peaks in Berastagi. Java's volcanic peaks, such as Gunung Merapi, can be a taxing climb, while spectacular Gunung Bromo is more of a stroll. Gunung Batur and Gunung Agung volcanoes in Bali are popular day trips. To see the destruction wrought by Mt Taal, a tiny volcano that packs a punch, take a boat tour around the incongruously picturesque lake. The volcano that dominates Lombok, Gunung Rinjani (3726m), offers a strenuous but worthwhile three-day jaunt.

Too hot to handle? Indonesia is a world-renowned destination for cool jungle treks, thanks to its huge tracts of uninhabited rainforest, second in size to Brazil's. There are more adventurous jungle-trekking opportunities in Kalimantan and Papua (Irian Jaya). Despite intense logging in Malaysia, Taman Negara National Park is a primal delight with deep, dark jungles, canopy walks and lots of insects. Sabah's main event is a climb to the top of Mt Kinabalu (4101m), which is half the height of Mt Everest.

In the mountainous regions of northern Thailand (Chiang Mai, Mae Hong Son and Chiang Rai), Laos (Luang Nam Tha) and Vietnam (Sapa), minority hill-tribe communities make popular trekking destinations.

Cycling & Motorbiking

Touring the region by bicycle is becoming more popular and many travellers combine cycling with buses for the boring or challenging stretches, or they take organised cycling tours. For long-distance touring, bring your own bike and gear, as bike shops aren't widespread or well stocked. In towns throughout the region, guesthouses rent out rickety bicycles for day trips.

Hands down, Vietnam is the most spectacular country in the region for cycle-touring, as the north–south highway predominately hugs the coast. Cycling is a great way to take advantage of the terrain in northern Vietnam (around Sapa) and Laos, and traffic is pretty light. Malaysia and Thailand also have viable touring routes, especially along the peninsula and the relatively flat terrain of the Mekong River. In the Philippines, areas around Moalboal on Cebu, and Guimaras Island, are other popular options. **Mr Pumpy** (www.mrpumpy.net) is a good place to start looking at routes and planning your two-wheeled odyssey.

Experienced bushbashing motorcyclists prize the rough roads of Cambodia, Laos and northern Thailand. You'll hear the put-put of a motorbike in most places you visit in the area, and many travellers hire a motorbike for excursions. Before hiring you'll need to give the bike a quick once-over (check tyre tread and obvious oil leaks), and pack some sunglasses in case goggles aren't supplied.

WILDLIFE

You'll definitely spot monkeys if you spend any time in Southeast Asia, usually cheekily swiping your lunch on hiking trails or around temples. In Sumatra and Kalimantan, look out for orang-utans, the only great ape species outside Africa. If you think you've seen birds, wait until you get to Thailand, which has more than 1000 different species. Then there are Borneo's rainforests that hide freakish fauna such as the hornbill, pygmy elephant and the extremely rare Bornean rhinoceros. Indonesia's east has the famous Komodo dragon and the cute Papuan tree kangaroo. Best of all, elephants are still ridden in parts of Thailand, Cambodia and Laos, so you can bounce your way on a mahout safari.

FESTIVALS

Religious festivals – Buddhist, Muslim and Christian – dominate the calendar in Southeast Asia. Here are a few highlights:

○ **Black Nazarene Procession** (Philippines) Locals prance a life-size statue of Jesus through the streets of Manila's Quiapo district on 9 January.

○ **Ati-Atihan** (Philippines) A three-day Mardi Gras celebrated on Panay in the third week of January.

○ **Chinese New Year** Widely celebrated in January or February with fireworks and parades in Bangkok (Thailand), Kuala Lumpur (Malaysia), Singapore and other Chinese communities.

○ **Tet** (Vietnam) Celebrates the lunar new year with large family gatherings and prolonged business closings.

○ **Lunar New Year** (Thailand, Cambodia, Laos) Celebrated in spring this water festival is an excuse to douse people in a huge water fight. Bangkok and Chiang Mai call it Songkran.

○ **Bun Bang Fai** (Laos) May's rocket festival is an animist celebration with processions and firing of bamboo rockets to prompt rain. A similar festival is held in northern Thailand.

○ **Tiet Doan Ngo** (Vietnam) Summer Solstice Day in June sees the burning of human effigies to satisfy the need for souls to serve in the army of the god of death.

○ **Trung Nguyen** (Vietnam) Wandering Souls' Day is held on the 15th day of the seventh moon (August); offerings are given to the wandering souls of the forgotten dead.

○ **Independence Day** (Indonesia) Marks the archipelago's release from colonialism on 17 August; fireworks and parades light up across the country.

○ **MassKara** (Philippines) Many Faces Festival is held in mid-October in Bacolod on Negros, filling the streets with dancing parades of oversized, smiling masked faces.

○ **Festival of Lights** (Myanmar) Celebrates the end of Buddhist Lent by illuminating the streets and houses with electric lights and paper lanterns.

○ **Bon Om Tuk** (Cambodia) The most important Khmer festival honours the wet season's end in early November.

○ **Elephant Roundup** (Thailand) Held in Surin during November; lumbering pachyderms indulge in races, tugs-of-war and football.

○ **Ramadan** (Malaysia, Indonesia, Brunei and southern Thailand) The Muslim fasting month requires believers to abstain from food, drink and sex between sunrise and sunset during the 9th month of the Islamic calendar.

PARTY SCENE

Pack your dance shoes – Southeast Asia is definitely a party place. Scenes rise and fall, but Bangkok and Jakarta have long been hotspots. Jakarta's Kota district is famous for its 'temples of trance' and ecstasy-fuelled weekenders. The massive Stadium club holds 4000 and runs the whole 48 hours of the weekend.

Bangkok's sometimes sleazy scene is massive, though smaller clubs are given over to 'working girls' and strip shows (steer clear of the area around Soi Patpong to avoid any confusion). Many Westerners prefer to head south to Ko Pha-Ngan and other coastal spots for the tribal full-moon parties. Singapore's scene is superclean with a strong drug-free element, while Vietnam offers booty-shaking in Hanoi and Ho Chi Minh City, particularly at the irony-laden Apocalypse Now clubs.

ROADS LESS TRAVELLED

Shhhh…there are still a few secret spots in Southeast Asia where you can find a beach to yourself. In Thailand, the underdeveloped beaches of Ko Tarutao National Marine Park won't be too crowded, and coastal Sihanoukville in Cambodia is a little further off the backpacker trail. You could try working your way up Vietnam's east coast to find a spot where you can unfurl a towel without anyone else on the beach. Similarly, the Philippines can be too far for some travellers, so you can often find quieter pockets.

COURSES

There are loads of courses you can do in the region, from the indulgence of a Vietnamese cooking course to the spiritual instruction of meditation to getting superfit with *muay thai* (Thai boxing). The **Council on International Educational Exchange** (www.ciee.org/study) is a good place to start as they offer programs in language, art and culture in Thailand and Vietnam, which are hosted by local universities.

WORKING

When you start to run out of cash, there are a few job opportunities in Southeast Asia, though local currency won't travel as well as what you might be paid at home.

Many expats (expatriates, who live outside their own country) survive in the region by teaching English. The pay may not be rewarding but you will get to interact with locals and make some friends. Bangkok, Ho Chi Minh City and Jakarta all have several language schools you can try. A good place to start looking for jobs and collecting information can also be **Dave's ESL Cafe** (http://eslcafe.com), a good source of information on work in the region.

If you've arranged work before leaving, you'll need to have organised the appropriate paperwork in your home country. Many visitors, however, just show up and organise work visas when they find work. Arrangements can be even more informal if you're working in a hostel, in a bar or as a dive instructor.

Alternatively, you could consider volunteering to give something back to the region (see p143).

WHEN TO GO?

Most of Southeast Asia, with the exception of northern Myanmar, lies within the tropics. You can expect warm or downright hot weather, with high humidity in lowland areas.

Mainland Southeast Asia (Thailand, Laos, Myanmar, Cambodia and Vietnam) experiences a three-season climate – cool and dry from November to March (average temperature 25°C/77°F to 30°C/86°F), followed by hot and dry from March to May (average temperature 30°C/86°F to 35°C/95°F), and hot and rainy from June to October (average temperature 25°C/77°F to 30°C/86°F). Highland areas are significantly cooler than the lowlands; for example, Hanoi is 5°C/9°F to 10°C/18°F cooler than Bangkok.

Oceanic Southeast Asia (southern Thailand, Myanmar, Brunei, Indonesia, Malaysia and Singapore) experiences two monsoons annually: one from the northeast (usually between October and April) and one from the southwest (between May and September). Rain is usually heavier during the northeast monsoon. Often you'll find better weather simply by crossing from one side of the island or country to the other. Travel is limited only during the peaks of the rainy season.

HE RICE TERRACES OF BANAUE (P213), PHILIPPINES, HAVE SERVED AS THE LOCALS' GARDENS FOR 2000 YEARS.

WHAT TO EXPECT?

LOCALS & OTHER TRAVELLERS

You can expect to see plenty of other travellers in Southeast Asia as it's a convenient holiday spot for many Australians and Asians. Lots of Brits and Europeans (particularly Scandinavians, Dutch and Germans) use it as a stopover on a round-the-world trip. Many French travellers pay homage to the former colonies of Vietnam, Laos and Cambodia. North Americans are discovering bigger destinations like Thailand and Vietnam. The east-coast islands of Thailand, especially Ko Tao and Ko Pha-Ngan, rank high with the twenty-somethings, with Ko Pha-Ngan famous for trippy full-moon raves. While stunningly beautiful, Phuket and Ko Samui attract older crowds (and larger wallets).

By and large, locals are curious about travellers and fire questions at you if you speak a common language.

The questions aren't nosey, they're measures for placing outsiders into their highly hierarchical society. Your status (primarily your age, but also your wealth) determines how much deference should be afforded to you. Also, chitchat is a well-practised art in the region and those who take the time to talk to you are extending their famed hospitality.

Unlike Western cultures which prize individuality, Asian cultures value the homogeneity, and the group, particularly the family, is paramount. The concept of 'face' – avoiding embarrassment for yourself or the group – is a guiding principle in social interactions. This translates into a host of baffling behaviours – sometimes locals will give incorrect information just to avoid admitting that they don't know something. Often the vaguer the answer, the closer you are treading to a face-saving game. Showing anger is a sure-fire way to make everyone lose face and is avoided at all costs. A better tool is a smile, which will be used when the bus breaks down and as a gracious excuse for minor cultural gaffes (such as putting your feet on chairs or tables, a no-no in this foot-phobic culture). A smile will endear you to market ladies, children and even water buffalo, but path-blocking monkeys and stray dogs are immune.

To avoid offence you should respect the 'sacred cows': the government, religion, and monarchy (in Thailand). Any negative opinions should be kept to yourself, even if you think no-one around understands English. Dress is an often overlooked cause of offence. Hot temperatures may make you feel like wearing skimpy clothing, but in Southeast Asia exposing your body may cause offence. You should wear clothes that cover to your elbows and knees, or even further in Muslim countries, where female visitors should even consider covering their heads (especially in rural areas). Standards are relaxed on the beaches due to tourist inundation, but topless sunbathing will draw a crowd of unabashed, gawking men and should be avoided.

FOOD
Prepare for some lip-smacking goodness as Southeast Asia has some of the most exciting dining you'll find anywhere in the world. Rice and fish are the basics, but chillies pep up most meals. Feel their kick in *sambal* (fried chilli and prawn paste) from Indonesia and Malaysia, or Thailand's *naam phrik* (chilli paste). Hotheads should also look out for Indian-inspired curries that crept south with migration. Noodles are another big travelling food, originally coming from China but reinterpreted in Malaysia's soupy *laksa*

(noodles in spicy coconut soup) and Vietnam's beefy signature dish, *pho* (beef-noodle soup).

With every country there's another 'must-try'. The Philippines has *adobo*, a stew that has Spanish influences but tastes of Filipino playfulness. The roadside favourite in Vietnam is the spring roll, stuffed with prawns, basil and mint. We could go on – green curries, chilli crab, banana pancakes and mango smoothies almost everywhere – if only our bellies and bursting belts would allow. There are a few culinary cautions to keep your adventures illness-free (see p46), but apart from these simple rules, eat up.

LANGUAGE
Linguistically, Southeast Asia has several different languages, including Thai, Bahasa (in Indonesia and Malaysia), Khmer (in Cambodia), Lao, Vietnamese and several hundred subdialects. That's the bad news. On the upside, in bigger, cosmopolitan cities (such as Bangkok, Singapore and Kuala Lumpur), you can get by with English. Less-developed nations such as Cambodia and Laos may present problems for English-only speakers and you'll probably need a phrasebook. In countries with large numbers of tourists, you'll find locals wanting to practice their English with you. Although it's fun at first, you might get frustrated with telling people your name, where you're from and answering the same clichéd questions.

You'll definitely get more out of your trip if you learn a few words and locals will appreciate you making the effort. Try the Lonely Planet phrasebooks if you want to master the lingo. The *Southeast Asia Phrasebook* is tailored for trips that cover several countries in the region.

COMMUNICATION

Most of Southeast Asia has internet access though wi-fi comes with a 'business' price tag. You might find mobile coverage dubious in some less-developed countries. Thailand and Malaysia probably have services similar to what you'd expect at home, while in Singapore they're probably a few steps ahead. Myanmar has government restrictions on some websites and restricts access to some email sites.

SAMPLE COSTS

	THAILAND (BAHT B)	SINGAPORE (SINGAPORE DOLLAR S$)	CAMBODIA (US$ OR RIEL CR)	INDONESIA (RUPIAH RP)	MYANMAR (KYAT K)
HOSTEL/ BUDGET ROOM	130–300B £2.20–5 US$4.20–9.70 A$4.80–11	S$30–60 £10.60–21 US$21–42 A$24–48	US$10–20 £5–10 A$11–23	RP15,000–50,000 £0.80–2.70 US$1.60–5.25 A$1.80–6	£5–8 US$10–16 A$11.50–18.50
CHEAP RESTAURANT MEAL	25–180B £0.40–3 US$0.80–5.80 A$1–6.70	S$3–20 £1–7 US$2–14 A$2.40–16	US$2–6 £1–3 A$2.50–7	RP3000–20,000 £0.15–1 US$0.30–2.10 A$0.35–2.40	£0.5–1 US$1–2 A$1.20–2.50
1L BOTTLE OF WATER	5–10B £0.08 US$0.16–0.32 A$0.20–40	S$0.90 £0.30 US$0.62 A$0.72	CR500–2000 US$0.12–0.50 £0.06–0.25 A$0.14–0.60	RP2000–4000 £0.10–0.20 US$0.20–0.40 A$0.25–50	K200 £0.10 US$0.20 A$0.25
SOUVENIR T-SHIRT	300B £5 US$10 A$11	S$13 £4.80 US$9.50 A$10	US$2 £1 A$2.50	RP20,000 £1 US$2.10 A$2.40	N/A
BOTTLE OF BEER	150B £2.50 US$4.75 A$5.60	S$8 £2.80 US$5.50 A$6.40	US$1.50–2.50 £0.75–1.25 A$1.70–2.90	RP15,000–25,000 £0.80–1.35 US$1.60–2.65 A$1.80–3	K1000–1500 £0.50–0.75 US$1–1.50 A$1.20–1.70
STREET SNACK	Serve of curry puffs 25–30B £0.40–0.50 US$0.80–1 A$1–1.10	Hawker noodles S$4 £1.40 US$2.80 A$3.20	Noodle soup CR2000–4000 US$0.50–1.00 £0.25–0.50 A$0.60–1.20	Market noodles or deep-fried cricket RP3000–8000 £0.15–0.45 US$0.30–0.85 A$0.35–1	Street noodles K150–250 £0.07–0.12 US$0.15–0.25 A$0.17–0.30
1L PETROL	25B £0.40 US$0.80 A$1	S$1.80 £0.67 US$1.35 A$1.40	CR3000 US$0.75 £0.40 A$0.90	RP4500 £0.25 US$0.45 A$0.55	K1000–2000 £0.50–1 US$1–2 A$1.20–2.50

COSTS

The most stable currencies are the Thai baht, Singapore dollar, Malaysian ringgit, Indonesian rupiah and Philippine peso. The local currencies of Vietnam (dong), Cambodia (riel), Laos (kip) and Myanmar (kyat) are used for small purchases on the street, but US dollars act as the second currency and are required for larger purchases (lodging and transport).

The table on p219 is useful as a planning guide only. Please don't use it to haggle with hotel owners – they really don't like that.

HEALTH

Get your arm ready to be pin-cushioned, because the World Health Organization recommends quite a few jabs before any travel to Southeast Asia. Start planning for vaccines eight weeks in advance and check with your travel clinic on current recommendations. At the time of writing the following made the list: diphtheria, tetanus, hepatitis A and B, measles, mumps, rubella and typhoid. Further vaccinations are recommended for travellers remaining in the region for longer than a month. Mosquito-borne diseases such as dengue fever, Japanese B encephalitis and malaria are a problem in certain rural areas.

Amoebic dysentery, giardiasis and traveller's diarrhoea often have the same initial symptoms – rushed trips to the bathroom. Rabies is a concern in the region as well. HIV/AIDS is now one of the most common causes of death in people under the age of 50 in Thailand. The epidemic is worsening in Cambodia, Myanmar and Vietnam. Heterosexual sex is the primary method of transmission, and most of these countries have unregulated sex industries.

Consult the Health & Safety chapter (p41) and seek professional medical advice for more travel-health information.

ISSUES

Every family has its problem child and the vast clan of Southeast Asia is no exception. Some nations have more headlines than actual incidents, but it's worth keeping an eye on the news in any country you're going to visit. It can also be worth checking warnings about the region from government bodies (see p41). The key is to be informed, not paranoid.

Thailand's Muslim separatists targeted tourist areas with bombings on New Year's Eve 2006, and areas in the remote southern provinces (Narathiwat, Yala, Pattani and Songkhla) can be dangerous. Similarly, the Thai–Myanmar border sees periodic border stoushes that make the area dangerous to travel in.

In Indonesia there are several active cells of the militant Islamic group, Jemaah Islamiyah (JI), which is responsible for atrocities such as the Bali bombings of 2002 and 2005, and the bombing of Jakarta's Australian Embassy in 2005. While the group seems to have slowed its activities at the time of writing, they are making tourism to areas such as Bali, Maluku Province and Central Sulawesi Province more difficult. Areas around East Timor's border are also volatile and visitors should have a close look at security warnings.

Insurgents in the Philippines also mean travel to Mindanao and Sulu archipelago is unsafe, though the security is improving. Check updates on government advisory sites for the latest.

With all these military problems, it seems insane that some travellers would make their trip even more risky

---

🦇 URBAN MYTHS – YABA DABA DON'T

Southeast Asia's backpacker trail is always whispering about the 'ultimate high' drug. Last time we checked it was yaba (or yama in Cambodia), the legendary drug that was reputedly invented by the Nazis to keep troops awake. What's sold under this name is usually a grubby mix that can include home-made methamphetamines produced in back-yard labs. Pills are often laced with heroin offcuts, mercury, lithium or whatever else the maker can find. Yaba is more addictive than users would like to admit, provoking powerful hallucinations (including the sensation of bugs crawling under the skin), sleep deprivation, psychosis and even suicidal urges. Like everything else about the Nazis, it's really past its use-by date unless your idea of the ultimate high is six feet under.

---

by smuggling drugs into countries such as Singapore and Malaysia, where it's not just illegal but can carry the death penalty. The so-called Golden Triangle of opium production is cleaning up its act, but it's targeting travellers rather than growers and dealers. And that means marijuana too. 'Soft' drugs can carry hard penalties for possession, including jail terms in Thailand, and in Indonesia not reporting possession can be a chargeable offence. Several high-profile cases (Australians will know the Bali Nine and Schapelle Corby cases) have been harsh lessons for travellers who didn't know the laws of the countries they were visiting and assumed that their own country would protect them. Simply put: they won't. Everyone wants to have a good time, but be aware of the risks by checking out warnings in guidebooks.

Attitudes towards women vary greatly across the region. Gender equality is reasonable in Singapore, Thailand and the Philippines, but Indonesia is an almost 'prefeminist' state. In Buddhist Indochina, solo women travellers are often perceived as a little odd, though this doesn't create hassles. In Indonesia the sight of solo women travellers can be found provocative and Western women are often perceived as 'loose'. Men and women should pay special attention to proper attire and behaviour required in the various temples and mosques across the region.

GETTING THERE

Southeast Asia has long been a hub of world travel with two key colonial ports (Bangkok and Singapore) that have made way to central airports in the jet age. Overland routes through the region were popularised during the flower-powered 1960s, but today many travellers use Asia as a stopover.

AIR
The major airports of Bangkok, Kuala Lumpur and Singapore are buzzing with aircraft, many refuelling on long-haul flights. Direct flights into these cities are frequent, so if you're flying on to Vietnam, Cambodia, the Philippines, Indonesia or Thailand it can be cheaper to catch a budget flight on from these hubs. Hong Kong is also a good entry point, with several budget carriers flying on from there.

Major players include:

- **British Airways** (BA; www.britishairways.com)
- **Cathay Pacific** (www.cathaypacific.com)
- **Garuda** (www.garuda-indonesia.com)
- **Malaysia Airlines** (www.malaysiaairlines.com)
- **Qantas** (www.qantas.com)
- **Singapore Airlines** (www.singaporeair.com)
- **Thai Airways International** (www.thaiair.com)

Budget options include:

- **Air Asia** (www.airasia.com)
- **Jetstar Asia** (www.jetstarasia.com)
- **One-Two-Go Airlines** (www.fly12go.com)
- **Pacific Airlines** (http://pacificairlines.com.vn)
- **Tiger Airways** (www.tigerairways.com)

SEA & OVERLAND
There are no passenger ferries into Southeast Asia, which means you'll have to fly between Southeast Asia and your next stop. There's always the chance, though, to pick up berths on yachts heading from Southeast Asia to Australia. The **Darwin to Ambon Yacht Race** (www.darwinambonrace.com.au) is a good place to start. Working your way overland to China through Vietnam is popular, and another route to try is across into India.

BEYOND SOUTHEAST ASIA

Travelling along the Mekong River, many travellers are heading north into China. Laos, Vietnam and, theoretically, Myanmar all have border crossings with China, though political differences can make this difficult, particularly in Myanmar, which can also serve as an excellent land-based route into India. Heading south you can hop across the Indonesian Archipelago into East Timor, then into Australia's remote north or over to Papua New Guinea as an entry point into the Pacific isles.

FURTHER INFORMATION

WEBSITES
- **Asia Times** (www.atimes.com) A news site with long articles and a vaguely US perspective.

- **Cambodian Information Center** (www.cambodia.org) Comprehensive list of links on culture, government and current events.
- **Ecology Asia** (www.ecologyasia.com) Profile of the region's flora, fauna and eco-organisations.
- **Indonesian homepage** (http://indonesia.elga.net.id) A great introduction to Indonesian culture, food and citizens' web pages.
- **Myanmar** (http://www.myanmar.com) A government-centric site that nonetheless has good general content.
- **Tanikalang Ginto** (www.filipinolinks.com) Largest web directory of Philippines-related online sites.
- **ThingsAsian** (www.thingsasian.com) Good portal to the whole region.
- **VientianeTimes.com** (http://www.vientianetimes.com) Not the official government mouthpiece that it first appears to be.
- **Vietnam Adventures** (www.vietnamadventures.com) Practical information on adventure travel.
- **Visit Mekong** (www.visit-mekong.com) General site on touring the Mekong River, the region's lifeblood.

- *Sightseeing* (Rattawut Lapcharoensap) A punchy collection of stories from a Thai-born American that looks inside modern Thailand.
- *The Sorrow of War* (Bao Ninh) A North Vietnamese perspective on the American War.
- *This Earth of Mankind* (Pramoedya Ananta Toer) The controversial (it was banned) recapturing of 100 years of Indonesia's colonial period.

FILMS
- *The Beach* (2001) A backpacker's search for an island paradise goes pear-shaped when the commune becomes a cult.
- *The Quiet American* (2002) The battle for 'hearts and minds' in the lead-up to Vietnam's conflict.
- *The Daughter from Danang* (2002) A harrowing documentary about a woman sent to the US for adoption as a child and her return to Vietnam.
- *Bombies* (2001) Looks at the legacy of unexploded ordnances left by the secret US war in Laos.
- *Mekong Full Moon Party* (2002) Takes a critical look at Thailand's spiritual faith being challenged by modern technological scepticism.

SWAP SHOPS

Book swaps are common on the Southeast Asian trail, so you'll rarely be without the printed word. At hostels and shops you can usually bring a book in and trade it for another. While the range may not be great, you'll definitely be able to read something. Recently, MP3 shops have begun to appear, offering music files for your iPod.

BOOKS
- *Tales from a Broad* (Fran Lebowitz) A woman's tale of charming her way around Singapore's expat community with more than a dash of sass.
- *Into the Heart of Borneo* (Redmond O'Hanlon) A cheerfully ill-prepared naturalist treks through the jungle into the remote interior of the island.
- *First They Killed My Father* (Luong Ung) A sometimes-harrowing tale of the Khmer Rouge coming to power as seen by an urban Cambodian family.

THE INDIAN SUBCONTINENT

Epic, squalid, triumphant and disastrous, the Indian subcontinent provides one of the world's most powerful travel experiences. This is the home of the highest, wettest, most remote and most crowded places on the planet. The range of experiences is breathtaking and intimidating – tiger-hiding jungles abutted by impenetrable concrete megalopolises, a new-found friend sharing his meagre meal alongside a scammer after your wallet, starving orphans in the streets trodden over by billionaires in Prada. It's intense.

India remains the region's epicentre. As political troubles in neighbouring Nepal, Pakistan and Sri Lanka take their toll on tourism stats, India continues to tear along frenetically. It's still cheap – the cost of food, transport and admission to many sights is rock bottom – but economic growth has changed the face of the region. Backpackers will find startlingly cutting-edge art and music scenes in the cities to go along with their temple visits and *chai*-sipping stints. But the quintessential subcontinental experience remains unchanged: a spiritual journey through mountains, rainforests, deserts and choked cities that culminates in jarring self-discovery.

The subcontinent is not for everyone. In most of the region, the crush of humanity and poverty is overwhelming. This, combined with the endless scams and the notorious bouts of Delhi belly, is enough to send unprepared travellers packing within days. In addition, violence afflicts several parts of the subcontinent.

But if you're up for it, the bustle and energy are addictive and the journey mind-blowing. After you've spent time on the subcontinent, other regions feel like they have the sound turned down and the lights dimmed. In the end, no-one goes away unchanged.

ITINERARIES

Most trips start from one of India's urban centres, but you can pick up the trail anywhere along the way.

EAST, NORTH OR WEST FROM DELHI

The following itineraries cram some must-have North India experiences into a packed trip. Start off contemplating **Delhi's** beautiful atmospheric Old City and many monuments before training off to Agra to witness India's signature memorial, the **Taj Mahal**. Make a detour to the ghostly abandoned city of **Fatehpur Sikri**, then head to **Khajuraho** for a peek at its risqué, erotic temples. Next, go farther east to the spiritual centre of **Varanasi**. From here you can make your way to **Kolkata** and then hop over to **Bangladesh**.

INDIAN SUBCONTINENT

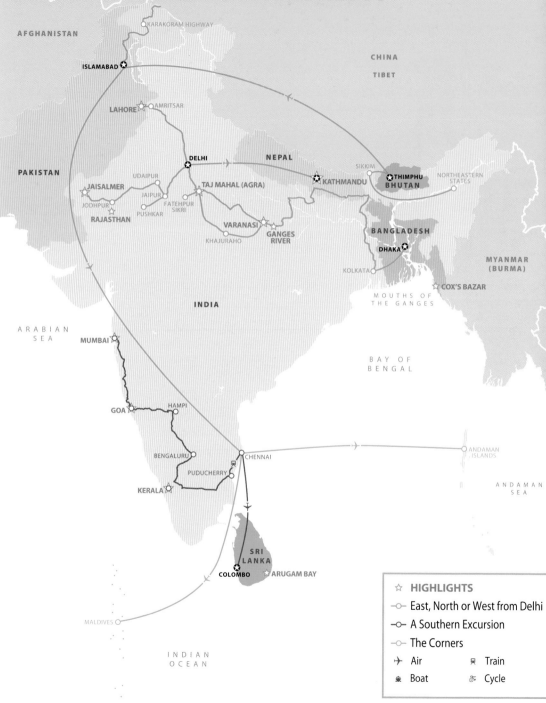

AFGHANISTAN

CHINA

TIBET

KARAKORAM HIGHWAY

ISLAMABAD

LAHORE • AMRITSAR

PAKISTAN

DELHI

NEPAL

SIKKIM

THIMPHU
BHUTAN

NORTHEASTERN
STATES

KATHMANDU

JAISALMER

UDAIPUR

JAIPUR

JODHPUR   FATEHPUR
PUSHKAR   SIKRI

RAJASTHAN

TAJ MAHAL (AGRA)

VARANASI

KHAJURAHO

GANGES
RIVER

BANGLADESH

DHAKA

MYANMAR
(BURMA)

KOLKATA

COX'S BAZAR

INDIA

MOUTHS OF
THE GANGES

ARABIAN
SEA

MUMBAI

BAY OF
BENGAL

GOA

HAMPI

BENGALURU

CHENNAI

PUDUCHERRY

KERALA

ANDAMAN
ISLANDS

ANDAMAN
SEA

SRI
LANKA

COLOMBO   ARUGAM BAY

MALDIVES

INDIAN
OCEAN

HIGHLIGHTS
- ○ East, North or West from Delhi
- ○ A Southern Excursion
- ○ The Corners
- ✈ Air
- ⚓ Boat
- 🚲 Train
- 🚲 Cycle

Alternatively, if you want to head towards Pakistan from Delhi, make your way through the Punjab to **Amritsar** and pause for a moment at the **Golden Temple**. Observe the entertaining one-upmanship at the India–Pakistan border before heading into **Lahore** to begin your exploration of Pakistan.

Of course, the most popular trip through the area goes through **Rajasthan**. From Delhi, take the train to **Jaipur**, from where you can hit **Amber Fort** and **Ranthambore National Park** – probably your best chance to see a tiger in the wild. Bus over to **Pushkar** and **Udaipur** for temples, palaces and lakeside relaxation. Next stop is **Jodhpur**, then on through the desert (perhaps by camel) to the ancient fortress of **Jaisalmer**.

Once you're back in Delhi, it's easy to catch a cheap flight up to **Kathmandu**, Nepal, to begin your trekking adventure.

A SOUTHERN EXCURSION

Mumbai is the easiest starting point for exploring India's steamy southern tip. Kick off in its cosmopolitan restaurants, nightspots and shops, then sashay south to **Goa's** lazy palm-fringed beaches. Head inland to historical, ruined **Hampi** and chill with yuppies in **Bengaluru**. Next, cruise south to **Kerala** and spend endless days on its languorous backwaters. Move over to French-flavoured **Puducherry** before catching a train to **Chennai**. Fill up on *idli* (spongy, round fermented rice cake) and finish up with a flight to **Colombo**, the starting point for your Sri Lankan holiday.

THE CORNERS

Feeling particularly intrepid? Head for the corners: the area's northeast, northwest, southeast and southwest. India's **northeastern states** (Assam and the surrounding regions) rarely see foreign travellers and provide amazing cultural diversity. The northeast also holds the incredible mountain state of **Sikkim** and mysterious neighbouring **Bhutan** – good luck getting a permit!

In the northwest, Pakistan's **Karakoram Highway** is the main draw. It's awe-inspiring and unforgettable, but it's also dangerous.

You can almost completely escape the travel crush with several lazy days on India's **Andaman Islands**. A flight from Chennai gets you there in hours.

Finally, if resorts are your style, jump off India's southwest coast and kick back in the **Maldives**.

WHAT TO DO?

HIGHLIGHTS

- Exploring endless sands by camel, starting from the honey-coloured fort at **Jaisalmer** (Rajasthan, India).
- Basking in the shade of the milky **Taj Mahal** (Agra, India), the ultimate monument to love.
- Soothing your soul with a gentle boat ride along the sacred ghat-lined **Ganges** (Varanasi, India).
- Diving into **Mumbai**, India's wild and wonderful melting pot.
- Kicking back on a languid boat cruise through the palm-fringed **Keralan** (south India) backwaters.
- Lying on the sand by day and dancing the night away on **Goa's** (west India) beaches.
- Exploring the laid-back beaches around **Cox's Bazar** (Bangladesh).
- Immersing yourself in **Kathmandu** (Nepal), one of the world's most backpacker-friendly cities.
- Spotting leopards, treading the mangrove forests and catching the waves at **Arugam Bay** (Sri Lanka).
- Spinning out with Sufis and experiencing some Mughal magic in **Lahore** (Pakistan).

GET ACTIVE

Even the simplest task (such as visiting temples) can be a major activity in North India and Nepal, where sheer mountain sides and winding paths demand fitness.

Ruins & Temples

The Taj Mahal, in Agra, is one of the few 'unmissable' experiences in life that isn't a letdown. More Mughal architecture abounds nearby at Fatehpur Sikri, in Delhi and in most of the towns in Rajasthan. Pakistan is also famous for its Mughal architecture, particularly around Multan and Lahore.

A good starting point for temple buffs is Nepal's Kathmandu Valley. In India, top spots include the erotic temples of Khajuraho and the ruins at Hampi.

Gompas (Buddhist monasteries) can be found all over north India, in Nepal and Bhutan and also in Pakistan and Bangladesh. The most impressive monasteries are

ENJOY A SPOT OF SHOPPING IN BETWEEN SUNBATHING AND PARTYING IN GOA, INDIA (SEE P225).

MEET SOME OF THE LOCALS AND EXPERIENCE NEPALI LIFE AT STOPS ALONG THE ANNAPURNA CIRCUIT (SEE P228), NEPAL.

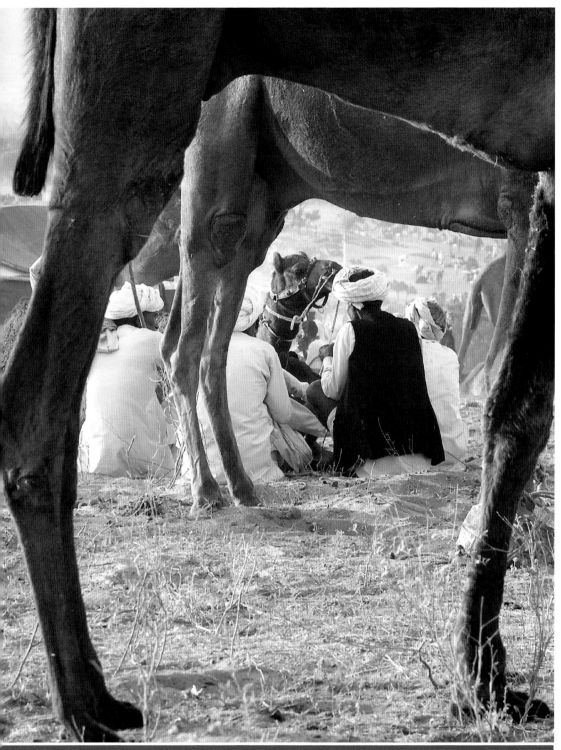

in Nepal and Bhutan, and in Sikkim, Arunachal Pradesh and Leh in India.

A different kind of Buddhist architecture is found in Sri Lanka. The most famous monuments in Sri Lanka are the giant Buddha statues at Gal Vihara and the Sri Dalada Maligwara temple in Kandy.

Trekking & Mountaineering

Now you're talking. Compared with the Himalaya, other mountain ranges aren't even trying. The world's highest mountains stretch all the way across the subcontinent from southern China to Afghanistan. These snowy mountains and lofty valleys offer some of the best trekking on the planet.

Traditionally, Nepal has been the easiest place to trek. No permits are required for the popular routes – including the Annapurna Circuit and the Everest Base Camp trek – and there are basic hotels and restaurants along the main trails. Beware of exhaustion and altitude sickness, which can be fatal.

The aftermath of the Maoist uprising has made Nepal scarier for many travellers. Although most visitors report no problems, check the security situation before setting off.

India is also well set up for Himalayan trekking. Sikkim has some of the best and no longer requires you to wade through acres of red tape to enter. However, you often have to be part of an organised group for high-altitude routes. Himachal Pradesh and Uttarakhand offer treks to remote temples and holy lakes, but you may need a permit and guide, and most routes are camping-only.

If you can afford to visit Bhutan, you'll experience some fantastic trekking routes. Mountain trekking is also possible in Pakistan, but most of the trekking areas are unsafe. Trekking is strictly low altitude in Sri Lanka.

For more information on trekking in any of these areas, consult the relevant Lonely Planet guidebook or trekking guide.

Rafting

The rivers that rush down from the Himalaya offer spectacular white-water rafting. Nepal is the best place to organise a trip – dozens of rafting companies offer trips on the Trisuli River near Kathmandu and the Sun Kosi River in east Nepal.

In India, you can go rafting on the Teesta and Rangeet Rivers in Sikkim and West Bengal, and the Beas, Ganges, Indus, Spiti and Kanskar Rivers in Himachal Pradesh. Rafting is also possible in Pakistan and Bhutan, but many operators in the former are new and have dubious safety records.

Cycling & Mountain-Biking

The subcontinent provides opportunities to experience mountain-biking in its most extreme form – but be sure to bring your own ride, as locally made bikes aren't up to the rugged terrain. Popular spots include the Kathmandu Valley in Nepal and Sikkim and Himachal Pradesh in India. There are also more challenging routes along the Thimphu and Paro Valleys in Bhutan and the Karakoram Highway in Pakistan.

Lowland cycling is also popular in central and southern India and Bangladesh, but you'll have to share the roads with wandering cows, speeding trucks and drivers with death wishes. Expect punctures, long days under the beating sun and endless questions from locals about your flashy foreign bike. On the upside, almost everyone will offer to help with minor fixes, and you'll have plenty of cyclist company everywhere.

Diving, Snorkelling & Water Sports

Sri Lanka, traditionally beach central, offers everything from water-skiing to parasailing. Surfers will find decent breaks at Hikkaduwa, Unawatuna and Arugam Bay.

Although India is surrounded by sea, the only decent scuba diving and snorkelling is in Sri Lanka (at Hikkaduwa and Unawatuna), on the touristy Maldives, or on India's Andaman Islands. India's mainstream beach destination is Goa, in the west.

All of these coastal places are gradually recovering from the effects of the 2004 tsunami, and many are finally back to full capacity. Others, however, are taking longer to rebuild.

Other Activities

Adventure sports are incredibly cheap in India, but tread carefully, as safety standards aren't always up to scratch. Himachal Pradesh, Goa and Maharashtra are the main centres for paragliding and hang-gliding, but there have been some tragic mishaps over the years.

Indian skiing has a better record and prices are possibly the lowest in the world. The main resorts are Solang Nullah in Himachal Pradesh and Auli in Uttar Pradesh. The ski season runs from January to March, and a day's skiing can cost you less than an incredible US$15 (£7.50, A$16).

Spectator sports are a popular diversion across the subcontinent, and there are countless opportunities to cheer on the local team. The most popular sports are cricket – a national obsession – football (soccer), field hockey and the bizarre traditional sport of *kabaddi* (similar to rugby but without a ball, teams of seven try not to be touched by an opposition player who has to keep chanting 'kabaddi').

WILDLIFE

As a 'megadiversity' country, India accounts for 70% of the world's biodiversity. Lovers of rare animals and plants will be thrilled by the opportunities its national-park system affords, from one-horned rhinos in the northeast to snow leopards in the Himalaya.

The huge draws are tigers and elephants. The most famous places to see tigers are the Ranthambore, Kanha, Corbett and Sunderbans national parks in India. Wild elephants can be seen in Periyar Wildlife Sanctuary and many of the national parks in Assam. For rhinos, head to Royal Chitwan National Park in Nepal or Kaziranga National Park in India. Conventional leopards can be seen in many national parks in Sri Lanka.

Other animals you may encounter include lions, bears, crocodiles and numerous species of deer and birds. Monkeys are ubiquitous (be wary of carrying bananas anywhere).

Some parks offer safaris on elephant back – a much more intimate experience than via jeep. A few parks can be explored by boat, including Sunderbans Tiger Reserve in West Bengal. Most parks have cheap government-run or private accommodation.

ECHU (P230), 'DAY 10', ARE BUDDHIST FESTIVALS IN BHUTAN HELD ON THE 10TH DAY OF A MONTH IN THE TIBETAN CALENDAR.

FESTIVALS

From the raucous exuberance of Holi to the anarchy of the Pushkar camel fair, festivals on the subcontinent are spectacular. Following is just a smattering of what's on offer.

○ **Holi Festival** (India) Held in February/March, it's when Hindus celebrate the arrival of spring and the defeat of the demon Holika by throwing tons of water and coloured powder over as many people as possible, including foreign visitors!

○ **Losar** (Tibetan Buddhist areas) Buddhists celebrate the Tibetan new year in February/March with masked dances and processions.

○ **Shivaratri** (India and Nepal) Hindus fast in February/March in honour of the cosmic dance performed by the god Shiva. *Sadhus* (holy men) make pilgrimages to Nepal and bathe in the Bagmati River in Kathmandu.

○ **Rath Yatra** (India) Held in June/July, it's when Hindus commemorate the journey of Krishna from Gokul to Mathura with processions of gigantic temple 'chariots' pulled by thousands of eager devotees. The most famous procession takes place at Puri in Orissa.

○ **Esala Perahera** (Sri Lanka) Kandy holds this huge and important pageant, with 10 days of candlelight processions and elephants lit up like giant birthday cakes. It's held in July/August.

○ **Kataragama** (Sri Lanka) Hindu pilgrims visit the shrine at Kataragama and put themselves through the whole gamut of ritual masochism. It's held in July/August.

○ **Durga Puja** (West Bengal, Northeast India and Bangladesh) Held in October, this is when Hindus make thousands of colourful statues of the goddess Durga and ritually immerse them in rivers and streams. At the same time, Nepal celebrates the Dasain festival with animal sacrifices, and central parts of India hold the Dussehra festival to celebrate the defeat of the demon king Ravana.

○ **Diwali** (India and Nepal) During October/November, Hindus across the subcontinent light oil lamps and let off firecrackers for five days to show the god Rama the way home from his period in exile. The festival is known as Deepavali in some parts of India and Tihar in Nepal.

○ **Pushkar Camel Fair** (India) One of the most famous events on the backpacker circuit, Pushkar's annual market day is now a chaotic free-for-all. You don't have to be in the market for a camel, as racing events and associated merrymaking make for a fantastic time. It's held in November.

○ **Eid al-Fitr** (Pakistan, Bangladesh) In Muslim areas, people fast throughout the holy month of Ramadan and many shops and restaurants stay closed. The fast is broken resoundingly during the feast of Eid al-Fitr. The festival moves with the lunar calendar, advancing 10 or 11 days each year.

○ **Tsechu** (Bhutan) In spring and autumn, Buddhist monasteries across Bhutan hold five days of masked dances in honour of Guru Rinpoche.

○ **Kumbh Mela** (India) Every three years, the world's largest festival (think tens of millions attending) takes place at either Allahabad, Haridwar, Nasik or Ujjain to commemorate an ancient battle between gods and demons.

PARTY SCENE

The unquestionable capital of nightlife is Mumbai (formerly known as Bombay). Ever wealthier and wackier, Mumbai's youth has adopted the region's most pro-Western, liberal views on drinking, dancing and drug use – despite the harsh legal penalties for the latter. There's a new hotspot every fortnight, while old ones fade into oblivion. Cover charges may cost the equivalent of a week's dorm stay. It's worth it, though, to shimmy along with Bombay's beautiful and feel the new India coursing through your veins.

The rest of the region packs up much earlier. While you'll be able to grab a late-night beer almost anywhere along the backpacker circuit, you won't get much in the way of nightlife. The university town of Bengaluru and the larger cities of Delhi and Kolkata have recently relaxed prohibitions against late-night carousing, but Berlin they're not. The use of alcohol is frowned upon in Pakistan, Bangladesh and Bhutan, and relatively rare in Sri Lanka and Nepal.

ROADS LESS TRAVELLED

Wanna really get away? Try Bangladesh. Chances are, once you're outside Dhaka you'll be the only foreigner.

You'll be able to explore temples, beaches and archaeological sites in peace and you'll get to see the magnificent Sunderbans Tiger Reserve in a way almost no-one does. Check the news and exercise caution when visiting Bangladesh, as periodic political violence – usually centred on election periods – can mar the travel experience.

India's northeast, with Assam and the surrounding states, offers great opportunities for wildlife-watching and ruin-exploring without the tourist crush as well. Sadly, several other spectacular regions – including Pakistan's mountainous north and Kashmir – are too dangerous for many travellers.

OTHER ACTIVITIES

India is the source of many 'alternative' therapies. Yoga was invented here around 500 BC, and Siddhartha Gautama (the Buddha) achieved enlightenment near Bodhgaya at the same time.

The best place to study yoga is Rishikesh, India. Most ashrams expect you to follow strict rules regarding silence, diet and behaviour. Those in search of inner peace can study Buddhist meditation in Bodhgaya and Dharamsala in India and Kathmandu in Nepal. For a total-immersion experience, consider staying at a famous ashram, such as **Aurobindo** (www.sriaurobindosociety .org.in) near Puducherry.

A word of warning: not all subcontinental spiritual experiences are entirely wholesome. Every year, Lonely Planet receives dozens of complaints about thefts, scams and overzealous proselytising at ashrams and retreats. Do your homework before signing up for anything.

WORKING

If you're looking to pay your way, you're out of luck: you can't compete with the throngs of workers who need the employment more than you do. Even teaching English, the staple of the pay-your-own-way rover, is a tough gig to come by. This is because most secondary schools in the area teach English as a required subject. A few organisations offer (poorly) paid teaching gigs, but do your homework as several of these are dodgy indeed.

Volunteering is a different story. India, Nepal and Sri Lanka have hundreds of humanitarian and conservation projects that need teachers, researchers, health-care staff and other support workers. Some accept direct applications, but most get staff through international volunteering organisations – see p143 for suggestions.

WHEN TO GO?

Peak season is between November and February, when views are clearest and the weather is relatively cool and dry. From February, the heat begins to build up. Travel can become unbearable until the monsoon arrives in June.

Some high-altitude areas – including Ladakh, Spiti and Lahaul in India and the Karakoram Highway in Pakistan – are accessible by road only from June to September. Check www.lonelyplanet.com for up-to-date information on the status of these regions.

WHAT TO EXPECT?

LOCALS & OTHER TRAVELLERS

You'll hear it constantly: 'Most people in India are great, *but…*' The truth is that the subcontinental experience is often soured for visitors by those who take advantage of the culturally unaware. Don't be one of them.

For starters, don't expect anything like privacy. Be prepared to answer questions on everything from your salary to how willing you'd be to marry a local belle. It can be completely overwhelming.

This is when it might get tough. For most of your trip, you'll be within shouting distance of touts, hawkers and con merchants, who hang around the main travellers' haunts in alarming numbers. As some of the most visible people you'll meet, they will do their best to give the rest of the population a bad reputation.

The important thing is to keep your sense of humour. Prices are almost always elevated for foreigners, but you can usually bargain down – keeping in mind that you'll be unimaginably rich in the eyes of many people you meet.

Of course, there are some real *badmashes* (scoundrels). Theft is a risk in some areas – often through the use of drugged food and drink on trains. Pakistan is now particularly dangerous for foreigners. In all Muslim areas, keep a low profile during public demonstrations and flash points of religious conflict.

URBAN MYTHS – INDIAN MYTHS DEBUNKED

There's good news and bad news.

Bad news first: many of the myths are true. Yes, hotel owners may spike your drinks. Yes, children may fling shit at you in order to distract you from your bags or pockets. Yes, you can be thrown in jail for your entire life if you hit a cow in Nepal.

But some stuff is just ridiculous. Take, for example, the paranoia-inducing legend that bottled-water sellers will replace the good stuff with tap water by drilling a hole in the bottom of the bottle. The claim is that the unsuspecting customer is tricked by the unbroken bottle-cap seal, so the vendor gets away with it. Nice story – but it makes no sense. You'd have to miss the fact that (if this story were true) the seller would be draining away perfectly good bottled water, which they could simply sell in the first place for the same price – without going to all the trouble of drilling.

There are several more insidious myths that need debunking. You will not wake up in a bathtub full of ice to find your kidneys missing. You will not get attacked by tigers or elephants in the streets. Practicing yoga in an ashram will not enable you to live to more than 200 years old. And you will not have to share a train carriage with goats, cows or chickens (that is, unless one of your fellow passengers has bribed the conductor).

The poverty will be confronting. Whether you give to beggars is a personal decision. If you wish to help, consider making a donation to a charity or development organisation.

Expect regular demands for *baksheesh* (tips) from everyone – including the porter who takes your bag and the bureaucrat who stamps your passport. It's a cross between a tip and a bribe, but it can open doors and make problems go away. Don't get bamboozled into doling out your cash left and right, though.

As for your fellow travellers, well, you'll probably never meet such a broad selection of freaks, do-gooders, adventurers, enlightenment seekers, beach bums, drug fiends, obsessive trekkers and bar-stool philosophers. Enjoy.

FOOD

The food may be the best in the world. It's impossible to do the vast array of regional cuisines justice in a short space.

India provides the region's most famous cuisine, and the offerings in the surrounding countries resemble Indian food. Roughly speaking, the north emphasises breads such as *naan* and *roti*, and the high Muslim population ensures the ready availability of meat dishes such as goat, lamb and chicken. Fiery chillies, rich creams and hearty potatoes add heft to meals.

In the south, rice is the staple carb, and fish and vegetables are the order of the day. Coconut milk and curry leaves add to the spicy mix.

Pakistani cuisine is meaty and spicy. Bangladeshi food tends to be less diverse, with fewer spices. Nepal's offering is frankly boring: think bland vegetable dishes. Luckily, the country is crammed with Indian, Chinese and European restaurants. Sri Lankan food is fresh and tasty, with emphasis on roasted spices and simmered curries. *Dhal* (lentils) is beloved throughout the entire subcontinent.

Fresh juices and lovely yogurty *lassis* are available everywhere, but stay clear from anything made from unboiled or untreated water. Stick with bottled water and make sure all fruits and vegetables have been peeled and that hot food is thoroughly and freshly cooked.

Alcohol is readily available on India's coasts and in Sri Lanka and Nepal; it's harder to come by, however, in Pakistan, Bangladesh and the conservative Indian interior.

LANGUAGE

English is widely spoken, but each region has its own dialects and languages. In India, Hindi is an official language, but 80% of the population speaks something else. Urdu is spoken by the northern and western Muslim population (especially in Pakistan), and Tamil and Sinhalese are the official languages of Sri Lanka. Bengali is spoken in Bangladesh, Nepali in Nepal and Dzongka (related to Tibetan) in Bhutan. Lonely Planet's *Hindu, Urdu, & Bengali* and *Nepali* phrasebooks will help you get your tongue around the local languages.

HEALTH

No matter how careful you are, chances are you'll develop a case of the runs. Most bugs are short-lived, and you should avoid taking blockers such as Imodium unless you have a long bus trip in store. If things stay dodgy for more than two days, see a doctor. See p46 for more information.

Before you go, get advice on vaccinations. Antimalarial medication is sensible if you're travelling in lowland

SAMPLE COSTS

	INDIA (RUPEE, RS)	PAKISTAN (RUPEE, RS)	NEPAL (RUPEE, RS)	SRI LANKA (RUPEE, RS)	BANGLADESH (TAKA, TK)
HOSTEL/ BUDGET ROOM	Rs 150 £2 US$3.50 A$4	Rs 200 £1.60 US$3.25 A$3.50	Rs 650 £5 US$10 A$11	Rs 200 £0.90 US$1.90 A$2	Tk 20 £0.15 US$0.30 A$0.31
CHEAP RESTAURANT MEAL	Rs 20 £0.25 US$0.50 A$0.55	Rs 50 £0.40 US$0.80 A$0.90	Rs 130 £1 US$2 A$2.15	Rs 100 £0.45 US$0.90 A$1	Tk 10 £0.08 US$0.15 A$0.16
1L BOTTLE OF WATER	Rs 8 £0.10 US$0.20 A$0.25	Rs 20 £0.15 US$0.30 A$0.35	Rs 15 £0.11 US$0.23 A$0.25	Rs 20 £0.10 US$0.20 A$0.22	Tk 20 £0.15 US$0.30 A$0.31
SOUVENIR T-SHIRT	Rs 80 £1 US$2 A$2.50	Rs 250 £2 US$4 A$4.50	Rs 400 £3 US$6 A$6.50	Rs 250 £1.15 US$2.30 A$2.50	Tk 100 £0.80 US$1.50 A$1.60
BOTTLE OF BEER	Rs 40 £0.50 US$1 A$1.25	Rs 80 £0.65 US$1.30 A$1.40	Rs 170 £1.30 US$2.60 A$2.80	Rs 80 £0.40 US$0.75 A$0.80	Tk 160 £1.15 US$2.30 A$2.50
STREET SNACK	Samosa Rs 6 £0.08 US$0.15 A$0.17	Samosa Rs 6 £0.05 US$0.10 A$0.11	*Momos* Rs 40 £0.30 US$0.60 A$0.65	*Lamprais* Rs 150 £0.70 US$1.40 A$1.50	Boiled egg Tk 4 £0.03 US$0.06 A$0.06
1L PETROL	Rs 55 £0.70 US$1.35 A$1.45	Rs 54 £0.45 US$0.90 A$0.95	Rs 67 £0.50 US$1 A$1.10	Rs 85 £0.40 US$0.80 A$0.85	Tk 35 £0.25 US$0.50 A$0.55

areas. Other health problems include cholera, dysentery, giardiasis and altitude sickness.

ISSUES

The most irritating aspect of your stay will most likely be the endless array of scammers, touts and con artists who will desperately try to part you from your money. The sad truth is that almost all the rumours are true, from gem scammers who sell you worthless 'jewellery' to shady hotel restaurateurs who drug clients. Get educated at Lonely Planet's **Thorn Tree forum** (www.lonelyplanet.com/thorntree), where you'll find the advice you need to stay relaxed and secure.

Periodic violence dots the region. Kashmir has been a no-go zone for a while, and civil war–style violence in Sri Lanka and Pakistan has also been a turn-off. Nepal and India's northeastern states also experience political tension. Check the situation at www.lonelyplanet.com before setting off.

GETTING THERE

Most people fly into Mumbai, Delhi, Chennai or Kolkata. Trekkers in Nepal will generally make a beeline for Kathmandu. Pakistan, Bangladesh and Sri Lanka are connected with the major Indian cities by cheap flights, but forget about getting to Bhutan unless you have a slew of permits and can fork out the cash for an expensive package tour.

In India and Bangladesh, most independent travellers get around by rail, which is cheap and relatively efficient. Budget airlines will whisk you around for reasonable prices, and in the more mountainous regions (as well as in Nepal and Pakistan) you'll rely on buses.

AIR

A host of international airlines, regular and budget, serve the region. Following are major national players:
○ **Air India** (www.airindia.com)
○ **Biman Bangladesh Airlines** (www.bimanair.com)

TAKE A CAMEL RIDE FROM THE INCREDIBLE 'GOLDEN FORTRESS' AT JAISALMER (P225) THROUGH THE DESERT IN RAJASTHAN, INDIA.

○ **Pakistan International Airlines** (www.piac.com.pk)
○ **Royal Nepal Airlines** (www.royalnepal-airlines.com)
○ **Sri Lankan Airlines** (www.srilankan.aero)

SEA & OVERLAND

It's theoretically possible to travel overland from the subcontinent to Tibet, Afghanistan or Myanmar, but these journeys are either prohibitively expensive or perilous. International ferries are nonexistent.

BEYOND THE INDIAN SUBCONTINENT

From India, you can catch relatively cheap flights to Singapore, Beijing, Hong Kong, Tokyo, the Middle East via Dubai, and Europe. Overland travel to or from the subcontinent is difficult and dangerous.

FURTHER INFORMATION

WEBSITES

○ **Bangladesh Parjatan Corporation** (www.bangladeshtourism.org) The national tourism organisation website, with a wealth of information.
○ **Best Indian Sites** (www.bestindiansites.com) Links to search engines, marriage matchmakers and information technology sites.
○ **Crazy Lanka** (www.crazylanka.com) A cheerfully silly website with lots of parodies of current news events.
○ **Discovery Bangladesh** (www.discoverybangladesh.com) A great place to kick off your research.
○ **Explore Nepal** (www.explorenepal.com) A good gateway information site with many links set up by category. Also try www.nepalhomepage.com or www.nepaltourism.info.
○ **Hi Pakistan** (www.hipakistan.com) News and views, fashion, music, showbiz and more.
○ **Incredible India** (www.incredibleindia.org) The official tourism site, with national travel-related information.
○ **Nepal Tourism Board** (www.welcomenepal.com) The official site: tourism news, a rundown of the country's sights and some glossy photos.
○ **Pakistan Tourism Development Corporation** (www.tourism.gov.pk) Official government tourism

site, with national travel-related fodder.
○ **Sri Lanka Tourist Board** (www.srilankatourism.org) The official tourism site, with tons of information.

BOOKS

○ *Midnight's Children* (Salman Rushdie) The epic, magic-realist tale of a boy born at the stroke of Indian independence. Incredible.
○ *The God of Small Things* (Arundhati Roy) A heartachingly beautiful story about a woman and her brother from Kerala.
○ *Amritsar to Lahore* (Stephen Alter) An insightful account of a journey across the border that divides Pakistan and India.
○ *Sam's Story* (Elmo Jayawardena) The simple, incisive tale of an illiterate village boy working in Colombo.
○ *Into Thin Air* (Jon Krakauer) A gripping account of the disastrous 1996 Everest expeditions.
○ *Rabindranath Tagore: An Anthology* (Krishna Detta and Andrew Robinson, eds) The masterworks of the greatest Bengali literary figure of all time.

FILMS

Bollywood (the Mumbai version of Tinseltown) cranks out hundreds of movies per year. No visit to India is complete without a cinema visit, with the attendant chilli popcorn and oohs, aahs and singalongs from the audience.

A few Indian films have reached canonical status:
○ *Sholay* (1975) The most popular Bollywood film of all time. A cross between a spaghetti western, a buddy flick and a classic myth, *Sholay* chronicles the adventures of two rugged vigilantes hired by the law to defeat a vile bandit leader and his army.
○ *Gandhi* (1982) The masterwork that chronicles the great man's life and the struggles of Indian-Pakistani Independence and Partition.
○ *Monsoon Wedding* (2001) A riotous and poignant affair directed by Mira Nair.
○ *Lagaan* (2001) Villagers from the pre-Partition subcontinent challenge their British rulers to a game of cricket.
○ *Devdas* (2002) A prodigal-son-gone-wrong tragedy, complete with betrayed love and hellfire. Considered actor Shahrukh Khan's masterwork.

NORTH AMERICA & THE CARIBBEAN

Supersized with preconceptions, the Americas family probably first made itself known to you through film, TV, music and most of popular culture. Big brother, the United States of America, steals most of the glory, stretching from sea to shining must-see, but 'me too' middle child Canada has its fair share of charms including the French-speaking and Inuit provinces. Youngest child, the Caribbean, is a misunderstood mix of nations such as troubled Haiti, rebellious Cuba and so-relaxed-it's-passed-out Jamaica.

Most visitors to the area spend some time in the USA, though the old British Commonwealth ties between Canada, Australia, New Zealand and the UK have meant working holiday visa arrangements between these countries see many travellers spending more time north of the border. A new work visa for Australians in the US (see p116) will probably change this.

The Caribbean is popular with North Americans but can be tricky for outside visitors, especially with the blockade on Cuba that means visitors have to reroute through Cancún, Nassau and Toronto. If you're interested in Mexico, check out the Mexico, Central & South America chapter (p251) – we've covered it there because most travellers visit Mexico during a trip to Latin America rather than North America.

ITINERARIES

Hitting the trail in North America usually involves a car, but think outside the metal box and you might find yourself catching the train or even walking the trails of the Rockies or Appalachians. However you get there, it's a big region, so don't be shy of taking the odd flight to cover some country.

CANADIAN CROSSING

Hike and munch your way through **Vancouver**, where mountain trailheads brush shoulders with nude beaches and Chinatown. From Vancouver, head north along Hwy 99 to **Whistler** for year-round skiing. Stop for a nibble in the **Okanagan Valley**, with various fruit harvests from late June to October, before bunking down in **Kelowna** on the lip of a lake. If time allows, laze your way on Rte 6 southeast to **Nelson**, an artist hang-out with many a bong raised to dull the pain from biking/skiing/boarding wipeouts. Back north on the Trans-Canada Hwy, hike up massive snowcapped mountains in **Banff National Park**. For more winter wonderland, take the Icefields Parkway north to **Jasper National Park**.

Warm up a little by heading out of the mountains into Saskatchewan, where plains stretch off forever in every

direction. **Saskatoon** breaks the monotony before **Winnipeg** with plenty of history, and a French quarter for good coffee and croissants. East of Thunder Bay in Ontario, the **Trans-Canada Hwy** skirts cliffs along **Lake Superior**. Skirt south to the car ferry 'short cut' to lake-studded **Bruce Peninsula** for top scuba and kayaking options. Snake south to the Canadian side at **Niagara Falls**, then plan on a couple of days in **Toronto**, with the quintessential Canadian experiences of tower views, the Hockey Hall of Fame and full-moon canoe trips on the harbour. Detour north to **Algonquin Provincial Park**, Canada's wild side with wolves howling from hilltops over clear lakes.

Southeast in the capital **Ottawa**, snack on a famed Beaver Tail, and, during winter, skate with commuters on the frozen canal. Crack open the French phrasebook for **Québec** and plan a few days for **Montréal**, with partying and bagels that hold their own with New York City's. Watch out for freshwater whales in the St Lawrence River, which leads northeast to the province's cobblestone capital, **Québec City**. Retell your trip's tale to the city's goat, Batisse.

WEST-COAST WANDERER

See the stars in **Los Angeles**, then take the fabled **Hwy 1**, built on landsliding fault lines and skirting rocky bluffs overlooking the Pacific. Stay a night in the college beach town **Santa Barbara**, for beaches and a Spanish Moorish–styled courthouse.

Pitch your tent at cliff-clutching **Big Sur** for hiking or diving at the **Point Lobos State Reserve**, then bunk down at Steinbeck's **Cannery Row** in Monterey. Leave Hwy 1 to head off to **San Francisco** for boho by the bay, then rejoin Hwy 1 on the **Golden Gate Bridge**. Follow **Hwy 1** to its end just south of the **Redwood National Park**, home to the famed big trees. Backtrack inland to get a glimpse of **Mt Shasta** on the way to Oregon. For more outdoorsy fun take in **Crater Lake National Park**, with drives along the country's deepest lake.

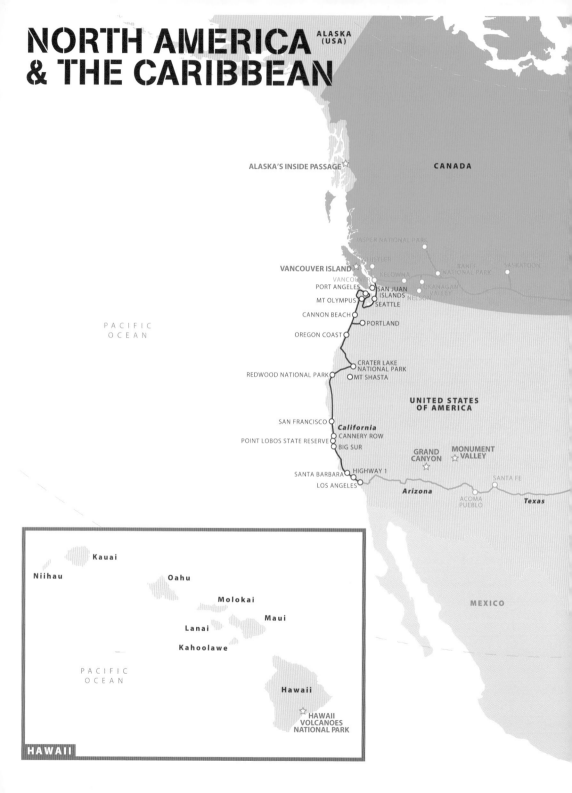

NORTH AMERICA & THE CARIBBEAN

ALASKA (USA)

CANADA

ALASKA'S INSIDE PASSAGE ☆

JASPER NATIONAL PARK

WHISTLER

SASKATOON

KELOWNA

BANFF NATIONAL PARK

VANCOUVER ISLAND ☆

VANCOUVER

PORT ANGELES

SAN JUAN ISLANDS

OKANAGAN VALLEY

NELSON

MT OLYMPUS

SEATTLE

CANNON BEACH

PORTLAND

PACIFIC OCEAN

OREGON COAST

CRATER LAKE NATIONAL PARK

REDWOOD NATIONAL PARK

MT SHASTA

UNITED STATES OF AMERICA

SAN FRANCISCO

California

CANNERY ROW

POINT LOBOS STATE RESERVE

BIG SUR

GRAND CANYON ☆

MONUMENT VALLEY ☆

SANTA FE

SANTA BARBARA

HIGHWAY 1

LOS ANGELES

Arizona

ACOMA PUEBLO

Texas

MEXICO

HAWAII

Kauai

Niihau

Oahu

Molokai

Maui

Lanai

Kahoolawe

PACIFIC OCEAN

Hawaii

HAWAII VOLCANOES NATIONAL PARK ☆

A LAND WITHOUT LANDMARKS? INUITS AND OTHER NATIVE PEOPLES BUILT THEIR OWN, CALLED INUKSUIT – FIND THEM TREKKING IN CANADA (SEE P243

VIBRANT COLOURS PERMEATE EVERY ASPECT OF LIFE IN THE CARIBBEAN AND BUILDINGS, LIKE THIS HOUSE IN THE DOMINICAN REPUBLIC, ARE NO EXCEPTIO

MARDI GRAS OR 'FAT TUESDAY', THE FINAL DAY OF FEASTING AND FUN BEFORE LENT, IS BACK IN A BIG RABBITY WAY IN NEW ORLEANS (SEE P242).

✪ **MOUNT RUSHMORE** I am so glad we came all the way to South Dakota with these tourist hordes and paid $8 for parking in order to see something that looks better on TV (and we even get to watch a breathtaking video about how some guy spent his life carving it)!

✪ **PEARL HARBOR** We waited in line for three hours to watch a video pumped full of patriotism, and then we took a little motorboat out to this platform where we had 10 minutes to look at what seems to be a ship in the water. Awesome!

✪ **HOLLYWOOD** Stars on the sidewalk are pretty sweet and all, but there has to be something else. The China Theater? Well, there it is. If I could only see through the smog, maybe I could admire those cool letters on the hillside...

✪ **SILICON VALLEY** It's famous the world over, but where is it? I guess it must be these miles upon miles of office parks surrounded by new subdivisions. Man, it is really inspiring to see such a centre of innovation!

✪ **ORLANDO/TAMPA** We can drop the kids off at Disneyworld, and then we can...we can explore...we can check out...wow, there really is nothing to do here. There are some flashy office buildings! Boy, this place really sucks.

✪ **THE WHITE HOUSE** Okay, after two days of waiting and multiple security checks, I have my ticket. What a rush! I am inside a building! And I get to see a couple of rooms! Wow, this was definitely worth it.

✪ **STATUE OF LIBERTY** This is it?!

www.lonelyplanet.com

Back on the **Oregon Coast**, throw down your towel on the sand at places such as **Cannon Beach**. Save at least a day for the college town of **Portland**, with tasty beers and lively locals. Make for Washington and stop in the seaport town **Port Angeles** near glaciated **Mt Olympus**. In **Seattle** take the local caffeine high up the **Space Needle**, where grunge got going all those years ago. Cycle or kayak around some of the 457 **San Juan Islands** before pulling into **Vancouver** and on into **British Columbia's** wilderness.

ROUTE 66 REVISITED

The Great Mother Road is a nostalgic drive through quintessential Americana. Only traces of the once-great highway remain, but this version is the States drive-thru style. Start in **Chicago**, Illinois and head for **St Louis**, a legendary blues town. Stop for gas in the cowtown-cum-metropolis **Kansas**, which has a whole 13 miles of the original Route 66 before it cuts across to the true

West of **Tulsa** and **Oklahoma City**.

Then the road grabs the panhandle of **Texas**, which includes the halfway point and the sculpture junkyard of cars stuck in the ground. There's more cow-poking in **New Mexico** as the road passes **Acoma Pueblo** and **Santa Fe**, and in **Arizona** you'll find the longest uninterrupted section of the original route as well as several small towns that are on a serious nostalgia binge. **California** is the home stretch with the original McDonald's, and at the end of the road is Los Angeles' **Santa Monica**, where a delicious beach and boardwalk await.

WHAT TO DO?

HIGHLIGHTS

○ Resurrecting Mardi Gras in **New Orleans** (USA), the comeback kid that proves it takes more than a hurricane to sink Creole and Cajun culture.

- Trekking down into the **Grand Canyon** (USA) will convince you this is more than a big ditch.
- Hailing a classic 1950s cab through **Havana** (Cuba) to cruise the Spanish-colonial streets while chomping on your hand-rolled cigar.
- Cruising **Alaska's Inside Passage** (USA) that boasts the continent's most stunning scenery and best chances for double entendre.
- Getting sprayed by **Niagara Falls** (Canada), Canada's top tourist attraction and notorious honeymoon spot.
- Stretching your legs on **Vancouver Island** (Canada) or whale-watching for a natural high in this handy wilderness.
- Feeling the earth expand under you at **Hawai'i Volcanoes National Park** (USA), an active lava landscape.
- Moseying through the freakish rock formations of **Monument Valley** (USA) that served as a backdrop to big Western movies and Marlboro man commercials.
- Wondering whether **New York** (USA) is the world's coolest capital from the bottom of a Manhattan or Long Island iced tea.

GET ACTIVE
North America and the Caribbean have world-class terrain for just about any outdoor pursuit you care to mention. No matter what makes you tick, you'll find a perfect spot to do it and plenty of gung-ho folks to do it with.

Skiing & Snowboarding
Snowboarding is almost as popular as skiing on northern American slopes. Canada's main slopes are in Ontario, Québec, Alberta and around Whistler in British Columbia. In the USA, the Rocky Mountain states (Colorado in particular) are known for the white stuff, including Aspen, Vail, Big Sky and Jackson Hole. Mammoth and Lake Tahoe in the Sierra Nevada are California's major downhill destinations. To get off the beaten track, take on Alaska's slopes around Juneau, Anchorage and Fairbanks.

Surfing & Kitesurfing
The USA has its stamp all over surfing, from the big *kahunas* of Hawai'i to legendary Californians such as Malibu, Rincon and Mavericks. Waves reach monstrous proportions, mostly on O'ahu's north shore, between November and February. Beginners get the basics at gentle Waikiki and then go gawk at the world-class big-wave pros. Maui attracts top international windsurfers like moths to a flame. Canada has some chilly (you'll need a dry suit) surfing off Nova Scotia and in the warmer waters off Melmerby and Cariboo near New Glasgow. There are a few surf spots in Cuba and some *super-bueno* secret breaks along the north and east coasts of the Dominican Republic.

Hawai'i is also a great place for kitesurfing, particularly at Waipulani Beach in Maui. San Francisco also catches the sweet summer winds that make the bay a good place to try kitesurfing, while Oregon has Hood River and Texas offers South Padre Island – both good spots to be blown away.

Trekking, Hiking & Rock-Climbing
If you're looking for a purely hiking holiday with a taste of the whole region, the Pacific Crest Trail zigzags from Canada to Mexico taking in the natural wonders of California, Oregon and Washington along the way. The USA has even more long-distance trekking options, ranging from the multiday Appalachian Trail to shorter strolls around Yosemite National Park. Desert trails and canyoneering in the southwest can be a good option in winter, and the mile trek down to the Grand Canyon is a must. At the other end of the thermometer, Alaska offers epic tracks including the Chilkoot Trail, Resurrection Pass Trail and Chena Dome Trail west of Fairbanks. You'll need to come well prepared for these advanced hikes, but the natural beauty is worth the effort.

In Canada, Ontario's Killarney Provincial Park has a long-distance trail around the tops of its rounded mountains. Other vertically oriented regions include Gaspésie Park and Mont Tremblant Park (Québec), Gros Morne National Park in Newfoundland and Cape Breton Highlands National Park in Nova Scotia. More hard-core trekking can be had in Pukaskwa National Park and on the Trans Canada Trail (can you spare 750 days?), slated to be the world's longest recreational trail upon completion. The Caribbean is not renowned for trekking, but Cuba has some good options such as the three-day trek over the Sierra Maestra via the 2000m-high Pico Turquino.

THE EERIE MONUMENT VALLEY, USA, (P243) FORMS PART OF THE LANDS OF THE DINÉ PEOPLE, MORE WIDELY KNOWN AS THE NAVAJO.

Rock-climbing and mountaineering are popular in California's Yosemite National Park (El Capitan and Half Dome are legendary big-wall climbs), the Sierra Nevada and the Rockies. Canadian climbing meccas include Collingwood, Sault Ste Marie and Thunder Bay in Ontario, Banff and Jasper in Alberta, and Squamish in British Colombia. In Alaska, Mt McKinley (6096m), the highest peak in North America, is the site of organised expeditions in late spring and early summer.

Diving

Keeping a US toe in the Pacific Islands, Hawai'i has awesome diving, with caves, canyons, lava tubes, vertical walls, WWII shipwrecks and the sunken volcanic crater of Molokini all awaiting you. There's casual snorkelling in Hanauma Bay Nature Preserve. Elsewhere in the USA, the Great Lakes, the Florida Keys (where you can dive with sharks) and southern California all feature top-notch underwater action. The Caribbean is where the diving really rocks: St Lucia, Dominica, Tobago, St Vincent and the Grenadines all boast world-class dive sites. Exploring the shipwrecks along the Dominican Republic's north coast and the coral gardens on the warmer south coast is deservedly popular. Haiti boasts black coral and stunning underwater geology and there are hundreds of picture-postcard coral reefs off islands in the Eastern Caribbean.

Cycling & Mountain-Biking

Mountain-biking is huge, particularly in northern California, where it was invented. Cycle-touring hotspots include the forests of New England, the Atlantic coast's offshore islands, the swamps of southern Louisiana, and California's west coast and wine country. In Canada, the Laurentian Mountains of Québec and the Rockies of Alberta and British Columbia are prime mountain-biking destinations. Cycling is the most budget-friendly way to get around the Caribbean islands.

WILDLIFE

Whale watching is popular in New England and in numerous places along the Californian coast and around the Caribbean. Killer whales are often spotted spyhopping off Vancouver Island and at numerous other spots in western Canada. Manatees can be seen in Florida, which is also a good place to dive with sharks. Baby seals await your adoration on the Magdalen Islands of Québec.

Bears rule the roost in northern Canada (beware the hefty polar bears in Churchill, Manitoba). Wolves, mountain lions and grizzly bears flourish in famous North American national parks such as Glacier and Yellowstone, which harbours the greatest unfenced concentration of charismatic (and photogenic) megafauna in the lower 48 states.

FESTIVALS

○ **Sundance Film Festival** (USA; www.sundance.org) January's chance to spot indie film-makers and stars – Paris and Tarantino are regulars.

○ **Québec City Winter Carnival** (Canada; www .carnaval.qc.ca) Features parades, ice sculptures, live music and dogsled racing. Held in February.

○ **Caribbean carnivals** (Caribbean; www.caribseek .com) Raucous parades and drinking throughout the region around February/March, with highlights in Havana (Cuba) and Santo Domingo (Dominican Republic).

○ **South by Southwest** (SXSW; USA; www.sxsw.com) In March. A gabfest and festival for film, plus indie, hip-hop and alternative music.

○ **Spring Break** (USA; www.springbreak.com) Students let loose for a week around Easter, descending on beach towns like migratory birds, to drink, dance and engage in ravenous mating rituals.

○ **Red Earth Native American Cultural Festival** (USA; www.redearth.org) Members of North America's 100 Native American tribes gather in Okalahoma in June to celebrate art, dance and more.

○ **Summer Solstice** (Alaska) Almost continuous daylight with midnight baseball, axe-tossing and tree-climbing competitions held in June across the state.

○ **Vodou Pilgrimages** (Haiti) A pilgrimage to the sacred waters of Saut d'Eau and Plaine du Nordin in Ville-Bonheur in July.

○ **Reggae Sunsplash and Reggae Sumfest** (Jamaica; www.reggaesumfest.com) Held about one week apart (in July/August) in Ocho Rios and Montego Bay respectively, these festivals are the island's biggest beach parties.

○ **Burning Man** (USA; www.burningman.com) A massive, arty happening held in the Black Rock Desert of northwestern Nevada in late August.

○ **Halloween** (USA and Canada) Spooky costumes and wild parties on 31 October in this North American tradition.

○ **Thanksgiving** (USA and Canada) The year's busiest travel period and a time of feasting and family get-togethers on the last Thursday in November.

PARTY SCENE

North America wrote the book on parties, then passed out on it and had its eyebrows shaved off. Spring break (around Easter) is a big chance for college students to go wild, with hotspots in and around Miami such as Panama City and Daytona Beach (though local residents have been pooping the party in the last few years). Many more make for Cancún (see p261) and Jamaica.

Outside the seasonal madness, there's plenty left in party keg. New York is known for its wild club scene, especially in the chic neighbourhoods of Tribeca and Soho, plus NYU students hang around Greenwich Village if you're looking to meet locals. San Francisco has had a strong dance culture since the 1990s, while Canada's Vancouver has been labelled 'Vansterdam' for the easy availability of marijuana (maybe that's why so many Hollywood movies are shot there). There are plenty of good watering holes in Los Angeles though particularly in Hollywood, West Hollywood and Santa Monica. Then there are the 'college towns' where university students rule the bars and an alternative culture blossoms – you'll find plenty of nose piercings and conversations about postmodernism in Boston, Austin (Texas) and Portland (Oregon). Fuelled by rum and the odd inhale of marijuana, the Caribbean party scene is insane; hotspots include Kingston (Jamaica), Barbados and Dominica.

ROADS LESS TRAVELLED

Looking for a new frontier? What about following America's early pioneers into the wilds of Alaska, but landing in the chilly capital of Juneau and exploring the Inuit traditions and taking the odd hike. You can also check out Canada's range of arctic provincial parks: Moose and mountain-goat mecca Stone Mountain, Muncho Lake with a dazzling blueness, and Liard River Hot Springs with soul-warming hot tubs to soak away the road.

If you're looking to head further out, the Caribbean has a few escape hatches from the tourist traps. Skip the big names (Bahamas, Jamaica) and seek out the tinier spots such as Aruba, St Kitts or Anguilla, where you might find a beach of your own. Cuba is another good getaway as travel is restricted for citizens from the United States.

WORKING

Getting a job in the States can be difficult. If you're from the United Kingdom, your best bet is to participate in a program run by **Bunac** (British Universities North America Club; www.bunac.org), which organises a variety of work and camp jobs. For Australians, there's a new class of visas created in 2007 as a work and holiday option in the US that's valid for a year (more info at www.unitedstatesvisas.gov).

Canada, as part of the Commonwealth, offers a working holiday visa (www.whpcanada.org.au) for 18- to 30-year-olds.

The Caribbean isn't a great place to look for work, with its high unemployment rate and low pay.

Once you have your visa sorted, you've got a few options for work (see p115). Working on a summer camp can give a unique insight into North America. Crewing on a boat in the Caribbean is one of the few opportunities in the area. You can start with Florida-based **Crewfinders** (www.crewfinders.com).

Working in North America without a visa isn't advisable, and border-security staff have been known to refuse entry to jobseekers if they find evidence that they'll be working in the country.

WHEN TO GO?

Most of North America is visitable year-round, though the climate could make or break your stay. East of the Rockies, the USA can be nastily humid during summer, especially in the south. North America's western and eastern coasts are sopping wet, though much of the precipitation falls during winter. The great North American prairies – lying in the Midwest between the Rocky Mountains and eastern seaboard – are fairly dry year-round and stay well below freezing point in winter. Florida enjoys a tropical climate and California's southern coast is comfortable year-round. Hawaii's balmy weather is near perfect, with northeasterly breezes – the rainiest period is between December and March. Alaska's climate is not known for its consistency (if you don't like the weather, just wait five minutes) but, like northern Canada, temperatures of -45°C/-49°F aren't uncommon in midwinter. High rainfall and moderate temperatures (15°C/59°F to 21°C/70°F) dominate summer, and there's an unpleasant thaw in May.

The Caribbean delivers warm weather, except during hurricane season from August to September. From mid-December to mid-April, the Caribbean is crowded by the so-called snowbirds – North American tourists dodging the colder weather further north.

WHAT TO EXPECT?

LOCALS & OTHER TRAVELLERS

It's just as common to see North Americans travelling around their own countries as it is to see international visitors. Backpacking in the States often means hiking and camping in the wilderness, so you might find North Americans on vacations, road trips or spring breaks (also known as 'March break' in Canada).

Most international visitors to North America head for the big cities – New York and LA are high on many must-visit lists, though national parks are becoming more popular. Backpackers are crowded out of the Eastern Caribbean by the bigger spenders who dazzle beaches with their bling. There are more young travellers in Cuba, Jamaica and the Dominican Republic, though package tourists are increasingly invading.

North Americans themselves suffer from some tough stereotypes. You won't be frisked for your preconceptions at the border, but you should probably leave them at home. Sure, you're likely to encounter full-figured, car-obsessed, parochial folks who've never been outside of their country. But Americans will surprise you. They're friendly (expect people to chat to you at bus stops and bars), polite (they seriously say 'sir' and 'ma'am') and very helpful people (handy when you're presented with 50 choices of bread in a café).

The rich history of immigration (forced or voluntary) gives America a unique sum-of-its-parts identity. Afro-American culture is strong in the south, with Mexican and Latin American culture increasingly influential in California, Texas, Colorado and the southwest. Don't underestimate the power of US patriotism with flags waved at every baseball or football game and most students swearing a pledge of allegiance to the US before starting lessons.

Most Canucks (Canadians) live along the border with the US, with the harsh northern frontier defining their character. Culturally, they're closer to the former colonial powers the United Kingdom and France (Québec is the centre of French loyalists). Compared to the US citizens, Canadians are often considered a little more reserved, more laid-back, more sensible – and far from boring.

You may not meet any native peoples travelling randomly through North America, but if you make the effort to visit a reservation or tribal lands be polite and respectful. Whatever you do, never snap photographs without permission.

The Caribbean is renowned as relaxed and laid-back, mon. Caribbean society and family structures are to some extent still shaped by Africa, a legacy of the region's population of the descendants of African slaves. The region also exhibits the flavours of France, Britain and the USA and, thanks to offshore financial opportunities, it is home to a large and growing contingent of expats.

FOOD

The nation that gave the world TV dinners and spray-on cheese will keep surprising you with its downright culinary weirdness. Avoid the Elvis diet (the King even deep-fried his toast) by seeking out good health-food (also called 'whole food') options born in the USA, plus a good dose of international cuisine washing in with immigrant cultures. Mexican food in California is as good as you'll get north of the border. The cuisine of the Deep South, Louisiana in particular, fuses its immigrant flavours (which include French, Sicilian and Choctaw Indian influences) with the bounty of the New World to produce dishes such as shrimp rémoulade, *beignets* (deep-fried donut) and *pain perdu* (sweet French toast).

In Canada food is similar to what you'd expect in the States, with a few more French flavours – try *poutine râpée* (boiled potatoes stuffed with pork) on for size. You can expect to have your fries drenched in *poutine* (gravy and cheese curds), though the condiment of choice is definitely maple syrup, which is best poured over pancakes or Beaver Tails (pastries).

Caribbean grub includes loads of seafood, but you'll also get a chance to build up a list of exotic fruits, such as soursop (a prickly-skinned fruit with tingly ice-cream flavoured flesh), guava and naseberry (usually used in ice creams and jams).

LANGUAGE

English is the lingua franca across North America, but it can be difficult to understand the Creole patois in

EDUARDO MUNOZ / REUTERS

CARIBBEAN PEOPLE, INCLUDING DOMINICANS, LOVE CARNIVAL (P245).

SAMPLE COSTS

	USA (US DOLLAR, US$)	CANADA (CANADIAN DOLLAR, C$)	CUBA (CUBAN CONVERTIBLE PESO, CUC$)
HOSTEL/BUDGET ROOM	US$12–60 £6.20–30.80 A$13–65.50	C$30–70 £15.20–35.50 US$29.50–69 A$32.25–75.50	CUC$15–30 £8.30–16.65 US$16.25–32.50 A$17.50–35
CHEAP RESTAURANT MEAL	US$3–10 £1.50–5 A$3.25–11	C$4–10 £2–5 US$4–10 A$4.25–10.75	CUC$2–5 £1.10–2.75 US$2–5.50 A$2.20–5.89
1L BOTTLE OF WATER	US$1 £0.50 A$1.10	C$1.50 £0.75 US$1.50 A$1.60	CUC$0.50 £0.25 US$0.55 A$0.60
SOUVENIR T-SHIRT	US$10 £5.15 A$11	C$12 £6.07 US$12 A$13	CUC$10 £5.50 US$11 A$12
BOTTLE OF BEER	US$1.50 £0.75 A$1.75	C$3 £1.50 US$3 A$3.25	CUC$1 £0.50 US$1 A$1.18
STREET SNACK	Hot dog US$1.50 £0.77 A$1.65	Coffee & donut C$2 £1.01 US$1.97 A$2.15	*Bocaditos* CUC$0.50 £0.27 US$0.55 A$0.59
1L PETROL	US$1.70 £0.87 A$1.85	C$1.15 £0.58 US$1.13 A$1.23	CUC$1 £0.55 US$1.08 A$1.25

the Caribbean. French and English are duelling official languages in Canada, but in only in Québec will you need your French phrasebook. Spanish is spoken in Cuba, the Dominican Republic and Puerto Rico. Thanks to immigration from Latin America, 'Spanglish' is increasingly spoken in El Norte (aka the USA) and Spanish is the USA's second most common language.

COMMUNICATION

Internet cafés and wi-fi hotspots are commonplace in both the USA and Canada – access is usually cheapest (often free) in public libraries. The Caribbean has internet access in most tourist areas, but wi-fi is still quite rare and you'll have to prepare yourself for sloth-like speeds.

The North American mobile-phone (or 'cell') system uses GSM 1900 or CDMA 800. The geek-free translation is that unless you have a tri-band model phone, you're better off renting or buying a pay-as-you-go option for the length of your stay.

HEALTH

North America is a pretty healthy place, which is just as well since being ill costs a fortune. You may have to get special insurance to cover you in the USA, so double-check that your coverage includes the States.

Outdoors, there's a small risk of tick-borne diseases (such as Rocky Mountain fever and Lyme disease), giardiasis (known locally as 'beaver fever'), caught by drinking contaminated water, and the odd case of rabies in the northern wilderness. Sharks are a rare health risk to surfers in Florida and northern California.

In the Caribbean a few more travel precautions are required. Some fresh water is contaminated with schistosomiasis (bilharzia) or leptospirosis, and mosquitoes in some areas carry dengue fever.

Consult the Health & Safety chapter (p41) and seek professional medical advice for more travel-health information.

ISSUES

Many travellers get the idea from TV and films that the US is a violent place and that everyone has a gun. The truth is that crime does occur, but much of it happens in 'bad neighbourhoods' and if you take a few precautions (see p50) you should avoid harm. If you're heading for bigger cities, find out where the unsafe areas are and steer clear. Rural America is generally safe, while Canada's tougher gun laws mean the country sees significantly less violent crime.

The Caribbean isn't so simple. Haiti has volatile security and travel is not advisable. Kingston in Jamaica has a reputation for violent crime and you should think hard before wandering the streets at night. You should check the latest on the safety in these regions by using government warning sites (see p41).

August to September is hurricane season in the Caribbean and the southern USA, with many places closing in August. New Orleans was hit by a devastating flood in August 2005 and islands in the Caribbean are also irregularly hit by heavy weather.

Borders are pretty easy-going throughout the region, though the US Department of Homeland Security can occasionally shake down the odd traveller. If anything is out of order or if they suspect you of intending to work illegally, they'll send you straight home. Beefed-up domestic security means that there are strict limits on what you can carry on domestic flights; check the **Transport Administration Authority** (http://www.tsa .gov/travelers/index.shtm) for details.

GETTING THERE

AIR

Chicago, Los Angeles, New York, Miami, San Francisco and Washington, DC are the USA's major international hubs, but flights into other US cities won't cost much more. Toronto, Montreal and Vancouver are the major Canadian air hubs. If you're coming from Australasia or Southeast Asia, it may be cheaper to hop on a flight to Hawaii and get a domestic flight within the US.

There are direct flights from London to a few former British colonies in the Caribbean, and flights from Paris to Guadeloupe and Martinique. The cheapest way to visit the Caribbean is often as part of a package deal, at least initially.

Transatlantic alliances and code-share agreements mean that reaching many major Caribbean and far-flung North American destinations, such as Hawai'i and Alaska, often requires at least one change of planes (in order to get the cheapest deal). Ask about the possibility of free stopovers on these routes.

There are literally hundreds of airlines flying to North America, with new budget providers appearing every day. If you're flexible with your travel dates, another option is flying stand-by with last-minute, space-available specialists such as **Airhitch** (www .airhitch.org) and **AirTech** (www.airtech.com).

SEA

Cruising to North America can be very pricey, though you might be lucky enough to score passage across the Atlantic or Pacific on a yacht or cruise ship. Ferrying from Iceland, then hoping for a passage to Greenland is a chilly possibility.

SPECIALIST TOUR OPERATORS

o **Go Native America** (www.gonativeamerica.com) A US-based organisation that offers tours into Native America.

o **Green Tortoise Adventure Travel** (www.green tortoise.com) Try their hostel-hopper that goes between San Francisco, Los Angeles and Las Vegas, with trips further afield to Alaska, Baja Peninsula and Mexico.

o **TrekAmerica** (www.trekamerica.co.uk) Trips taking in a combination of big cities, national parks, out-of-the-way towns and remote beaches.

BEYOND NORTH AMERICA & THE CARIBBEAN

The most obvious route out of the region is overland south into Central and South America. You can take the Pan-American Hwy into Mexico and roll through Central America all the way to Buenos Aires with a couple of pit stops.

With some patience, you can hop from the islands of the Eastern Caribbean to Güiria in Venezuela by ferry, landing on the doorstep of South America. It's also possible to catch a boat from Jamaica and other Caribbean islands to Central America (normally Belize, Honduras or Panama).

From Greenland you can set sail for Copenhagen and Reykjavík, and continue on to the rest of Europe.

FURTHER INFORMATION

WEBSITES

For specific country overviews, the lowdown on travel in the region and hundreds of useful links, surf Lonely Planet's website (lonelyplanet.com).

The portals listed here provide a different slant on the region:

o **Canadian Tourism Commission** (www.travelcanada .ca) Official tourist site packed with details.

o **Canada's Cultural Gateway** (www.culture.ca) All the facts about Canada, including what Mounties actually do out there on the prairies.

o **caribbean-on-line.com** (www.caribbean-on-line .com) Caribbean travel portal.

o **Caribseek** (www.caribseek.com) Popular portal into all things Caribbean.

o **National Park Hotel Guide** (www.national parkhotelguide.com) A guide to hotels throughout the wilderness of USA and Canada.

o **Road Trip USA** (www.roadtripusa.com) Ace guide to the USA's best off-the-beaten-blacktop road trips.

o **Travel.org** (www.travel.org/na.html) Huge North American travel directory.

BOOKS

o *Bury My Heart at Wounded Knee* (Dee Brown) The book that brought Native American experience to the mainstream.

o *On the Road* (Jack Kerouac) The blueprint for American road trips with the odd drug-fuelled detour; if you're over classics, *Dharma Bums* will blow your hair back.

o *Tell My Horse: Voodoo and Life in Haiti and Jamaica* (Zora Neale Hurston) Follow a voodoo disciple into the spooky other world of magic.

o *Dread: The Rastafarians of Jamaica* (Joseph Owens) Beyond the *ganja* (marijuana), this is a deep examination of Jamaica's cultural cornerstone.

o *The Lost Continent* (Bill Bryson) An American travel writer turns his pen on his own country with some chuckle-worthy observations.

o *Seek: Reports from the Edges of America and Beyond* (Denis Johnson) A look at America from fundamentalists to fun-lovers contrasted with the author's global wanderings.

FILMS

o *Into the Wild* (2007) After university a top student gives away his life savings and hitches to Alaska to see the country.

o *Traffic* (2000) The US war on drugs from both sides of the Mexican border.

o *Les Invasions Barbares* (The Barbarian Invasions; 2003) An intellectual Québec film (in French) following a son's efforts to make his father's last days perfect.

o *Hollywood North* (2003) A mockumentary about the Canadian film industry.

o *Garden State* (2004) A New Jersey escapee is forced to return for his mother's funeral and some home truths.

MEXICO, CENTRAL & SOUTH AMERICA

Latin America is an epic destination that lures in first-time travellers with its extraordinary terrain and captivating history. The region stretches from the arid northern border of Mexico to the glacial southerly tip of Patagonia in South America. But in between these distant frontiers lie idyllic beaches, lush jungles, pristine lakes, pulsating cities and towering mountains.

The heady mix doesn't stop there – add the voices of the ancient Aztec, Mayan and Incan civilisations, and you have yourself a potent cocktail of potential travel experiences. Mexico's magnificent Aztec heritage is a huge draw, while Guatemala, Belize and Honduras form the heartlands of the complex and learned culture of the Maya. Further south in Peru, trekkers can uncover the breathtaking beauty of Machu Picchu at the heart of the former Inca empire.

Ecotourism is huge these days, which is why Costa Rica is grabbing headlines in every travel magazine from New York to London and Sydney. Indeed, vast swaths of the country are either private reserves or national parks, and the government has progressive environmental policies. But there are other countries that also boast spectacular landscapes and amazing creatures – as well as fewer tourists. The Honduran Bay Islands and Belize are prized for their diving and snorkelling, while the Andes mountain range stretches from Colombia to the tip of Patagonia like a continental backbone. And of course, the lungs of the New World are the lush and fertile Amazon jungle that carpets much of the interior.

People lose their hearts to Latin American cities too. Buenos Aires' wide, grand boulevards, and the sensual melancholy melody of its tango, have cast a spell on many a visitor, while the *joie de vivre* and sights of Rio de Janeiro and Brazil's legendary Carnaval are known the world over.

Whether you find yourself taking a siesta in a hammock on the Mexican Riviera, or trekking along the ancient Inca Trail, you could easily amble around the region for months and never tire of it.

ITINERARIES

A trip from Mexico to Argentina is entirely within the realm of possibility and remains one of the planet's great overland adventures. However, it takes time, energy and a whole lot of patience to travel the vast expanse of two continents. For those with less time, however, you can still cover a lot of ground in a few months, especially if you focus your energy on a particular area or two. Although it's hard to generalise a region as varied as Latin America, it helps to break things down: think Mexico, Central America, the Andes and Amazonia.

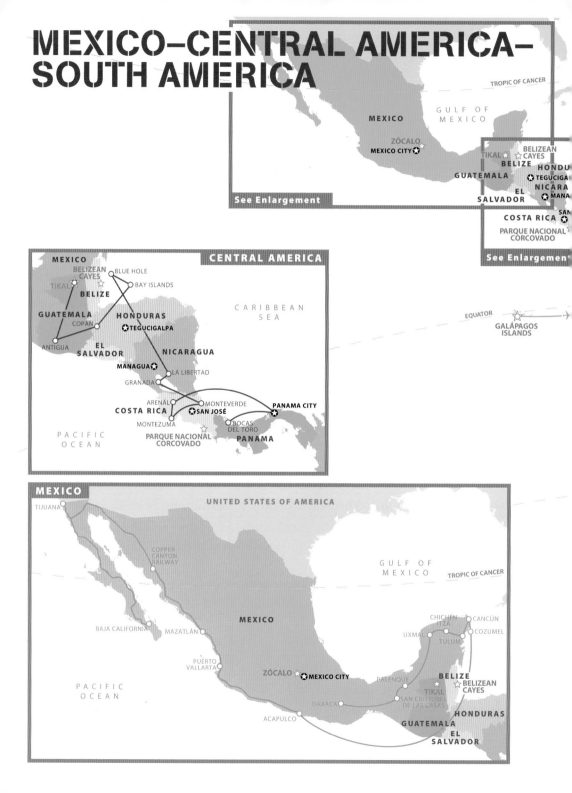

MEXICO–CENTRAL AMERICA–
SOUTH AMERICA

TROPIC OF CANCER

GULF OF
MEXICO

MEXICO

ZÓCALO
MEXICO CITY

TIKAL ☆ ★ BELIZEAN
CAYES

BELIZE HONDU

GUATEMALA ★ TEGUCIGA
NICARA

EL ★ MANA
SALVADOR

See Enlargement

SAN
COSTA RICA ★

PARQUE NACIONAL
CORCOVADO

See Enlargemen

CENTRAL AMERICA

MEXICO
BELIZEAN
CAYES BLUE HOLE
TIKAL ☆ BAY ISLANDS
BELIZE

GUATEMALA HONDURAS
COPÁN ★ TEGUCIGALPA

ANTIGUA EL NICARAGUA
SALVADOR
MANAGUA ★ LA LIBERTAD
GRANADA

ARENÁL MONTEVERDE PANAMA CITY
COSTA RICA ★ SAN JOSÉ
MONTEZUMA BOCAS
DEL TORO
PARQUE NACIONAL PANAMA
CORCOVADO

PACIFIC
OCEAN

CARIBBEAN
SEA

EQUATOR
GALÁPAGOS
ISLANDS

MEXICO

UNITED STATES OF AMERICA

TIJUANA

COPPER
CANYON
RAILWAY

GULF OF
MEXICO TROPIC OF CANCER

MEXICO

BAJA CALIFORNIA MAZATLÁN

CHICHÉN CANCÚN
ITZA
UXMAL COZUMEL
TULUM

PUERTO
VALLARTA

ZÓCALO ★ MEXICO CITY

PALENQUE BELIZE
TIKAL ☆ BELIZEAN
CAYES

PACIFIC
OCEAN

OAXACA SAN CRISTOBEL
DE LAS CASAS
HONDURAS
ACAPULCO
GUATEMALA
EL
SALVADOR

CARIBBEAN
SEA

EASTERN
CARIBBEAN
ISLANDS

UBA

HAITI

MAICA

SANTA
MARTA

AMA
TY

CARTAGENA

★ CARACAS

VENEZUELA

★ GEORGETOWN

NAMA

PARAMARIBO

BOGOTÁ ★

COLOMBIA

GUYANA

SURINAME

French
Guiana
(FRANCE)

ATLANTIC
OCEAN

★ QUITO

CUADOR

DEVIL'S NOSE

MANAUS

LETICIA

AMAZON
RAINFOREST

PERU

MACHU
PICCHU

BRAZIL

LIMA ★

INCA
TRAIL

CUSCO

★ LA PAZ

BRASÍLIA
★

BOLIVIA

SALAR
DE UYUNI

PARAGUAY

RIO DE JANEIRO

TROPIC OF CAPRICORN

SAN PEDRO
DE ATACAMA

☆ SUGARLOAF
MOUNTAIN

ASUNCIÓN
★

CHILE

IGUAZU
FALLS

URAGUAY

MENDOZA

VALPARAISO

SANTIAGO
★

BUENOS
AIRES ★

MONTEVIDEO
★

ARGENTINA

Falkland Islands
(Islas Malvinas)

TORRES
☆ DEL PAINE

TIERRA DEL
FUEGO

☆ **HIGHLIGHTS**
—○— Mexican Margaritas
—○— Cervezas En Centro
—○— Andean Highs & Chilean Wines
—○— Rainforests & Rum
✈ Air   ⊞ Train
⚓ Boat   ⚲ Cycle

THE GREAT BLUE HOLE (SEE P256), MADE FAMOUS BY JACQUES-YVES COUSTEAU, IS A POPULAR DIVE SPOT OFF THE COAST OF BELIZE.

WHERE MESOAMERICAN AND SOUTH AMERICAN NATIVE CULTURES MET: COSTA RICA BOASTS THE LUSH PARQUE NACIONAL CORCOVADO (SEE P257).

DEAD RELATIVES ARE WELCOMED BACK WITH SKULLS AND THEIR FAVOURITE FOODS ON DÍA DE LOS MUERTOS (SEE P260), 'DAY OF THE DEAD', IN MEXICO.

MEXICAN MARGARITAS

Mexico is as varied as its world-famous cuisine, which means that you can kick off your travels in a few tourist hotspots. If you're coming down from Gringo Land (USA), **Tijuana** is the country's notorious gateway. But Mexico is much more than cheap tequila and donkey shows, which you'll quickly learn once you start surfing the wilderness beaches of **Baja California**.

If you cross the border at Texas, consider riding the legendary **Copper Canyon Railway**, which cuts through canyons and winds around dizzyingly high cliffs on its way from Chihuahua to the Pacific. Once you arrive on the coast, **Mazatlán, Puerto Vallarta** and **Acapulco** are traditional destinations for sun-worshippers and siesta-seekers.

If you want to combine some quality beach time with visits to spectacular ruins, the Yucatán Peninsula is just the place. A few margarita-fuelled nights in **Cozumel** and **Cancún** could be followed by a healthy dose of visits to pre-Columbian sites, including the stunning cliff-top ruins at **Tulum,** and the famous Mayan sites of **Uxmal** and **Chichén Itzá**.

Continuing on the same theme, don't miss the Indiana Jones–esque lost jungle city of **Palenque**, before kicking it colonial style in either **Oaxaca** or **San Cristóbal de las Casas**.

CERVEZAS EN CENTRO

Nothing beats the tropical heat of Central America like an ice cold *cerveza* (beer). After scaling temples in Guatemala's **Tikal**, the crown jewel of the old Mayan cities, pop the top on a Gallo lager in the beautiful volcano-ringed colonial city of **Antigua**. This backpacker paradise is a great place to spend a few weeks studying Spanish in an affordable language school, but be sure to press on to the **Copán** ruins just within Honduras.

A jaunt out to the **Bay Islands** for a spot of diving or snorkelling is an understandably popular diversion, as is kicking back and savouring a bottle of Salva Vida. In neighbouring Belize, the **Blue Hole** is regarded as one of the world's top dive sites, and the Belikin beer ain't half bad either!

In this narrow waist of the Americas, it's not difficult to make rapid headway down through El Salvador and Nicaragua. Surfers rave about the empty beaches and

Suprema beers of **La Libertad**, while history buffs are happy to brave the potholed roads of Nicaragua for a chance to sip a Tona in the colonial city of **Granada**.

For many, the Gringo Trail stops at the eco-haven of Costa Rica, where you can down bottles of Imperial lager in the rainforests of **Monteverde**, on the beaches of **Montezuma**, or in front of the volcano at **Arenal**. But those who continue south to Panama are richly rewarded. From the chic clubs of **Panama City** to the Caribbean climes of **Bocas del Toro**, this country (and its Balboa lagers) remains bewilderingly underexplored.

Some intrepid folk skirt around the dangerous no-man's-land of Darién Gap by freighter or yacht, but it's far safer to get a flight if you're continuing down to South America.

ANDEAN HIGHS & CHILEAN WINES

Many travellers, lured by the **Galápagos Islands**, pick up the Gringo Trail in Ecuador. Ecuador's capital, **Quito**, is a stunning city more than worthy of its World Heritage status. There is also a memorable **Devil's Nose** (El Nariz del Diablo) train journey leading from Riobamba to Durán on the coast, which is worth working into your jaunt around Ecuador – it's often referred to as South America in miniature.

Heading south to Peru, almost all travellers will pass through **Lima** (once one of the most glorious colonial cities, now fallen on harder times) on their way to the **Inca Trail**. The Southern Railway to **Cuzco** provides a wonderful rickety ride close to **Machu Picchu** itself.

From there, the laid-back, altitudinous climes of **Lake Titicaca** draw in a lot of backpackers, as do the breathtaking Bolivian **Salar de Uyuni** salt plains and Chile's laid-back oasis of **San Pedro de Atacama**.

Most travellers to Chile arrive in **Santiago** at some point, either by bus or by plane. After savouring a sophisticated glass of Chilean red or white, it's a short hop to the charming, faded grandeur of the port city of **Valparaíso**, and a pivot for the exhilarating trans-Andean bus ride over to the colonial Argentinian city of **Mendoza**. In recent years more and more travellers are venturing to the very tip of the continent to see the majestic **Torres del Paine** and/or the stark **Tierra del Fuego**.

MY FIRST
~ JUNGLE NIGHT ~

The jaguars didn't bother me much during the day. Adonis, our local guide who was leading us deep into the Guatemalan jungle, assured us they were elusive, shy creatures. The most recent time he had seen one was more than a year ago when he had surprised a pair in the act of jaguar love. Last week, he had spotted some jaguar spoor, which was probably about as close to the animals as we would get, he said.

But his reassurance meant little that night as I cowered in my hammock under the Central American stars. Now my mind turned every rustle into a prowling big cat full of murderous intent (probably to get back at the rude human who had interrupted a moment of feline passion). And, if it wasn't a jaguar poised to spring, it was a poisonous fer-de-lance viper, picking which of my buttocks to sink its fangs into.

Tiredness calmed my overactive imagination and I dozed. Next day, big surprise: no death by either snakebite or jaguar mauling. We packed up our stuff and continued towards our destination, El Mirador, the site of the tallest temple in the Mayan world, and two days' trekking from the small village of Carmelita at the end of the road.

Although we may have questioned why we had left a perfectly nice Honduran beach to come here, that night no doubts remained. Just before sunset we took our places at the top of the unexcavated temple mound. A Mayan astrology priest had probably sat in the same place 2000 years before and honed his knowledge of the galaxy. Tonight, as with every night, the howler monkeys screeched their farewells to the setting sun as spectacular pink shades streaked the western skyline. The sky darkened and, one by one, the stars shimmered into life.

Jolyon Attwooll is a Lonely Planet author who worked at the Santiago Times *where he was introduced to tango and pisco sours.*

RAINFORESTS & RUM

To the east, a sort of Gringo Triangle has formed around rum-soaked **Rio de Janeiro** through to the towering **Iguazú Falls** and **Buenos Aires**, the cosmopolitan capital of Argentina. Although they're decidedly different in character, sultry Rio and stately Buenos Aires are two of Latin America's most attractive cities. At the thundering Iguazú Falls on the edge of Amazonia, you'll catch a glimpse of the vast expanse of rainforest that lies beyond.

The **Amazon Rainforest** is almost like a continent unto itself, with a whole network of miniroutes within its borders. However, one of the best ways to tackle this huge landscape is by taking an unforgettable river trip from the jungle city of **Manaus** in Brazil to **Leticia** in Colombia.

Elsewhere in the region, travellers are fewer and farther between, though there are many diversions for the truly intrepid. Colombia and Venezuela definitely fall into the category of tough travel, though people rave about the old-world cities of **Cartagena** and **Santa Marta**. In neighbouring Venezuela, you can check out

Angel Falls, the world's highest waterfall, and the world's longest cable car at **Mérida**.

The possibilities for off-the-beaten-path adventure don't stop there. Island-hopping off the coast of Rio is one option, as is a trip into the unsung but captivating nation of **Uruguay**.

WHAT TO DO?

HIGHLIGHTS

○ Heading deep into the jungles to discover the lost city of **Tikal** (Guatemala), one of the great wonders of the Mayan world.
○ Getting your dive on in the **Belizean Cayes** (Belize), the site of the world's second largest barrier reef.
○ Coming face to face with rare wildlife in **Parque Nacional Corcovado** (Costa Rica), a biodiversity hotspot.
○ Snapping pics of **Sugarloaf Mountain** (Rio de Janeiro, Brazil), the quintessential sight of this spectacularly located city.

- Following Darwin's storied tracks through the far-flung **Galápagos Islands** (Ecuador).
- Exploring the end of the world at **Torres del Paine** (Chile), home to turquoise lakes, granite pillars and pristine glaciers.
- Entering a seemingly alien landscape when you drive on the world's largest salt flats at **Salar de Uyuni** (Bolivia).
- Trekking along the Inca Trail to **Machu Picchu** (Peru), one of the wonders of the ancient world.
- Standing in awe before **Iguazú Falls** (Argentina, Paraguay, Brazil), which are more than 2km wide.
- Viewing Mexico in a single frame at the **Zócalo** (Mexico City), which blends colonial architecture with Aztec ruins.

GET ACTIVE

Latin America has its fair share of hammock-strung beaches, which is good news – you'll want a *siesta* after getting your adrenaline fix.

Caving

Central America has a labyrinth of caves, many of which were used as ceremonial sites by the Maya. Lanquín is the best known in Guatemala, and has a spectacular exodus of bats at dusk. Mexico's Cuetzalan cave system is renowned amongst cavers, as is Sótano de las Golondrinas, which is reputedly the world's second-deepest cave entrance. In South America, Venezuela is riddled with cave systems – Cueva del Guácharo (inland from Cumaná) is definitely up there on the speleology must-do list. In the northeast of Brazil, close to 200 deep underground caves are known to exist in the Terra Ronca region, one of the largest networks in Latin America – many caves are still unexplored.

Cycling & Mountain-Biking

In Central America, Costa Rica is best geared to the two-wheeled traveller. Potholes in other parts of the region can put off some pedalling fans, but with a bit of patience, successful journeys can be made. Extreme mountain-bikers might fancy biking down 'Death Road' in Bolivia. Statistically the most dangerous road in the world, its sweeping downhill run still attracts many a saddled daredevil. An increasingly popular biking option is to cycle the spectacular forests and lakes of southern Chile and Argentina.

Diving & Snorkelling

Belize has the planet's second-largest barrier reef, some crystal-clear waters and breathtaking dive sites. Cozumel in Mexico is also known as a great destination for lovers of underwater life. If you're on a tight budget, you could head to the Honduran Bay Islands, particularly Utila, which offers cheap PADI courses. But don't ignore the Pacific coast – there is still some memorable diving here, including off Panama's Coiba Island. Down in South America, the best diving is off the Galápagos Islands. Only experienced divers take the plunge here, but they get a privileged glimpse into a world of sea lions, hammerhead sharks and eagle rays.

Skiing & Snowboarding

Some world-class slopes are located in Argentina and Chile. The most renowned resort is Chile's Portillo, just over an hour and a half away by car or bus from Santiago, where off-season training and competitions are often run for northern-hemisphere downhillers. El Colorado, La Parca and Valle Nevado are also not far away from the Chilean capital, and all of them have decent facilities. Termas de Chillán is the main destination for slope junkies in the south of Chile. Across the Andes in Argentina, Las Leñas, Chapelco and Cerro Catedral all have decent powder from June to September.

Surfing

The Pacific Ocean off Central America has some great surfing. Costa Rica draws its fair share of jet-setting surfers, especially since you can choose from two oceans. The Pacific has more consistent waves, but the swells on the Caribbean coast can be more impressive during the right season. El Salvador is often overlooked, but its beaches have some great breaks – mainly in the La Libertad region. The powerful Mexican Pipeline break at Puerto Escondido in Baja California is also a big draw for wave fans. In South America, try the Chilean town of Pichilemu for more low-key (and colder) surf, while Brazil's coastline is almost one uninterrupted line of surfing nirvana.

ZÓCALO (P258), 'THE PLINTH', FORMALLY KNOWN AS LA PLAZA DE LA CONSTITUTIÓN, IS THE MAIN SQUARE IN MEXICO CITY.

Trekking & Mountaineering

Pick any spot in Central America, and chances are there will be a volcano looming nearby. One of the most accessible is Volcán Pacaya near Antigua, Guatemala. A stream of tourists treks to the summit for a noxious waft of sulphur and the chance to stride on the volcanic ash.

If the Andes look awesome from below, they are even more breathtaking once you are in amongst them. Among the cognoscenti, the peaks in Peru are thought to provide the best climbing opportunities. The Cordillera Huayhuash is one for hard-core climbers, while the Cordillera Blanca includes some of the more popular peaks around the town of Cuzco.

In the north of Chile, San Pedro de Atacama is a popular launching point for treks. Further down, many *andinistas* (as opposed to alpinists) get tempted by the mountains that encircle Santiago. Los Leones is a good one for the enthusiastic but inexperienced climber. On the other hand, Argentina's Mt Aconcagua (6962m) is the highest summit in the western hemisphere, and should only be undertaken by the very experienced – it can take weeks simply to acclimatise to the thin air.

White-Water Rafting

When it comes to water sports, Costa Rica, once again, got there first in Central America. The Reventazón and Pacuare rivers in Costa Rica are in a stunning virgin-forest setting. However, other countries are now getting in on the white-water action. Both Honduras and Guatemala have some decent rafting opportunities with varying levels of difficulty. In Mexico, visit the state of Veracruz for some hair-raising white-water rafting.

Chile arguably has the best (and most challenging) rapids in South America, with exhilarating runs for both rafters and kayakers on the Maipó, Trancura and Futaleufú rivers. Just across the Andes in Argentina, Mendoza offers plenty of scope to satisfy white-water thrill-seekers. There's also rafting just outside of Cuzco in Peru, and Ecuador's many rivers bubble with possibilities.

INTI RAYMI, 'FESTIVAL OF THE SUN', SACSAYHUAMAN INCAN RUINS, PERU.

WILDLIFE

Latin America hogs more than its fair share of all creatures great and small. In Central America, you can banter with spider monkeys in Nicaragua, recoil from tarantulas in El Salvador, and view a kaleidoscopic range of birds, from macaws to the elusive quetzal, in Guatemala. Costa Rica, with its rainforest-canopy walkways, is the most developed nation for wildlife-spotters, but the ecosystem is equally broad in most of its neighbours. For instance, Panama has around 940 different types of birds to spot.

In South America you are even more spoilt for choice. The Amazon has an estimated 15,000 animal species, with around 1800 species of butterfly alone! Less feted, but with far more visible wildlife, the Pantanal wetlands in the west of Brazil teem with pumas, anacondas, giant river otters and a myriad of other exotic creatures. The same accessibility is also available in the Esteros del Iberá marshlands in Corrientes (Argentina), while the Península de Valdés in the same country is a great place to watch whales.

Then, of course, there are the legendary Galápagos Islands, where a couple of the giant tortoises may even have been around to welcome Darwin ashore back in the old days.

FESTIVALS

From sacred indigenous ceremonies in Peru to Carnaval in Rio, Latin Americans are never ones to shirk an opportunity for a full-blooded celebration. Try to fit as many of the following into your trip as possible:

○ **New Year's Eve** (Chile) Not, strictly speaking, a festival, but the spectacular fireworks extravaganza and New Year's celebration at Valparaíso is one of the finest of its kind anywhere.

○ **Carnaval** (Brazil) The February carnivals in Rio, Olinda, Recife and Salvador are some of the most spectacular festivals on earth. Parades, dancing, music and song combine for the most hedonistic of celebrations.

○ **Oruro Carnaval** (Bolivia) Tub-thumping raucous festival where costume parades and hedonistic festivities enthral thousands of visitors in February each year.

○ **Semana Santa** (Guatemala) The Easter celebrations in the delightful colonial town of Antigua include colourful parades, elaborate ceremonies and beautiful yet fragile decorations.

○ **Los Diablos Danzantes** (Venezuela) Held on Corpus Christi (usually the ninth Thursday after Easter) in San Francisco de Yare; a fiery parade and devil-dancers cap off the festivities.

○ **Inti Raymi** (Peru) The 'sun festival' of Cuzco (24 June) culminates with a re-enactment of the Inca winter-solstice observance at Sacsayhuamán.

○ **Festival of Yamor** (Ecuador) Otavalo's biggest shindig in early September has fireworks, parades and an all-round party atmosphere. The Reina de la Fiesta procession is a highlight.

○ **Día de Los Muertos** (Day of the Dead; Mexico) Mexicans welcome the souls of their dead back to earth across the country (Pátzcuaro is especially colourful) on 2 November.

○ **Día del Tango** (Argentina) Informal celebration of the birthday of tango great Carlos Gardel (11 December) and a good time to hit Buenos Aires to see tango, an integral part of that city's character.

○ **Día de Nuestra Señora de Guadalupe** (Mexico) The day (12 December) of Mexico's patron saint, Guadalupe. Festivities culminate with a huge procession and party at the Basílica de Guadalupe in Mexico City.

PARTY SCENE

The Gringo Trail is full of classic backpacker towns and cities where you can congregate with like-minded people, drink, smoke and chill out.

○ **Antigua** (Guatemala) Ringed by volcanoes, buzzing with nightlife and steeped in history, this is a delightful place to relax.

○ **Cuzco** (Peru) The former Inca capital is not only the gateway to Machu Picchu, but is also a happening town in its own right.

○ **Isla Montecristo** (El Salvador) Tranquil community on the Pacific Peninsula.

○ **Jericoacoara** (Brazil) This is the latest off-the-beaten-track beach to get popular with the laid-back travelling crowd.

○ **Lago de Atitlán** (Guatemala) One of the most gorgeous settings imaginable. No place for stress here.

○ **Lake Titicaca** (Bolivia and Peru) A massive high-altitude lake with accessible islands in the middle and colourful locals.

○ **Montañita** (Ecuador) Bohemian little place with the best surf in the country.

○ **Pucón** (Chile) One for action fans, this picturesque town also has plenty of sedate trekking options on offer.

○ **San Cristóbal de las Casas** (Mexico) Charming colonial town with a distinct bohemian vibe, perched in the invigorating air of the Chiapas highlands.

○ **San Juan del Sur** (Nicaragua) Magnificent Pacific bay and party town.

○ **San Pedro de Atacama** (Chile) Sleepy, laid-back stopoff for travellers to the moonlike surroundings of the Chilean desert.

You can add to this list the classic party capitals such as Mexico City (Mexico), Cancún (Mexico), Tamarindo (Costa Rica), Rio de Janeiro (Brazil) and Buenos Aires (Argentina).

ROADS LESS TRAVELLED

How many people can you get onto a Latin American bus? Answer: two more. Not the funniest joke perhaps, but the punch line has a point – travelling in rural Latin America is not for the nervous or claustrophobic!

However, a ride on the region's infamous 'chicken buses' is an essential part of the Latin American travelling experience. Often, you'll find yourself sandwiched between two locals (and maybe their infants too) in a space designed to accommodate two school children. And as you get a little off the beaten track, paved roads give way to dust, mud and the occasional river crossing.

VOLUNTEER TRAVELLING

Latin America is awash with volunteer positions, with something to suit almost everyone. You could work with street kids in Lima, build houses in Honduras, teach orphans in Buenos Aires, conserve sea turtles in Costa Rica, support women's groups in Chile – the range of options are simply huge.

Before arriving, many first-timers prefer to sort out their volunteer work through an organisation in their home country, which is good for peace of mind. These groups usually arrange projects before you arrive, and provide backup and support in case things go wrong. However, don't rule out the possibility of finding volunteer work once you are in the region. It often works out to be cheaper in the long run, and you can get a feel for a project before you agree to join in. For more on how to organise a volunteering trip, see p143.

COURSES

Get beyond *una cerveza por favor* (a beer, please), and you will dig a lot deeper into the local culture – and that truly is what travel is all about. If you want a few lessons just to help you get by, there are cheap language schools in the popular tourist towns such as Antigua, Mexico City and Buenos Aires. If you're a would-be linguist, however, try somewhere slightly more off the beaten track, where you are less likely to be sharing a beer each night with 10 other gringos and speaking in English. Homestays are good for this, though like with anything else in life, practice makes perfect.

WORKING

Speaking English as a first language is no longer the guaranteed ticket to employment it once was. Many language schools no longer take on teachers without a degree or a TEFL qualification – so go armed with one or the other, or have an alternative plan to make ends meet. Possibilities also exist for crewing on foreign yachts that stop along the Pacific, especially on the Guatemalan, Costa Rican, Venezuelan, Ecuadorian and Peruvian coasts. Deck hands are occasionally taken on by yachts at either end of the Panama Canal. In popular tourist areas, jobs for tour leaders, trekking guides, hostel managers, bar hands or shop workers do crop up – but don't expect to make much more than *cerveza* money.

WHEN TO GO?

The busiest time for tourism tends to be from December to March, when many gringos seek shelter from cold, northerly climes. July and August are also popular. In such a vast region with great geographical extremes, there is, unsurprisingly, a huge variety in climate. And the best time to go will depend largely on what you plan to do. There are no seasonal patterns that apply everywhere in Latin America, so be careful to check the weather cycles for each of your destinations when you are planning your trip.

WHAT TO EXPECT?

LOCALS & OTHER TRAVELLERS

In Mexico and Central America there is a large North American travelling contingent, while in South America the backpacker balance is slightly more European. Plenty of Aussies and Kiwis frequent most of the Gringo Trail in Latin America, and there is a growing number of Korean and Japanese visitors.

   The Latin Americans' reputation for being extrovert, warm and always up for a fiesta is generally true, although you may find isolated indigenous communities are more reserved. Female travellers should be aware that a machismo attitude is widespread in Latin America (although not universal), meaning attention from the opposite sex is much more obvious.

FOOD

Throughout most of Latin America, food tends to centre on the hearty and healthy staple combination of rice and beans. But fresh fruit (especially in the tropics) is never far from the menu, nor is fresh seafood along the coasts. And there are a few noteworthy culinary hotspots, namely Mexico, with its richly varied regional cuisines, and the Argentinian pampas, home to some of the world's most sumptuous steaks.

LANGUAGE

Spanish is the official language in every Latin American country with the exception of Brazil (Portuguese), Belize (English), Suriname (Dutch), French Guiana (French) and Guyana (English). English is on the rise and often spoken in big cities and tourist areas, but learning the rudiments of the Spanish and/or Portuguese is strongly advised. There are also hundreds of indigenous languages still being used in Latin America, although the number of speakers are dwindling.

COMMUNICATION

Internet cafés are springing up in all the tourist areas, and the prices have come down while the speed of connection has accelerated. Mobile-phone technology is also spreading. Calls in some countries (especially in Central America) are surprisingly cheap – worth looking into if you're sticking around for a while. Those on the move often find net phones in the well-frequented hostels along the Gringo Trail. With a good connection, these are a cheap way of keeping in touch.

COSTS

Although Latin America is generally still very good value for travellers, it is not always quite as cheap as some expect. The amount you need to spend will fluctuate a lot within the region, and will obviously depend on how comfortable you want to make yourself.

HEALTH

If you're going to a tropical region of Latin America, the list of recommended vaccinations can seem intimidating. Don't let this faze you – the most serious condition you're likely to encounter is a bad case of the runs. Malaria, however, is a risk, especially in lowland tropical areas, while yellow fever is endemic in Panama and most of the top half of South America. If you are going on a jungle trip, do take proper precautions.

Climbers should be wary of altitude sickness, which can be fatal. If you start feeling its effects, go down the mountain immediately. In the desert, the tropics or on a mountain, the sun can be dangerous – make sure your skin is properly protected.

ISSUES

While Latin America is no longer the hotbed of civil unrest that it once was, some countries still have fairly shaky political situations. Colombia in particular is noted for the armed conflict between its government and FARC (the Revolutionary Armed Forces of Colombia) rebels. Kidnappings, murders, paramilitary reprisals and counterreprisals are still depressingly common.

SAMPLE COSTS

	MEXICO (MEXICAN PESO, $)	COSTA RICA (COLÓN, ₡)	GUATEMALA (QUETZAL, Q)	BRAZIL (BRAZILIAN REAL, R$)	ARGENTINA (ARGENTINE PESO, $)
HOSTEL/ BUDGET ROOM	$110–220 £5.25–10.50 US$10.25–20.50 A$11.25–22.50	₡2500–12500 £2.55–12.75 US$5.05–25.25 A$5.55–27.75	Q40–160 £2.65–10.60 US$5.20–20.80 A$5.70–22.80	R$10–45 £3.00–13.10 US$5.70–25.70 A$6.25–28.00	$20–100 £3.25–16.25 US$6.35–31.75 A$7.00–35.00
CHEAP RESTAURANT MEAL	$20–80 £0.95–3.80 US$1.85–7.40 A$2.05–8.20	₡1500–4500 £1.55–4.65 US$3.05–9.15 A$3.35–10.05	Q10–40 £0.65–2.65 US$1.30–5.20 A$1.45–5.70	R$4–20 £1.15–5.75 US$2.30–11.50 A$2.5–12.5	$7–20 £1.15–3.25 US$2.25–6.35 A$2.45–7.00
1L BOTTLE OF WATER	$6 £0.30 US$0.55 A$0.65	₡300 £0.30 US$0.60 A$0.65	Q7 £0.45 US$0.90 A$1.00	R$2 £0.60 US$1.15 A$1.25	$4 £0.65 US$1.30 A$1.40
SOUVENIR T-SHIRT	$110 £5.25 US$10.25 A$11.25	₡4500 £4.65 US$9.15 A$10.05	Q40 £2.65 US$5.20 A$5.70	R$18 £5.25 US$10.25 A$11.25	$30 £4.85 US$9.50 A$10.45
BOTTLE OF BEER	$20 £0.95 US$1.85 A$2.05	₡500 £0.55 US$1.00 A$1.10	Q14 £0.90 US$1.80 A$2.00	R$3 £0.90 US$1.80 A$2.00	$6 £1.00 US$1.90 A$2.10
STREET SNACK	Nachos $10 £0.45 US$0.95 A$1.00	Churro ₡500 £0.55 US$1.00 A$1.10	Taco Q4 £0.25 US$0.50 A$0.60	Meat skewer R$2 £0.60 US$1.15 A$1.25	Empanada (stuffed pastry) $4 £0.65 US$1.25 A$1.40
1L PETROL	$6 £0.30 US$0.55 A$0.65	₡300 £0.30 US$0.60 A$0.65	Q7 £0.45 US$0.91 A$1.00	R$1 £0.30 US$0.60 A$0.70	$2 £0.30 US$0.65 A$0.70

Venezuela, too, has teetered dangerously towards civil unrest, following a frosty standoff between the government and the opposition. The situation is potentially volatile, so keep up with the latest developments if this country is on your wish list. The same applies to Bolivia and, to a lesser extent, Peru.

The economic crash in Argentina caused a well of resentment that still simmers today, although this is directed towards the government and banks rather than foreigners. Elsewhere, there is still tension in parts of the Mexican state of Chiapas.

Petty and violent crime is an issue in some Latin American cities and even in some tourist areas. Be vigilant, don't keep any more money than is necessary with you, and stick to tried and trusted routes.

GETTING THERE

You'll most likely need to fly direct. However, it is of course possible to fly to the USA, and then go overland into Latin America.

AIR
Latin America is extremely well connected via a number of international travel hubs. From roughly north to south, you can choose to start your travels in Mexico City, San José (Costa Rica), Panama City, Caracas (Venezuela), Bogotá (Colombia), Quito (Ecuador), Lima (Peru), Rio de Janeiro (Brazil), Santiago (Chile) or Buenos Aires (Argentina), as well as several other lesser-known hubs.

Budget airlines are nonexistent in Latin America, though several major players service the region:
o **Air France** (www.airfrance.com)
o **American Airlines** (www.aa.com)
o **Continental Airlines** (www.continental.com)
o **Delta Airlines** (www.delta.com)
o **Iberia Airlines** (www.iberia.com)
o **Lufthansa** (www.lufthansa.com)
o **Mexicana Airways** (www.mexicana.com)
o **TACA** (www.taca.com)
o **United Airlines** (www.united.com)

SEA & OVERLAND
If you're planning on travelling from Mexico to Argentina, you will most likely need to bypass Darién Gap to get between Panama and Colombia. One option for doing this is to sail from Colón to Cartagena (of course, you can always fly!). Otherwise, travelling by sea is not a particularly practical option.

Travelling overland through Latin America is a wonderful way of exploring the region, especially since border crossings are generally safe and secure. Some travellers even buy cars before hitting the open road, but you really need to be confident you know your stuff, both mechanically and drivingwise, to even contemplate this option.

SPECIALIST TOUR OPERATORS
Although crossing Darién Gap on foot isn't a wise decision, the region is ripe for exploration if you're young at heart and seeking some serious adventure. The exclusive operator in this vast wilderness region is **Ancon Expeditions** (www.anconexpeditions.com), which operates out of Panama City (Panama) and offers a variety of tailored treks.

BEYOND MEXICO, CENTRAL & SOUTH AMERICA

There are plenty of flights to Australia and New Zealand from Chile, Brazil and Argentina. You may get a stopover in the South Pacific, but the cheapest way to arrange this is with a round-the-world (RTW) ticket. Flights to North America (Miami is the cheapest destination) are frequent and often good value. There are also some cheap deals to Johannesburg from São Paulo and Buenos Aires – it could even be worth getting a return ticket if you fancy a quick blast in a different continent.

FURTHER INFORMATION

WEBSITES
o **About.com: South America Travel** (http://gosouthamerica.about.com) Portal with a range of links to Latin America–related sites.
o **Buenos Aires Herald** (www.buenosairesherald.com) The most established English-language daily in the region.
o **Latin America Press** (www.latinamericapress.org) News on political issues from across the region.

THE SUBLIME SALT FLATS OF SALAR DE UYUNI (P258), BOLIVIA, ARE THE DRIED-UP REMAINS OF A GIGANTIC PREHISTORIC LAKE.

- **Latin American Network Information Center** (www.lanic.utexas.edu) One of the best resources for Latin America.
- **Larutamayaonline.com** (www.larutamayaonline.com) Concentrates on Guatemala and Central America.
- **Santiago Times** (www.santiagotimes.cl) Daily English-language update on Chilean current affairs, with a broader South American perspective too.
- **South America Daily** (www.southamericadaily.com) Good place for a lowdown on the region's news.
- **South American Explorers** (www.saexplorers.org) Travel-club site with bulletin board and volunteer information.
- **Tico Times** (www.ticotimes.net) News source relied upon heavily by expats in Costa Rica.

BOOKS

- *One Hundred Years of Solitude* (Gabriel García Márquez) A masterpiece on the metaphorical history of Latin America.
- *House of Spirits* (Isabel Allende) An intimate account of the author's impressions of her native Chile.
- *I, Rigoberta Menchú* (Rigoberta Menchú) Brought the world's attention to the plight of the Maya in Guatemala.

- *The Old Patagonian Express* (Paul Theroux) Tells of a train journey from Boston to Patagonia; written in a cantankerous fashion.
- *Touching the Void* (Joe Simpson) Brilliantly captures the drama of an Andes mountaineering disaster.
- *Voyage of the Beagle* (Charles Darwin) Describes the trip that stirred the English scientist to form his theory of evolution.

FILMS

- *Maria Full of Grace* (2004) A portrait of a young and beautiful Colombian woman who becomes a mule in the cocaine trade.
- *The Motorcycle Diaries* (2004) An epic retelling of a young Che Guevara's motorcycle trip through South America.
- *City of God* (2003) A harrowing yet artistic portrait of life in the slums of Rio from the 1960s to the mid-1980s.
- *Y Tu Mamá También* (2002) Follows an uncensored coming-of-age road trip through the Mexican countryside.
- *Amores Perros* (2001) Hailed as the Mexican *Pulp Fiction* – an incredible tale of overlapping narratives set in Mexico City.
- *Evita* (1996) A controversial Hollywood recountal of the life of Argentina's Eva Perón, played by Madonna.

AFRICA

Africa is a travel destination known to strike fear into the hearts of parents, but to hell with that. This frequently misunderstood continent is home to no less than 53 countries, each of which offers a seemingly endless number of potentially life-changing experiences. Do believe the hype, as few destinations on the planet are as challenging and rewarding as the birthplace of humankind.

Africa is a place you need to explore, work at and put something into in order to get the maximum out. Not that this is an easy proposition of course, especially since the sheer scale of the continent can quickly overwhelm even seasoned travellers. You have to be up for the odd hard journey through this largely rural continent. And there are a few ugly and frantic cities, some of which are home to the poorest people on earth.

Africa will slap your senses silly, and leave your reeling for more – but it's all worth it, one hundred times over. It is a continent with a legacy of ancient civilisations and with diverse cultures that demand your attention. It's a place of majestic landscapes, stunning wildlife and adventurous overland journeys.

Pack your bags and check your expectations – you're in for a long and bumpy road. But, we promise that when you get to the end, you'll never look at life the same way.

ITINERARIES

Africa is the second-largest continent on the planet. It is home to dense jungles, bone-dry deserts, sprawling savannas, jagged mountains and seething cities. Choosing a place to start isn't as easy as slipping on your favourite jeans. However, it certainly doesn't have to be as difficult as figuring out what you want to do with your life. Trying to break down this hulking continent is also no small task, though it helps to think of Africa as having roughly four regions: north, south, east and west.

SOUTHERN SAFARI

Most first-time travellers to Africa choose to start in **Cape Town**, a dreamy and romantic ocean-side city on the western coast of South Africa. From here, you can get your booze on by visiting the vineyards along the **Garden Route**, and then following the backpacker trail to the legendary surfing mecca of **Jeffrey's Bay**. For your first face-to-face encounter with a horned oryx or a horny baboon, don't miss the wildlife-packed **Kruger National Park**.

If you're looking for a bit more adventure, press on to the **Kalahari** in Botswana and Namibia. Adrenaline junkies will want to go skydiving over the sand dunes in **Swakopmund**, while elephant-lovers can join the

ONG A BASE FOR ARAB SPICE TRADERS, ZANZIBAR (P272) NOW ATTRACTS TOURISTS WHO COME TO ENJOY ITS UNSPOILED BEACHES.

herd (tens of thousands strong) at **Chobe National Park**. Or, why not climb the world's tallest sand dunes at **Sossusvlei**, or spot hippos and crocs in the **Okavango Delta**?

If you're looking to head deeper into the continent, cross into either Zambia or Zimbabwe, which are divided by the legendary **Victoria Falls**. For rasta vibes, reggae nights and a whole lot of herb, kick it for a few days on the tranquil shores of **Lake Malawi**.

EASTERN ESCAPE

Another classic African gateway is **Nairobi**, the infamous capital city of Kenya. You're probably going to want to leave 'Nai-robbery' ASAP with your valuables in hand and make a beeline straight for **Masai Mara National Park**. Depending on the time of the year, you can follow the wildebeests on their annual migration to **Serengeti National Park** in neighbouring Tanzania.

As this is safari country, don't miss the veritable Lost World that is **Ngorongoro Crater**, or the stunning, arid and inhospitable **Lake Turkana**, the cradle of mankind. Mountain men (and women) will want to scale the lofty heights of **Mt Kenya** and **Mt Kilimanjaro**, though beach bums probably won't be able to leave the sun-kissed beaches of **Zanzibar** or **Lamu**.

Few experiences in Africa rival that of trekking through the rainforest in search of the rare mountain gorilla. Face-to-face encounters with the gentle giant take place at Uganda's **Bwindi Impenetrable National Park** and Rwanda's **Parc National des Volcans**.

Heading north into Ethiopia, travel gets distinctively tougher. But it's worth it to visit the birthplace of Haile Selassie, the physical incarnate of Jah Rastafari. Travellers also swoon over the rock-hewn churches at **Lalibela** or the ancient biblical city of **Aksum**.

NORTHERN NOMADS

Few travellers can resist the pull towards **Cairo**, the ancient Egyptian city on the Nile. Although the Mother of Africa is a bit rough around the edges, no trip to Africa is complete without visiting the **Great Pyramids at Giza**. From Cairo, you can also sail down the Nile River on a *felucca* (traditional sail boat), and pay a visit to the temples and tombs of **Luxor**.

Heading west, Libya is beginning to open up to independent travellers. **Leptis Magna** is worth the red tape, especially since it's regarded as the best Roman site in the Mediterranean. For Star Wars fans, cross into **Matmata** in neighbouring Tunisia, which was the filming location of the Mos Eisly space port on the desert planet of Tatooine. Continuing west, **Timimoun** in Algeria is a storybook Saharan oasis town of palm trees, salt lakes and sand dunes.

Morocco's medieval cities enchant even the most hardened of travellers. The vibrant souqs of **Marrakesh** and the elegant mosques of **Fès** recall a time when this country was the centre of the learned world. For nature-lovers, a visit to the graceful orange and red sand dunes at **Merzouga** is a must, while wind- and kitesurfers should flock to the coastal town of **Essaouira**.

WESTERN WANDERLUST

It's tough travel through West Africa, though the best place to get your bearings is Senegal's capital of **Dakar**. With Parisian trappings, this charmer of a city attracts an entourage of internationally known musicians. For a reminder that the Africa bush is just around the corner, spot monkeys and antelopes at the international bioreserve of **Parc National du Niokolo-Koba**.

For the most coveted of passport stamps, head to **Timbuktu** in Mali, a historic centre of learning that is home to several storied mosques. A boat trip up the **Niger River** also reveals castelled mosques made entirely of mud, and pink sandstone villages carved into cliff faces.

For a taste of postcard-perfect Saharan landscapes, look no further than the **Ténéré Desert** in Niger. Here, you'll find everything from sand dunes and gravel plains to cave paintings and dinosaur fossils.

The award for the friendliest people in West Africa goes to the Ghanaians, and you'll agree once you land

---

MY FIRST
~ AFRICAN TRACK ~

When I made the short journey across the Rovuma River and into northern Mozambique in a dugout canoe, I felt like a trailblazer. This is what I'd come to Africa for – crossing remote, slightly sketchy borders and exploring countries well off the beaten track (Mozambique had been at war 18 months earlier). A rotting hippo carcass and a couple of backpackers coming the other way didn't dampen my spirits and, passport stamped (in a mud hut), I boarded a beaten-up Land Rover and sped towards the coast.

I had known my journey south from Dar es Salaam was going to be bad when my bus window fell out in the city's bus station just as the heavens opened. It was 32 hours later before I reached Mtwara, the border town. 'Recovering' in a ramshackle bar, I was befriended by a bunch of second-hand clothing dealers and, bemused by my ramblings about white-sand beaches and 'undiscovered' northern Mozambique, they helped me reach the remote border trail.

I fell in love with the country and the days flew by. I remember doing quite a lot of snorkelling, wandering about the village trying to buy beer and local biscuits, and catching a dhow out to a tiny offshore coral island where the remains of a 16th-century Portuguese fort stood. Although the region had been isolated and improvised, my corner of Mozambique seemed untouched by war. Nowhere in Africa have I had such a warm local welcome or enjoyed such an exciting, guidebook-free travel experience. I never wanted to see the beaten track again.

Matt Fletcher traded his damp English flat for African camp sites and an international camel derby that kickstarted his freelance writing career.

FIESTY FISHERMEN GOING TO SELL THEIR WARES AT DAR ES SALAAM, THE EVER-GROWING CENTRE OF BUSINESS AND TRADE IN TANZANIA.

WATCH OUT FOR HIPPOS WHILE TRAVELLING THROUGH THE WILDERNESS OF THE OKAVANGO DELTA (SEE P272), BOTSWANA.

THE SMOKE THAT THUNDERS, BETTER KNOWN AS VICTORIA FALLS (SEE P272), ZIMBABWE.

in the breezy capital of **Accra**. For a world-class wildlife-viewing experience, don't miss nearby **Mole National Park**, which is famous for its bus-sized elephants and roving gangs of baboons.

WHAT TO DO?

HIGHLIGHTS

- Spotting a pride of sleeping lions in the tall grass at **Kruger National Park** (South Africa).
- Navigating a canoe through the croc- and hippo-infested waterways of the **Okavango Delta** (Botswana).
- Standing in awe before **Victoria Falls** (Zambia and Zimbabwe), one of the natural wonders of the world.
- Being humbled by the wildebeest migration in **Masai Mara** (Kenya) and the **Serengeti** (Tanzania).
- Standing on the rooftop of Africa at the summit of **Mt Kilimanjaro** (Tanzania), the continent's highest peak.
- Chilling out on the pristine beaches of **Zanzibar** (Tanzania), East Africa's exotic spice island.
- Exploring **Dogon Country** (Mali), home to a stunning escarpment and a unique, animist culture.
- Trekking through the **Ténéré Desert** (Niger), a Saharan landscape of surreal beauty.
- Putting on your best Indiana Jones hat, and penetrating the depths of the **Great Pyramids of Giza** (Egypt).
- Navigating the winding, narrow alleys of **Fès** (Morocco), one of North Africa's most dynamic cities.

GET ACTIVE

Africa is all about getting into the wilds – but make sure you're getting your sport on in the presence of qualified guides and/or tour operators.

Diving & Snorkelling

Arguably, Africa's best diving and snorkelling is found in the Red Sea. Egypt is the most obvious place to get your feet wet, though nearby Eritrea and Sudan also have some superb reefs if you're up for a bit of adventure. Of course, the whole east coast of Africa is peppered with great dive locations, especially up-and-coming Mozambique. Far-flung São Tomé & Príncipe is an expensive but exotic place to dive, while the shores of Lake Malawi are cheap and decidedly more humble in scale.

Rafting & Kayaking

White-water rafting on the Zambezi River below Victoria Falls (Zambia/Zimbabwe) is simply incredible – it's the hardest commercially run rapid in the world. You can also raft in Ethiopia, Kenya, Namibia, Swaziland and at the Nile's source in Uganda. The Okavango Delta in Botswana and the Zambezi River in Zambia are the ultimate locations for multiday kayak safaris, while Lake Malawi is a good place for renting canoes. Pole-propelled *pirogues* (dugout canoes) can give you a taste of local life on the continent's waterways – exploring the thatched huts of Ganvié, perched on stilts above Lake Nokoué in Benin, is a classic African experience – and you could always bring your own canoe (buy a flat-pack craft) and paddle the great rivers of the continent at your own pace.

Safaris

Going on *safari* (Swahili for 'journey') is undoubtedly an African highlight. East and South Africa have the highest density of the 'big five' (buffaloes, elephants, lions, leopards and rhinoceroses), which are showcased in many excellent parks. The wildebeest migration (July, August and October) between the Serengeti and Masai Mara reserves on the Tanzanian–Kenyan border is one of the world's great wildlife spectacles. Safaris are possible year-round, but best at the end of the dry season when animals are concentrated around dwindling water sources. At the end of the rains, the grass can be just too damn high to see much. Budget camping safaris are easily arranged, but going cheap often means fewer smiles per mile.

Surfing

Between April and July, there's world-class surfing to be had all along the coast of South Africa. The most famous break on the continent is at Jeffrey's Bay, which dishes out a fierce ride that can last several minutes. However, you'll find less crowds (and sometimes no-one at all) if you go beyond the surfer trail and explore Madagascar, Mozambique, Senegal and Namibia. If you prefer to surf with a sail or a kite, the Cape Verde islands and Morocco are emerging as internationally recognised wind- and kitesurfing destinations.

Trekking

From the Drakensberg in South Africa to the Atlas in Morocco, Africa boasts some superb mountain ranges. Mt Kilimanjaro (5895m), the continent's highest peak, is a tremendous challenge, but the less ambitious can still break in their hiking boots elsewhere. Places such as the Fouta Djalon Highlands (Guinea), Dogon Country (Mali) and Fish River Canyon (Namibia) offer easy-going trekking. The continent has many curious little corners where you can pick up a guide, shoulder a pack, walk through beautiful countryside and meet local people on their own terms. Donkeys, horses or camels will extend your range, or could be your sole means of transport if you're truly out in the wilderness.

WILDLIFE

Don't focus all your attention on Kenya and Tanzania – you can mix it with wildlife across the continent. There's the wondrous weirdness of Madagascar's wildlife, lions in Benin, great white sharks off South Africa, mountain gorillas in Uganda and Rwanda, desert elephants in Burkina Faso and chimpanzees in Guinea. And there are wildlife-rich countries you wouldn't immediately think of: Cameroon, Ghana, Senegal and the prosperous, stable (but expensive) Gabon, where 11% of the country has been declared national park in the hope it'll become an ecotourism paradise. Old hands at Africa often get more into Africa's bird life than its big beasts – great birding spots include Nigeria, Senegal, the Gambia, Ethiopia, Kenya and South Africa. Needless to say, binoculars are an essential accessory in Africa.

FESTIVALS

Festivals take place across the continent and almost every nation hosts a handful of religious and cultural events. Islamic festivals are widely celebrated in the north, west and coastal regions of East Africa. The end of Ramadan and Eid al-Adha are celebrated big-style

JT ON YOUR SAFARI SUIT AND CHECK OUT THE WILDEBEESTS AT MASAI MARA NATIONAL PARK (SEE P272), KENYA.

One of the biggest decisions made by first-timers heading to Africa is whether or not to travel the continent on an organised tour by overland truck. These behemoth vehicles, which follow a variety of touristy routes from Cape to Cairo, provide all-inclusive budget safaris for a few dozen travellers at a time.

If you're fearful about travelling overland across the continent, joining an overland-truck tour is an attractive option for those who want their adventure packaged for risk-free consumption. Although they're certainly not cheap, it's hard to put a price on the peace of mind that comes with safe and secure travel.

However, to say that overland trucks cheapen the experience of travelling in Africa is an understatement, to say the least. Common complaints are that interaction with Africans is minimal to nonexistent, and that the continent is sadly reduced to a collection of wildlife-watching experiences.

Perhaps more than any other continent, Africa can be intimidating to inexperienced and veteran travellers alike. However, the reality rarely mimics the envisioned stereotypes, and most independent travellers leave the continent empowered by their experiences.

So trust us – if you can, take a chance, go at it alone and prepare to be overwhelmed and enchanted by this incredibly diverse continent.

---

in Foumban (Cameroon) – expect horse racing and all-night parties. Christian festivals are common elsewhere in Africa. Here are some of the highlights:

○ **Leddet & Timkat** (Ethiopia) The Ethiopian Christian Orthodox festivals are celebrated in grand style in Gonder. They mark the birth and baptism of Jesus on 7 and 19 January respectively.

○ **Festival Pan-Africain du Cinema** (Fespaco or Pan-African Film Festival; Burkina Faso; www.fespaco.bf) This festival is held over nine days in Ougadougou during late February/early March in odd-numbered years. Fespaco's Oscar equivalent is the Étalon de Yennenga.

○ **Dogon festivals** (Mali) Agguet, Ondonfile and Boulo (the rain-welcoming festival) include complex masked dances and take place in April and May. The Sigui takes place roughly every 60 years in Dogon Country, depending on the position of the star known as Sirius.

○ **Grahamstown Festival** (South Africa) A 10-day celebration of arts and crafts with an associated fringe festival in June/July.

○ **Festival of the Dhow Countries** (Zanzibar; www.ziff.or.tz) East Africa's largest cultural event showcases the film, literature, music, culture and art of coastal countries and is held in July. Numerous open-air gigs make it quite a party.

○ **Maralal International Camel Derby** (Kenya; www.yaresafaris.com/camelderby.htm) Held in August/September, this raucous event is staged in the 'wild west' of northern Kenya. Anyone can enter and there's a cycle race too.

○ **Umhlanga** (Reed Dance; Swaziland) This is a week-long debutante ball for marriageable young women, held in August/September. The reed dance, when reeds are presented to the Swazi queen mother, is the finale.

○ **/Ae//Gams Arts & Cultural Festival** (Namibia; www.windhoekcc.org.na) Windhoek's extravaganza of music, dance and ethnic dress takes place in September.

○ **La Cure Salée** (Niger) Held in late September, the most famous version of this celebration is the Gerewol festival, which includes the male beauty contest of the Woodaabé people (Fula cattle herders).

○ **Odwira** (Ghana) Held in Kumasi, this is a huge Ashanti purification festival taking place in the ninth month (or Adae) of the Ashanti calendar (usually December or January).

PARTY SCENE

Africa is not a coin-op party paradise, but there are a few hang-outs dotted around the continent where travellers seem to congregate, kick back and let the good times roll. You'll rarely be short of a buddy or two in the following spots:

- **Cape Maclear and Nkhata Bay** (Malawi) Classic, bleary-eyed, lakeside hang-outs.
- **Casamance** (Senegal) Beachside chill-outs a plenty.
- **Chefchaouen** (Morocco) Hashish-scented town where weeks pass unnoticed.
- **Kokrobite** (Ghana) Great seafood, palm-fringed beaches and drumming lessons.
- **Lamu** (Kenya) Unique, historic, small-scale Swahili island.
- **Swakopmund** (Namibia) Desert 'n' coast party town for adrenaline junkies.
- **Tofo** (Mozambique) Surf, dive, relax and party off the beaten path.

You can add to this list the classic party capitals such as Dakar (Senegal), Bamako (Mali), Maputo (Mozambique), Kampala (Uganda), Kigali (Rwanda) and Cape Town (South Africa).

ROADS LESS TRAVELLED

One of the joys of travelling through the vastness of Africa is exploring off the beaten track. People are often warm and welcoming in these places, and it's often much easier to connect with local people and get a proper insight to a country. Africa is a fantastic place for an expedition, and it's relatively easy to join a Saharan camel caravan leaving from Timbuktu (Mali) or Agadez (Niger), to reach the source of the Niger River (Guinea/Sierra Leone), or to retrace the first, struggling footsteps of European explorers. If that sounds a bit much, simply look into places covered sparsely (or not covered at all) by your guidebook. Think northern Mozambique, eastern Zambia and the back roads of Transkei (South Africa), rather than the big backpacker draws.

COURSES

Africa is not exactly one of the world's most popular study-abroad destinations. But there are some potentially interesting courses out there if you're willing to take the time to look. Why not study Swahili on the island of Zanzibar, crack the code of Arabic in Cairo, or brush up on your French in Dakar? If you have any interest in wildlife and conservation, many of the continent's national parks offer specialised courses.

WORKING

For those without specialist skills and training, getting paid work in Africa is hard, and usually you'll need to spend a lot of time chatting up the expat community. A few travellers get lucky and land tourist-industry jobs (tour guiding, bar work etc) in eastern and southern Africa's Western-oriented backpacker destinations, but don't expect great (if any) wages. Travellers with a degree can sometimes get teaching work, most commonly in private schools.

WHEN TO GO?

The equator cuts through the middle of Africa and the continent enjoys a huge variety of climates, so there's never a bad time to visit – the weather is always perfect somewhere.

The rains in West Africa begin between March and June and finish between September and October – their exact timing is influenced by distance from the coast. Temperatures are generally higher just before the torrential downpours begin.

North Africa has seasons similar to southern Europe, but summer is terribly hot, even in the High Atlas. Winters can be cold, grey and nasty.

In East Africa the 'long rains' occur between March and May, while the 'short rains' are between October and December. June and July are the coolest months, with temperatures and rainfall varying less along the coast.

The southern African summer (that's November to March) is hot and wet, while winter can be surprisingly cold.

WHAT TO EXPECT?

LOCALS & OTHER TRAVELLERS

Africa attracts a huge cross section of nationalities, though the French are more prevalent in West Africa, where French is an official language. East and South Africa's huge tourist profile ensures the widest variety (and number) of nationalities, including the most English-speakers.

By and large, Africans are easy-going and polite. Good manners are respected, and hospitality to travellers

THE MEDINA FES EL BALI, FÈS (SEE P272), MOROCCO, A UNESCO WORLD HERITAGE SITE AND HOME TO A RICH ARRAY OF SOUNDS, COLOURS AND SMELLS.

is common – occasionally it's overwhelming. In a few (and this is an exception rather than the rule) tourist hotspots, hospitality sometimes comes with a catch, and travellers are exploited for income rather than offered genuine friendship.

FOOD

It's hard to generalise the cuisines of 53 countries, but rest assured that you will be well fed in Africa. The gastronomic jewel of the continent is arguably Morocco, home to fragrant tajines and savoury couscous. Of course, these two dishes make an appearance in some form or another throughout much of the north.

In sub-Saharan Africa, food is a much more modest affair. Whether it's called *ugali* in the east or *pap* in the south, boiled corn meal is the staple that feeds much of the masses. It fills the belly by itself, but also serves as a nice accompaniment to hearty African stews of beef, goat and chicken.

Along the coasts, seafood can be a luxurious affair, while various river and lake fish are always good eating.

Don't eat bush meat – it's illegal in most places and just plain wrong.

LANGUAGE

Africa is a place of, quite literally, thousands of languages, but English is widely spoken, except in the west where French is the most common second language. Portuguese is good for Angola, Mozambique and São Tomé & Príncipe, while Swahili is the trading language of East Africa, just like Hausa in West Africa and Arabic in North Africa. A number of pidgins and creoles (mixtures of local and European languages) are spoken on the coast of West Africa.

COMMUNICATION

Cheap internet cafés are readily available in major towns and cities from Transkei to Timbuktu.

Connections vary in speed and quality, but almost all allow you to access web-based email in a reasonable amount of time.

Mobile-phone technology is changing telecommunications in Africa. Unreliable land-line networks are being usurped by affordable pay-as-you-go mobile services, so buying a SIM card and/or mobile phone can be a good idea if you're spending a long time in one country.

COSTS

Compared with most of the developing world, Africa is expensive. Travellers commonly blow big chunks of their budget on 4WD hire and internal flights. However, you should try to save some cash for something worthwhile, such as going on safari or arranging an expedition.

The actual cost of living (food, transport etc) varies only a little around the continent, and this table should give you a rough idea.

SAMPLE COSTS

	SOUTH AFRICA (RAND, R)	KENYA (KENYAN SHILLING, KSh)	EGYPT (EGYPTIAN POUND, E£)	MOROCCO (DIRHAM, DH)	SENEGAL (WEST AFRICAN FRANC, CFA)
HOSTEL/ BUDGET ROOM	R40–150 £2.65–10.00 US$5.20–19.50 A$5.80–21.50	KSh300–1000 £2.20–7.25 US$4.30–14.25 A$4.70–15.70	E£15–50 £1.40–4.65 US$2.75–9.10 A$3.00–10.00	Dh30–300 £2.00–10.00 US$3.90–19.50 A$4.30–21.50	CFA4500–13400 £5.15–15.30 US$10–30 A$11.10–33.05
CHEAP RESTAURANT MEAL	R20–50 £1.35–3.30 US$2.60–6.50 A$2.90–7.20	KSh80–500 £0.60–3.65 US$1.15–7.10 A$1.25–7.85	E£12–25 £1.10–2.35 US$2.20–4.55 A$2.40–5.05	Dh25–45 £1.65–2.95 US$3.25–5.85 A$3.60–6.40	CFA450–2230 £0.55–2.55 US$1–5 A$1.10–5.50
1L BOTTLE OF WATER	R5 £0.35 US$0.65 A$0.75	KSh35 £0.25 US$0.50 A$0.55	E£1.50 £0.15 US$0.25 A$0.30	Dh5 £0.35 US$0.65 A$0.70	CFA225 £0.25 US$0.50 A$0.55
SOUVENIR T-SHIRT	R60 £4 US$7.85 A$8.65	KSh475 £3.45 US$6.75 A$7.45	E£40 £3.75 US$7.25 A$8.05	Dh100 £6.60 US$13.00 A$14.25	CFA3575 £4.10 US$8.00 A$8.80
BOTTLE OF BEER	R7 £0.50 US$0.90 A$1.00	KSh80 £0.60 US$1.15 A$1.25	E£10 £1.00 US$1.75 A$2.00	Dh5 £0.35 US$0.65 A$0.70	CFA335 £0.40 US$0.75 A$0.85
STREET SNACK	Meat pie R2 £0.15 US$0.25 A$0.30	Roti KSh30 £0.20 US$0.45 A$0.50	Pita E£0.50 £0.50 US$0.85 A$1.00	Pastry Dh10 £0.70 US$1.30 A$1.40	Roasted meat CFA670 £0.80 US$1.50 A$1.70
1L PETROL	R7 £0.50 US$0.90 A$1.00	KSh55 £0.40 US$0.80 A$0.85	E£0.50 £0.50 US$0.85 A$1.00	Dh9 £0.60 US$1.15 A$1.30	CFA335 £0.40 US$0.75 A$0.85

HEALTH

Sadly, all the world's major diseases are found in Africa. Malaria is a problem from the southern fringes of the Sahara down to the South African border, so take antimalarials if you're passing through a hot zone. Yellow fever is a problem across a similar area, but not endemic south of Namibia and Zambia – you'll need to show a Yellow Fever Vaccination Certificate when applying for some visas.

It's impossible to overstate the disaster wrought by HIV/AIDS in sub-Saharan Africa. Infection rates of over 30% of the adult population aren't uncommon in southern Africa, and there are literally thousands of new infections per day, the huge majority from heterosexual intercourse.

Schistosomiasis (bilharziasis) is sadly present in many beautiful (and inviting) lakes and waterways, including the ever popular Lake Malawi. The risk to tourists is pretty low, but if you do get wet (especially after tramping through standing water on reedy shorelines) dry off quickly and dry your clothes well.

ISSUES

Crossing borders in Africa is relatively easy and usually straightforward. However, at remote frontiers and disputed borders, bureaucratic obstacles and demands for 'fines' can be thrown your way. As you'd imagine, corruption is quite common in Africa.

Dangerous and tricky African regions include the fringes of the Sahara, central Sierra Leone, Côte d'Ivoire, Liberia, parts of Nigeria, northern Algeria, northern Chad, eastern/southern Sudan, the Central African Republic, Congo, the Democratic Republic of Congo and Somalia. In addition, rebel activity continues in parts of Burundi, Rwanda and Uganda, and there are pockets of banditry and general lawlessness in northern Kenya and southern Ethiopia, Sudan, Libya, plus eastern Eritrea – travel permits are required here. Normally safe and stable countries bordering the above states occasionally import problems. Sierra Leone and Angola are getting better, but there are huge problems with unexploded ordnance and banditry.

Zimbabwe, once a fantastic travel destination, is beset by political and social unrest and commodity shortages. However, travellers have not been targeted and some destinations such as the town of Victoria Falls are still attracting tourists. Check the situation carefully before travelling.

GETTING THERE

Africa has a number of international air hubs, which makes it easy for travellers the world over to arrive by plane. European travellers also take advantage of the numerous intercontinental ferries that ply the Mediterranean.

AIR

Two of Africa's most popular gateways for international arrivals are Johannesburg and Cape Town in South Africa. In East Africa, the most popular arrival city is Nairobi, though Dar es Salaam (Tanzania) is also busy. In West Africa, Accra (Ghana) and Lagos (Nigeria) are the busiest gateways, but considerable traffic heads into Dakar (Senegal) as well. Casablanca (Morocco) and Cairo (Egypt) are the busiest gateways in North Africa.

Budget airlines are nonexistent in Africa, though several major players service the continent:

- **Air France** (www.airfrance.com)
- **British Airways** (www.britishairways.com)
- **Brussels Airlines** (www.brusselsairlines.be)
- **Ethiopian Airlines** (www.ethiopianairlines.com)
- **Kenya Airways** (www.kenya-airways.com)
- **KLM Royal Dutch Airlines** (www.klm.com)
- **Lufthansa** (www.lufthansa.com)
- **South African Airways** (www.flysaa.com)

SEA & OVERLAND

The days of working your way to Africa aboard a cargo ship are over, though frequent ferries link Spain and France with Morocco, France with Algeria and Tunisia, Italy with Tunisia, Malta with Libya, and Egypt with Jordan.

The only land access to Africa is across the Sinai from Israel to Egypt. However, you can only cross at the Taba–Eilat border post, not at Rafah in the troubled Gaza Strip.

SPECIALIST TOUR OPERATORS

Dozens of tour operators run trips in Africa. Region-specific operators include:

- **African Trails** (www.africantrails.co.uk) Offers truck tours through East Africa plus a trans-African route.
- **Point Afrique** (www.point-afrique.com) Offers cheap charter flights to, and French-speaking tours around, Saharan West Africa.
- **Truck Africa** (www.truckafrica.com) Runs overland truck safaris from London to Cape Town and shorter tours around East Africa.

BEYOND AFRICA

From Cape Town at the bottom of the continent, flying is your only option, though there are occasionally good deals to Australia, India and South America. If you're doing it the other way round, it's easy to continue (by bus) into the Middle East before heading east into Asia or northeast towards Russia. You could also go by rail through China or Europe. Cheap flights to India are often found in Nairobi and Dar es Salaam.

FURTHER INFORMATION

WEBSITES
- **Africa Centre** (www.africacentre.org.uk) A cultural centre and education resource for all things African.
- **All Africa** (www.allafrica.com) A real gateway to all things African, this website posts around 1000 articles a day, collated from over 125 different news organisations.
- **BBC News Africa** (www.news.bbc.co.uk/2/hi/africa /default.stm) A comprehensive daily review of the leading African news stories.
- **Justice Africa** (www.justiceafrica.org) Campaigns for improved human rights across the continent.
- **News Africa** (www.newsafrica.net) The latest African news and country backgrounds.

BOOKS
- *Africa by Road* (Bob Swain and Paula Snyder) Invaluable reading for those driving around the continent.
- *A History of Africa* (JD Fage) A comprehensive yet digestible overview of the entire continent.
- *A Traveller's Literary Companion* (Oona Strathern) A recommended compendium of African literature.
- *Dark Star Safari* (Paul Theroux) The famed travel writer weaves pessimism and anger into his trans-African tale.
- *In the Footsteps of Mr Kurtz* (Michela Wrong) Tells the long, sorry tale of Mobutu's reign in the Democratic Republic of Congo (formerly Zaïre).
- *My Traitor's Heart* (Rian Malan) An excellent autobiography of an Afrikaner in the 'new' South Africa.
- *Shadows Across the Sahara* (John Hare) A personal account of the author's remarkable trans-Saharan camel trek.
- *Things Fall Apart* (Chinua Achebe) An African literary classic by the much revered Nigerian author.
- *Travels in West Africa* (Mary Kingsley) A remarkable account of a woman's travels in 19th-century West Africa.

FILMS
- *The Last King of Scotland* (2006) Forrest Whitaker brings the violent and bone-chilling dictatorship of Idi Amin to life.
- *Blood Diamond* (2006) Leonardo di Caprio scours the continent's worst war zones in search of conflict diamonds.
- *Tsotsi* (2005) Academy Award–winning film about life in the black townships of Johannesburg, South Africa.
- *Hotel Rwanda* (2004) The true story of one hotel manager's efforts to save thousands from the genocide.
- *Lumumba* (2000) A French film about the assassination of Patrice Lumumba, the first elected leader of Congo, at the hands of the CIA.
- *Out of Africa* (1985) Depicts an idealised image of colonial Kenya, starring Meryl Streep and Robert Redford.
- *The Battle of Algiers* (1965) This French black-and-white classic is centred on the bloody Algerian War of Independence.

THE MIDDLE EAST

The Middle East is the cradle of civilisation, the place where the greatest empires in history left behind an astonishing legacy carved from the stones of a remarkable landscape. Here the great ruins of antiquity (Baalbek, Petra, Palmyra and Persepolis) rub shoulders with living cities equally steeped in history (Damascus, Jerusalem and Esfahan). And then there are Dubai and Tel Aviv, whose embrace of all that is modern signals the region's arrival in the 21st century.

Beyond the cities, there's so much more to the region than deserts. Yes, you can venture into the Sahara Desert, the Empty Quarter or Wadi Rum. But snowcapped mountains rise above Lebanon and Iran and another world awaits beneath the Red Sea. But perhaps the Middle East's greatest treasure is its people, who are renowned for their hospitality and who bear scant resemblance to what you may have read in the headlines. If you don't believe us, you'll be missing out on the journey of a lifetime.

ITINERARIES

There are three stumbling blocks to overland travel in the Middle East: Iraq; Saudi Arabia, thanks to the near impossibility of getting a visa; and Israel, as an Israeli stamp in your passport prevents entry into Iran, Lebanon, Libya, Syria and all Arabian Peninsula states. However, travellers have got around the issue of the Israeli passport stamp by asking officials to stamp on a separate entry card.

ISTANBUL TO CAIRO
Few journeys allow you to get to know a region quite like this one. From **Istanbul** head down through **Turkey** and further into **Syria** where you know you've entered the Middle East proper, especially in the evocative bazaar of **Aleppo** and incomparable **Damascus**, one of the Arab world's most glorious cities. After a side trip to **Beirut** with, despite everything, its Mediterranean *joie de vivre*, and the epic ruins at **Baalbek**, return to Syria and go on into **Jordan**. After a pause in cosmopolitan **Amman**, float in the **Dead Sea**, marvel at rock-hewn **Petra**, disappear into the desert at **Wadi Rum** and don't miss a detour to **Jerusalem**. From there it's down to the **Red Sea**, where the diving and snorkelling is some of the best in the world, either at **Aqaba** or across the waters from Egypt's Sinai Peninsula at laid-back resorts such as **Dahab**. The clamour of **Cairo** is not far away, not to mention the sophistication of **Alexandria** or the antiquities of the **Nile Valley**.

ISTANBUL TO SHIRAZ

Travelling east across Turkey from **Istanbul** is a gradual process of leaving Europe behind and entering the Middle East. Crossing Turkey's border with **Iran** takes you onto the old Silk Road. The bazaar at **Tabriz** is a roiling introduction to the country, and while **Tehran** wouldn't win any beauty contests, it resonates with the intriguing contradictions of modern Iran. Further south, the beautiful blue-tiled **Esfahan** is a living monument to the glories of ancient Persia. The mud-brick architecture of **Yazd** will draw you in, while at journey's end, **Shiraz** is studded with fine mosques and serves as the gateway to the astonishing ruins of **Persepolis**.

THE GULF & ARABIAN SEA

Take advantage of the attempts to turn the Qatari capital **Doha** into a Dubai-style regional hub, and make it your gateway to the Gulf. Doha is a gentle introduction to the region, but **Dubai** is being transformed into one of the world's most glamorous, most talked-about cities. Nearby **Abu Dhabi** is heading down a similar path, while the coast around **Khor Fakkan** is spectacular, as is the **Musandam Peninsula** which actually belongs to Oman. By road or by air, head to **Muscat**, the capital of Oman which surrounds a beautiful arc of bay and is home to a souq (market) without peer. Travel inland to **Jebel Shams**, the Grand Canyon of Arabia, and to the imposing fortress at **Nakhal**, then down across the **Empty Quarter** to the blowholes at **Mughsail**. Yemen is just across the border with the mud skyscrapers of **Wadi Hadramawt**, one of the jewels in an extraordinary country. The beautiful old town at **San'a** is a world away from the riches of the Gulf.

WHAT TO DO?

HIGHLIGHTS

○ Emerging, Indiana Jones–like, into glorious rose-red, rock-hewn **Petra** (Jordan).
○ Imagining yourself as Lawrence of Arabia in **Wadi Rum** (Jordan).
○ Wondering at the wisdom of the ancients in blue-tiled **Esfahan** (Iran).
○ Losing yourself in **Damascus** (Syria), one of the world's oldest cities.

○ Following in the footsteps of pilgrims to **Jerusalem** (Israel and the Palestinian Territories).
○ Returning to the glories of the Phoenicians and Romans at the ruins of **Baalbek** (Lebanon).
○ Delving into the labyrinth of **San'a** (Yemen), a labyrinthine 2500-year-old walled city.
○ Embracing the future in **Dubai** (United Arab Emirates), one of the 21st century's most exciting cities.

GET ACTIVE

Diving, scaling summits of rock and of sand or skiing the slopes, there's not much you can't do in the Middle East.

Camel Trekking & 4WD Safaris

The deserts of Wadi Rum (Jordan) and the Empty Quarter (Saudi Arabia and Oman) are among the most spectacular deserts on earth. In Jordan, travelling by camel is the perfect vehicle for desert contemplation, but Saudi Arabian and Omani deserts are the preserve of 4WD enthusiasts.

Cycling & Mountain-Biking

Mountain-biking is popular in Israel, Jordan and to some extent Lebanon (Mt Lebanon Range), while cyclists enjoy the flatter roads of Syria. The only drawbacks? The heat can be a killer (avoid May to September) and you should be self-sufficient as spare parts are scarce.

Skiing & Snowboarding

Beirut is famous for the fact that you can swim in the Mediterranean in the morning, then ski on the slopes of Mt Makmal, northeast of Beirut, in the afternoon. A no less improbable experience awaits in the Alborz Mountains north of Tehran, where Iran's slowly re-emerging middle class takes to the slopes.

Trekking, Mountaineering & Climbing

Jordan is a trekkers' and climbers' paradise, most notably in and around Wadi Rum, Petra and the Dana Nature Reserve. Maktesh Ramon (the world's largest crater) and the canyons and pools of Ein Avdat in Israel's Negev Desert are great trekking areas, as are the higher, cooler Upper Galilee and Golan regions of

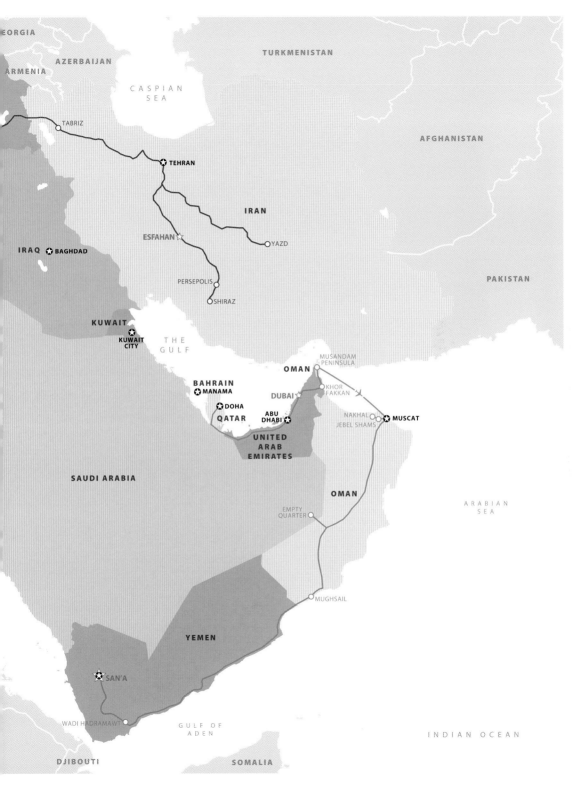

THE MILLENNIA-OLD TEMPLE OF BACCHUS, LOCATED IN BAALBEK (SEE P281), BEKAA VALLEY, LEBANON, WAS DEDICATED TO DIONYSUS, THE GOD OF WIN

CAMP UNDER THE STARS IN THE OLD STOMPING GROUNDS OF LAWRENCE OF ARABIA, WADI RUM (SEE P281), JORDAN.

the country. North of Tehran, it's possible to climb Mt Damavand (5671m), which is the highest peak in the Middle East. The surrounding Alborz Mountains also offer some marvellous trekking and mountaineering to the adventurous traveller.

Water Sports
The Red Sea along the Sinai coast of Egypt, Saudi Arabia (if you can get in), Eilat (Israel) and Aqaba (Jordan) have world-class coral reefs, while Khor Fakkan in the United Arab Emirates is also outstanding. At any Red Sea coast resort worth its salt, your passion for a variety of water sports from sailing to water-skiing will find an outlet. On Egypt's Sinai coast, Moon Beach is a renowned windsurfing destination. The United Arab Emirates is also geared up for high-adrenaline jet skis. For something completely different, try pearl diving in Bahrain.

WILDLIFE
Most mammals have been hunted into extinction across the Middle East, but a few relics survive, such as the highly endangered cheetah in Iran and the iconic Arabian oryx, which is making a comeback in Jordan; you may be able to see the latter in captivity. Migrating bird species pause in their millions in Israel and Jordan's Wadi Araba. The Red Sea is home to more than 1000 fish species.

FESTIVALS
Major festivals in the Middle East fall into two categories: religious ones that change according to the lunar calendar, and which are marked by feasting and religious observance, and cultural festivals that draw an international audience.

Religious Festivals
○ **Ras as-Sana** (Islamic New Year) The start of the Muslim year is marked by family feasts and a few public festivities.
○ **Eid al-Moulid** (Moulid an-Nabi) The Prophet Mohammed's birthday. Celebrated with feasts and large gatherings of extended family.
○ **Ramadan** Muslims fast during daylight hours and eat till they drop after sunset.
○ **Eid al-Fitr** Marks the end of Ramadan with a three-day eating extravaganza.
○ **Eid al-Adha** Muslims make the haj (pilgrimage to Mecca).
○ **Eid al-Kebir** (Tabaski) Commemorates Abraham's willingness to sacrifice his son on God's command; rams are eaten in great quantities.
○ **No Ruz** (Persian New Year) Celebrated in Iran around 21 March.
○ **Easter & Christmas** The region's Christians attend church services and gather for celebratory feasts and, in some countries, processions at Easter.
○ **Pesah** (Passover) Honours the exodus of the Jews from Egypt and lasts for a week.
○ **Purim** (Feast of Lots) Celebrates how the Jewish people living in Persia were saved from massacre.

Other Festivals
○ **Jenadriyah National Festival** (Al Jenadriyah, Saudi Arabia) In late February or early March, a major cultural event featuring traditional songs, dances and poetry competitions, demonstrations of falconry and exhibitions of traditional crafts.
○ **Dubai World Cup** (Dubai, UAE) The world's richest horse race held at the end of March.
○ **Palmyra Festival** (Palmyra, Syria) Popular folk festival amid the ruins, held in April/May.
○ **Baalbek Festival** (Baalbek, Lebanon) Famous arts festival in July/August.
○ **Jerash Festival** (Jerash, Jordan) Stunning setting in ancient Roman city with performances in July/August.
○ **Bereshet Festival** (Megiddo Forest, Israel) Bohemian gathering in the spiritual Megiddo Forest in September.
○ **Bosra Festival** (Bosra, Syria) Festival of music and theatre, held in Roman amphitheatre in September every second year.

PARTY SCENE
You wouldn't come to the Middle East for its nightlife, but the situation is more nuanced than you might think. Tel Aviv and Israel are undoubtedly the home of the Middle East's most vibrant party scene, but Beirut and Dubai both have terrific nightlife. Amman also has sophisticated venues beloved by middle-class locals and travellers alike.

ROADS LESS TRAVELLED

Qala'at Samaan in northern Syria sees far fewer travellers than it deserves, just like the Egyptian oasis towns (eg Dakhla and Bahariyya) that serve as gateway towns for the Sahara. Garmeh and Masuleh in Iran offer desert or mountain seclusion, while Anjar and Tripoli in Lebanon are far from the glitz and ghosts of modern Lebanon.

COURSES

If you'd like to be able to say more than *shukran* ('thank you' in Arabic) or *toda* ('thank you' in Hebrew) and really want to get beyond surface conversations, learn Arabic in Beirut or Amman, and Hebrew in Jerusalem or Tel Aviv.

WORKING

The Middle East is the sort of place where you keep your CV stashed and get down to the serious business of travelling. Short-term job possibilities are limited to teaching English and working in backpackers hostels (especially Israel) and in the kibbutz or moshav systems in Israel. For archaeology buffs, joining a dig as a volunteer, especially in Israel and Jordan between May and September, won't feel like work, but these opportunities also require months of advance planning.

WHEN TO GO?

The best times to visit the Middle East are spring and autumn. Summer is way too hot, especially in desert regions and along the Gulf and Red Sea coasts. Winter can bring some surprisingly miserable weather to the northern Middle East.

The coasts of the Red Sea, Arabian Sea and the Gulf range from hot to extremely hot, often with 70% humidity; summer daytime temperatures can exceed 50°C/122°F. The shores of the Mediterranean enjoy a milder, more European climate. Much of Iran and Yemen is above 1000m and, together with highland

XPLORE THE AMAZING MAZE THAT IS THE YEMENI CAPITAL OF SAN'A (SEE P281).

~ STORYTELLER CAFÉ ~

O n my first trip to the Middle East back in 1998, I found that I just couldn't leave Damascus. Part of it was the hospitality of the people, the warmth and graciousness of every encounter. But central to the city's charms was the storyteller café in the heart of the old city, just down the steps from the Umayyad Mosque. Every night for three months, the same storyteller would don his traditional costume, take to the stage and tell the same story to what was usually the same audience. Everyone knew the story and the storyteller was the master of his audience, pausing for effect, then pausing for the usual cast of locals to add their own interpretations. It was theatre with the same script, but every night was somehow different, like A Thousand and One Nights with a permanent replay of everyone's favourite story.

Anthony Ham's travel writing career continuously draws him back to the cities where he first fell irretrievably in love with the Middle East, and to the silence of the desert.

---

areas in Lebanon, northern Israel and the Hajar Mountains of Oman, these parts experience very cold winters. Southeastern Iran, Yemen and southern Oman are affected by Indian monsoonal systems from March to May and July to August.

Apart from climate, you'll need to factor in Ramadan, when the whole region is on a go-slow.

WHAT TO EXPECT?

LOCALS & OTHER TRAVELLERS

The Middle East is dominated by two very Islamic characteristics: conservative codes of social behaviour and an honouring of guests with boundless hospitality. The latter ensures that most travellers are treated with great civility, and invitations to sit, talk and drink tea are seemingly endless. At the same time, the social conservatism requires a careful adherence to local norms; women travellers in particular should dress modestly and in Iran and Saudi Arabia are required to wear full Islamic dress. Jordan, Syria, Lebanon and Israel are quite liberal societies, at least as experienced by travellers.

Historic links ensure that British travellers are fairly common throughout much of the region and French travellers are quite common in Syria and Lebanon. American travellers are also drawn to Israel. Plenty of Europeans, Aussies and Kiwis also frequent the region, but, as a general rule, the more prominent a country's military is in the region, the less likely you are to see travellers from these countries.

Destinations where travellers congregate in large numbers include Wadi Musa (around Petra in Jordan), Cairo, Damascus, Jerusalem and Dahab.

FOOD

The Middle East is a feast for the senses and your taste buds are in for a treat. *Mezze* is the Middle East's answer to Spanish tapas and Italian antipasto and is almost infinite in its variety from Lebanon to Egypt. Dips (such as *hummus* and *baba ghanooj*) are staples, as are *shwarmas* (kebabs), *felafel* (mashed chickpeas with spices), fresh salads, *fuul* (fava beans cooked with garlic and garnished with herbs and spices), piping hot bread and the sweetest of sweets. There are subtle culinary differences from country to country. But they all share an emphatic belief in the importance of good food.

LANGUAGE

Arabic is the official language everywhere except Iran and Israel, where Farsi (Persian) and Hebrew, respectively, are spoken. English is widely spoken in the region, and older Syrians and Lebanese still speak a little French

COMMUNICATION

The internet is widely accessible throughout the region, even in formerly recidivist states such as Syria and Saudi Arabia. In these and other countries (eg Iran) where information is strictly controlled by government censors, many political and other websites are blocked. However, you shouldn't encounter problems logging on to your Yahoo, Hotmail or Gmail account.

Mobile-phone networks nowadays cover much of the region. Lebanon and the United Arab Emirates regularly figure as having the highest number of mobile phones per capita in the world.

COSTS

The region's surfeit of oil and government subsidies mean that transport costs are generally low, while the basic necessities of life remain quite reasonable. The cheapest places to travel are Syria and Iran. Lebanon,

SAMPLE COSTS

	ISRAEL (NEW ISRAELI SHEKEL, NIS)	SYRIA (SYRIAN POUND, S£)	UAE (UAE DIRHAM, DH)	IRAN (IRANIAN RIAL, IR)
HOSTEL/ BUDGET ROOM	22–95NIS £3.10–13.15 US$6–25 A$6.50–28	up to S£1050 up to £10.55 up to US$20 up to A$22.50	up to Dh200 up to £27.40 up to US$55 up to A$58	up to IR190,000 up to £10.45 up to US$20 up to A$22.50
CHEAP RESTAURANT MEAL	20–50NIS £2.80–6.90 US$5.50–14 A$5.90–14.80	S£75–150 £0.75–1.50 US$1.50–3 A$1.60–3.20	Dh50–100 £6.85–13.70 US$13.50–27.50 A$14.50–29	IR30,000–40,000 £1.65–2.20 US$3.30–4.40 A$3.50–4.70
1L BOTTLE OF WATER	6NIS £0.85 US$1.70 A$1.80	S£25 £0.25 US$0.50 A$0.55	Dh1.50 £0.25 US$0.40 A$0.45	IR2500 £0.15 US$0.30 A$0.30
SOUVENIR T-SHIRT	15–20NIS £2.10–2.80 US$4.15–5.20 A$4.50–5.90	S£500 £5 US$10 A$10.75	Dh25 £3.45 US$6.80 A$7.35	IR35,000 £1.95 US$3.85 A$4.20
BOTTLE OF BEER	18NIS £2.15 US$5 A$5.30	S£60 £0.60 US$1.20 A$1.30	Dh20 £2.75 US$5.45 A$5.90	NA
STREET SNACK	*shwarma* 15NIS £2.10 US$4.15 A$4.50	*shwarma* S£25 £0.25 US$0.50 A$0.55	*shwarma* Dh3 £0.45 US$0.85 A$0.90	*sausis* sandwich IR3500 £0.19 US$0.40 A$0.42
1L PETROL	5.5NIS £0.80 US$1.75 A$1.65	S£25 £0.25 US$0.50 A$0.55	Dh4 £0.55 US$1.10 A$1.20	IR800 £0.05 US$0.09 A$0.09

A FORMER POWERHOUSE OF PERSIA, ESFAHAN (SEE P281), IRAN, IS RENOWNED FOR ITS HISTORIC ARCHITECTURE.

Jordan and Yemen aren't much more expensive, while Israel and the Gulf States are certainly not budget destinations. The most expensive place (and with the least to see) is Kuwait.

HEALTH

The Middle East poses few health risks. Nevertheless, malaria is periodically present in a few rural areas (eg desert oases) and waterborne diseases are also common. For more information on health matters, see the Health & Safety chapter (p41) and seek professional medical advice.

ISSUES

Hostility towards Western countries, particularly the US, is certainly increasing in the Middle East, largely because of the conflicts in Iraq and between Israel and the Palestinian Territories. However, the region remains one of the most hospitable in the world (especially Syria, Jordan and Iran), and many locals will argue vociferously on matters of foreign policy, then invite you home to dinner to continue the discussions over a banquet of bountiful food and mint tea. Be careful with whom and where you talk politics – public political dissent can lead to unpleasant consequences for locals.

All countries of the region, except Egypt and Jordan, refuse to admit anyone whose passport has been tainted by evidence of a visit to Israel. Israeli immigration officials will, *if asked*, stamp only a separate entry card and not your passport, but entry/exit stamps into those countries will be no less incriminating than an Israeli stamp, and other missing stamps can later raise questions. A safer option includes returning to the country (Jordan or Egypt) from which you started. Even better, make Israel your final stop in the region.

GETTING THERE

The Middle East, with Dubai and Doha leading the way, is fast becoming a transport hub for air travellers, either as entry points to the region or as stopovers en route elsewhere.

AIR

The region's major air hubs are Cairo, Tel Aviv, Beirut, Dubai, Doha and, to a lesser extent, Amman.

Major airlines include:

- **British Airways** (www.britishairways.com)
- **EgyptAir** (www.egyptair.com)
- **El Al** (www.elal.co.il)
- **Emirates** (www.emirates.com)
- **Gulf Air** (www.gulfairco.com)
- **Iran Air** (www.iranair.com)
- **Lufthansa** (www.lufthansa.com)
- **Middle East Airlines** (www.mea.com.lb)
- **Qatar Airways** (www.qatarairways.com)
- **Royal Jordanian Airlines** (www.rja.com.jo)

SEA & OVERLAND

Ferries shuttle reasonably regularly from Greece and Cyprus to Israel or Egypt. Less frequented routes connect Egypt with Sudan.

Transport is plentiful for crossing the Turkey–Syria, Turkey–Iran and Iran–Pakistan borders, although less so between Egypt and Sudan.

SPECIALIST TOUR OPERATORS

- **The Adventure Company** (www.adventurecompany .co.uk) Small-group adventure tours with structured itineraries to Jordan.
- **Crusader Travel** (www.crusadertravel.com) Diving and adventure tours from Israel and Turkey.
- **Dragoman** (www.dragoman.com) The largest of the overland companies takes in Turkey, Syria, and Jordan, not to mention just about everywhere else on the planet.
- **Exodus** (www.exodus.co.uk) Overland and adventure trips covering Iran, Jordan, Lebanon, Syria and Turkey.
- **Explore Worldwide** (www.exploreworldwide.com) Small-group exploratory holidays which take in Iran, Jordan, Lebanon, Syria and Turkey.
- **The Imaginative Traveller** (www.imaginative -traveller.com) Highly professional, established outfit with a vast range of tours offered to Iran, Jordan, Syria and Turkey.
- **Kumuka** (www.kumuka.com) Masses of routes offered, including dedicated explorations of Jordan or Syria.
- **Oasis Overland** (www.oasisoverland.co.uk) Turkey, Syria and Jordan.

URBAN MYTHS – DANGER ZONE?

Don't believe everything you read. Outbreaks of violence and acts of terrorism against Western targets in the Middle East are rare, although you should always check out the latest security warnings before travelling. Okay, so you probably shouldn't be planning a trip to Iraq or Gaza any time soon, and rambling around the Israel–Lebanon border is not a smart move. Turkey's extreme southeast, close to the border with Iraq, should also be avoided, and check the prevailing security advice before heading to Yemen. But the region's problems are invariably highly localised, leaving most places safe to visit. Isolated acts of terrorism aside, personal safety is rarely an issue in the region. You're far less likely to be mugged on the streets of Damascus, Tehran or Cairo than in London. Although female travellers will grow weary of suggestive comments, violence against women is extremely rare.

○ **On The Go** (www.onthegotours.com) Egypt and Turkey specialists, with the odd detour into Jordan.

BEYOND THE MIDDLE EAST

Standing as it does at the crossroads of three continents, the Middle East can be a launch pad for an epic overland journey. Egypt enables you to travel south into the heart of Africa and on to Cape Town. An alternative is the so-called 'hippie trail', running from Turkey to Iran, the Indian subcontinent and on to Kathmandu. If you're flying, Dubai is good for cheap deals to the Indian Subcontinent. A final option is to head north through southern and eastern Europe.

FURTHER INFORMATION

WEBSITES

○ **Al-Bab** (www.al-bab.com) Arab-world gateway with links to news services, country profiles, travel sites and maps.
○ **Al-Bawaba** (www.albawaba.com) News, entertainment and Yellow Pages directories, with online forums and kids' pages.
○ **Arabnet** (www.arab.net) Saudi-run encyclopedia collecting news, articles and other resources.
○ **BBC News** (www.bbcnews.com/middleeast) Comprehensive regional news that's constantly updated.
○ **Great Buildings Online** (www.greatbuildings.com) Explore digital 3D models of the Pyramids and other Middle Eastern monuments.

BOOKS

○ *A History of the Arab Peoples* (Albert Hourani) A highly readable sweep through centuries of Arab history.
○ *Mezzoterra* (Ahdaf Soueif) A searing critique of Western stereotypes and the gritty realities of the Arab-Israeli conflict.
○ *Jerusalem: One City, Three Faiths* (Karen Armstrong) The most balanced study of the city claimed by Jews, Muslims and Christians.
○ *Nine Parts of Desire* (Geraldine Brooks) An outsider-insider look at the role of women in the region.
○ *Seven Pillars of Wisdom* (TE Lawrence) A great read by one of the Middle East's most legendary figures.

○ *Arabian Sands* (Wilfred Thesiger) His crossing of the Empty Quarter is an all-time travel classic.
○ *From the Holy Mountain* (William Dalrymple) An engaging trip through Turkey, Syria, Israel and the Palestinian Territories.

FILMS

○ *Lawrence of Arabia* (1962) David Lean's masterpiece captures all the hopes and subsequent frustrations in the aftermath of WWI.
○ *Chronicle of a Disappearance* (1996) Palestinian director Elie Suleiman evokes the lives of Palestinians living under occupation.
○ *Secret Ballot* (2001) Unrivalled treatment of the contradictions between revolutionary and democratic Iran.
○ *Yol* (1982) Yilmaz Guney's epic follows five Turkish prisoners on parole as they travel around their country.
○ *West Beirut* (1998) Ziad Doueiri's powerful work is the finest film on Lebanon's devastating civil war.
○ *Nina's Tragedies* (2003) A nuanced exploration of the Arab-Israeli conflict from the Israeli side of the fence.

RUSSIA, CENTRAL ASIA & THE CAUCASUS

Bigger than Africa and Australasia put together, this massive region could use Texas as a handkerchief. Central Asia alone (the famous 'stan' brothers: Kazakhstan, Uzbekistan, Kyrgyzstan, Tajikistan, Turkmenistan and Afghanistan) is about the size of Europe; Russia itself spans half the globe. It's an area that makes you wonder how we know so little about a place that is so big.

Throw in Belarus, the Caucasus and Ukraine and this is an area of huge contrasts, covering everything from permanently frozen tundra to baking desert, and embracing Christianity, Islam, Buddhism and Borat. The ghosts of great empires still haunt historic centres from St Petersburg (Russia) to Samarkand (Uzbekistan), and outside the cities there are enough blanks on the maps, enough wilderness, to keep you exploring for years.

With the collapse of the Soviet Union in 1989, a brave new world opened to backpackers. Sure, there won't be beachside frolics or fine dining, but if you like history and a diverse culture, you'll be mesmerised. Russia has European tradition plastered over with grim Soviet aesthetic, and more recently a confusing catch-up capitalism that sees Hummers rolling over medieval streets and past onion-dome churches.

Central Asia is completely different. The Eurasian steppe quickly turns to untamed jagged mountains, expansive deserts, and lush alpine valleys dotted with the yurts of Mongolian-looking horsemen. Down in the plains and valleys lies a string of ancient Silk Road cities and Islamic architectural treasures that stretches from Tbilisi (Georgia) to China. Reality may not quite gel with romantic images of camel caravans, caravanserais (pit stops for trade caravans as they travelled across the Silk Road) and turbaned Silk Road merchants, but in some places you can definitely get the sense that you are travelling directly in the footsteps of Marco Polo. The Iron Curtain that once shrouded this area has been drawn open and the show has just begun.

ITINERARIES

Air travel on the big airlines – **Aeroflot** (www.aeroflot.com), **Transaero** (www.transaero.ru) and **Uzbekistan Airways** (www.uzairways.com) – is usually reliable, but smaller carriers have more dubious safety and punctuality records. Train travel is the best way to get around the region, though packing a Dostoevsky-sized novel is essential for the epic rides, and you should expect anything under second class to be cramped, uncomfortable and insecure. In Russia and the west, boat travel on canals, rivers and lakes is a great way to get about. There's also a ferry service from Baku (Azerbaijan) to Turkmenbashi (Turkmenistan).

RUSSIA, CENTRAL ASIA & THE CAUCASUS

ARCTIC
OCEAN

UNITED
KINGDOM

NORTH
SEA

NORWAY

DENMARK

SWEDEN

FINLAND

BARENTS
SEA

KARA
SEA

FRANCE

GERMANY

BALTIC
SEA

ESTONIA

WHITE
SEA

RUSSIA

CZECH
REPUBLIC

POLAND

LATVIA

LITHUANIA

RUSSIA

☆ THE HERMITAGE
(ST PETERSBURG)

AUSTRIA

SLOVAKIA

HUNGARY

BELARUS

✪ MINSK

YAROSLAVL ✪

MOSCOW ✪

✪ SUZDAL

CHERNOBYL ☆

VLADIMIR

RUSSIA

KAZAN

ROMANIA

KIEV ✪

RYAZAN

NIZHNY
NOVGOROD

MOLDOVA

UKRAINE

YEKATERINBURG

BULGARIA

☆ ODESSA

BLACK
SEA

KURGAN

PETROPAVLOSK

OMSK

NOVOSIBIRSK

TURKEY

GEORGIA

TBILISI ✪

CASPIAN
SEA

ASTANA ✪

KAZAKHSTAN

ARMENIA

ARAL
SEA

CYPRUS

AZERBAIJAN

KHIVA ☆

BISHKEK

URUMQI

☆ HIGHLIGHTS

Trans-Siberian Railway

Golden Ring

Silk Road

✈ Air   Train

Boat   Cycle

TURKMENISTAN

UZBEKISTAN

BUKHARA

TASHKENT ✪

ALMATY ✪

KOCHKOR

KYRGYZSTAN

ASHGABAT ✪

SAMARKAND

FERGANA
VALLEY

TORUGART PASS

CHINA

MERV

DUSHANBE ✪

PAMIR
HIGHWAY

KASHGAR

IRAN

TASH RABAT

TAJIKISTAN

A FORMER JEWEL IN THE CROWN OF IMPERIAL RUSSIA, THE BLACK SEA PORT TOWN OF ODESSA (SEE P299), UKRAINE, HAS A BURGEONING NIGHTLIFE.

MERV (SEE P299), TURKMENISTAN, HAS HISTORICAL BUILDINGS AND RUINS FROM SEVERAL DIFFERENT ERAS TO EXPLORE, SOME DATING BACK 5000 YEARS.

CHURCH OF THE SAVIOUR ON SPILLED BLOOD, LESS MORBIDLY KNOWN AS THE CATHEDRAL OF THE RESURRECTION OF CHRIST, ST PETERSBURG, RUSSIA.

URBAN MYTHS - BORAT'S CENTRAL ASIA

When British comedian Sacha Baron Cohen wanted a far-out face to give an outsider's perspective on the UK and later the US, he created a Kazakhstani character who innocently hits on feminists and sings anti-Semitic rants in the snappily titled film, *Borat: Cultural Learnings of America for Make Benefit Glorious Nation of Kazakhstan*. Borat pretends that in his homeland horses have the vote and women are only allowed to ride outside buses. It's all high satire from Cohen (himself Jewish), but some people thought there was truth in the Kazakhstan jest.

In fact, the world's ninth-biggest country is a cosmopolitan place and not at all like the Romanian village used to portray Borat's Kazakhstani home town. The country's chief rabbi has publicly praised the government's treatment of Jewish people and women not only ride the buses but often drive them. The region is wealthy in natural gas and even exports diamonds as well as potassium (as Borat's fictional national anthem indicated with the chorus: 'Kazakhstan is number-one exporter of potassium.') Recently, neighbouring Turkmenistan committed to looking after its citizens by supplying free natural gas, electricity, water and salt until 2030, making it a long way from the grim poverty Borat pokes fun at.

Many folks in Kazakhstan appreciate that Borat is just a character, though the government banned him from using the '.kz' web address and the country's foreign minister threatened to sue Cohen. The Kazakhstani newspaper *Karavan*, however, got the joke, declaring it was the best film of the year and that it was not 'anti-Kazakh, anti-Romanian or anti-Semitic' but 'cruelly anti-American'. Kazakh novelist Sapabek Asip-uly went one step further, suggesting Cohen get a national award as he had 'managed to spark an immense interest of the whole world in Kazakhstan – something our authorities could not do during the years of independence.'

Trans-Siberian Railway

The seven-day Trans-Siberian railway links **Moscow** to **Vladivostok** on the Pacific coast, clanking through eight time zones and across 9289km of mountain, steppe, forest and desert. More popular is the Trans-Mongolian railway, which branches south two-thirds along the route, passing through **Mongolia** en route to **Beijing**. If you don't plan to stop in Mongolia to or from Beijing, you can take the Trans-Manchurian route, which cuts through northern China instead of Mongolia.

Golden Ring

The **Golden Ring** (Zolotoe Koltso) allows the exploration of historic old towns (such as **Suzdal** and **Yaroslavl**), Russian Orthodox churches and magnificent monasteries northeast of **Moscow**. It's not going to take months (a week would take in the highlights), but will give you a real taste of what old Russia must have been like.

Silk Road

This ancient trade route links **Xi'an** (China) to the Mediterranean via a tangle of alternate routes. Ours starts at **Ashgabat**, then heads overland to **Merv** and the Silk Road cities of **Bukhara**, **Samarkand** and **Tashkent**. From here dip into the fertile **Fergana Valley** before swinging north on the mountainous road to **Bishkek**. Skip the border with **Kazakhstan** into cosmopolitan **Almaty** and then catch the train on to **Urumqi** in China. Alternatively, from Bishkek cross the rugged **Torugart Pass**, visiting the *jailoos* (summer pastures) around **Kochkor** and the caravanserai of **Tash Rabat** before crossing over to **Kashgar**, then down into **Pakistan**.

WHAT TO DO?

HIGHLIGHTS

- Discovering hidden treasures in St Petersburg's (Russia) top art house, the **Hermitage**.
- Rambling through **Khiva** (Uzbekistan), the last independent khanate with fortifications frozen in time amid the desert.
- Paddling for as long as you can in **Lake Baikal** (Russia), the Pearl of Siberia ringed by daunting mountains.

- Meeting **Merv** (Turkmenistan), a maze of ruins where you can reconstruct ancient empires from the leftover foundations and pottery shards.
- Celebrating in **Samarkand** (Uzbekistan), a city of stone minarets and ancient architecture that's still buzzing long after its 2000th birthday.
- Taking the long road on the **Pamir Highway** (Tajikistan), with its awe-inspiring mountain scenery and views into Afghanistan's Wakhan corridor.
- Feeling a chill down your spine at **Chernobyl** (Ukraine), the eerie site of a nuclear leak that makes *The Simpsons'* reactor jokes less funny.
- Hanging out in **Almaty** (Kazakhstan) before you try to scale the majestic Tian Shan ranges.
- Saluting faded hammer-and-sickle logos in **Minsk** (Belarus), complete with a dominating former KGB building.
- Re-enacting the *Battleship Potemkin* at **Odessa** (Ukraine) or embracing the Black Sea's wildest nightlife.

GET ACTIVE

The outdoors is being embraced by a new generation in Russia and Central Asia. New adventure-travel possibilities are appearing everywhere and if you like it extreme in the extremities, there are loads of expeditions into the Arctic, Siberian wilderness and mountains of Central Asia.

Trekking, Mountaineering & Climbing

Wherever the country is wild and difficult it usually draws mountaineers and trekkers. Central Asia is no exception, with fantastic walking and trekking kicking off right at city limits, notably in Almaty in Kazakhstan and Bishkek and Karakol in Kyrgyzstan. Further afield, the alpine valleys of the Fan Mountains in Tajikistan and pyramid peaks of Khan Tengri and Tian Shan range in eastern Kyrgyzstan provide impressive goals for climbers, trekkers and mountaineers. Eastern Tajikistan and remoter parts of Kyrgyzstan offer more ambitious treks and never-climbed peaks for the truly intrepid or insane.

Other good mountains with scope for adventure include:
- **Carpathian Mountains** (Ukraine)
- **Lapland Biosphere Reserve** (Russia)
- **Elbrus Area** (Russia–Georgia border)
- **Altay Mountains** (southern Russia and Western Mongolia)
- **Ural Mountains** (central Russia) – the divide between Europe and Asia
- **Sayan Mountains** (Mongolian border)
- **Kamchatka Peninsula** (Russia)

Cycling & Mountain-Biking

Mountain-biking can be organised by local and international tour companies in areas also recommended for walking and trekking (above). If you're cycle-touring, you might find lakes masquerading as potholes on back roads, but spares will be rare so bring your own in most cases.

Horse & Camel Trips

Ride the ranges like a Kyrgyz cowboy with Central Asia's rich culture of nomadic horsemanship. Trips vary from a couple of days to three-week-long expeditions, but Kyrgyzstan and Kazakhstan are good places to start. You can saddle up with these cowpokes:
- **Alexandra Tolstoy** (Kyrgyzstan; www.alexandra tolstoy.com)
- **AsiaRando** (Kyrgyzstan; www.asiarando.com)
- **DN Tours** (Turkmenistan; www.ridingholidays.com)
- **Kasachstan Reisen** (Kazakhstan; http://kasachstanreisen.de)
- **Shepherd's Way** (Kyrgyzstan; www.kyrgyztrek.com)
- **Wild Frontiers** (www.wildfrontiers.co.uk)

Skiing & Snowboarding

Ski facilities are found outside Almaty in Kazakhstan and in the central Caucasus region around Elbrus (5642m). Russia has several solid downhill ski resorts including Abzakovo, Asha, Baikalsk, Kirovsk, Krasnaya Polyana and Dombay. For the ultimate downhill rush join a group for some high-altitude heli-skiing in both areas.

The Kola Peninsula north of Moscow, the Altay Mountains on the Kazakhstan–Russia border and the Carpathians in Ukraine provide cross-country skiing *par excellence*, and locally made gear of reasonable quality is readily available.

Other Activities

You can explore Siberia by ferry on the Irtysh, Yenisey and Ob rivers, or float down the Volga from Nizhny Novgord to Volgograd (former Stalingrad). Boating around the Black Sea coast is popular between May and mid-October. The remote Altay area has some of the region's most intense white-water rafting. If you fancy a dogsled trek or snowmobile zoom into the wilds of Russia, there are tour groups such as **Megatest** (www .megatest.ru) to get you there (and hopefully back).

You can go caving in Kyrgyzstan and Kazakhstan, where local speleological societies lead guided hiking, caving and mountain expeditions. In Siberia, a Russian sauna (complete with the optional back-beating with birch twigs and a naked roll in the snow) is an experience you won't forget in a rush.

You can dive in the icy Siberian Lake Baikal (Russia) or within the Arctic Circle with diving operators such as **Diveworldwide** (www.diveworldwide.com) or Moscow's **MGU** (www.dive.ru).

WHEN TO GO?

Generally, the region has an extreme continental European climate. Summers are very warm, but Russia's long, dark, very cold winters are truly extreme – much

HOLY SPIRIT CATHEDRAL, MINSK (SEE P299), BELARUS, THE RELIGIOUS CENTRE OF THE CITY'S ORTHODOX COMMUNITY AND A POPULAR MEETING POINT

— PEEK BEHIND THE IRON CURTAIN —

Rasa and I became firm friends while studying Russian at university. From early on we knew that all the textbooks in the world would not make us fluent (Exercise 1: Translate 'Ivan works on the collective farm and is very proud of his tractor.'), so we headed to St Petersburg University to study Russian. St Pete was sensory overload – ideal for puzzling over verb conjugations and noun declensions. It's a stunning city custom-made for guidebook clichés – 'city of contrasts' really is apt here. Elaborate, candy-coloured royal palaces and staggering collections of art existed alongside grinding poverty and crumbling housing blocks; pimped-up mafia-mobiles cruised potholed roads next to rust-bucket Ladas.

Just to prove how small the world really is, Rasa bumped into a friend of a friend from Australia on Nevsky Prospekt (St Pete's main street); he and his musician friends were in town busking, so the party we threw at the student dorm went down in history thanks to our very own live band, squeezed into our tiny flat. Our grammar improved alongside our tolerance for rough-as-guts vodka and short-lived holiday romances (the two seemed inexplicably intertwined). After morning classes we'd spend most afternoons at museums and historic sites, soaking up the drama and bloodshed this city specialises in. By night – well, the dorm building was the scene of some memorable parties, but the long white nights, live music and backstreet bars of the city also beckoned. We were pretty chuffed to find our familiarity with the language opening plenty of interesting (bar) doors.

Carolyn Bain is a Lonely Planet author and near-fluent in Russian after a couple of vodkas.

---

of the country is well below freezing point for over four months of the year (November to March). In February and March the sun shines, there's a lack of humidity and it doesn't feel so cold. The coast bordering the Sea of Japan experiences a northern monsoonal climate, which means there's a 30% to 40% chance of rain each day between May and September.

WHAT TO EXPECT?

LOCALS & OTHER TRAVELLERS

You'll meet a few travellers in western Russia, but the rest of the country and Central Asia are strictly for the hard-core European travellers. Tourist hang-outs are tough to find, though you'll discover plenty of travellers in Russia's Golden Ring, on the Trans-Siberian railway and, to a lesser extent, around Lake Baikal and the Black Sea coast, and in the Central Asian towns of Bukhara, Samarkand and Bishkek.

The people of the region have some big PR problems, probably not helped by Borat. Images of Cold War dorks are probably as accurate as 1970s stereotypes about Americans or Brits. The downright rudeness of the region's bureaucracy and service industry is often countered by genuine friendliness and unconditional hospitality from people on the street. Respond with a small gift and be careful not to take advantage of others' generosity. Vodka is often forced upon guests, even in Muslim Central Asia. 'Vodka terrorism' is also common on train journeys and during other chance social encounters. Saying 'Well, just a small one then' puts you on the slippery slope to hangover oblivion… 'I'm an alcoholic' might get you out of trouble.

Immigrants from former Soviet republics make up 20% of Russia's population, while Central Asian nations all have an ethnic majority bearing their names, such as the Kazakhs of Kazakhstan. Millions of Russians and Ukrainians living in Central Asia are referred to as Slavs. Generally, attitudes are conservative, particularly in Central Asia where care should be taken around religious sites – skimpy clothing is a no-no. Central Asia is staunchly Muslim but experiences little religious extremism (Chechnya is the violent exception). The Orthodox Church is enjoying a revival in Russia, Georgia and Armenia, all of which have some of the world's oldest and most spectacularly located churches.

FOOD

No-one comes to this region for the food and few people come home raving about the cuisine. The food in the former Soviet Union is a triumph of bland. Cardboardy dumplings, bowel-disturbing beetroot borscht and thick black bread that needs to be washed down with vodka. Then there's *kvas*, the local beerlike beverage that's made from…bread.

This is food you'd eat for a dare. Central Asian cuisine remains a bleak choice between *shorpa* (mutton fat in a bowl), *shashlik* kebabs (mutton fat on a stick) or *plov/pilau* (mutton fat in rice). Vegetarians really suffer here.

Okay, so there are some high points: markets groan with fruit in summer and the region's melons, grapes and nuts (not to mention the caviar) are world-class.

SAMPLE COSTS

	RUSSIA (ROUBLE, R)	UKRAINE (HRYVNIA, UAH)	BELARUS (BELARUS ROUBLE, BR)
HOSTEL/ BUDGET ROOM	R235–1055 £5–23 US$10–45 A$11–49	80–130uah £8–13 US$16–25.75 A$17.25–28	BR10,720–53,600 £2.50–13 US$5–25 A$5.50–27.25
CHEAP RESTAURANT MEAL	R110–200 £2.50–4 US$4.50–8 A$5–9	5–25uah £0.50–2.50 US$1–5 A$1–5.50	BR2400–7200 £0.50–1.50 US$1–3 A$1–3.25
1L BOTTLE OF WATER	R12 £0.25 US$0.50 A$0.50	2.50–3.50uah £0.25–0.35 US$0.50–0.75 A$0.50–0.75	BR1200 £0.30 US$0.50 A$0.75
SOUVENIR T-SHIRT	R150 £3 US$6 A$6.75	25–35uah £2.50–3.50 US$5–7 A$5.50–7.50	BR15,000 £3.50 US$7 A$7.50
BOTTLE OF BEER	R70 £1.50 US$3 A$3	5–12uah £0.50–1.25 US$1–2.50 A$1–2.50	BR900 £0.25 US$0.40 A$0.50
STREET SNACK	*Blini* R30 £0.75 US$1.25 A$1.50	Kebab 2.50uah £0.25 US$0.50 A$0.50	*Blini* BR1500 £0.35 US$0.75 A$0.75
1L PETROL	R15–20 £0.30–0.40 US$0.60–0.80 A$0.70–0.90	5uah £0.50 US$1 A$1	BR2400–2600 £0.50–0.75 US$1–1.25 A$1.25–1.50

Most towns have Turkish, Korean, Chinese and Western restaurants, so you won't starve.

LANGUAGE
Russian is the second language of most people in Central Asia, where numerous Turkic ethnic languages (and occasionally Persian) are also used locally. Learning the Cyrillic alphabet is a must, as even a few characters will help you decipher Russian, Central Asian, Ukrainian and Belarusian languages. English, however, is not widely spoken, so you'll need to learn some language before you go. Lonely Planet's *Russian* and *Central Asia* phrasebooks will get a battering if you're travelling through the area.

COMMUNICATION
You'll find plenty of internet cafés and some wi-fi in Russia, but good connections are scarce in Central Asia. The same holds true for mobile communication (except in Kyrgyzstan, where the only function of your mobile will be to weigh your bag down), the use of which is spreading out of big cities in Russia and Ukraine and further out.

COSTS
In Russia, Ukraine and Belarus a two-tier pricing policy exists (local prices and a mark-up tourist amount), which means tourists will be bitten harder in the hip pocket in many hotels, museums and attractions, though not for train and air tickets.

HEALTH & ISSUES
Start planning for the usual armful of jabs. There are also a few other health issues to consider. Tick-borne encephalitis, Lyme disease and Japanese encephalitis (spread by mosquitoes) are major problems in eastern Siberia during the summer, especially for trekkers. Cholera is not uncommon in southern regions, and you can catch malaria in southern Tajikistan. Diphtheria is on the increase in Ukraine. Short-term visitors are at little risk from the region's well-known nuclear pollution – you can even take a tour of radioactive Chernobyl in Ukraine or the disappearing Aral Sea in Uzbekistan and Kazakhstan.

Getting a visa will be a danger to your mental health, so plan ahead at least three months before you leave – getting it on the road is a bureaucratic nightmare and expensive. Clusters of countries, snake-like borders, complicated regulations and fixed visa dates demand more pretrip planning than most other regions. The visa situation has improved greatly in recent years. Only Turkmenistan remains a significant problem – you are required to book a tour and guide for a visa. The nightmare doesn't end there, though, as some countries still require you to register with police when you arrive (check local embassies for details as they take this very seriously).

At the time of writing, the following were no-go zones for travellers: Afghanistan, Azerbaijan–Armenia border, Nagorno-Karabakh and surrounding borders, and some regions within Russia (Chechnya, Dagestan, North Ossetia, Stavropol, Ingushetia, Karachayevo-Cherkessia and Kabardino-Balkaria, and the surrounding borders). The Azerbaijan–Armenia border remains closed. Afghanistan and its surrounding borders remain war zones with land mines and irregular skirmishes occurring throughout.

The casual repression of human rights, a lack of press freedom, massive corruption and occasional acts of terrorism all feature in the colourful life of the region, but it's only the sporadic violent drunk (including the occasional policeman) that you are likely to come face to face with.

GETTING THERE

Vexing visa arrangements and border boredom are bound to start your journey to the region. You can come by land from Iran, China and Europe, though flying into the region's hubs – Kiev, Moscow, Almaty and Baku – is more common. Many flights into the

HOP OFF THE TRANS-SIBERIAN RAILWAY TO EXPLORE THE FROSTY WINTER WONDERLAND THAT IS LAKE BAIKAL (SEE P298), RUSSIA.

region won't appear on your standard RTW ticket. Moscow is serviced by dozens of airlines but Central Asia has limited options – often it's Lufthansa (which has great connections and alliances in the region) and **BMI** (www.flybmed.com) that offer the best deals. Smaller players such as **Estonian Air** (www .estonian-air.ee) or **FlyLAL** (www.flylal.com) can be good options if you're heading into Moscow and don't mind a stopover in Estonia or Lithuania.

By land there are hundreds of routes into the region from all directions. Trains are the easiest option. Before you make any plans, carefully check out the border crossings you want to use.

Despite an amazing network of ship canals and sea ports, there are only a few scheduled services into Russia (from Japan) and only a little traffic across the Black and Caspian Seas.

SPECIALIST TOUR OPERATORS

These local operators can get you out and about in the region:

○ **Ayan Travel** (www.ayan-travel.com) Turkmenistan and Uzbekistan tour specialists.

○ **Celestial Mountains** (www.celestial.com.kg) Kyrgyzstan's finest tour group.

○ **Great Game Travel** (www.greatgametravel.co.uk) Specialising in Tajikistan and Afghanistan with horse treks and 4WD tours.

○ **Lenalptours** (www.russia-climbing.com) A group based in St Petersburg that does mountain treks and climbs.

- **Salom Travel** (www.salomtravel.com) Has good tours of the 'stans'.
- **Stantours** (www.stantours.com) Covering the region but best for Turkmenistan.
- **Wild Russia** (www.wildrussia.spb.ru) Operating out of St Petersburg. Also has a representative in Scotland.

BEYOND RUSSIA, CENTRAL ASIA & THE CAUCASUS

From Russia and Central Asia you can branch out almost anywhere. Once you've travelled overland to Europe, you can roll on into the Middle East or Eastern Europe. Head for western China to follow the Karakoram Highway (one of the world's most breathtaking overland trips) down into the Indian subcontinent, or take the Tran-Manchurian railway all the way to Beijing.

FURTHER INFORMATION

WEBSITES
- **Central Asia News** (www.centralasianews.net) Just the facts on this regional news service.
- **EurasiaNet** (www.eurasianet.org) Good news source and portal for Central Asia.
- **Kabul Caravan** (www.kabulcaravan.com) First port of call for travel information to Afghanistan.
- **Oriental Express Central Asia** (www.orexca.com) Lots to explore in this virtual travel guide focusing on Uzbekistan, Kyrgyzstan and Kazakhstan.
- **Pamirs** (www.pamirs.org) Excellent travel info for exploring the Pamirs in Tajikistan.
- **Russian National Group** (www.russia-travel.com) Russia's tourist site.
- **Trans-Siberian Railway** (www.transsib.ru/Eng) Trans-Siberian info.
- **UA Zone** (www.uazone.net) Ukrainian information.
- **Unesco** (www.unesco.kz) Website of the Unesco regional office for Central Asia, with lots of cultural info.
- **Virtual Guide to Belarus** (www.belarusguide.com) A homespun website for Belarus.
- **WayToRussia.Net** (www.waytorussia.net) Good travel-agency guide.

BOOKS
- *Journey to Khiva* (Philip Glazebrook) Following the footsteps of Britain's 19th-century spies, the author digs deep in Central Asia and the Caucasus.
- *A Short Walk in the Hindu Kush* (Eric Newby) Anything but a lazy stroll, Newby's funny take on the region.
- *The Gulag Archipelago* (Alexander Solzhenitsyn) A look into the harsh Soviet-era camps in the north by one of Russia's modern greats.
- *The Great Game* (Peter Hopkirk) History with thriller twists as it follows the 19th-century Cold War between Britain and Russia across Eurasia.
- *The Railway* (Hamid Ismailov) A satirical novel about the end-of-the-line town of Gilas in Soviet Uzbekistan; so good they banned it in Uzbekistan.

FILMS
- *Nochnoi Dozor* (*Night Watch*, 2004) Moscow comes to life (and death) in this supernatural thriller that pits good against evil with a uniquely Russian twist.
- *Statsky Sovetnik* (*The State Counsellor*, 2005) Another 2005 blockbuster set in early-20th-century Russia.
- *Russian Ark* (2002) If you can't get to St Petersburg's stunning Hermitage, this film will walk you through it with insights into Russia's history.
- *Luna Papa* (1999) A Central Asian coming-of-age tale that shows off the region's markets and people.

TRAVELLER TALES

NAME Lewis Webster **AGE** 29
FAVOURITE COUNTRY Australia
MY BIG TRIP I spent the year in Australia on a one-year working-holiday visa. I flew into Melbourne, bought a car and more or less followed the coast anticlockwise. My first big stop was Brisbane, where I spent about two months before continuing up the east coast. Then I worked as a dive master on a live-aboard dive boat on the Great Barrier Reef out of Cairns, for about three months, followed by a couple of months camping around the Northern Territory and Western Australia. I stopped off in Perth over Christmas and finally headed back to Melbourne to sell the car and fly home.
TOP TIP My 'top tip' would be to not plan too rigidly. Although a bit of structure is necessary for your trip, you'll have more fun if you value the unplanned and unexpected.

NAME Molly Bird **AGE** 18/19
FAVOURITE COUNTRY India!!!!!!!!!!!!
MY BIG TRIP I worked as a cook in a small catering company for six months to earn the money I needed for the big trip. My friend Jess and I travelled to India, Nepal, Vietnam, Singapore, Australia, New Zealand and Fiji in six months. I was absolutely intoxicated by India. It's so different, so beautiful, so smelly, so exciting, so never-on-time and absolutely bursting with life at every seam. I got so much from our 4½ months there and I'm desperate to go back. With a small charity, I taught English in a primary school in a remote village in the foothills of the Himalayas. I lived with a family and we had no electricity, modest water facilities and there were no other Westerners in the village. Teaching was an experience which far exceeded my expectations. The three months whizzed by in a flurry of games, picnics, lessons, songs, homework and laughter. I found teaching much more rewarding than just travelling. When you're living and working in a place you cease to be a tourist and that's when it really gets interesting. I absolutely loved India and the volunteering I did there.
TOP TIP Working and travelling are two different experiences; don't miss either.

NAME Jonathan Williams **AGE** 18
FAVOURITE COUNTRY Fiji, in particular the islands of Taveuni, Tavewa and Ovalau.
MY BIG TRIP I decided to plan my year out so that I would be able to do a little bit of everything I wanted to do, rather than one particular activity in great depth. I began the year by setting off on a world trip immediately after receiving my exam results from school. My first stop was Fiji, where I taught in a primary and secondary school for four months. As it was my first international trip alone, I decided to go with an organisation who would offer support unavailable to independent travellers during any arising emergencies. My eye-opening experience in Fiji was absolutely amazing, and I would recommend volunteering to anybody, par-

ticularly in a country where life is so different to that in the Western world. After Fiji, I joined the 'backpacker route', visiting the Cook Islands, New Zealand, Australia and Singapore over a two-month period. When I arrived in the UK, I got a job working for a member of parliament at the House of Commons. The six months I spent in Westminster gave me a fascinating insight into the world of politics – which I later went on to study to degree-level at the University of Birmingham.

TOP TIP Make sure that you don't waste your year – have something planned from the beginning to the end. This will prevent you getting bored and consequently wishing that you hadn't taken a year out in the first place.

NAME Rebecca Grossberg Joseph **AGE** 29
FAVOURITE COUNTRY Poland
MY BIG TRIP After I finished university in the USA, I came to France and planned to stay for only three months to house-sit and help an American tour guide before returning home to a real job. I ended up spending an entire year in the south of France as an au pair. I then moved to Paris to look for a job, did a lot of babysitting and did an internship at a major news company. I also did a lot of travelling in France, Spain and Italy, and around the rest of Europe.

TOP TIP The best advice I can give is to not be scared of being alone or going somewhere different. Listen to other travellers because the best advice comes from the people you meet in trains, bars, youth hostels etc.

NAME Sarah Collinson **AGE** 18
FAVOURITE COUNTRY Chile
MY BIG TRIP In November I left to go to Peru with 10 others through the company VentureCo. Once we had arrived, we spent a week travelling down from Lima to Cusco. In Cusco we lived with Peruvian families. During the week we went to Spanish language school, while on the weekends we did miniexpeditions in the surrounding area. At the beginning of December we left for our aid project. We spent a couple of weeks living in tents while we finished building a community house. We then walked to our next aid project; an ecological survey on the endangered *Polylepis* trees. The next two months of the group trip were spent travelling, sightseeing and trekking down through Bolivia, Chile and Argentina. One of the most challenging aspects of this was having to take it in turns to 'lead' the group. This meant that it was up to us where we stayed, how we got there and what we did when we were there. This gave us invaluable experience for when we were travelling by ourselves. Along the way many of us decided to change our flights and stay in South America longer. Once we had finished the group trip, I travelled back up through Argentina, Brazil and then back to Buenos Aires via Uruguay with a couple of others from the group.

TOP TIP Never miss out on any experiences offered to you...

NAME Damien Rickwood **AGE** 18
FAVOURITE COUNTRY Belize – there is something for everyone there.

MY BIG TRIP Six months spent working in my mind-numbing local supermarket seemed like a distant memory when I eventually reached the exotic lands of Belize, Guatemala and Honduras on my Trekforce expedition. I soon realised that shelf-stacking was a justifiable means to realising the adventure of my dreams.

Here are some my indescribable experiences and accomplishments: completed jungle survival training, built a ranger station, logged an insane number of plants, trekked for weeks through dense jungle, acquired a Latin American Spanish accent, observed the best Semana Santa celebrations in Central America, watched the sunrise from an ancient Mayan temple, was integrated into a remote indigenous community, spent four months washing in rivers, tried my hand at teaching, plunged through countless waterfalls, experienced many unforgettable parties, dived a coral reef, climbed an active volcano, explored the depths of bustling markets, spent days travelling in rickety buses, ate an unhealthy amount of tortillas and made some brilliant friends. I don't think there is a single word that could sum up my roller-coaster ride of senses and emotions.

TOP TIP Spending a lot of your time in the same country or area gives you a real insight into the culture and allows you to become part of the community.

NAME Graham MacPherson **AGE** 18
FAVOURITE COUNTRY Botswana
MY BIG TRIP I spent a year teaching in a primary school in the southern suburbs of Cape Town, South Africa. My main duties were as a boarding house master and rugby coach and I also taught Maths and English to small groups of two or three to help with extra lessons. The rest of the work was completely varied: I drove school teams around, went as a supervisor on canoeing trips on the Orange River, played a hairy Ishmaelite in the school play *Joseph and the Amazing Technicolor Dreamcoat*. It was never boring, not always easy but very worth it.

TOP TIP I know everyone says have a sense of humour, keep an open mind or make a diary. These are useful, but really the best top tip available is save some time for travelling at the end of your trip to see a bit of the world.

NAME Amanda Akass **AGE** 19
FAVOURITE COUNTRY Bolivia
MY BIG TRIP I left for South America in March with a group from Quest Overseas, a gap-year organisation. We spent a month studying Spanish in the beautiful city of Sucre in Bolivia, which was invaluable, and then a month working in the jungle for a conservation charity called Inti Wara Yassi. As well as learning to be dab hands at cement mixing, we also looked after parrots, monkeys and jaguars in the

charity's care. I spent two weeks walking through the jungle and swimming in rivers with a three-month-old puma, too tame to be released into the wild. We then travelled up through Peru and Bolivia, trekked in the mountains, explored ancient ruins and partied on beaches! After finishing my three months with Quest at Machu Picchu, I travelled on to Chile, Argentina and Brazil with friends from the group. On returning home, I volunteered at some youth camps, dazzled my poor family with my Spanish skills and dramatic anecdotes and went back to work for a bank to save up for university.

TOP TIP Don't worry if none of your friends are having gap years, I can guarantee you'll make friends for life travelling!

NAME Kate Wilkinson **AGE** 19
FAVOURITE COUNTRY Cuba – the people are so friendly and the country is so unlike anywhere I have ever been before.

MY BIG TRIP I worked for most of a year in a geriatric ward, knowing that every moment I spent there was paying for three months of freedom. I started planning where to go and budgeting early on in the year to maximise the amount of money that I could save for travelling. In April I left England and went to Cuba to learn Spanish for a month with a host family. That was an awesome experience as the country was so different from capitalist Western Europe. Af-

terwards, I travelled around Costa Rica, which was more for fun than for experiencing anything different – it's pretty much Westernised. I moved on to the USA next and used the Greyhound bus to get up to Vancouver, where I saw old friends and revisited old places I used to go when I lived there. My trip was for learning something new, and returning to some places I hadn't been for years. By working hard for six months, I could do that and it left me with a huge wealth of experience to take to university.

TOP TIP Keep your money in your bra. You know where it is and if someone is going for it!

NAME Phil Vintin **AGE** 27
FAVOURITE COUNTRY New Zealand
MY BIG TRIP I travelled with my girlfriend for eight months in Australia, two months in Southeast Asia and two months in New Zealand. Most of this was pure laziness, beer-drinking and sightseeing, but it did involve two months of actual working in Sydney. The work in Sydney was cold calling over the phone, trying to sell people credit card insurance. Although dull, it was a great way to meet fellow backpackers and earn a bit of extra cash.

TOP TIP If I was to do the whole thing again, I would have taken much more cash with me and done the work as early in the trip as possible – I met some great people and you never know when you might need a floor to sleep on.

BIG TRIP PLANNER

JANUARY

FEBRUARY

MARCH

APRIL

MAY

JUNE

JULY

AUGUST

SEPTEMBER

OCTOBER

NOVEMBER

DECEMBER

DIRECTORIES

BRITISH TRAVELLERS

PAPERWORK

GETTING A PASSPORT
○ **UK Passport Service** (www.passport.gov.uk/passport)

VISAS
○ **Thames Consular Services** (www.thamesconsular
.com) Comprehensive visa agency.

AIR TICKETS
Online Bookers
○ **Airline Network** (www.airlinenetwork.co.uk)
○ **Austravel** (www.austravel.com)
○ **Bridge the World** (www.bridgetheworld.com)
○ **ebookers** (www.ebookers.com)
○ **Expedia** (www.expedia.co.uk)
○ **Flight Centre** (www.flightcentre.co.uk)
○ **Fly Thomas Cook** (www.flythomascook.com)
○ **Opodo** (www.opodo.co.uk)
○ **Quest Travel** (www.questtravel.com)

○ **Trailfinders** (www.trailfinders.com)
○ **Travel Bag** (www.travelbag.co.uk)
○ **Travel Mood** (www.travelmood.com)
○ **Travelocity** (www.travelocity.co.uk)

Specialist Travel Agents
○ **STA Travel** (www.statravel.co.uk)
○ **Student Flights** (www.studentflight.co.uk)
○ **USIT** (www.usit.ie) Ireland's top student travel
company.

OVERLAND TICKETS
○ **InterRail** (www.interrail.com) Budget train tickets
for under-26-year-olds.

INSURANCE
○ **Campbell Irvine** (www.campbellirvine.com)
○ **Endsleigh** (www.endsleigh.co.uk) Has several
customised travel policies.
○ **Insure & Go** (www.insureandgo.co.uk)

MONEY & COSTS

DISCOUNT CARDS
○ **UK Youth Hostels Association** (www.yha.org.uk) This local affiliate of Hostelling International (HI) can supply you with a card for use in any country.

HEALTH & SAFETY

VACCINATIONS
○ **Fit For Travel** (www.fitfortravel.scot.nhs.uk) Scottish service that details where to get immunised and offers other pretravel tips.
○ **Immunisation** (www.immunisation.nhs.uk) Website with information on immunisation and its benefits.
○ **Travel Doctor** (www.traveldoctor.co.uk/vaccines .htm) Lists immunisation recommendations and requirements; also has good clinic list.
○ **World Health Organisation** (www.who.int/ ith/en) WHO's last word on health everywhere around the globe.

FIRST-AID COURSES
○ **Adventure Lifesigns** (www.adventurelifesigns.co.uk)
○ **British Red Cross** (www.redcross.org.uk)
○ **St John Ambulance** (www.sja.org.uk)
○ **Wilderness Expertise** (www.wilderness-expertise.co.uk)
○ **Wilderness Medical Training** (www.wildernessmedicaltraining.co.uk)

OTHER TRAVEL-SAFETY COURSES
○ **Objective** (www.objectivegapyear.com)
○ **Planet Wise** (www.planetwise.net)

TRAVEL CLINICS
○ **Globetrotters Health Clinics** (www.globetrotters travelclinics.com) Clinics in Durham, London and Hounslow.
○ **MASTA** (www.masta.org) Travel clinics all over Britain.
○ **Nomad Travel Clinics** (www.nomadtravel.co.uk) Clinics in London, Bristol and Southampton.
○ **Royal Free Travel Health Centre** (www.travel clinicroyalfree.com) Provides vaccinations and advice in London.

GET PACKING

Good outfitters (most with online stores) include:
○ **Blacks** (www.blacks.co.uk) Affordable gear.
○ **Cotswold** (www.cotswold-outdoor.com) Outdoor stockist.
○ **Gear Zone** (www.gear-zone.co.uk) Good range of outdoor gear including backpacks, mosquito repellents and sleeping bags.
○ **Itchy Feet** (www.itchyfeet.com)
○ **Nomad Travel & Outdoor** (www.nomadtravel .co.uk) Some shops include travel clinics so you can get immunisations while browsing backpacks.
○ **Travel with Care** (www.travelwithcare.com) General supplies, but especially good for health supplies.

TAKEOFF

○ **HM Revenue & Customs** (www.hmrc.gov.uk) Search this site for the latest information on customs regulations on bringing duty-free and more back with you to the UK.

STAYING IN TOUCH

PHONE
The following company offers calling cards:
○ **BT Calling Cards** (www.payphones.bt.com /callingcards) Has one, nine or unlimited numbers as call options, but cost increases.

TRANSPORT OPTIONS

AIR
Round-the-world (RTW) Tickets
○ **Great Escapade** (www.thegreatescapade.com) UK-only RTW tickets (for more information, see Sample Round-The-World Tickets, p88–9).

Budget Airlines
Here are a few reliable airlines from the UK's ever-changing budget market:
○ **Bmibaby** (www.bmibaby.com)
○ **easyJet** (www.easyjet.com)
○ **Flybe** (www.flybe.com)

- **Jet2** (www.jet2.com)
- **Ryanair** (www.ryanair.com)
- **Thomsonfly** (www.thomsonfly.com)

Carbon Trading
- **AtmosFair** (www.atmosfair.de)
- **Carbon Neutral** (www.carbonneutral.com)
- **Future Forests** (www.futureforests.co.uk)
- **Greenseat** (www.greenseat.nl)

OVERLAND
Car & Motorcycle
Apply for your international licence at:
- **RAC** (www.rac.co.uk)

JOBS & TEMPING

GENERAL JOB SITES
- **Eurojobs** (www.eurojobs.com) Extensive job website for Europe.
- **Expatica** (www.expatica.com/jobs) Western European site with good job search engine.

INTERNSHIPS & WORK PLACEMENTS
- **ABN AMRO** (www.graduate.abnamro.com) International bank accepting interns at its European offices.
- **BUNAC** (www.bunac.org/uk) Offers several overseas programs (including cultural exchange).
- **Changing Worlds** (www.changingworlds.co.uk) Provides work placements in Australia and New Zealand.
- **English-Speaking Union** (www.esu.org) For UK undergrads only, this program has 11 placements per year in the US Congress.
- **FreshMinds** (www.freshminds.co.uk) Recruits high-performing graduates for corporate research projects.
- **Grampus Heritage & Training Ltd** (www.grampus.co.uk) Offers work experience in Europe for art students.
- **InterExchange** (www.interexchange.org) Does work-exchange programs to the US for under 28-year-olds.
- **International Employment & Training** (IET; www.jobsamerica.co.uk) Offers internships in the US.

- **International Exchange Centre** (IEC; www.isecworld.co.uk) Offers placements in Russia, South Africa and beyond.
- **Interspeak** (www.interspeak.co.uk) Arranges internships (one to six months) in Europe including host families and targeting your interests.
- **IST Plus** (www.istplus.com) An organisation offering internships in the US, Canada, Australia, New Zealand and China.
- **USIT** (www.usit.ie) Ireland's top student travel company organises work-abroad programs.
- **Visitoz** (www.visitoz.org) Offers work placements on Australian farms.
- **Work & Travel Company** (www.worktravelcompany.co.uk) Does a variety of work programs in Australasia, Africa and Asia that can be good for continuing university students.

TOURISM & HOSPITALITY
Ski Jobs
- **Jobs in the Alps** (www.jobs-in-the-alps.co.uk) Provides ski and chalet jobs as well as 80 hospitality jobs in summer.
- **Mark Warner** (www.markwarner-recruitment.co.uk) Recruits for chalet and ski-host work for European resorts.
- **Ski Staff** (www.skistaff.co.uk) Recruitment agency that staffs British ski companies in the French, Swiss, Austrian and Italian Alps.
- **Total Holidays Ltd** (www.skijob.co.uk) Has winter jobs for instructors, reps and chalet and catering staff, mostly in Europe, with some in Canada.

WORKING WITH KIDS

AU PAIRS & NANNIES
- **A-One Au Pairs & Nannies** (www.aupairsetc.co.uk) Offers work in Australia, Canada, New Zealand, Europe, the US and South Africa.
- **Au Pair in America** (www.aupairamerica.co.uk) Places people in the US and Canada.
- **Childcare International** (www.childint.co.uk) Placements in Australia, Canada, Europe and the US.
- **Childcare Solution** (www.thechildcaresolution.com) Recruits nannies and nurses for the ski

resorts and summer beach resorts in Europe and the US; qualifications required.

- **Just Au Pairs** (www.justaupairs.co.uk) Places people in Europe and the US.
- **Matchmaker Au Pair Agency** (MMAPA; www.matchmakeraupairs.co.uk) Specialises in Europe.
- **Quickhelp Agency** (www.quickhelp.co.uk) Sends nannies to France, Germany and Spain.

CAMP COUNSELLORS

- **BUNAC** (www.bunac.org/uk) Offers several overseas programs (including camp counsellors in the US).
- **Camp America** (www.campamerica.co.uk) Local site of international recruiters for US summer camps.
- **Village Camps** (www.villagecamps.com) European camps in Austria, England, France, Holland and Switzerland.

TEACHING ENGLISH

- **Bell Language School** (www.bell-centres.com) Runs CELTA programs in the UK with affiliated language schools worldwide.
- **British Council** (www.britishcouncil.org /learning-elt-teach-english.htm) Has advice about training and job searches, and a language-assistants program for those with no experience or qualifications.
- **EF English First** (www.englishfirst.com) An international school with several UK training branches offering TEFL and TESOL courses and good placements afterwards.
- **Inlingua International** (www.inlingua -cheltenham.co.uk) Offers TESOL training in Cheltenham, with the option to work at schools upon completion.
- **International House London** (www.ihlondon .co.uk) Offers good distance programs in CELTA courses with jobs in partner schools globally.
- **Saxoncourt UK** (www.saxoncourt.com) Offers CELTA training in London, with placements in private language schools in 20 countries upon completion.
- **Via Lingua** (www.vialingua.org) Offers TEFL certificate training plus job placements.

VOLUNTEERING

VOLUNTEERING HOLIDAYS

- **Go Differently** (www.godifferently.com) Specialises in short-term volunteering in Southeast Asia.
- **Hands Up Holidays** (www.handsupholidays.com) Does good tours – at least a third of the tour is spent volunteering on a variety of projects.
- **Madventurer** (www.madventurer.com) Combines volunteering and holidaying in several Asian, African and South American countries.
- **Travellers Worldwide** (www.travellersworldwide .com) Combines volunteering with in-country courses such as tango or photography.

ORGANISED PROGRAMS

- **Azafady** (www.azafady.org) Madagascar-based trips that include saving lemurs or health work.
- **Biosphere Expeditions** (www.biosphere -expeditions.org) Hands-on wildlife and conservation research such as snow-leopard research in the Altai Mountains or whale studies on the Azores.
- **British Trust for Conservation Volunteers** (BTCV; www.btcv.org) The UK's largest conservation charity, which offers two- or three-month placements.
- **BUNAC** (British Universities North America Club; www.bunac.org/volunteer) Offers several volunteer programs such as school-based projects in Ghana, rainforest conservation in Costa Rica and community work in South Africa or China.
- **Changing Worlds** (www.changingworlds .co.uk) Offers a variety of paid and volunteering experiences, including teaching, conservation, farming, law, journalism and medical placements.
- **GAP Activity Projects** (www.gap.org.uk) With over 33 years of experience, GAP offers experiences teaching English, caring for the disadvantaged and working in medical clinics in 23 countries.
- **Global Xchange** (www.globalxchange.org.uk) A youth exchange program for under-25-year-olds that places people in developing countries for three months and follows up with three months in the UK for a citizen from a foreign country.

- **Inter-Cultural Youth Exchange (ICYE) UK** (www.icye.co.uk) Six- to twelve-month placements in community projects across the world.
- **International Voluntary Service** (IVS; www.ivs-gb.org.uk) Sends volunteers on short-term work camps which assist conservation, inner-city children, orphanages, community arts projects and people with disabilities.
- **The Leap** (www.theleap.co.uk) Specialises in ecotourism projects in Africa and South America for up to 12 weeks.
- **Link Overseas Exchange** (www.linkoverseas.org.uk) Focuses on informal teaching and volunteers work in pairs in India, Sri Lanka, China, Nepal and Georgia. For under-25-year-olds.
- **Outreach International** (www.outreachinternational.co.uk) Selective volunteer program that tackles conservation, education and social issues with year-long placements, though a one-month option recently added.
- **Raleigh International** (www.raleigh.org.uk) Five- or ten-week personal programs in Africa and Central America for under-24-year-olds.
- **Youth for Development** (YfD; www.vso.org.uk) Another youth-oriented development program that works with VSO (Voluntary Service Overseas) partners.

CHARITIES, NGOS & SENDING AGENCIES
- **2Way Development** (www.2way.org.uk) This organisation arranges individual volunteer place-ments by matching the skills of participants with appropriate needs within grass-roots development organisations in the developing world.
- **Christians Abroad** (www.cabroad.org.uk) Volunteer placements in various fields around the world.
- **Coral Cay Conservation** (CCC; www.coralcay.org) Runs expeditions to collect scientific data in coastal areas of Fiji, Tobago and the Philippines.
- **Experiment in International Living** (EIL; www.eiluk.org) Homestays around the world (including the UK) that include English teaching, working with people with special needs or recreating national parks.
- **MondoChallenge** (www.mondochallenge.org) Provides volunteer support to schools and small businesses in developing countries.

USEFUL WEBSITES
- **British Overseas NGOs for Development** (BOND; www.bond.org.uk) Forums and information about the UK's contribution to international development.
- **Network of International Development Organisations in Scotland** (NIDOS; www.nidos.org.uk) A network of 55 Scottish-based volunteer organisations.
- **One Life** (www.onelifelive.co.uk) London event that showcases the UK's international voluntary organisations.
- **Volunteering Options** (www.volunteeringoptions.org) Irish site that has lots of information about international volunteering.

COURSES

- **Art History Abroad** (www.arthistoryabroad.com) Six-week and full-summer courses in Italy as well as a two-week option in London.
- **Càlédöñiâ Languages Abroad** (www.caledonialanguages.co.uk) Offers holidays with language, culture and dance programs in Latin America and Europe.
- **Don Quijote** (www.donquijote.org) Offers Spanish language learning in Spain and Latin America.
- **Susan French Belly Dancing Holidays** (www.bellydancingholidays.co.uk) Takes regular tour classes to Turkey.
- **Tasting Places** (www.tastingplaces.com) A UK-based company offering cooking tours to France, Thailand, Italy, Spain and Greece, as well as masterclasses in London restaurants.

EXCHANGE PROGRAMS
- **DAAD German Academic Exchange Service** (http://london.daad.de) Has regular placements in Germany.
- **En Famille Overseas** (www.enfamilleoverseas.co.uk) Family-stay exchanges in France, Germany, Italy, Spain and around the UK.
- **English-Speaking Union** (www.esu.org) Offers scholarships and other opportunities in the US and Canada.

NORTH AMERICAN TRAVELLERS

PAPERWORK

GETTING A PASSPORT
- **US State Department**
  (http://travel.state.gov/passport)
- **Passport Canada** (www.ppt.gc.ca)

VISAS
Here are a few services that will apply for visas on your behalf (most will also help you out with passports):
- **A Briggs** (www.abriggs.com) Promises overnight passport services.
- **Travel Document Systems** (www.traveldocs.com)
- **Travel Visa Pro** (www.travelvisapro.com)
- **Travisa** (www.travisa.com)

- **Visa Connection** (www.visaconnection.com)
- **Visa HQ** (www.visahq.com)
- **Zierer Visa Services** (www.zvs.com)

AIR TICKETS
Online Bookers
- **Airfare Watchdog** (www.airfarewatchdog .com) Good for domestic fares, but also has some international surprises.
- **Auto Europe** (www.autoeurope.com) Specialises in flights and car rental in Europe.
- **Hotwire** (www.hotwire.com) Books hotels, flights, cruises and car rentals.
- **Last Minute** (http://us.lastminute.com) Flights, hotels, car rental and a unique 'boss is watching' function.

- **Priceline** (www.priceline.com) Offers hotels and car rental.
- **Sky Auction** (www.skyauction.com) Bid on hotel accommodation, flights, cruises and car rentals.

Specialist Travel Agents
- **Travel Cuts** (www.travelcuts.com) Canada's national student travel agency that has offices in all major cities.
- **Travelosophy** (www.itravelosophy.com) US student/youth travel company.

INSURANCE
- **Gateway Plans** (www.gatewayplans.com)
- **Highway To Health** (www.highwaytohealth.com) Offers student policies.
- **Travelguard** (www.travelguard.com)
- **Wallach & Company** (www.wallach.com)

MONEY & COSTS

DISCOUNT CARDS
These local affiliates of Hostelling International (HI) can supply you with a card that you can use in any country.
- **Hostelling International USA** (www.hiusa.org)
- **Hostelling International Canada** (www.hihostels.ca)

HEALTH & SAFETY

VACCINATIONS
- **CDC Vaccination** (www.cdc.gov/vaccines) Information on US vaccination programs.
- **National Vaccine Information Centre** (www.nvic .org) Alternative to vaccination pundits.
- **Travel Doctor** (www.traveldoctor.info) Good information on diseases and immunisations.
- **World Health Organisation** (www.who.int/ith/en) WHO's last word on health everywhere around the globe.

FIRST-AID COURSES
- **American Heart Association** (www.americanheart .org) Has CPR courses.

- **American Red Cross** (www.redcross.org)
- **Canadian Red Cross** (www.redcross.ca)
- **Healthy World** (www.healthy.net) Features a series of online treatments for the basics.
- **Medic First Aid** (www.medicfirstaid.us) A portal to centres across the US that offer accredited courses.
- **Wilderness Medical Associates** (www.wildmed .com) Specialising in first-aid and survival skills for the great outdoors.

OTHER TRAVEL-SAFETY COURSES
- **School for Field Studies** (www.fieldstudies.org) Offers a variety of international health and safety courses.

TRAVEL CLINICS
- **American Society of Tropical Medicine and Hygiene** (www.astmh.org) Has a directory of travel clinics.
- **Public Health Agency of Canada** (www.phac-aspc .gc.ca) Navigate to Travel Health and find their list of travel clinics.
- **Traveler's Medical Service** (www.travelersmedical .com) Clinics in Washington and New York.

GET PACKING

Here are a few equipment suppliers:
- **Magellans** (www.magellans.com) Online travel supplies store.
- **North Face** (www.thenorthface.com) Quality luggage, tents and clothing.
- **Packing Light** (www.packinglight.net) Travel goods with an emphasis on keeping weight down.
- **US Outdoor Store** (www.usoutdoorstore.com) Good backpacks and specialised outdoor sports gear.

TAKEOFF

- **US Customs** (www.customs.ustreas.gov/xp/cgov /travel) Details what you can take and bring back, including duty-free limits.
- **Canadian Border Services Agency** (www.cbsa -asfc.gc.ca/travel-voyage/canadians-eng.html) Duty-free and customs limits for Canadians.

STAYING IN TOUCH

PHONE

The following companies offer calling cards:

- **AccuGlobe** (www.accuglobe.com) Offers pay-as-you-go calling cards with access from 45 countries.
- **AT&T** (www.usa.att.com/traveler) Has several options for calling cards and web-based calling.
- **ConnexPhone** (http://connexphone.com) Offers callback and other international options.
- **FlexTelOne** (http://flextelone.com) Products include calling cards and cellular international (roaming).

Mobile phone

- **Telestial** (www.telestial.com) Specialises in international cell phones including prepaid SIM cards and handset rental.
- **United World Telecom** (www.uwtcallback.com) Their CallMyGlobalNumber can redirect your home calls to another country.

TRANSPORT OPTIONS

AIR

Some good air ticket bookers in North America include:

- **Airtreks** (www.airtreks.com)
- **Cheap Tickets** (www.cheaptickets.com)
- **Expedia** (www.expedia.com)
- **Hotwire** (www.hotwire.com)
- **ITN** (www.itn.net)
- **Lowest Fare** (www.lowestfare.com)
- **Orbitz** (www.orbitz.com)
- **Sidestep** (www.sidestep.com)
- **Student Travel Association** (STA; www.sta.com)
- **Travel Cuts** (www.travelcuts.com) Canada's national student travel agency that has offices in all major cities.
- **Travelocity** (www.travelocity.com)
- **Travelosophy** (www.itravelosophy.com) US student/youth travel company.

See also the Paperwork chapter, p31.

Round-the-world (RTW) Tickets

- **Air Timetable** (www.airtimetable.com) 'Around the world' fares and links to airports.

Budget Airlines

As well as local budget operators, North America has the following cheap ways to get out of the country:

- **Alaska Airlines** (www.alaskaair.com) Flies between Canada, the US and Mexico.
- **ATA Airlines** (www.ata.com) Flies to Mexico and Hawaii.
- **Frontier Airlines** (www.frontierairlines.com) Serves Canada, US, Costa Rica and Mexico.
- **Jet Blue Airways** (www.jetblue.com) Flies between US, Mexico and Caribbean destinations.
- **Spirit Airlines** (www.spiritair.com) Flights to select destinations in the Caribbean, US, South and Central America.
- **Sun Country Airlines** (www.suncountry.com) Does the Caribbean, US and Mexico.
- **USA3000 Airlines** (www.usa3000.com) Flights from the US to Costa Rica, Jamaica, Dominican Republic and Mexico.
- **West Jet** (www.westjet.com) Heads to Canada, US, Mexico and the Caribbean.
- **Zoom** (www.flyzoom.com) Canadian-based operator flying to US, South America, Europe and the Caribbean.

Carbon Trading

These initiatives include a flight-offset calculator:

- **My Climate** (www.my-climate.com) Offsetting programs in India, South Africa and Madagascar.
- **Offsetters** (www.offsetters.com) Promotes 'next generation energy' (basically sustainable) with offsets in Canada, Cambodia and Uganda.

OVERLAND
Car & Motorbike

Apply for an international driving licence from these organisations:

- **AAA** (www.aaa.com) Add your zip code and you'll get your nearest regional office in the US.
- **CAA** (www.caa.ca) For Canadians.

THE ADVENTURE TRAIL

○ **Great Outdoors Resource Page** (http://gorp.away
.com/index.html) Index for North Americans taking
on the outdoor world.

JOBS & TEMPING

GENERAL JOB SITES

○ **Escape Artist** (www.escapeartist.com) Has three
different e-zines aimed at North Americans moving
overseas; one has good coverage of jobs.
○ **Global Placement** (www.globalplacement.com)
Registration service that posts jobs around the
world. Pay €30 (US$45) when you get a job.
○ **Jobaroo** (www.jobaroo.com) Designed for finding
work in Australia.
○ **Overseas Jobs** (www.overseasjobs.com) Search portal
for North Americans looking for overseas work.
○ **Yahoo! Hotjobs** (http://hotjobs.yahoo.com) Reset
options for various countries.

INTERNSHIPS & WORK PLACEMENTS

○ **Abroad China** (http://abroadchina.net) Offers
internships in China.
○ **Alfa Bank Fellowship** (www.alfabank.com
/community/fellowship_programme) Placements
in Moscow for US citizens.
○ **Alliance Abroad** (www.allianceabroad.com)
Organises internships both in the US and
inter-nationally.
○ **British University North America Club** (BUNAC;
www.bunac.org) Offers work placements in the UK,
Australia, New Zealand and Canada.
○ **CDS International** (www.cdsintl.org) Portal for
placements in US and international businesses.
○ **Connect 123** (www.connect-123.com) Offers
internships in South Africa.
○ **Cross Cultural Solutions** (www.crosscultural
solutions.org) Offers programs throughout
South America.
○ **European Internships** (www.europeaninternships
.com) Portal to a variety of opportunities across
Europe.
○ **Institute for Central American Development**

Studies (www.icads.org) Has social-justice positions
in Central and South America.
○ **Intern Jobs** (www.internjobs.com) Portal for
internships worldwide.
○ **Proworld** (www.myproworld.org) Offers
opportunities in South America, India, Mexico
and Thailand.

WORKING WITH KIDS

AU PAIRS & NANNIES

○ **Club Aventure** (www.aventuresjeunesse.com) Jobs
for au pairs in the UK, France, Denmark, Iceland and
Netherlands.
○ **Globetrotters** (www.globetrotterseducation.ca) Au
pair work for North Americans in Europe.
○ **Scotia Personnel** (www.scotia-personnel-ltd.com)
A Canadian agency that arranges au pair jobs in
Europe and Australia, as well as summer-camp work
in Italy or the UK.

TEACHING ENGLISH

○ **Dave's ESL Cafe** (http://eslcafe.com) Loads of jobs,
especially in Northeast Asia, but also in Southeast Asia.
○ **Language Magazine** (www.languagemagazine
.com) US language-teaching magazine with Job
Shop for US opportunities.
○ **Overseas Digest** (www.overseasdigest.com) Tips
for Americans heading overseas, particularly for
teaching work.
○ **TESL Canada** (www.tesl.ca) Official TESL site with
links for schools and teachers throughout Canada.

VOLUNTEERING

VOLUNTEERING HOLIDAYS

○ **Aquila Tours Inc** (www.voluntouring.ca) A
Canadian company that seamlessly integrates
a volunteering experience with the traditional
elements of travel.
○ **PEPY Ride** (Protect the Earth, Protect Yourself;
www.pepyride.org) Cycling-based fundraising in
Cambodia that contributes to education; also offers
tours that highlight sustainability.

ORGANISED PROGRAMS

○ **Amigos de las Américas** (www.amigoslink.org) High-school and college-aged volunteers work five to eight weeks in South and Central America.
○ **Amizade** (www.amizade.org) Offers two-week to six-month placements in several destinations.
○ **Global Volunteers** (www.globalvolunteers.org) Offers one- to three-week programs in Africa, Asia and the Pacific, working with communities on education and health care.
○ **Por Un Mejor HOY** (www.hoycommunity.org) Mexico-based organisation that seeks Spanish-speakers for one- to two-week community work.

CHARITIES, NGOS & SENDING AGENCIES

○ **Oceanic Society** (www.oceanic-society.org) The Oceanic Society is a nonprofit organisation dedicated to protecting wildlife and marine biodiversity in Belize, Costa Rica, Suriname and Brazil.
○ **Peace Corps** (www.peacecorps.gov) A byword in volunteering for North Americans, with a choice of many countries.

USEFUL WEBSITES

○ **Transitions Abroad** (www.transitionsabroad.org) Navigate to 'Volunteer Work Abroad' for a hefty offering of expert US articles on international volunteering; also offers excellent opportunities.
○ **University of Minnesota Learning Abroad Center** (www.umabroad.umn.edu) A self-service centre for volunteering that's not just for U of M students.

COURSES

○ **Amerispan** (www.amerispan.com) Offers study options in several different languages.
○ **Center for Study Abroad** (www.centerfor studyabroad.com) A Seattle-based outfit offering study programs that can get credit in your school.
○ **Centers for Interamerican Studies** (http://cedei .org) Offers exchanges and courses in South America, including the popular 'Semester in the Andes'.
○ **Epiculinary** (www.epiculinary.com) Tours to Spain, Italy and France that involve hands-on cookery.

○ **National Registration Center for Study Abroad** (www.studyabroad.nrcsa.com) Evaluates programs around the world and offers the best of them, usually in a huge variety of languages.
○ **School for Field Studies** (www.fieldstudies.org) Does courses in conservation that can be credited to some college courses.

EXCHANGE PROGRAMS

○ **American Institute for Foreign Study** (AIFS; www.aifs.com) College study exchanges with five different countries.
○ **Council on International Educational Exchange** (www.ciee.org) The first port of call for North Americans studying overseas – with courses on languages, culture, business and more.
○ **Swap Canada** (www.swap.ca) Solid site for Canadians who want to go on exchanges overseas.

AUSTRALASIAN TRAVELLERS

PAPERWORK

GETTING A PASSPORT
- **Australian Passport Information Service** (www.passports.gov.au)
- **New Zealand Department of Internal Affairs** (www.dia.govt.nz/diawebsite.nsf)

VISAS
- **Overseas Working Holidays** (www.owh.com.au)
- **Visa Link** (https://visalink.com.au)

AIR TICKETS
Online Bookers
- **Airfares Flights** (www.airfaresflights.com.au) Comparison tool.
- **Flight Centre** (www.flightcentre.com.au)
- **travel.com.au** (www.travel.com.au)
- **Zuji** (www.zuji.com.au)

Specialist Travel Agents
- **Best Flights** (www.bestflights.com.au)
- **Student Flights** (www.studentflights.com.au)

INSURANCE
- **Cover More** (www.covermore.com.au)
- **iTrek** (www.itrektravelinsurance.com.au)
- **World Nomads** (www.worldnomads.com) Has New Zealand offices.

MONEY & COSTS

DISCOUNT CARDS
These local affiliates of Hostelling International (HI) can supply you with a card that you can use in recognised HI hostels in any country in the world.
- **YHA Australia** (www.yha.com.au)
- **YHA New Zealand** (www.yha.co.nz)

HEALTH & SAFETY

The Australian government issues travel warnings on the website of the **Department of Foreign Affairs and Trade** (www.smartraveller.gov.au).

VACCINATIONS
- **Immunisation Advisory Centre** (www.immune.org.nz) Check 'Health Professionals' section for information on Kiwi immunisation policy.
- **Immunise** (www.immunise.health.gov.au)

FIRST-AID COURSES
- **First Aid International** (www.firstaidinternational.com.au) Offers courses and kits.
- **First Aid Melbourne** (www.emergency.com.au) Kits and courses in Melbourne only.
- **First Aid Store** (www.firstaidstore.com.au) Has good hiker kits.
- **Red Cross New Zealand** (www.redcross.org.nz)
- **RedR** (www.redr.org/australia) Offers training in humanitarian-relief fields.
- **St John Ambulance Australia** (www.stjohn.org.au)

TRAVEL CLINICS
- **Travel Clinic** (www.travelclinic.com.au)
- **Travel Doctor** (www.traveldoctor.co.nz) Several branches throughout New Zealand.
- **Traveller Medical & Vaccination Clinic** (www.tmvc.com.au)

GET PACKING

- **Go Go Gear** (www.gogogear.com.au) Online travel goods store.
- **Kathmandu** (www.kathmandu.com.au)
- **Mountain Designs** (www.mountaindesigns.com)
- **Paddy Pallin** (www.paddypallin.com.au) Outdoor specialist with good tents.

TAKEOFF

- **Australian Customs Service** (www.customs.gov.au) Look for the 'Know before you go' PDF for details on what you can take out and bring back.

- **New Zealand Customs Service** (www.customs.govt.nz/travellers) Information on what you can take when departing and returning to New Zealand.

STAYING IN TOUCH

PHONE
- **Telecom** (www.telecom.co.nz) Head for 'Personal' and then 'Calling Card'.
- **Telstra** (telstra.com.au/callingcardshop/phoneaway.htm) Offers the PhoneAway card to call home.

TRANSPORT OPTIONS

AIR
Budget Airlines
- **Jetstar** (www.jetstar.com.au)
- **Tiger Airways** (www.tigerairways.com)
- **Virgin Blue** (www.virginblue.com.au)

Carbon Trading
- **Carbon Neutral** (www.carbonneutral.com.au)
- **Climate Friendly** (https://climatefriendly.com)
- **Greenfleet** (www.greenfleet.com.au) Also covers car and other overland transport.

OVERLAND
Car & Motorcycle
- **Australian Automobile Association** (www.aaa.asn.au) Find your state's association on this umbrella website.
- **New Zealand Automobile Association** (www.aa.co.nz)

JOBS & TEMPING

GENERAL JOB SITES
Like recruitment companies, the following sites can help you with your job quest:
- **Anywork Anywhere** (www.anyworkanywhere.com) Lists jobs and gives overviews of several industries.
- **Going Overseas** (www.goingoverseas.net.au) Advice on work in the UK, Canada and Japan.
- **Gumtree** (www.gumtree.com.au) Massive bulletin board for information on work, moving overseas and more.

- **Hays** (www.hays.com.au/overseas) International recruiter that's good for work in Britain.
- **International Working Holidays** (www.iwh.co.nz) Work options for Kiwis, from nannying and camps to hospitality and ski-resort jobs.
- **Overseas Working Holidays** (www.owh.com.au) Great organisation with jobs in Canada, the UK and Russia; they even offer information nights in several capital cities.

INTERNSHIPS & WORK PLACEMENTS
- **Monash Professional** (www.monashprofessional .com.au) Monash University's link to international and local internships.
- **Student Placement** (www.studentplacement.com .au) Has internships as well as nanny and summer work in the US.

WORKING WITH KIDS

- **Au Pair Australia** (www.aupairaustralia.com.au) Recruits for international positions.
- **Au Pair in America** (www.aupairamerica.com.au) Great for US jobs.
- **Australian Nanny and Au Pair Connection** (www .australiannannies.info) Places internationally.
- **Family Match** (www.familymatch.com.au) No-fee option for Australian and international placements.
- **JCR Australia** (www.jcraus.com.au) Strong international links make this a good option for overseas placements.
- **Milestonz** (www.milestonz.com.au) Recruits for Australia and New Zealand.
- **Nannies Abroad** (www.nanniesabroad.co.nz) Recruits Kiwis for nanny jobs internationally.

TEACHING ENGLISH

- **Career One** (www.careerone.com.au) Has plenty of English-teaching jobs in China and Southeast Asia.
- **Dave's ESL Cafe** (http://eslcafe.com) Loads of jobs especially in Northeast Asia, but also in Southeast Asia.
- **Global TESOL Australia** (http://globalteacher.com .au) Offers teaching jobs around the world along with certification.

- **Languages International** (www.languages.ac.nz) Teacher training in Auckland and Christchurch.
- **Seek Learning** (www.seeklearning.com.au) Offers TESOL qualifications; attached job site has positions for teachers.
- **Teach International** (www.teachinternational.co.nz) Offers courses and placements for canny Kiwis.

VOLUNTEERING

VOLUNTEERING HOLIDAYS
- *Add*venture VSA (Volunteer Service Abroad; www.vsa.org.nz) Navigate to '*Add*venture' to find out more about this volunteer organisation's short-term community-project options in Southeast Asia.
- **Hands Up Holidays** (www.handsupholidays.com) Does good tours – at least a third of the tour is spent volunteering on a variety of projects.
- **World Expeditions** (www.worldexpeditions.com) An adventure-travel outfit offering community-project trips to developing countries.

ORGANISED PROGRAMS
- **AFS Intercultural Programs** (www.afs.org.au) Offers international community service in several countries with projects ranging from four to 12 weeks.
- **Australian Volunteers International (AVI) Youth Program** (www.australianvolunteers.com) Sends volunteers around the globe on self-funding placements. Also offers a Youth Program for 18- to 30-year-olds.
- **Australian Youth Ambassadors for Development** (AYAD; www.ayad.com.au) Government scheme to send 18- to 30-year-olds overseas in a variety of roles for three to 12 months.
- **Conservation Volunteers** (www.conservation volunteers.com.au) Environmental-volunteering options in Australia, New Zealand and beyond.
- **World Youth International** (www.worldyouth .com.au) Takes people aged from 13 to 30 on five-week community-development trips in Kenya, Uganda, Peru, Cambodia, Laos, Nepal and Australia.

CHARITIES, NGOS & SENDING AGENCIES

○ **Australian Volunteers International** (AVI; www .australianvolunteers.com) Longer programs of up to two years are available with Australia's peak international volunteering body.

○ **Global Volunteer Network** (www.volunteer.org .nz) A huge variety of global programs open to all nationalities, though it's especially strong in Asia and Africa.

○ **Volunteer Service Abroad** (VSA; www.vsa.org.nz) Offers longer assignments across Africa, Asia and the Pacific.

○ **Volunteering for International Development from Australia** (VIDA; www.vidavolunteers.com.au) Places skilled Australians in developing nations of the Asia-Pacific region with most projects running more than 18 months.

USEFUL WEBSITES

○ **Volunteering Australia** (www.volunteering australia.org) A site by Australia's governing body on volunteering with links to nonprofit organisations. Has answers to questions and offers ways to get involved.

○ **Volunteering New Zealand** (www.volunteeringnz .org.nz) The resource epicentre of the New Zealand volunteering world.

COURSES

EXCHANGE PROGRAMS

○ **AFS Australia** (www.afs.org.au) Offers high-school and university exchanges.

○ **Society for Australian-German Student Exchange** (www.sagse.org.au) Scholarships to visit Germany for short-term study.

○ **Student Exchange Australia** (http://student exchange.org.au) Offers semester-, summer- and year-long programs.

○ **Youth For Understanding** (YFU; www.yfu.com .au/exchange) Runs several programs for under-25-year-olds.

BEHIND THE SCENES

THE AUTHORS

CO-ORDINATING AUTHOR
GEORGE DUNFORD
Parts One, Two and Four; Europe, Australia, New Zealand & the Pacific, Northeast Asia, Southeast Asia, North America & the Caribbean, and Russia, Central Asia & the Caucasus chapters

For a Melbourne-based freelance writer, George sure has had some sweet gigs – attending Scottish music festivals to make podcasts for www.lonelyplanet .com, getting lost in New Zealand for the *Micronations* book and also writing a couple of guidebooks along the way. He writes for the *Big Issue*, *Get Lost!* and other publications. He sometimes finds time to update the travel writing and journalism blog Hackpacker (http://hackpacker.blogspot.com).

Thanks from George
First up thanks to all the authors who've fed into this book – whether people who posted on www .lonelyplanet.com, specialist contributors or guidebook authors. The biggest salute to Bridget Blair for listening to all my talking to myself and making this a fun and flexible project. Cheers to Carolyn Boicos and Emma Gilmour for

reading chapters and supplying their regional expertise. A cheeky wink to Simon Hall for climbing the Thorn Tree for fruits. A hefty good onya to Jane 'Is this anything?' Ormond for reading drafts and making it more snap than crap. Also a cheers to Felice Howden for her top work on currencies. Thanks to my generous contributors, especially Rosie Mulready (for fool's errands) and Carolyn Bain (for truckstop lunch dates). In house, thanks to Mark Adams for his lustrous design, James Hardy for masterly tweaks, Kate Morgan for first-class contracting and Shawn Low for finding the manuscript in the mess. Finally thanks to Nikki for reading and nodding at the dumb jokes and being a good travel companion.

CONTRIBUTING AUTHORS
MATTHEW D FIRESTONE
Africa, Mexico, and Central & South America chapters
Matthew is a trained biological anthropologist and epidemiologist who is particularly interested in the health and nutrition of indigenous populations. He has worked alongside the San of the Kalahari in Botswana and Namibia, as well as the Cabecare in the highlands of Costa Rica. As a freelance travel writer, he has visited over 50 different countries on six continents, and has authored more than a dozen different books for Lonely Planet. When he's not travelling, home is a shoebox apartment above a ramen noodle shop in Tokyo, Japan.

ANTHONY HAM
The Middle East chapter

Anthony Ham's gap year started with a one-way ticket to Bangkok and ended with a motorcycle accident in Turkey. En route, he experienced a life-changing moment of clarity while sitting on the running boards of a Thai train and he decided to become a writer. He also fell irretrievably in love with Damascus. He now lives in Madrid and has a master's degree in Middle Eastern politics under his belt. He keeps returning to the Arab world whenever he can and has written Lonely Planet's *Libya* and *Saudi Arabia* guides and contributed to, among others, *Jordan, Iran* and the *Middle East*.

VIVEK WAGLE
The Indian Subcontinent chapter

Born in India, Vivek started Big Tripping at the age of three, when he moved to Pakistan and then the USA. His first solo round-the-world trip came at the age of 14 (Amsterdam is *not* an appropriate place for naïve teenage boys!), with several that followed. He returns to India every two years to catch up with relatives, drink coconut water and be mocked for his terrible Hindi. Now living in Melbourne, Australia, he has written guidebooks to Southeast Asia, India, the USA, Mexico and Europe.

CREDITS

Much of the text in this book is based on *The Gap Year Book*, published by Lonely Planet in July 2005. The authors of that book were Charlotte Hindle, Joe Bindloss, Bradley Mayhew, Jolyon Attwooll, Heather Dickson, Matthew Fletcher, Anthony Ham, Andrew Dean Nystrom and China Williams.

This book was produced in Lonely Planet's Melbourne office. It was commissioned and project managed by Bridget Blair and overseen by associate publisher Chris Rennie. It was edited by Shawn Low, Robyn Loughnane and Branislava Vladisavljevic, designed by Mark Adams with assistance from James Hardy and laid out by Cara Smith. Image research was done by Pepi Bluck, and Ryan Evans and Gerard Walker managed pre-press preparation of the photographs. The maps were created by Paul Piaia, Wayne Murphy and Joshua Geoghegan. Thanks to Jane Atkin, Rebecca Dandens, Ben Handicott, Graham Imeson, Kate Morgan and Mary Nelson Parker.

INDEX

000 map pages